Whistling Past the Graveyard

Whistling Past the Graveyard
Constitutional Abeyances, Quebec, and the Future of Canada

David M. Thomas

Toronto   Oxford   New York
OXFORD UNIVERSITY PRESS
1997

Oxford University Press
70 Wynford Drive, Don Mills, Ontario M3C 1J9

Oxford New York
Athens Auckland Bangkok Calcutta
Cape Town Chennai Dar es Salaam Delhi
Florence Hong Kong Istanbul Karachi
Kuala Lumpur Madrid Melbourne Mexico City
Mumbai Nairobi Paris Singapore
Taipei Tokyo Toronto Warsaw

and associated companies in
Berlin Ibadan

Oxford is a trademark of Oxford University Press

Canadian Cataloguing in Publication Data

Thomas, David M. (David Martin), 1943–
    Whistling past the graveyard

Includes bibliographical references and index.
ISBN 0-19-541215-X

1. Canada – Constitutional history. 2. Federal government – Canada.
3. Nationalism – Quebec (Province). I. Title.

JL65 1997.T46 1997   342.71'029   C97-930842-9

Cover Design: Sonya Thursby
Text Design: Max Gabriel Izod
Formatting: Janette Thompson (Jansom)

Copyright © Oxford University Press Canada 1997

1 2 3 4 — 00 99 98 97

This book is printed on permanent (acid-free) paper ∞.

Printed in Canada

Contents

Preface vii

Acknowledgements viii

Introduction xi

1 The World of Abeyances 1

2 The Term and the Temperament 19
　Unsuspecting Confidence 33

3 Settled Unsettlements 51
　'Circumstances' 52
　Ambiguities 60
　Triumphs 71

4 The Way We Were: Abeyance Maintenance 89
　Different Worlds 99
　Special Status 106
　Formal Change 117

5 Unsettlement 137
　Well-known Entities 142
　Major Surgery 148
　What If? 156

6 Unsettled Settlement 174
　Altered States: Meech Lake 178
　States of Mind: Pierre Trudeau 185
　States of Being 192
　The State We're In 198

Conclusion 219

Bibliography 231

Index 258

To Maureen

Preface

As events move inexorably on, writing about the Canadian constitution seems increasingly irrelevant, at least as far as formal constitutional change is concerned. Anguished debate over whether or not something should be placed in the preamble or the body of the text now pales beside the deconstruction and reconstruction of an economy, the restructuring of the workforce, ecological crises that cause the destruction of a community's way of life, the decline of Keynesianism, and the *political* realities of Quebec nationalism, Western populism, and aboriginal discontent. All such questions have constitutional implications, but the constitution itself seems at the mercy of larger political, social, and economic forces. As I wrote I could see myself becoming one of a declining band of what Allan Tupper has called 'constitutional stalwarts', one of those who still labour to interpret the last two decades of constitutional activity in new and useful ways. To put it perhaps more vividly, do I have to see myself as a member of the ship's orchestra, playing 'Nearer my God to Thee', as the waters rise and she sinks by the bow?

But the hope remains that there is yet something useful to say, useful in that it may make us view our past and present somewhat differently. The words we use, and the ways in which we use them, play a key part in our construction of 'reality'. Ideas, as Ralph Heintzman has said, 'live outside of time waiting for us to make them our own' but, in order to enter time, they do so in words, which then take on an independent existence. People fight at least as much over images, myths, symbols, what is and is not to be stated, and over how we are to define our reality, as they do over economic choices, Marx's fading ghost notwithstanding. I argue that we should add to our vocabulary the notion of constitutional abeyances, and in Canada's case should note how they have been inextricably linked to the questions that surround the role and place of a small nation within a larger state. An awareness of abeyances, and of the approaches taken previously, could affect our thinking on the dilemmas we face, the terms we use, the linkages between them, and the political temperament necessary for the solution to our problems—or their avoidance if this is still possible.

Acknowledgements

I owe a debt of gratitude to particular institutions and to the people who run them. My thanks must go first to Mount Royal College. The College provided me with a professional leave of absence and has also consistently supported my attendance and participation in conferences, at which it has been possible to make contact with many of the scholars whose work I have relied upon, and which have given me the opportunity to test and discuss my own ideas. It would have been easy, in very difficult budgetary times, for the College to curtail such activities. Secondly I wish to acknowledge the assistance that I received from various libraries: at Mount Royal College, the University of Calgary, the Ontario Archives, the National Archives, and the Archives of the Quebec Liberal Party at the University of Montreal, I received unfailingly helpful and courteous service. This meant a great deal for I was often saved both time and fruitless effort thanks to staff who went out of their way to be of help.

I have numerous individuals to thank, starting with Dr Roger Gibbins. Without his support, this book simply would not have been written: I cannot thank him adequately for all his help. Also at the University of Calgary I wish to thank Dr Stan Drabek, Dr Keith Archer, Dr Gretchen MacMillan and Dr Donald Smith. Numerous others also contributed to the content and to my thinking and gave extremely generously of their time and hospitality. My meetings with them were not so much interviews as conversations with people who have given years of devoted service to their country. I wish to thank, in alphabetical order: Senator Gérald-A. Beaudoin, Dr Edwin Black, the Honourable Edward G. Broadbent, Dr David R. Cameron, the Right Honourable Joe Clark, Dr Alain-G. Gagnon, Dr Ralph Heintzman, Dr Muriel Kovitz, Josée Legault, Dr Alan McDougall, Robert Normand, the Honourable Jean-Luc Pepin, Dr Gordon Robertson, Dr François Rocher, Dr Richard Simeon, Senator Arthur Tremblay, and Dr Ronald Watts.

From the above I must single out the late Jean-Luc Pepin. On a chilly day in Edmonton we revisited the heady days of the Task Force on National Unity. A planned two-hour interview turned into a whole day of debate and discussion. Even though he had been gravely ill, his wit, enthusiasm, capacity for work, and devotion to Quebec and to Canada were inspiring. He subsequently provided me with detailed written comments on an earlier draft of this work, even as he was preparing to visit his daughter and her family in Africa. I was very fortunate to have met him as I did.

At the end of the project, Monsieur Claude Ryan very kindly consented to read and comment upon the manuscript. He too is in the tradition of those federalists in Quebec who have spent a political lifetime trying to deal with matters constitutional, and who are still searching for acceptable answers.

As the roster of names above indicates, I have been able to consult a veritable who's who of constitutional experts. (In one sense this was depressing, for it brought home forcibly the realization that we have employed many of our very best legal and political minds, but to little or no avail.) They may well be responsible for much of what I have to say, but they are not responsible for the conclusions drawn, the linkages made, or the way in which it has been said. I think it fair to say that they should share only the credit for whatever has merit.

I owe major intellectual debts in particular to Dr Michael Foley and to Dr Alan C. Cairns. Professor Foley's seminal work *The Silence of Constitutions* got me thinking about Canada's abeyances; Professor Cairns's interest in my initial paper on the subject made me realize that I should consider a more detailed investigation of the topic, and his own extensive work has I know had a considerable influence on me. I am also indebted to the works of numerous historians whose understanding of events is far more detailed than mine could ever hope to be.

I have tried to provide a somewhat new perspective on our constitutional history; I have not attempted to rewrite it. This book is in a sense an essay, and is therefore selective in approach. It is also, unavoidably, a form of intervention in a political debate. I have attempted to use Foley's concept of abeyances to illuminate and to link, and I am suggesting that it provides an important addition to our constitutional vocabulary. And in terms of constitutional vocabulary I must also mention the work of Edmund Morgan on political fictions, for his analysis of popular sovereignty proved especially helpful.

I have tried to write in a manner that is clear and interesting without oversimplifying what is, without doubt, very complex material. In the search for clarity of expression it is always a pleasure to read Bernard Crick and to use his work as a model. In his essay 'On the Orwell Trail', Crick, quoting Hugh Kenner, reminds us, however, that plain style, and prose that appears clear as an Orwellian window pane, can be 'a rhetorical device, to inspire trust' just as much as a complex 'high' style may be calculated 'to inspire respect'. I have tried to avoid falling into either trap.

I must of course thank my family and my friends. My wife and I are lucky in that we have friends to whom a discussion of such matters as politics and the constitution has always been interesting, and who bring to these debates a lifetime of experience and informed comment. In particular I want to thank the Honourable Mr Justice Roger P. Kerans; he suggested pursuing the Burke connection, and many a constitutional problem has been discussed with him before, during, and after dinner. I also wish to thank the friends who housed me as I journeyed across the country; without them, fieldwork would have been both expensive and solitary. My wife Maureen provided invaluable support and assistance throughout the project, from incisive editorial comments to gracefully putting up with all the inconveniences that inevitably arise as a book takes over a large part of one's life. And for the title chosen, I must thank Dr David R. Cameron, for it was he who first suggested the image of whistling past our constitutional graveyard.

Finally, I wish to thank Euan White, Acquisitions Editor at Oxford University Press, for his willingness to commission yet another book on Canada's constitutional crises, and to acknowledge the very able editorial assistance of Olive Koyama, Jane McNulty, and Phyllis Wilson, Managing Editor.

I am sure that all to whom I owe so much believe, as I do, that we are not merely prisoners of our time and circumstance as our present becomes our future. How we choose to see things, and the explanatory frameworks we provide, are matters of more than merely academic interest.

Introduction

For over a quarter of a century, Canada has been in a state of ongoing constitutional and political crisis. The situation worsens with every passing decade. Most scholars are now deeply pessimistic about our ability to keep the country united. In the *Canadian Journal of Political Science*, book reviews discussing matters constitutional now almost invariably end with a disclaimer stressing the intractable nature of the problems and the lack of viable options.[1] Reviewers write 'with a profound sense of sadness'; there is 'no agreement on constitutional fundamentals'; we used to think we knew what was right, now we can only agree on what seems 'politically wrong'. The political highway is littered with the wreckage of constitutional proposals, including several that came close to success. What are we to make of this?

Have we spent the past three decades trying merely to slow the inexorable flow of Quebec nationalism? Has dealing with this question so fractured the country's political culture that we cannot now agree upon an acceptable course? This would help account for our lack of preparedness. However, before we start to talk about Plans A or B and about how the country will be carved up, it behooves us to take a longer and closer look at our history, and then ask ourselves if there are not other ways of looking at the questions that surround the successful integration of small nations within larger states. On this score, it is perhaps best to put my cards, face up, on the table at the outset. I believe that Quebeckers do constitute a nation, at least by any of the normal standards by which we make such a judgment. Like the Scots, the Irish, the Lithuanians, or any number of other examples, those who live in Quebec believe that they constitute a definable 'people'. I am *not*, it must be noted, arguing that Quebec should be a nation–state. I am not proposing that Quebec become sovereign (whatever that means these days). I do not wish to disparage other groups. I recognize also the depth and complexities of aboriginal claims. But I will argue that our history shows us trying to grapple with, and avoid having to provide, hard answers to the issues surrounding a small nation within a much larger federation, which is itself situated next to a political and economic superpower.

Before we blame ourselves and our predecessors too much for their and our lack of foresight, we should recognize the magnitude of the problem. We also must realize that constitutions conceal as well as reveal, and that much of our previous success came from avoidance of the intractable as well as from reliance upon British traditions acccepted by all. The theme of avoidance leads to the notion of constitutional abeyances, a key part of the discussion of how we got from there to here.

When writing, in Canada, on any topic of constitutional importance, difficulties come in many ways and in different guises.

One must first wrestle with a mountain of material, for what strikes one immediately is the sheer amount that has been written since the mid-1970s:

> Such a plethora of material might appear to suggest that there is little chance of saying anything new, and that this generation of constitutional commentators can only be parasitical on what has gone before.[2]

The number of significant constitution-related commissions and task forces set up from 1979 to 1991 totalled 16.[3] The three volumes of the *Report of the Royal Commission on the Economic Union and Development Prospects for Canada* (the Macdonald Commission) were almost 2,000 pages in length and they were accompanied by a series of 300 research studies, covering nineteen areas and released in some seventy-one volumes.[4] The 1991 edition of *Canada: The State of the Federation* contained a select bibliography on 'Constitutional Reform in the Post Meech Era' that ran to nine pages, and much more has come out since.[5] The vast assemblage of commentaries, studies, reports, analyses, and sources in English is accompanied by a formidable array of writings in French, only some of which are available in translation, and most of which are available not at all in English Canada except via inter-library loans.[6] Quebec too has had a veritable cottage industry of constitution-related studies: how this industry survives, how many of these works the general public buy, and how much it all costs, could be a book in itself.[7]

It is possible to see such a wealth of information as an asset, for one can surely choose carefully from the writings of Canada's ablest political scientists, historians, sociologists, philosophers, and legal scholars. Yet this output, although it contains many pieces written with passion, clarity, and style, has been criticized as generally lacking in both iconoclasm and theoretical originality:

> [But] social scientists have remained close to the policy makers' agenda, have failed to provide new prisms through which to interpret the Constitution and have undertaken little research which links constitutional politics with other important Canadian issues.... Canadian political scientists are too generous in their public assessments of each others' work to the detriment of its quality.[8]

This appears to have led to a dearth of policy studies and—with a few notable exceptions—neglect of policy effectiveness 'as an important criterion for the evaluation of democratic constitutions'.[9] Sociologists in particular, it seems, have not taken up the challenge presented them, and have been guilty of theoretical sloppiness in general, and the avoidance of specific and central issues, including the debate over sociological terms such as 'distinct society'.[10] The problems to be faced by those who examine Canadian constitutional questions are hard to overestimate.

Where so much has become interconnected and where the topics themselves are like giant jigsaw puzzles, there are, firstly, serious difficulties of focus and scope. Federalism itself as an idea, and federations as its institutional manifestation, are obvious examples. Interconnectedness means that choosing to discuss anything other than a minor and highly arcane topic inevitably leads on to larger questions, and doing research on anything that does not have larger significance is likely to leave one open to the charge that one's work is divorced from the 'real' world of constitutional debate. Roger Gibbins has argued, apropos of federalism, that one must build the jigsaw out of smaller, albeit central, components. What he has to say regarding the difficulties students of federalism face applies equally to constitutional studies:

> One of the most difficult problems for students of federalism arises from the vast scope of the subject matter. . . . Indeed, given a bit of imagination there are few aspects of Canadian political life that could not be brought under the umbrella of federalism.[11]

Secondly, excellent though it is, much of the available constitutional and political analysis is secondary material; it was not written by the participants, whose discussions and decisions are hidden behind a veil of cabinet and official secrecy. Canada lacks the British tradition of vigorous memoirs by key cabinet-level participants that serve to supplement, and offer a corrective to, academic analysis. Such accounts as do exist are usually lacking in balance and perspective and are often of the 'I was right and they obviously were not' school of analysis.[12]

The question of objectivity and personal involvement constitutes a third problem, for when writing about the constitution it is very difficult indeed to contain—or even identify—one's own values. Constitutional questions matter a great deal to those who write about them, for scholars are also citizens. In the social sciences (and, to be fair, in the sciences also) it is always difficult to disentangle oneself from the climate of opinion prevailing in an era or within a school of thought. It is doubly difficult to do so when one is drawn to a particular side in a struggle that is still a part of one's civic life.[13] Stephen Brooks and Alain-G. Gagnon (and others) have discussed the roles of intellectuals in a larger sense within capitalist societies and, more particularly, in terms of Canadian and Québécois nationalism and the Canadian state.[14] One's origins and socialization also matter. Edwin R. Black has noted that a certain denigration of Canadian politics may be due in part, whether consciously or unconsciously:

> to the astonishing number of political participants who are the product of foreign socialization processes . . . they cannot escape the continual screening of all political reality which their childhood images provide throughout much of their lives.[15]

We would all undoubtedly like to take the Eugene Forsey view that sometimes the people you respect and like are wrong, and people you dislike are right, and that we can discern the difference.[16] Who is to say that even Eugene Forsey could separate reason and passion so easily? As is almost always the case, Alan Cairns has already noted the problem:

> Trudeau is fond of quoting Thucydides, who attributed greatness to Themistocles, who could dispassionately accept that Athens was not immortal. . . . For most of the professoriate, however, who are neither gods, historians, nor Themistocles, such divine disinterestedness or insouciance is neither what we feel nor seek to attain when our own country is our subject.[17]

The temptation to make political use of academic work is perhaps nowhere more graphically illustrated than in the uses that have been made of history and of historical 'facts'. The testimony given to the Commission on the Political and Constitutional Future of Quebec (the Bélanger-Campeau Commission)[18] is a clear example of the use of history to legitimize views and mobilize support: 'À la limite donc, les faits sont indifférents; ce qui compte, c'est l'effet produit, c'est l'efficacité de la performance discursive.'[19] From the Conquest (was it even a conquest; should it be written with a capital C?) to the 1981 'Nuit des Longues Couteaux', where you sit tends to be where you stand. Thus the use of a label such as the one above, purporting to describe what happened to the Quebec delegation in 1981, can be seen as a misuse of a particularly odious historical incident that is in no way parallel or comparable. 'Is its use in a Canadian context totally innocent? It is permissible to doubt this.'[20]

The highly emotional nature of our constitutional discourse should come as no surprise. We are and have been dealing with matters of great import and, within a federal system such as ours, territorial and jurisdictional issues are dangerously tied to all of our cultural, social, economic, historical, and philosophical problems. One of the key reasons for the study of history, and why we need good historians, is not to learn the assumed lessons of history but to prevent its overt and outright misuse. The eminent British historian Eric Hobsbawm made precisely this point in a lecture given in that cauldron of historical revisionism, the Balkans. Speaking at the opening of the Central European University he said:

> History is the raw material for nationalist or ethnic or fundamentalist ideologies, as poppies are the raw material for heroin addiction. The past is an essential element, perhaps *the* essential element in these ideologies. If there is no suitable past it can always be invented. Indeed, in the nature of things there is usually no entirely suitable past, because the phenomenon these ideologies claim to justify is not ancient or eternal but historically novel. . . . The past legitimizes. . . . In this situation historians find themselves in the unexpected role of political actors. I used to think that the profession of history, unlike that of, say, nuclear physics, could do no harm. Now I know that it can.[21]

Any discussion of these larger issues takes us into a fourth area of great difficulty: the realm of cause and effect. Here we confront the kind of problems that have faced those who have studied the English civil war period, with the important proviso that they, unlike us, are not actors on the stage at the same time. Those who study the mid-seventeenth century and the struggle between King and Parliament that split the country, have asked what brought events to such an impasse. There is a confusing array of probable and plausible causes: the rise of a mercantile bourgeoisie; changes in the forces and modes of production; demography; the clash of religious principles and ideas; new political doctrines; town versus country; the accidents of circumstance and personality. In the words of Braudel and others this is the problem of the interplay between features that are supposedly of 'longue durée', which set conditions and boundaries, and those that are 'événementielle' and which are transitory or momentary, usually driven by reasonably practical responses to long-term and slow-moving features. At best this approach sees the fluctuating and circumstantial as 'conjonctures' playing a part somewhere between the long term and the immediate. This is a matter which will be discussed in far more depth in Chapter Five; it raises the problem of the distinctions that we make 'between those states of affairs or events which could have been altered by agency and those, it is supposed, which could not have been.'[22] It therefore raises the problems surrounding historical what-ifs and what-might-have-beens and the debate surrounding counterfactual explanation and understanding. What if Pierre Trudeau had not returned to power; what if the 1995 referendum had passed; what if?... and so on.[23]

In the case of the English civil war in the 1600s, each of the explanations (longue, moyenne, or événementielle) offers fertile and plausible arguments, as do almost any of them in combination.[24] And so it is with Canada. Today's constitutional crises can be seen as due to Quebec's Quiet Revolution, which also lends itself to a Marxist perspective.[25] There were enormous economic and social changes, particularly in western Canada, including the rise of far stronger provincial governments as well as new class 'fragments'.[26] There has been demographic change (as I write, a new book on generational demography tops the best-seller lists); immigration has changed the face of our cities and the realities of our politics; there are ongoing concerns about the Americanization of values and culture; and there has been the erosion of religion and its replacement, especially in Quebec, by secular, state-oriented values.[27] To this list can be added debates over institutional failure, geography, provincialism, and province building.[28] We have witnessed the rise and now contemplate the fall of the Keynesian embedded state.[29] There are renewed debates over the meaning of citizenship, and conflicts over the essence of Canadianness.[30] The party system has undergone cataclysmic change, particularly if one is a federal conservative.[31] And, of course, there are always questions about the actions or inactions of key players.[32] Our explanations for change can thus range from the pull of the universal homogeneous state and the loss of civility to the fact that René Lévesque was late for breakfast one fateful morning.[33] ('I went to breakfast and discovered that the seven had got together to tear up the agreement signed by everybody.'[34])

It is difficult to find a more graphic illustration of the fact/value and cause/effect interpretive dilemmas than the public exchange of letters, in late October of 1992, between former Prime Minister Pierre Elliott Trudeau and his long-time advisor and former Secretary to the Privy Council, the Honourable Gordon Robertson.[35] These are two men of great intelligence and vast experience, confidants and colleagues for many a year who were part of the same events and the same debates. Yet they agreed on nothing, not even the most basic 'facts'—let alone their consequences. The substance of their argument will form part of a later chapter; for the moment this correspondence is simply mentioned as an astonishing testimony to the problems noted above. It represents totally diverging views of history, of cause and effect, of what the constitution says and does, and of the impact of proposed changes. One has only to read such an exchange (as well as many of the Meech Lake debates) to understand the intractable nature of current constitutional discourse.[36]

Words—the same words—mean different things to different people. It is not so much a legal world of terminological hair-splitting and exactitude but an Orwellian universe where the 'boo' and the 'hurrah' words can be the same: it all depends on the observer. It is a world of code-words and subtext, of images and rhetoric and myth, of historical revisionism and justification, and of 'discourse'.[37] It is often a narrow realm, self-absorbed at a time when global forces press in upon a beleaguered federal state.

Within this overall context of analytical difficulty, briefly sketched above, this work is written. Its subject matter is the notion of constitutional abeyances developed by the British scholar Michael Foley in *The Silence of Constitutions: Gaps, 'abeyances' and political temperament in the maintenance of government.*[38] Foley's discussion of abeyances deals only with Britain and the United States. It is my contention that his thesis can also cast light on the constitutional difficulties that Canada has encountered; charting the emergence of one key abeyance will reveal, starkly, what happens when abeyances are unearthed or disinterred. Thinking in terms of abeyances provides a perspective on Canadian constitutional dilemmas that is both different and potentially useful. As such it could add important theoretical and practical pieces to the Canadian constitutional puzzle regarding what we can and should expect from our constitution, how mature and successful constitutions work, and how far we have moved from the temperament—and the gaps—needed to enable us to achieve constitutional peace.

It is therefore particularly important to establish, at the outset, what constitutional abeyances are, how they fit into the overall constitutional scheme of things, and why the idea appears to be so useful a notion in a Canadian setting. It is equally important, indeed vital, to establish at the outset what they are not. And throughout, it must be remembered that any discussion of larger constitutional issues will to some extent bear the imprint of the author's own values and value judgments, try as one might to be even–handed. We are all subject to the 'availability error'. We often will judge things not after careful, logical, empirical analysis but rather by what is uppermost in our mind and most readily available because it is recent, dramatic, concrete, symbolic, or emotional, and accords with our predispositions. In a recent work on the subject, Stuart Sutherland concludes that the unexamined primacy of certain assumptions 'permeates all reasoning'[39] even though we would wish it, and often believe it, to be otherwise. As Bernard Crick has argued, 'Political theory is itself political.'[40] It may, he says, be disguised as method but we must be on our guard against 'the dangers of a descriptivism or empiricism which lacks self-consciousness about its own assumptions.'[41] I have tried to be on guard, and also to bear in mind another of Crick's dictums, namely that 'the academic student of politics should be committed to saying things from the head that the heart might wish were otherwise.'[42]

This book is intended both for academic readers and for a more general audience interested in our ongoing search for constitutional calm. The notes at the end of each chapter provide background information and discursive comments but they are not essential reading, unless one wishes to pursue a topic in more detail. The following outline of each chapter is intended to provide an overview of the structure of the book, but it too can be omitted by readers who want to start immediately on the main argument.

Chapter One analyses Foley's use of the term abeyances and shows that they are not the product of imprecise legal images, conventions, or an unwritten constitution. Chapter Two contrasts abeyances with more commonly used and seemingly related notions, such as instrumentalities, myths, fictions, and taboos, and investigates the relationship between abeyances and the kind of constitutional wisdom to be found in the writings of Edmund Burke. This discussion of the utility of the concept is followed, in Chapter Three, by the general application of the idea to the settlement of 1867 and to our central abeyance: the status and recognition of Quebec as something other than a province. The nature of this and numerous other points of suspended irresolution is outlined, as are our reasons for tolerating ambiguity. What will be emphasized is that in 1867 the circumstances were appropriate for successful abeyance creation and maintenance and that the way in which we approached our problems did indeed have much that was Burkean about it. Our desire to avoid defining and constitutionalizing the differences between Quebec and English Canada (I use this term advisedly for historical reasons) will therefore be charted. This is neither to argue that there has been no legal recognition of difference, for there has, particularly regarding religion and language, nor is it to assume that we have lacked pragmatic asymmetrical arrangements. This is precisely the point: such definable measures, be they legal or fiscal, jurisdictional or denominational, have not attempted to constitutionalize the essence of the problem. They have, rather, been ways of avoiding it: watertight doors to prevent the entire ship from foundering; constitutional fictions so as to avoid having to tackle our deepest incompatibilities and inconsistencies. Chapter Four, therefore, traces why an acceptable settled unsettlement lasted so long, and how our abeyances came to the surface.

It is not my intent to venture at any length into the general political culture debate; this would take us too far afield. Mention must be made of specific elements of our political culture, such as parties, patronage, consociationalism, élitism, and ties to Britain, for they are vital parts of the political glue that held the system together and kept our abeyances in check. Political 'temperament' is an essential part of the Foleyan analysis and a discussion of Canadian temperament and Canadian political sophistication cannot be avoided. Nevertheless, these features of political culture will be seen only as context. The analysis presented relies heavily upon the work of specialists. It does not attempt to reinterpret or add to their work except in that it uses the notion of abeyances to provide a different prism through which to view our political history. It attempts to show why our abeyances—one in particular—were so different from those of either Britain or America, as were and are the ways in which we deal with them.

Chapter Four also discusses when, why, and how the abeyance of Quebec's status as a distinct society finally surfaced, and how we became engaged in the overt attempt to constitutionalise Quebec's distinctiveness. In so doing, a number of associated abeyances rose to the surface, at a time when their original context had changed out of all recognition, and when the temperament necessary for their avoidance had fallen out of fashion. Those politicians, such as Robert Stanfield, who attempted to deal with the abeyances surrounding Quebec's distinctiveness, became names on a lengthening casualty list of those who fell in the expanding constitutional wars. Their failure shows, above all, how intractable our abeyances were and why we disinter them at our peril: Canada, like Bram Stoker's Transylvania, has been haunted by the (constitutionally) undead.[43] At the heart of it all lies the question of smaller nations within larger states, and the considerable difficulties this poses.

Chapter Five discusses the ways in which the government of Pierre Trudeau sought to deal with our emergent constitutional disjunctions and the open claim for Quebec sovereignty that manifested itself with the victory of the Parti Québécois in 1976. It focuses specifically upon the work of *The Task Force on Canadian Unity*, reluctantly created in July of 1977, and otherwise known as the Pepin-Robarts Commission after its co-chairs, Jean-Luc Pepin, a former federal cabinet minister and head of the Anti-Inflation Board, and John P. Robarts, the former Premier of Ontario. The Task Force's report, *A Future Together: The Observations and Recommendations of the Task Force on Canadian Unity*, represents the most extensive and logically interconnected of the attempts to deal with and engage our abeyances, at least until the emergence of the Charlottetown Accord.[44] Chapter Five shows how it attempted to deal with the 'mega-abeyance' of duality. Pepin-Robarts can be seen as a follow-up to the *Report of the Royal Commission on Bilingualism and Biculturalism* (Laurendeau-Dunton) and as attempting to settle some of our greatest gaps of unsettlement.[45]

Accounts of what transpired and what *might* or *could* have taken place, if compelling, will 'suggest alternatives as they reduce them'.[46] The question of 'what-ifs' can be of more than passing interest as we now contemplate what is.

The Pepin-Robarts Report was intended to be window dressing; the Commissioners were to 'hold hands with the public' while the federal government marshalled its forces.[47] They exceeded their mandate and did not have the backing of Trudeau, to whom their recommendations were anathema. Some scholars see a clear thread running from the Report of the Tremblay Commission to the work of the Royal Commission on Bilingualism and Biculturalism (Laurendeau-Dunton) to Pepin-Robarts, then to the Meech Lake Accord and, finally, to the Charlottetown Accord and the reports and debates that preceded it.[48] However we assess the present state of our abeyances and the place of Quebec in Confederation, it is vital to understand the Trudeau approach that was to hold sway as a result of the great patriation debate and the events of 1981–2.

Chapter Six discusses the effects of Trudeau's actions upon our treatment and perception of abeyances and upon views of how Quebec should be treated. Trudeau's attitude, and the events leading up to the Constitution Act of 1982, have been exhaustively analysed and commented upon elsewhere. What is stressed in this context is his refusal to see Quebeckers as constituting a nation, and his determination to outflank the Quebec abeyance rather than confront it. This is the reverse of much of the conventional wisdom and as such is one reason for revisiting such a well-worn subject. (Kenneth McRoberts's analysis of the ironies of the Trudeau approach is a notable exception.) Trudeau's strategy of going around the abeyance as if it did not matter carried a high price. He was forced, or was inclined, to pit one abeyance against another and, in so doing, brought into play perhaps the most intractable abeyance of all: where is the locus of sovereignty in Canada and how is it to be exercised? In the effort to avoid confronting the Quebec question head on, the question of Quebec's distinctiveness was not laid to rest. When it did return, in the form of the 'distinct society' clause of the Meech Lake Accord, followed by the Charlottetown Accord, Trudeau intervened and confronted it directly and savagely. His comments are contrasted with the kind of political as well as moral advice to be found in Burke, and with the temperament and approach necessary to achieve an acceptable constitutional resolution of such a volatile question as the existence of more than one nationalism within a liberal state.

This leads naturally to the conclusion and to the question of the state of our abeyances now, and the future of Quebec within Canada. Can we just leave our abeyances alone? Should we do so, or must we now be imaginative, proactive, and magnanimous? Can we learn anything of significance by comparing Quebec's situation with that of another small nation, Scotland, within a larger state? In Canada matters are settled in that the arrangements of 1982 are deeply entrenched, highly federalized, and extremely complex; any attempt to change them is fraught with obvious difficulties, particularly since the referendum of October 1992 on the Charlottetown Accord. Yet constitutional issues remain unsettled in the eyes of those who believe that 1982 was a flawed and unfortunate compact that, in particular, left out Quebec, violated our constitutional continuities, and paradoxically did not tackle our greatest abeyance. We are still in a constitutional no man's land and no cease fire has been sounded.

Canada's experience with abeyances, and with one in particular, casts further light on Foley's thesis. All who have tried to tackle the Quebec abeyance can be listed as missing in action, with the possible exception of Pierre Trudeau. His failure may be yet to come, when historians examine his role after his retirement in 1984. We have now put in place significant new constitutional provisions and have heightened expectations. At the same time, the legal rules for constitutional change are so gridlocked that formal change is almost out of the question. What we have now is the reverse of the Foleyan wisdom, for we have neither *settled unsettlement* (where there is suspended but acceptable irresolution) nor even *unsettled unsettlement* (where there would at least be agreement that matters are indeed unsettled and cannot remain so). These are the two conditions that Foley envisages, and mature constitutions contain the former, not the latter. I argue that we have instead a third and uniquely Canadian variant, namely *unsettled settlement*, and time alone may not be a sufficient cure. A change of heart and perspective may be our best, and last, hope if the country is to stay united.

Notes

1 See, for example, the recent reviews of the following books: *Canada: Reclaiming the Middle Ground*; *Negotiating with a Sovereign Quebec*; *Canada's Century: Governance in a Maturing Society*; *Seeking a New Canadian Partnership: Asymmetrical and Federal Options*; *Trudeau and the End of a Canadian Dream*; *Thinking English Canada*. Such titles in themselves illustrate our difficulties.

2 Alan C. Cairns, 'Ritual, Taboo, and Bias in Constitutional Controversies in Canada, or Constitutional Talk Canadian Style' in *Disruptions: Constitutional Struggles from the Charter to Meech Lake*, ed. Douglas E. Williams (Toronto: McClelland and Stewart, 1991), 201.

3 See the Canada West Foundation's summary document, *A Roadmap for Constitutional Change* (Calgary: Canada West Foundation, 1991). This figure is approximate. It depends upon what one counts as 'significant'. The *Roadmap* omits one or two of importance, and includes certain others that had little significance. Between 1950 and 1990 there were twenty-two constitutional conferences. See Nelson Wiseman, 'In Search of Manitoba's Constitutional Position, 1950–1990', *Journal of Canadian Studies* 29, 3 (Fall 1994), 85–107.

4 Ronald L. Watts, 'The Macdonald Commission and Canadian Federalism' in *Canadian Federalism: Past, Present and Future*, ed. Michael Burgess (Leicester: Leicester University Press, 1990).

5 Douglas M. Brown, ed., *Canada: The State of the Federation 1991* (Ottawa: Renouf Press, 1992). A bibliography on federalism produced by Darrell R. Reid for the period 1980–5 lists 3,418 separate sources. See *Bibliography of Canadian and Comparative Federalism* (Kingston: Institute of Intergovernmental Relations, 1988).

Introduction xxi

6 Daniel Latouche, with the collaboration of Guy Falardeau and Michel Levesque, has edited an exceptionally useful and comprehensive new bibliographic guide: *Politique et Société au Québec: guide bibliographique* (Montreal: Boréal, 1993). It includes English as well as French sources. To further illustrate the point I am making, the section which covers 'Cadre constitutionnel et régime fédéral' runs to 47 pages and almost 2,000 titles without listing sources that cover institutions, parties, ideologies, foreign relations, or a number of other important areas. Note also the extensive bibliography of over 1,000 sources organized by Michael Seymour, ed. *Une nation peut-elle se donner la constitution de son choix?* (Montreal: Bellarmin, 1995).

7 This is not to suggest that English-speaking Canadians would not benefit from, and be surprised by, the rich variety of literary sources now available, as a visit to a good Quebec bookstore will demonstrate. One does, however, hear complaints that Quebec authors see little of the subsidy monies that are made available to publishing houses, and many important works do not get translated.

8 Allan Tupper, 'English Canadian Scholars and the Meech Lake Accord', *International Journal of Canadian Studies* 7–8 (Spring-Fall 1993), 347–57 at 348. Scholars have also been accused of a perhaps inevitable parochialism. See, for example, the comments made in the introductory chapter to Keith G. Banting and Richard Simeon, eds, *Redesigning the State: The Politics of Constitutional Change in Industrial Nations* (Toronto: University of Toronto Press, 1985).

9 Tupper, 350.

10 Claude Denis, 'Quebec-as-distinct-society and conventional wisdom: the constitutional silence of anglo-Canadian sociology', *Canadian Journal of Sociology* 18, 3 (1993), 252–69. He provides an extremely interesting critique of our use of such terms, albeit from a particular perspective. The separation of English- and French-Canadian sociologists should also be noted. Dennis P. Forcese has argued that 'The development of Canada's two sociologies has occurred with infrequent contact with one another.' See 'Sociology in Canada: A View from the Eighties', *International Journal of Canadian Studies* 1–2 (Spring-Fall 1990), 35–53. Canada's historians have also come in for criticism. The British historian Ged Martin, after quoting some outrageous observations by Arthur Lower on French-Canadian character, has commented rhetorically, 'Sometimes I ask myself whether Canada has been well served by its historians.' See 'What We Know and What We Think We Know: The Great Coalition of 1864 in The Province of Canada', paper presented at the Annual Conference of the British Association of Canadian Studies (Nottingham, 1991), 46. See also D.G. Creighton, 'Sir John A. Macdonald and Canadian Historians' in *Approaches to Canadian History*, eds Ramsay Cook, Craig Brown, and Carl Berger (Toronto: University of Toronto Press, 1967), 55–6: 'Canadian historians, in all too many cases, commit Macaulay's mistakes, without the exercise of his virtues ... their views seem to have a disturbingly close approximation to the planks of one of the party platforms of their period of study.' In both the United Kingdom and Canada there has been an ongoing debate about the role that historians should play in the telling of national stories.

11 Roger Gibbins, 'Federal Societies, Institutions, and Politics' in *Federalism and the Role of the State*, eds Herman Bakvis and William M. Chandler (Toronto: University of Toronto Press, 1987), 15.

xxii **Introduction**

12 As British examples of detailed and analytical memoirs see the three volumes of Richard Crossman's *The Diaries of a Cabinet Minister* (London: Hamish Hamilton, 1975) and, more recently, the highly acclaimed and entertaining account of his political years by Roy Jenkins entitled *A Life at the Centre* (New York: Random House, 1993). In the bibliography provided on the Prime Minister and Cabinet in a widely used, major text on Canadian government and politics (Rand Dyck's *Canadian Politics: Critical Approaches* (Scarborough: Nelson, 1993), one insider's account only is noted, that of Sir Robert Borden, written in 1938! Anthony King's comment regarding the debate over prime ministerial power 'being conducted largely on the level of a barroom brawl' applies also to memoirs. Not surprisingly, this plethora of British diarists has been resented by colleagues. The Scottish MP Willie Ross had a hearty dislike of his 'chattering English colleagues, who flooded the bookstores with their diaries'. See Arnold Kemp, *The Hollow Drum: Scotland Since the War* (Edinburgh: Mainstream Publishing, 1995), 107–8.

13 See Robert Young, ed., *Confederation in Crisis* (Toronto: James Lorimer, 1991), 90–5. Young quotes Peter Russell's heartfelt remark in defence of his constitutional position: 'But I guess I'm speaking as a patriot. I love my country. I know patriotism is the refuge of scoundrels, but I don't mind.'

14 Stephen Brooks and Alain-G. Gagnon, *Social Scientists and Politics in Canada: Between Clerisy and Vanguard* (Montreal and Kingston: McGill-Queen's University Press, 1988). The introductory chapter to this study provides a wide-ranging summary of the issues. See also Doug Owram, *The Government Generation: Canadian Intellectuals and the State 1900–1945* (Toronto: University of Toronto Press, 1986); Stephen Brooks and Alain-G. Gagnon, 'Politics and the Social Sciences in Canada' in *Canadian Politics: an introduction to the discipline*, eds Alain-G. Gagnon and James P. Bickerton (Peterborough: Broadview Press, 1990); Peter Wagner and Bjorn Wittrock, *Social Scientists, Policy and the State* (New York: Praeger and Co., 1989); Marc Henry Sulet, *Le silence des intellectuels: radioscopie de l'intellectuel québécois* (Montreal: Éditions Saint-Martin, 1987). Sulet discusses Quebec's 'loss' of its intellectuals and, in turn, their loss also.

15 See the introductory remarks in E. Black, *Divided Loyalties: Canadian Concepts of Federalism* (Montreal and Kingston: McGill-Queen's University Press, 1975), 4. I may also be a victim of this phenomenon, even though all of my working life has been spent in Canada. I have a Welsh-speaking father and an English mother. Thinking in terms of lives also raises the problem of political generations, and, in this case, the effects of generational change on attitudes towards matters constitutional. Stephen Schechter has argued that in the United States there have been clearly discernible generational factors driving the way in which the amending process has been used. See Stephen L. Schechter, 'Amending the United States Constitution: A New Generation on Trial' in *Redesigning the State*, 160–203. Although I think that there are difficulties with his argument, it does raise the question of the connections between generational and constitutional change in Canada as something worthy of study. See, for example, John C. Pierce, et al., 'Generational Differences in the Public's Policy Preferences in British Columbia', *International Journal of Canadian Studies* (Winter 1993), 23–38. Note also the debate over post-materialism, values, and support for sovereignty. See Pierre Martin, 'Générations politiques, rationalité économique et appui à la souveraineté au Québec', *Canadian Journal of Political Science* 27, 2 (June 1994), 345–59.

16 Eugene Forsey, *A Life on the Fringe: The Memoirs of Eugene Forsey* (Toronto: Oxford University Press, 1990), 125.

17 Alan C. Cairns, 'The Growth of Constitutional Self-Consciousness' in *Disruptions*, 33.

18 '*L'avenir politique et constitutionnel du Québec*' (Québec: Éditeur Officiel du Québec, 1991).

19 'Ultimately, then, [the] facts don't matter; the important thing is the effect produced, how effectively the argument is presented.' Jacinthe Ruel, '*Le passé au service du présent. Les mémoires de la Commission Bélanger-Campeau, entre la mémoire et la rhétorique*', paper presented at the annual meeting of the British Association for Canadian Studies (Cambridge, 1993), 19. See also John English, 'The Second Time Around: Political Scientists Writing History', *Canadian Historical Review* 67, 1 (1986), 1–16. English criticizes political economists in particular. Historians do at least try to provide as accurate a portrayal as they can of a world that was, and show how it is linked to the one that came to be. Political theorists, however, work with ideas from the past but are present- and future-oriented. The danger is, as Gordon S. Wood notes, that 'they are, as historians like to say, very "Whiggish"; they usually see the past simply as an anticipation of our present, and thus they tend to hold people in the past responsible for a future that was in fact inconceivable to them.' *New York Review of Books* (23 May 1996), 53. This point must be borne in mind when discussing the settlement of 1867.

20 Max Nemni, 'Le "des"accord du Lac Meech et la construction de l'imaginaire symbolique des Québécois' in *Le Québec et la restructuration du Canada—1980–1992*, eds Louis Balthazar, Guy Laforest, and Vincent Lemieux (Quebec: Sillery, 1991), 179. Nemni's article is a wholesale attack on myths and Quebec historical interpretations in general, and is a powerful contribution to the debate, even though it is hotly contested. See also his recent appraisal of the historical significance of the work of the commission. Max Nemni, 'La Commission Bélanger-Campeau et la construction de l'idée de sécession au Québec', *International Journal of Canadian Studies* 7–8 (Spring–Fall 1993), 285–314. Wherever a source is in French but the quotation used in the text is in English, the original has been translated. Otherwise, I have left the quotation in French, and a translation is provided in the notes.

21 Eric Hobsbawm, 'The New Threat to History', *The New York Review of Books* (16 December 1993), 62–4. See also his work on nationalism in general. E.J. Hobsbawm, *Nations and Nationalism since 1780: Programme, Myth, Reality* (Cambridge: Cambridge University Press, 1990). For a critical review of the approach taken by Hobsbawm (and also by Benedict Anderson in *Imagined Communities: Reflections on the Origin and Spread of Nationalism*, rev. edn (London: Verso, 1993), see Elias José Palti, 'Liberalism vs. Nationalism: Hobsbawm's Dilemma', *Telos* 95 (Spring 1993), 109–26. Also see the review by Tony Judt, 'The New Old Nationalism', *The New York Review of Books* (26 May 1994), 44–9. Judt also comments of Anderson's work that its 'metaphorical reach exceeds its historical grasp'. The harm done is graphically illustrated in Michael Ignatieff's *Blood and Belonging: Journeys into the New Nationalism* (Toronto: Penguin Books, 1993).

22 Geoffrey Hawthorn, *Plausible Worlds* (Cambridge: Cambridge University Press, 1991), 30. For a discussion of Braudel's work and a list of commentaries, see the

xxiv **Introduction**

extensive footnotes accompanying the discussion on pp. 28–30. The question of how major changes occur in a complex federation—such as Canada's—is something that should concern us. John E. Trent and others have pointed out that the Meech Lake and Charlottetown Accords may be seen as clear failures or 'they can be perceived as stepping stones in a much longer process that requires attitudinal adjustments to new concepts prior to symbolic and institutional power shifts'. See John E. Trent, Robert Young, and Guy Lachapelle, eds, *Québec–Canada. What Is the Path Ahead?* (Ottawa: University of Ottawa Press, 1995), 15.

23 Ibid. Hawthorn's ideas are discussed and utilised in Chapter Five.

24 For a still useful discussion of the problems of the philosophy of history see W.H. Walsh, *Introduction to the Philosophy of History* (London: Hutchinson and Co., 1967). Walsh attacks the view that historians must retreat into less exposed and very limited interpretive positions. He uses the analogy of travel abroad. 'To go backwards in time is in many ways comparable to going outwards in space, and not the least in the circumstances that those who undertake the journey feel the need both to report and to assess' (186).

25 There is now a very extensive literature on the Quiet Revolution, covering everything from questions about its origins and when it began, to whether or not it really was a revolution. For an overview of the changes in Quebec in their entirety, it is difficult to find a more readable source than Kenneth McRoberts's text *Quebec: Social Change and Political Crisis*, 3rd edn (Toronto: McClelland and Stewart, 1993). For full bibliographic details on Quebec see *Politique et Société au Québec*, ed. Latouche.

26 See especially Garth Stevenson's discussion of class fragments in his well-known text *Unfulfilled Union: Canadian Federalism and National Unity* (Toronto: Macmillan, 1989). See also Larry Pratt and John Richards's classic work *Prairie Capitalism: Power and Influence in the New West* (Toronto: McClelland and Stewart, 1979).

27 See for example the explanation in Richard Simeon and Ian Robinson, *State, Society, and the Development of Canadian Federalism*, Research Studies of the Royal Commission on the Economic Union and Development Prospects for Canada (Toronto: University of Toronto Press, 1990), vol. 71, 145ff. Their views are representative of the standard explanations of the end of the Duplessis era. I think that it is extremely difficult for those who live outside Quebec to really come to terms with the political role that religion has played in the province and how recently and dramatically this changed. As late as 1956 so perceptive an observer as Michael Oliver wrote: 'If nationalism is a basic datum in Quebec, Roman Catholicism is even more fundamental. It can be taken as axiomatic for the foreseeable future that only social and political movements that are capable of operating within a Catholic context can gain strength in French Canada.' See Michael Oliver, *The Passionate Debate: The Social and Political Ideas of Quebec Nationalism 1920–1945* (Montreal: Véhicule Press, 1991), 16. As Oliver now points out in his preface, although he significantly overestimated the staying power of the Church, this does not mean, however, that ways of looking at the world 'that are predominantly Catholic' have vanished.

28 Much of this debate focuses of course on such questions as the merits of inter- versus intrastate federalism, the empirical evidence for and against the effects and realities of province building, the workability of executive federalism and the failures of the party and electoral systems to focus debate on national rather than regional issues. For an

excellent discussion of the struggles of the late 1970s to the mid-1980s, and the problems to be faced when analysing them, see David Milne, *Tug of War: Ottawa and the Provinces Under Trudeau and Mulroney* (Toronto: James Lorimer, 1986).

29 See in particular the work of Alan C. Cairns, for example, 'The Embedded State: State-Society Relations in Canada' in *State and Society: Canada in Comparative Perspective*, Research Studies of the Royal Commission on the Economic Union and Development Prospects for Canada (Toronto: University of Toronto Press, 1986), vol. 31; 'The Governments and Societies of Canadian Federalism' in *Constitution, Government and Society in Canada*, ed. Douglas E. Williams (Toronto: McClelland and Stewart, 1988); and 'The Politics of Constitutional Conservatism', also in *Constitution, Government and Society in Canada*.

30 For example see R. Kenneth Carty and W. Peter Ward, 'The Making of a Canadian Political Citizenship' in *National Politics and Political Community in Canada*, eds R. Kenneth Carty and W. Peter Ward (Vancouver: University of Vancouver Press, 1986); Charles Taylor, 'Legitimacy, Identity and Alienation in Late Twentieth Century Canada' in *Constitutionalism, Citizenship and Society in Canada*, eds Alan Cairns and Cynthia Williams, Research Studies of the Royal Commission on the Economic Union and Development Prospects for Canada (Toronto: University of Toronto Press, 1985), vol. 33, 183–229. Also, in the same volume, note Alan Cairns and Cynthia Williams, 'Constitutionalism, Citizenship and Society in Canada: An Overview', 1–50; for a discussion of our current difficulties over citizenship, see Jean Bethke Elshtain, *Democracy On Trial*, CBC Massey Lectures Series (Concord: Anansi Press Ltd, 1993). Peter Russell's important overview and analysis of the problems of citizenship, nationalism, and sovereignty must also be mentioned and has been widely quoted: Peter H. Russell, *Constitutional Odyssey: Can Canadians Become a Sovereign People?* 2nd edn (Toronto: University of Toronto Press, 1993); for an earlier version of the idea of the lack of agreement see Kenneth McNaught's comment that 'As a nation Canada has never had any conclusive debate about the fundamental assumptions of her national polity.' 'Ottawa and Washington Look at the U.N.', *Foreign Affairs* 33 (July 1955), 666. Note also Donald V. Smiley's powerful and succinct work *The Canadian Political Nationality* (Toronto: Methuen, 1967).

31 See, for example, the changing role of parties and patronage as discussed by David Elkins, 'Parties as National Institutions: A Comparative Study' in *Representation, Integration and Political Parties in Canada*, ed. Herman Bakvis, Royal Commission on Electoral Reform and Party Financing (Toronto: Dundurn Press, 1991), vol. 14, 3–62; David Smith, 'Perennial alienation: the prairie west in the Canadian federation' in *Canadian Federalism*, ed. Michael Burgess; Gordon T. Stewart, 'Political Patronage Under Macdonald and Laurier 1878–1911', *Canadian Political Party Systems*, ed. R.K. Carty (Peterborough: Broadview Press, 1992). Stewart's work is particularly useful for an understanding of a key mechanism of political accommodation in the first half-century following Confederation. See also his earlier work, *The Origins of Confederation* (Vancouver: University of British Columbia Press, 1986). The literature on new parties and on populism is too extensive to review, and will be referred to in a subsequent chapter.

32 This takes us back to the problems of 'histoire événementielle' and causation, and to the roles of individuals and circumstance. In Canada's case there may be a strong argument that leadership has indeed made a huge difference, at least insofar as national

xxvi **Introduction**

parties are concerned. See David E. Smith, 'Party Government, Representation and National Integration in Canada' in *Party Government and Regional Representation in Canada*, ed. Peter Aucoin, Research Studies of the Royal Commission on the Economic Union and Development Prospects for Canada (Toronto: University of Toronto Press, 1985), vol. 36.

33 The loss of civility and the consequences for democracy, society, and politics are entertainingly and clearly discussed by Jean Bethke Elshtain in her 1993 Massey Lecture, *Democracy on Trial*. For a provocative discussion of the state in a new global context see Peter Emberley, 'Globalism and Localism: Constitutionalism in a New World Order' in *Constitutional Predicament: Canada After the Referendum of 1992*, ed. Curtis Cook (Montreal and Kingston: McGill-Queen's University Press, 1994).

34 *The Gazette*, 6 November 1981. The historic deal-making First Ministers' Conference was held in the first week of November, 1981. On the evening of the third day (and into the early hours of the fourth) discussions were held which would lead to seven premiers breaking ranks with Lévesque and dissolving what had been known as 'the gang of eight' versus Trudeau. The Quebec delegation was not a party to this last-minute turnaround (it was staying across the river in Hull), and Lévesque only found out about it the next morning when he arrived late for breakfast—and had little or no time to react. See Russell, *Constitutional Odyssey*, Ch. 7.

35 *The Globe and Mail,* 8, 21, and 24 October, 1992.

36 Not to mention the difficulties of communicating coherently using different networks and languages. See Marc Raboy, 'Des vases non communicants; les communications québécoises dans le système fédéral canadien' in *Bilan québécois du fédéralisme canadien*, ed. François Rocher (Montreal: VLB éditeur, 1992).

37 Note the comments made on this subject in Claude Denis, 'Quebec-as-distinct-society and conventional wisdom: the constitutional silence of anglo-Canadian sociology'. Denis attempts to 'deconstruct' the term 'distinct society', as well as several others in current usage.

38 Michael Foley, *The Silence of Constitutions: Gaps, 'abeyances' and political temperament in the maintenance of government* (New York: Routledge, 1989).

39 Stuart Sutherland, *Irrationality: The Enemy Within* (London: Constable and Company, 1992), 16.

40 Bernard Crick, *In Defence of Politics*, 4th edn (London: Weidenfeld and Nicholson, 1992), 186. This and the following quotations are taken from an essay entitled 'A Footnote to Rally the Academic Professors of Politics', which has been added to the fourth edition, along with two other such 'footnotes'.

41 Ibid., 190.

42 Ibid., 194.

43 I was taken by the use of a similar expression in A.T.Q. Stewart's work on the problems of Irish nationalism, *The Narrow Ground: The Roots of Conflict in Ulster* (London: Faber and Faber, 1989). This analysis is particularly useful for the light that it sheds on the relationships between the deeper patterns of history and the effects of contemporary events. The outbreaks of 'the Troubles' in Ireland have always been linked to what was happening outside the country. Political events else-

where, and external support, have been extremely important. In addition, Stewart argues that 'Not only are the lessons of the past disregarded; the community is actually instructed on all sides to disregard them, and at all costs. . . . Even if the community succeeded in forgetting the past, however, it is not likely that the past would forget it. The consequences of ignoring basic precepts are now all too obvious' (184). Patterns do not get changed or broken easily, and in a struggle for political and constitutional power, history, as Stewart notes, is a quarry in which we find rocks to throw. The same is true in Canada.

44 Canada, *A Future Together: Observations and Recommendations*, Task Force on Canadian Unity (Ottawa: Queen's Printer, 1979). The Task Force also produced two accompanying documents, *Coming to Terms: The Words of the Debate*, and *A Time to Speak: The Views of the Public*.

45 *Report of the Royal Commission on Bilingualism and Biculturalism* (Ottawa, Queen's Printer, 1965–70). Note also Christopher R. Adamson, 'The Unpublished Research of the Royal Commission on Bilingualism and Biculturalism', *Canadian Journal of Political Science* 7, 4 (December 1974), 709–20.

46 Hawthorn, *Plausible Worlds*, 33.

47 For a discussion of this and other events surrounding the creation of the Task Force see Cristine Andrea Beauvais de Clercy, 'Holding Hands With The Public: Trudeau and the Task Force on Canadian Unity' (MA thesis, Saskatchewan, 1992). A succinct discussion of the writing of the Report is to be found in David R. Cameron, 'Not Spicer and Not the B & B: Reflections of an Insider on the Workings of the Pepin-Robarts Task Force on Canadian Unity', *International Journal of Canadian Studies* 7–8 (Spring-Fall 1993), 333–46.

48 See Cameron, 'Not Spicer and not the B & B'. For a defence of Charlottetown as a *principled* settlement that took into account the deeper questions of Canadian federalism see Ronald Watts, 'The Reform of Federal Institutions' in *The Charlottetown Accord, the Referendum, and the Future of Canada*, eds Kenneth McRoberts and Patrick Monahan (Toronto: University of Toronto Press, 1993), 17–36.

1

The World of Abeyances

Abeyance: 'A state of suspension, temporary non-existence or inactivity: dormant or latent condition liable to be at any time revived.'

Any Canadian scholar who reads Michael Foley's *The Silence of Constitutions* could not fail to be struck by its possible applicability to the Canadian situation and the Canadian condition. Foley's elegant analysis is densely packed with observations and conclusions that are thought-provoking: what he has to say about the workings of the British and American constitutions and the political temperament necessary to sustain them has an eerie applicability to Canada. Foley's ideas, as the noted British political theorist Bernard Crick has pointed out, are 'outstandingly subtle, important and well argued'.

Foley posits a constitutional universe where we must recognize a new category of phenomena, which he calls 'abeyances'. The awkward thing about them, however, is that they are noticeable by their seeming absence rather than their overt presence. This entails, as we shall see, some analytical difficulties. For the moment it is perhaps useful to provide an illustrative metaphor. Abeyances can be thought of as constitutional black holes: they are detectable largely by the behaviour of things around them. In spite of a good deal of evidence, their existence may be doubted and alternative explanations will be offered to account for the way things are. But we will still feel their gravitational attraction. A real black hole is surrounded, it is theorized, by an 'event horizon, the boundary of the region of space-time from which it is not possible to escape' and which acts like a one-way membrane. Once something passes through it, there is no getting out.[1] Constitutional abeyances may also have an event horizon, for abeyances will be densely packed with material of an intensity and power that is qualitatively different to other constitutional phenomena; getting too close to one is dangerous, for one can be sucked into its core, and into a debate which had not been anticipated. Luckily we are only using a metaphor, and these should not be pushed too far, or be allowed to carry the full weight of an argument.[2] Whether or not one can escape from the constitutional gravitational pull of an abeyance and retreat through the membrane (or come out the other side) remains an open question. It will be argued that we may be able to return an abeyance to necessary obscurity, and to act as if it were not there. Nevertheless, the black hole comparison is useful to bear in mind as we enter the Foleyan universe.[3]

He explains these 'perverse phenomena' as an intermediate but vital layer to be found between the metaphysical and moral adjuncts to constitutions (the world of Aristotelian values and teleological ends) and the largely unwritten constitutional conventions which are, nonetheless, accepted, acceptable and, in the main, understood. But abeyances rest in a 'twilight zone' and this is where, in Foley's view, we should leave them. His definition of abeyances is that they are:

> constitutional gaps which remain vacuous for positive and constructive purposes. They are not, in any sense, truces between two or more defined positions, but rather a set of implicit agreements to collude in keeping fundamental questions of political authority in a state of irresolution. Abeyances are, in effect, compulsive hedges against the possibility of that which is unresolved being exploited and given meanings almost guaranteed to generate profound division and disillusionment. Abeyances are important, therefore, because of their capacity to deter the formation of conflicting positions in just those areas where the potential for conflict is most acute. So central are these abeyances, together with the social temperament required to sustain them, that when they become the subject of heightened interest and subsequent conflict, they are not merely accompanied by an intense constitutional crisis, they are themselves the essence of that crisis.[4]

Thus, in the Foleyan constitutional cosmology, constitutional conventional wisdom is reversed.

Constitutions are usually seen as unfolding, as being progressively refined, as having 'gaps' filled in, as developing into tightly constructed edifices with both solid foundations and tried, tested, and well-thought-out additions. Foley's thesis is that such a view, with its emphasis on 'the rule of law . . . legal precision, ascertainable rights, and determinable powers'[5] flies in the face of constitutional, historical, and socio/cultural reality, for it ignores the existence of extremely awkward, 'even perverse' phenomena, namely the need for 'gaps of unsettlement'. It is therefore a mark of constitutional maturity when a constitution is 'incoherent' but accepted; when its values are contradictory and unsettled in some fundamental ways.

This does not mean that there is not an *appearance* of settlement: far from it. For constitutions to work there must exist the constitutional equivalents of the Emperor's new clothes. Perhaps this goes too far and gets too close to a Platonic noble lie (although Foley does not use this term). What is really being defended is the idea that a constitution must be '*acceptably* imprecise and agreeably *elusive*'[6] (Foley's words, my emphasis) and that the furies of opposing principles must not be allowed to run rampant. Abeyances are thus understandings: tacit, ambiguous, geared to order and tradition and deference; based upon fear of change and the resolve, consciously or unconsciously, to exclude fundamental dissent:

It is recognized that any attempt to define them would be not merely unnecessary or impossible, but positively misguided and even potentially threatening to the constitution itself. This is because such 'understandings' only remain understood as long as they remain sufficiently obscure to allow them to retain an approximate appearance of internal coherence and clarity, while at the same time accommodating several potentially conflicting and quite unresolved points of issue. The resolution of conflict in such cases is that of suspended irresolution—either consciously secured or, far more probably, unconsciously and unintentionally acquired. These packages of aggregated positions are preserved by studied inattention. They may include contradictions, tensions, anomalies, and inequities, but the fragility and, at times, total illogicality of such packages are kept intact through a convention of non-exposure, of strategic oversight, and of complicity in delusion—in short, through an instinctive reversion to not breaking ranks when confronted with the constitutional equivalents of the emperor's clothes.[7]

Perhaps, at this stage, it is useful to apply the abeyance idea to two well-known situations where it is easier to see abeyances at work than it is in the constitutional arena. The first of these is the situation in a long-standing marriage. In most successful relationships there will be areas of exclusion and of complicity in this exclusion. There are likely, almost inevitably, to be 'no go' zones where there is suspended irresolution of certain matters. Neither spouse has won the battle over the points at issue and to resume the battle is fruitless (in fact they may have different opinions about what these points even are). Such matters may seem minor, certainly to an outsider, but because of their subtext they are not. Avoiding these areas is to escape from conflict over precisely those matters about which conflict is most acute; such debates strike at the very heart of the relationship and bring back old wounds and deep scars. To commence an argument is to invite a crisis in which the specific point at issue, or whatever triggered it, becomes secondary to the new crisis itself and the emotions it produces. Abeyances raised inevitably attract other problems. To avoid activating an abeyance, marriages develop conventions of avoidance: there will be 'wilful neglect, protective obfuscation, and complicity in non-exposure'[8] (to use Foley's terminology). In a column written after the October referendum Lysiane Gagnon used precisely this marital analogy, quoting Josh Freed to the effect that:

> I've come to the conclusion that constitutions are like marriage contracts. They are easy to sign before the wedding, when both parties share a rosy optimism about their future. But they are impossible to renegotiate once you've lived together too long. Imagine trying to spell out the unspoken rules of your relationship after ten years with your partner.[9]

It may be the case that the people involved do not really understand what the situation is and why the 'rules' operate as they do.[10] R.D. Laing has argued that in families and in the social world in general there may be (i) 'rules that certain values must not be challenged, *questioned* or even *seen* [and] (ii) there may be a rule not only against seeing that there is such a value, and that there is such a rule.' There may also be rules against seeing the rule that the values cannot be questioned or seen![11]

A more theoretical illustrative abeyance, but one of considerable importance, may lie buried within our Anglo-Saxon jury system, for if we think at all deeply about juries there would appear to be a serious paradox at the core of the notion of a trial by one's peers. We choose 'peers' so that a jury will in some important ways be 'like' the accused and can therefore place him or her in context. Jury members will, it is assumed, not be so dissimilar that they do not understand the sort of circumstances that surround the case and therefore understand the kinds of actions that peers would regard as acceptable in the situation. Yet, at the same time, these peers are required to have little or no knowledge of the accused or of the case. They are supposed to be average citizens, opinionless, influenced only by the evidence they hear. The abeyance is the incompatibility between these two ideas, one requiring a jury of individuals who will understand what happened because they can place the accused in a comprehensible setting, the other demanding a group of jurors who know as little as is humanly possible about the case or the community's feelings. If we really believed in one or the other of these views exclusively, juries and results would be very different indeed. But we do not push these questions to their limits; we leave a gap of unsettlement *at their core* and pretend that the technicalities of jury selection provide an answer. They only do so because we avoid the logic of the underlying questions.

A true jury of one's peers would mean that police officers should try other police officers, or accountants should sit in judgment on accountants, as professional societies are supposed to do. Clearly this creates unacceptable problems. At the same time it is difficult to believe that a jury comprised predominantly of female members of the lower middle class, or the working poor, have much in common with a male plastic surgeon accused of malpractice; this does not look much like judgment by one's neutral peers. This set of contradictory problems arises in terms of the selection of juries for aboriginal cases being tried in, or close to, the accused's community. This, the demand to be tried by peers, taken to its logical extreme, involves the concept of cultural differences. Here the argument is more subtle, and it hinges upon the view that certain identifiable cultural groups have a right to a trial by the standards of the group, or at least in a way that takes such standards into consideration. This is a demand for a jury who will understand the context and the 'real' nature of the evidence and whose verdict will be acceptable to the community; but there is often deep reluctance to sit on such a jury, and outside suspicion is that it would be biased. There are obviously enormous unresolved issues here. Should a black person be tried by a black jury? If a poor black is tried by successful, professional, educated blacks, could this be challenged? What cultural (or socioeconomic) groups are to count, and how? We cannot expect to find satisfactory answers if we push the problem to its limits.[12]

Foley's views thus raise a host of intriguing questions about the applicability of the idea of constitutional abeyances in a Canadian setting. (His application is, first of all, to the relationship between the Stuart Kings and Parliament, when James I and Charles I challenged the abeyances surrounding royal powers. Secondly he deals with the presidency of Richard Nixon, when the tacit silences surrounding the powers and role of the president became controversial.) Even if we agree that the idea of abeyances is a very useful corrective to the assumption that constitutions simply set out clear statements of rights and principles, a key question will aways lurk in the background: as with a marriage, should we not seek greater clarity on important matters? Is there not a need to recognize and articulate certain things and not take them either for granted or as matters to be avoided? How many abeyances, and of what type, is it healthy to support?

These are particularly important problems in Canada's case, and will be a central part of later discussions. But first we must be sure that the scene has been set by establishing that a constitution is far more than a set of legally definable rules, and by emphasizing that although constitutional practice is often driven by unwritten conventions, whether a constitution is largely written or unwritten does not in itself account for the need for abeyances, nor does it indicate the forms that abeyance preservation will take—and whether it will be successful.

To determine what a constitution 'is', it might seem straightforward enough to rely on standard textbook definitions, and where better to start than with Peter Hogg's *Constitutional Law of Canada*. Hogg points out that:

> In Canada (as in the United Kingdom) there is no single document comparable to the Constitution of the United States and the word 'Constitution' accordingly lacks a definite meaning. The closest approximation to such a document is the British North America Act, 1867, which was renamed the Constitution Act, 1867 in 1982.[13]

He goes on to point out that in the Constitution Act, 1982, there is, for the first time, provision for a definition of the phrase 'Constitution of Canada'. It is defined, in s. 52 (2), as including:

(a) the Canada Act, 1982, including this Act;
(b) the Acts and orders referred to in the schedule; and
(c) any amendment to any Act or order referred to above in paragraph (a) or (b).[14]

The word 'includes' would seem to imply that this definition is not complete, but Hogg contends that this is highly unlikely to be the case, given the specificity and length of the list referred to in (b) above. It comprises 30 Acts and orders including, of course, the Constitution Act, 1867 itself and its amendments, as well as the orders in council and statutes creating or admitting provinces, and the Statute of Westminster. Hogg sees it as 'only realistic to regard the definition as exhaustive'[15] and to also therefore recognize that making any alterations would entail grave consequences. The definition of what is entrenched provided above is clearly inadequate for our purposes, for it is far too narrow. As Hogg recognizes, not only does it omit pre-1867 instruments and statutes of importance (including, for example, the Royal Proclamation of 1763, the Quebec Act of 1774, the Constitutional Act of 1791, and the Act of Union of 1840), it also does not deal with Imperial Statutes, ordinary Canadian statutes, case law, Orders-in-Council, matters of Royal prerogative, and the all-important conventions and usages of the constitution. What the Constitution Act, 1982 does is tell us *only* that which is entrenched; it reveals our constitutional priorities, for 'any law that is inconsistent with the provisions of the Constitution is, to the extent of the inconsistency, of no force or effect.'[16] We thus have a 'capital C' constitution and an overall 'small c' one as well, one that encompasses unwritten rules and practice as well as statutes and the common law.

To emphasize the importance of such a variety of written and unwritten sources is to remind ourselves that the 'small c' constitution is equally as important as its entrenched big brother. Yet this is still to remain highly legalistic in approach and, in a political sense, a constitution involves far more than that which we will find in legal texts. By way of contrast—and it is probably as far removed from a legal approach as one can get—according to some scholars we should see the constitution reflected and manifested in our overall culture, including its artistic, symbolic, and popular expression. David Howes, for example, has argued that we can learn as much about the constitution from the art of Alex Colville and Norman Rockwell as we do from a Peter Hogg or a Lawrence Tribe![17] (In their paintings, says Howes, they reveal the differences which underlie our constitutional structures and values.) I would argue that even if most citizens, let alone legal experts, are unlikely to appreciate the constitutional nuances in art, the essential point is nonetheless important: constitutions are also a state of mind and reflect 'habits of the heart'.[18]

This need to broaden our views and move away from an institutional and legal-rational approach as the guide to constitutional interpretation is made in a rather different way by Charles Conklin. In his *Images of a Constitution,* Conklin deconstructs what courts and judges do and how the judicial image of what is being done is all-important in terms of constitutional interpretation.[19] Thus the ways in which the members of the Supreme Court approached the crucial 1981 Patriation Reference case provided, says Conklin, a classic illustration and articulation of the boundaries, and competing constitutional images and approaches, that are 'embedded within the consciousness' of those who wrestle with constitutional questions.[20] A constitution is therefore something we also carry around in our heads, so to speak; it is not merely the written and unwritten rules for the sharing and use of power. His arguments are detailed and complex (and his prose style makes him difficult to read) and full justice cannot be done to them here. What is important from the point of view of my argument is that Conklin attacks the idea that a constitution is 'a thing' external to the observer. 'A constitution is an image; it is a product of the legal community's imagination. A constitution does not live except through the consciousness of the legal community.'[21] Because lawyers are a part of a larger community they experience a shared consciousness with it: 'I [says Conklin] call this shared consciousness an image. Its parameters make up what has hitherto been called a constitution.'[22]

Conklin then deconstructs the images and the 'shared signposts of communication', and identifies the boundaries of our legal discourse. He sees three images at work: historicist, rationalist, and one that he labels 'teleological'. The image in use sets the approach and frames the result:

> So long as the image goes unchallenged, it reflects the ideology of the community—an ideology because the image shapes or pre-censors how one understands the self and the other. But once the image is challenged the deliberator must defend his/her image vociferously. The image no longer protects against intruders. His/her self is open to brutal and raw attack. . . . That is why, I think, critical constitutional discourse is political discourse.[23]

Precisely because it is political there can be images and counter-images; élites may hold or cling to one view, perhaps subconsciously, but citizens may not share the dominant image. The images evolve subconsciously and grow in meaning. Thus an image is not a 'conception' for this is definable, nor is it a 'fundamental value' which also connotes 'a determinate entity' which one consciously chooses. Like abeyances, images are therefore hard to find or to define; they are 'networks of prejudgments'.[24]

Conklin's work was chosen as a recent illustration of a comprehensive, legally based, constitutional analysis that is innovative and well aware of the importance of subjectivity, context, and the dominant paradigms. It expands our ideas as to what a constitution is and does. His notion of prejudgments comes close to describing, in part at least, the nature of an abeyance. Our images affect our prejudgments as to how to deal with constitutional matters and whether or not to leave them in abeyance—but they do not constitute abeyances in themselves. The only time that Conklin uses the term abeyance is when he argues that 'The legislative use of section 33 of the Charter and section 2 of the Constitution Act, 1867 as amended by the Meech Lake Accord . . . initiates deep issues of "what is a constitution" rather than the abeyance of those issues.'[25] This is using the term in its legal sense of cessation and suspension, and although this contains the germ of Foley's usage (i.e., the idea that certain things should well be left alone), it certainly does not convey the meaning and importance that he has given to it. *Images of a Constitution* is still a work produced by a member of the legal community for that community, and it still sees the constitution living through the exercise of legal imagination.

This imagination is, however, 'ill-suited for achieving paradigmatic shifts in interpretation and approach'.[26] It does not look forward, it looks backward; it tends to look not at fundamental aims but focuses upon the wording of specific rules and the compartmentalization of powers. Putting it bluntly, the courts will usually work at the constitutional margins and will not deal with the political and social essence of the debate; if they do, there will be a backlash of criticism.[27]

In Canada it is our political imagination (or perhaps our lack of it), our political structures, our institutional and social realities, and our history and the way we interpret it, that have shaped the constitutional debate and our abeyances. The courts have been important, but, as David Smith has eloquently argued, we owe far more to 'The Invisible Crown' and its workings:

> the position and powers of the Crown in the Canadian constitution have moulded and influenced the operation of the country's courts, laws, legislatures and executives at both the federal and provincial levels of government; they have determined the evolution and administration of the public services of Canada; and they have exercised a singular force upon the growth of Canada's form of federalism. Lest it be overlooked, the monarchical principle also informs relations between the branches of government. In short, the pervasive influence of the Crown reaches into all areas of Canadian politics, including the very perceptions ruled and rulers hold of the 'realm' of government.[28]

Smith's focus is not on the symbolic Crown and what this means, but upon the Crown and the royal prerogative as an organizing principle of Canada's governments. His arguments and the evidence presented are further proof that 'at the core of every country's constitution lie understandings and agreements that confound the easy adaptation of abstract principle.'[29]

And above all, if we believe Foley, it is our political temperament that matters. We must, however, keep in mind Conklin's point that our legal images have indeed been going through a period of brutal reassessment and change. Historicism with its focus on institutional relationships and precedents (this is the way things have been done; this is what was meant), gives way to policy rationalism and sociology (what are the posited values), or to teleology and the idea that the constitution is unfolding as it should as we get closer to our democratic goals. The teleological view is perhaps the furthest from an appreciation of abeyances, and it can be seen graphically in the argument that Canada has now become (or is becoming) a fully fledged, rights-giving, liberal democratic republic.[30]

This observation brings us, for the moment, too close to present events and to the difficulties confronting us. The point to be made is that abeyances, like Conklin's images and Smith's invisible Crown, significantly expand our notion of what a constitution is, what it does, and how it does it. Seen in this light, constitutions become more equivocal, personal, intuitive, discreet, indeterminate, nuanced, porous, and political; less legal, clear, written, known, knowable, and rational. A constitution is thus an amalgam of history, law, politics, philosophy, and temperament both individual and collective *as well as* the overt network of rules and procedures by which states are run and citizens protected.

Alan Cairns has also taken a very broad view of the nature, role, and importance of a constitution: it is reflected in almost all of his writings. The argument presented above does not, in some ways, go as far as he does. He has stressed the 'moulding effects' of élites, institutions, and big governments[31] and has assigned an absolutely central role to constitutional thinking as a condition of our continued national existence:

> A constitution is not just a bundle of machinery, a big tinker toy with substitutable parts facilitating easy assembling and dismantling. It is also a body of understandings, norms, and identities of those who live the ongoing life of the country. From this perspective, we are all part of the constitution, and the evolution of our inner life has a constitutional component and significance.[32]

Thus legal, institutional, and constitutional forces are at least as important in the Cairnsian cosmos as socio-economic factors. He has written extensively on the constitution's role in shaping citizen identity, and echoes Bertrand Russell when he speaks of our collective need to have constitutional 'intellectual furniture' with which we can feel comfortable and at home. Whether or not he is correct to ascribe such force to our constitutional identity (or identities) and to the meanings and constitutional values 'we carry in our heads'[33]—as causal forces rather than dependent variables—is not the point at issue here.[34] What I wish to stress is that in order to appreciate how Foley's abeyances work one must take an expanded constitutional view of the Cairns type and accept the links between constitutional thoughts, political actions, political culture, and political institutions, bearing in mind that the legal community's images, and our history, also play a crucial role whenever an issue actually gets into court.

Even if the case for an expanded view of constitutions is accepted as reasonable and is linked to questions of the essential spirit that animates a political community, be it federal or otherwise, this is still not a particularly powerful argument for the acceptance of abeyances as a useful new category and way of thinking.[35] Do not other terms, *already in widespread use*, in fact deal adequately with these areas of uncertainty?

The first of these terms are constitutional conventions—the vitally important informal rules that have arisen through political practice:

> As many areas of the constitution are structured by archaic or incomplete laws, the political arena has given birth to binding conventions and customary usages that not only direct political action in these matters, but ultimately determine the full substance and character of the Canadian constitution.[36]

Andrew Heard, in *Canadian Constitutional Conventions: The Marriage of Law and Politics*, has given a closely argued analysis of the debate as to what a convention is, and what definitional difficulties we face. His review makes abundantly clear that a constitutional convention is not a constitutional abeyance.

Heard argues that there have been two tendencies at work in Canada:

> One tendency is to draw a clear boundary between law and convention. In its opinions on the 1981 reference questions about the amendment of the Constitution, the Supreme Court of Canada drew a sharp distinction between conventions, as political rules, and the rules enforced by the courts. . . . The second major trend lies in an increasing propensity to seek the legal regulation or judicial resolution of issues normally governed by convention.[37]

He then places conventions into four categories ranging from 'fundamental' conventions, with a major and direct effect on the constitution, to 'infra-conventions' whose existence is disputed and unclear.[38] The answer to the question of the relationship between law and convention, especially as exemplified in the Patriation Reference case, has indeed had an effect on our abeyances.[39] But even though the crucial question (at least for Laskin) is whether or not the parties act and speak as if they were bound by the convention, just as one might argue they feel bound and constrained by an abeyance, the fact remains that their sense of obligation is open, recognized, operative, public, and based upon political precedents. The point at issue is justiciability and whether a convention has the full force of law. Therefore even if we agree that the sanctions for non-observance of a convention lie in the political world, we have to recognize that in the realm of Heard's 'fundamental' conventions we are dealing with 'generally accepted principles embedded in institutional history' and these serve 'to legitimize the posited legal framework'.[40] Clearly such conventions are not abeyances but are, in some senses, the basis upon which the law rests.

But can the same be said for very weak conventions (infra- and semi-conventions) and for usages? Brun and Tremblay have argued that 'La convention constitutionnelle s'élabore sous la forme d'une entente. Un usage, une pratique ou une façon de faire y fait un objet d'un accord.' They go on to add that this agreement/entente may be written, oral, 'ou tacite'.[41] This last sounds far more like an abeyance, and in Heard's view this notion of a tacit entente 'poses many problems, not the least of which is trying to establish its existence'.[42] Heard, as noted, is indeed willing to recognize that there is a category of conventions that are so weak that their existence is hotly contested, but his analysis of all forms of conventions (and even usages) assumes that we are always, none the less, talking about rules and their applicability. However, as soon as the discussion turns to tacit and undefinable agreements rather than rules, we should admit that we are moving closer to abeyance territory rather than studying the role of conventions as such.

Any discussion of constitutional conventions raises the possibility that a largely unwritten and convention-dependent constitution will be more likely to house abeyances, for so much remains unstated. Are not abeyances merely a manifestation of the lack of both precision and clarity that is the hallmark of the British constitution? Unwritten constitutions may indeed be particularly suited to abeyances. The British constitution's ability to tolerate abeyances is rooted in its historical complexity: 'History has traditionally been seen by the British as a substitute for a properly conceived and fully worked out constitution.'[43] Royal prerogatives remain abstruse. Parliamentary sovereignty is assumed and covers a multitude of constitutional sins.[44] It is seen as compatible with the rule of law, for it is assumed that Parliament will exercise restraint and will uphold common-law traditions. Political sovereignty, embodied in the electorate, and legal sovereignty, embodied in Parliament, are seen as separable. Many constitutional conventions are a line of defence behind which abeyances lurk. The British constitution 'remains constructively vacuous'; it equivocates, it is a *mélange* of co-existing constitutions dating from different eras, and it lacks a major, single, written document: 'It is replete with great yawning gaps of unsettled sources of authority and unresolved issues of procedures, powers and rights.'[45] The possibilities for constitutional conflict are therefore rife, the disjunctions serious, the unsettlement profound.

An illustrative example of a British constitutional inconsistency is the role of the Lord Chancellor. Traditionally, the Lord Chancellor spoke for judges and insulated them from public opinion. Yet he also sat in cabinet and was a party to policy making—at the same time as he was the head of a supposedly independent judicial system and as such the senior member of the Law Lords, Britain's final court of appeal. If he were to be asked how he reconciled his political job with his legal one he would, likely, reply that it really all depended on the chap himself: the right fellow could rise above mere politics and would see his legal and constitutional duties.[46] Thus the assumptions of fair play and character serve to hide a much deeper abeyance: the independence of the judicial system itself and its democratic role. What keeps such indeterminate and arbitrary arrangements in check remains an ongoing issue.[47] The point at issue here is whether or not this ability to avoid abeyances is rooted in an *unwritten* constitution and in the realistic, pragmatic, determination to make it work, and the lawyer's commonly held belief that historical accretions are the secret of constitutional success.

One can make several objections to this line of reasoning. The first of these is that the distinction between written and unwritten constitutions has been overdone; no such easy distinction is to be made. No constitution is completely written or codified and all mature constitutions rely heavily upon conventions. The British constitution in written form is to be found in all sorts of texts and documents and decisions as well as in statutes, as obviously was the Canadian constitution even before the Constitution Act, 1982. Numerous scholars therefore regard the written-unwritten distinction as redundant and unhelpful, or even misleading.[48]

Michael Burgess argues that in Britain there is a myth of unitary government which ignores 'the British tradition of federalism' and which has a powerful and unjustified stranglehold on the British body politic and on the prospects for meaningful constitutional change. It has enabled British governments, until relatively recently, to disguise constitutional questions as mere political issues.[49] Burgess is therefore arguing that, in the British case, abeyances have gone too far, and their presence and power now obstruct serious reform and debate over fundamental issues.

The point about abeyances is that they posit another level of the 'unwritten', another dimension to the written-unwritten distinction, but one which is not the same as attributing everything to conventions, pragmatism, and the common law. To mistake it for such is to lose an important, indeed vital, perspective. A convention that becomes operative can usually be written down without disastrous results, even if it is open to dispute and the constitution does not have its source in a single document. But an abeyance is not only unwritten; the assumption is that it cannot and should not be written. This can be seen even more clearly when considering a further objection to the view that abeyances are of peculiarly British origin, and owe their existence to the great weight of history and tradition, and to an unsystematical constitutional order, governing in the name of previous generations beyond the constitutional grave. Compelling as this may seem, and even if 'unassembled' constitutions seem ideal for the continued existence of abeyances, a brief review of the United States' experience reveals that, in Foley's view, such 'assembled' constitutions, if workable, must also house both abeyances and means of circumvention, evasion, avoidance, and equivocation—and the willingness to accept the results.

How can this be? Surely a constitution based upon clear principles, such as the separation of powers, plus federalism itself must resolve what Peter Russell calls 'mega-constitutional' questions, so that few if any abeyances need exist? Russell defines these as going beyond ordinary constitutional politics and as addressing 'the very nature of the political community on which the constitution is based. Mega-constitutional politics, whether directed towards comprehensive constitutional change or not, is concerned with reaching agreement on the identity and fundamental principles of the body politic.'[50] Was not the United States' Constitution a logical and comprehensive arrangement that had its parts and its principles meshing smoothly together; was it not the very model of an enlightenment, age of reason, Newtonian, agreement that solved its mega-problems? A reading of any of the detailed analyses of the ingredients of the American situation, and the unfolding of the Constitution, reveals that the reality was far more ambiguous. The initial role and place of the Supreme Court itself is a classic illustration of this.[51] Foley himself, in two other works, has outlined the case against the widely held view that the American Constitution was directly influenced by Newtonian principles and that it, along with so much else in American society, is deeply mechanistic in nature.[52] He argues, for example, that 'the principle of separated powers and the principle of checks and balances originally represented two quite distinct and different notions of government,' even though it is now difficult to think coherently of the one without the other.[53] He has also argued that to see the United States as non-ideological, or as ideological merely in spasms, or as a problematic mix of the two, does not do justice to the complexity of the American ideological and constitutional conglomeration or to its political history and past experience:

> It would appear that there is a clear potential for deep and irreconcilable tensions amongst America's basic ideals. But this has to be squared with the fact that these contradictions rarely become apparent. The impulse for following the individual components to their logical conclusions and to their respective priorities seems continually to be inhibited by the American tradition of regarding such principles as mutually assimilable in the context of the United States.[54]

Reading Foley's discussion of the intricacies and subtleties of the American system—the brevity and ambiguity of the Constitution, its adaptability, and its longevity; the institutional structure and architecture; the respect for the Bill of Rights and a higher law; the extraordinary role of the judiciary; the ability to dress up the public philosophy in constitutional clothes; and perhaps, above all, the veneration for the Constitution, and the ability to substitute it for ideology—is to pose a sharp reminder to Canadians who wish to emulate American practice.[55] America's ideological approach to matters is so deeply rooted in its history and in the unique ways that this historical pool of experience is used, that to see it as simple universal liberalism in action, a liberalism that can and should be copied, is to make a gigantic leap of ahistorical political faith. Canada was founded on very different principles, has wrestled with totally different issues, and has had a different sort of constitutional maturity, as shown in the way core values and abeyances are handled. Canadians who are led to believe that we are a particularly befuddled non-sovereign people in search of constitutional clarity should remember not only the idiosyncratic complexity of American arrangements, but also that constitutional abeyances are as important a part of the American experience as they are of the British. For the moment the point to be made is that the seeming clarity of American arrangements, and the power of their traditions of behaviour, hide their abeyances very effectively.

Additionally, the prominence of and reverence for the Constitution (with a capital C) turns political questions into constitutional problems: and this is precisely the point, for it is the *kind* of constitutional questions that are posed and answered, and how this is done, that prevents constitutional turmoil and mayhem from exploding. Americans are indeed used to thinking in constitutional terms, used to analysing legal decisions and philosophy; used to open debate over deep principles such as 'freedom'. Yet this debate is carried on largely within the narrow confines of the law and the Courts. There *is* a state of continuous constitutional turmoil (over rights, for example) but the Supreme Court is able to defuse it by self-imposed limitations too numerous and detailed to mention here. What the Court does is answer constitutional questions while leaving the door open to change and preserving the Constitution's ambiguities. The focus of what is so eagerly sought is, of course, that some action or rule be designated as constitutional or unconstitutional and this is particularly desired these days by constitutional conservatives.[56] But even if an abeyance could have been aroused from its slumber by a case, this will not happen: the abeyance will be ignored, and legal precision and/or obfuscation takes the place of debate over constitutional gaps and illogicalities. When the Court is called upon to deal with a particularly thorny constitutional question it can classify the question as 'political' in addition to the other means it has of evasion and equivocation.[57] Even the whole issue of judicial supremacy is itself an abeyance—for to raise it seriously would call into question the work of the court, and the work of the court is to avoid answering key political questions like this, whilst doing enough to maintain a semblance of judicial coherence and principle. The Supreme Court is thus a key abeyance avoidance mechanism.

The fact that the Supreme Court can and does reverse itself and is not bound by precedent helps significantly in this regard. Political battles do take place but these are focused on the appointment process and on the President's choice as much as upon constitutional issues. This moves the focus away from the underlying problems and into the realms of personality, partisan politics, and legal history. Canada may now be moving in this direction. F.L. Morton argues that the Canadian Supreme Court's 'activist Charter jurisprudence' after 1982 has ensured that there is a new form of judicialized politics, without which 'there would have been no great rush to climb aboard the constitutional bandwagon of 1992.'[58] This has also meant that the role of the legislature in protecting rights has receded to such an extent that the courts are now seen as a form of protection *against* legislative power, rather than the other way around. There may have been 'a wholesale change in the way Canadians think about parliament, and parliamentary debate. It is wrong to assume that under the Charter parliament has merely given up "legislative room" to the courts, and otherwise carries on business as before. Something far more drastic has occurred.'[59]

Thus, while it is true that Canada's constitutional origins have bequeathed to her a constitution that has large British-style gaps in it, to lay all Canada's abeyances at the doorstep of a partially unwritten and ambiguous constitution, dependent upon the existence of innumerable conventions and customary usages, and the extension of the royal prerogative, would be wrong. The United States shows us that mature democracies differ greatly in the way abeyances are handled, yet avoidance there must be if the political system is not to be in an untenable state of real and permanent crisis. And mature democracies, ostensibly committed to the preservation of the same kinds of democratic rights and freedoms, will not do so in the same ways nor will they have to wrestle with similar abeyances. Each system has its own peculiar inner demons, its own constitutional undead 'liable at any time to be revived', and each will face its own particular difficulties when attempting to deal with political problems that go far beyond the normal demands made in pluralist societies; problems that democracies, and their legal systems, may not be very well equipped to handle.

Notes

1 Stephen W. Hawking, *A Brief History of Time* (Toronto: Bantam Books, 1988), 89.

2 Metaphor, says British historian Ged Martin, 'is a dangerous tool for historians, and should be accompanied by the scholarly equivalent of a health warning.' *Britain and the Origins of Canadian Confederation, 1837–67* (Vancouver: University of British Columbia Press, 1995), 241.

3 In *The Narrow Ground: The Roots of Conflict in Ulster* (London: Faber and Faber, 1989), 49, A.T.Q. Stewart uses an interesting hidden-planet metaphor to describe unseen historical effects. 'Like an unseen planet whose presence is revealed only by its influence on other celestial bodies, the rebellion (of 1641) betrays its significance in later events.' I came across this usage after deciding on the idea of black holes as an explanatory device; both are intended to convey a similar general idea, namely the distortions caused by something that we do not believe is there.

4 Michael Foley, *The Silence of Constitutions: Gaps, 'abeyances' and political temperament in the maintenance of government* (New York: Routledge, 1989), xi.

5 Ibid., 129.

6 Ibid.

7 Ibid., 9.

8 Ibid., xi.

9 Lysiane Gagnon, 'Canada, where compromise is the stuff of daily life', *The Globe and Mail*, 21 November 1992, D3. David Cameron makes the important point that 'The language of politics feeds on analogy [and that] the richest and most fertile analogy which the language of politics possesses [is] the analogy between human groups and the individual.' In the case of Quebec it has always been popular to refer to marital or family analogies. Cameron notes that 'This was the period when the images of a Canadian "family" and an English and French speaking "marriage" were popular, with Quebec typically cast in the role of a demanding wife.' This has been replaced of late with Quebec seen as a demanding teenager. So much for metaphorical progress. See David Cameron, *Nationalism, Self-Determination and the Quebec Question* (Toronto: Macmillan of Canada, 1974), 47 and 116. Michael Ignatieff observes that 'It could almost be said that Quebec was bound to Canada only so long as it could construct a rhetoric of resentment around the relationship. Federalism is like some marriages which cohere, paradoxically, because both parties are united in their grievances towards each other.' *Blood and Belonging: Journeys Into The New Nationalism* (Toronto: Viking, 1993), 123. C.E.S. Franks cautions us, correctly, against the multiple meanings that inhere in such metaphors. See *The Myths and Symbols of the Constitutional Debate in Canada* (Kingston: Institute of Intergovernmental Relations, 1993).

10 See R.D. Laing, 'Intervention in Social Situations' in *The Politics of the Family and Other Essays* (New York: Pantheon Books, 1971), 33.

11 Ibid., 'Rules and Metarules,' 106. Laing adds that 'If my view is right, we at this moment (of crisis) may not know we have rules against knowing about certain rules' (111).

12 I am indebted to Dr Edwin R. Black for some of these insights and to Mr Justice R.P. Kerans for suggesting the jury problem in the first place.

13 Peter Hogg, *Constitutional Law of Canada*, 2nd edn (Toronto: Carswell, 1985), 2.

14 Ibid., 6.
15 Ibid.
16 *Constitution Act 1982*, s. 52.1.
17 David Howes, 'In the Balance: The Art of Norman Rockwell and Alex Colville as Discourses on the Constitutions of the United States and Canada', *Alberta Law Review* 29, 2 (1991), 475–97. Howes' general argument is an interesting one; it brings into play the idea of the visual representation, in Colville, of a constitution which is 'juxtaposing' and 'diathetical'.
18 See, for example, Eugene Forsey's comment that 'What we are dealing with in constitutional change is not paper or things. It is human lives.' *Freedom and Order: Collected Essays* (Toronto: McClelland and Stewart, 1974), 309.
19 William E. Conklin, *Images of a Constitution* (Toronto: University of Toronto Press, 1989). For a review and critique of the images chosen see Katherine Swinton, *University of Toronto Law Journal* 41, 1 (1991), 291–4.
20 Conklin, 63. In 1981, the Trudeau Government was forced by events to ask the Supreme Court the crucial question as to whether the federal government could unilaterally ask the British parliament for major constitutional changes, or whether provincial consent was also a requirement. The court came down on both sides of the fence. A clear majority held that in a strictly legal sense there was no requirement of provincial consent, but a majority held also that in terms of constitutional convention, there was a requirement for a 'substantial degree' of provincial consent. Trudeau was, later, to bitterly condemn this outcome. For an account of these events see Peter H. Russell, *Constitutional Odyssey: Can Canadians Become a Sovereign People?*, 2nd edn (Toronto: University of Toronto, Press, 1993). For Pierre Elliott Trudeau's critique see his 'Convocation Speech at the Opening of the Bora Laskin Law Library', *University of Toronto Law Journal* 41, 1 (1991), 295–306.
21 Conklin, 3.
22 Ibid.
23 Ibid., 10.
24 Ibid., 11.
25 Ibid., 248. The book was published in 1989 and it is assumed in this quotation that the Meech Lake Accord would be ratified.
26 Byron M. Sheldrick, 'Constitutional Evolution and Constitutional Reform: Prospects for the Judicial Modification of the Canadian Federal "Arrangement"', paper presented at the annual meeting of the Canadian Political Science Association (St Catharines, 1996), 3.
27 There will sometimes be extraordinary cases: the Patriation reference case was one, and the latest reference on the issues surrounding the legalities of unilateral secession is another.
28 David E. Smith, *The Invisible Crown: The First Principle of Canadian Government* (Toronto: University of Toronto Press, 1995), 5.
29 Ibid., 175.
30 David J. Bercuson and Barry Cooper, 'From Constitutional Monarchy to Quasi Republic: The Evolution of Liberal Democracy in Canada' in *Canadian*

Constitutionalism 1791–1991, ed. Janet Ajzenstat (Ottawa: Canadian Study of Parliament Group, 1992). In this essay the authors argue that Canada is now becoming a democratic republic of rights-bearing citizens in which 'the people of Canada are sovereign'. Others will simply see this as a choice of American values and the triumph of a particular view of rights. See also Barry Cooper's essay 'Looking Eastward, Looking Backward: A Western Reading of a Never-Ending Story', and Alain Nöel's critical comments, in *Constitutional Predicament: Canada After the Referendum of 1992*, ed. Curtis Cook (Montreal and Kingston: McGill-Queen's University Press, 1994), 89–111.

31 'Studies of Canadian politics have suffered from a disciplinary mobilization of bias that grossly underestimated the autonomy of élites, the weight of government, and the moulding effect of institutions on political behaviour.' Alan C. Cairns, 'The Governments and Societies of Canadian Federalism' in *Constitution, Government and Society in Canada*, ed. Douglas E. Williams (Toronto: McClelland and Stewart, 1988), 169.

32 Cairns, 'The Canadian Constitutional Experiment' in *Constitution, Government and Society in Canada*, 245.

33 Ibid.

34 There has been a recent, vigorous, debate over precisely this point. See Ian Brodie and Neil Nevitte, 'Evaluating the Citizens' Constitution Theory', *Canadian Journal of Political Science* 26, 2 (June 1993), 235–59, and the ensuing defence (by Cairns) and rejoinder (by Brodie and Nevitte), also in the same issue.

35 There is now a great deal of renewed interest in the ideas underlying federalism. Carl Friedrich's well-known phrase (from *Trends of Federalism in Theory and Practice* [New York: Praeger, 1968]) about there being 'many rooms in the house that federalism builds' is echoed by a spate of recent works on the development of federalism, especially in Europe. See, for example, the collection of essays in *Comparative Federalism and Federation*, eds Michael Burgess and Alain-G. Gagnon (Toronto: University of Toronto Press, 1993).

36 Andrew Heard, *Canadian Constitutional Conventions: The Marriage of Law and Politics* (Toronto: University of Toronto Press, 1991), 1.

37 Ibid., 2.

38 Note in particular Chapter 7 in Heard for a review of these categories.

39 See, for example, James Tully's discussion of conventions of justification in practice, and the patriation reference and Quebec veto reference cases in particular. 'Diversity's Gambit Declined' in *Constitutional Predicament*, especially 165–74. In the Quebec veto case he accuses the Court of 'a misunderstanding that is typical of legal positivism' and argues that there are three conventions of justification that have stood the test of time and federal practice. One of these is the consent of those affected. There is certainly no doubt that the Supreme Court's decision to rule on a convention was an unprecedented decision in itself.

40 Conklin, *Images of a Constitution*, 83.

41 Henri Brun and Guy Tremblay, *Droit Constitutionnel* (Cowansville: Éditions Yvon Blais, 1982). 'Constitutional conventions are worked out in the form of agreements. A particular usage, practice, or way of doing things becomes the subject of an agreement.'

42 Heard, *Canadian Constitutional Conventions*, 11. Heard notes, for example, that an

embryonic convention of non-use may be developing surrounding the future use of the notwithstanding clause.

43 Foley, *The Silence of Constitutions*, 85.
44 Bernard Crick pursues this point in his essay 'The English and the British' in *National Identities*, ed. Bernard Crick (Oxford: Basil Blackwell, 1991), 90–104.
45 Foley, *The Silence of Constitutions*, 92.
46 This question was put to Lord Hailsham (as Lord Chancellor) by a Canadian jurist, and, as recounted to me, this was the gist of his answer. In fairness, it should also be noted that Lord Hailsham did campaign for a charter of entrenched rights that would curb the powers of police, parliament, and government—but to no avail.
47 The problem arising from the fact that legalized politics are not democratic politics, and that the Charter opens the door to expansive application, has been dealt with in several studies. For a recent useful discussion of the very complex questions this raises, see Thomas M.J. Bateman, 'Charter Application and Democratic Life in Canada', paper presented at the annual meeting of the Canadian Political Science Association (St Catharines, 1996).
48 And a typology that encompasses only one case is not particularly helpful.
49 Michael Burgess, *The British Tradition of Federalism* (London: Leicester University Press, 1995), 3.
50 Russell originally called these volatile problems 'macro' rather than 'mega' questions, and first broached them in his Presidential Address to the 1991 Annual Meeting of the Canadian Political Science Association. He now prefers the latter term as it sounds more 'ominous' and better 'captures their crisis-like nature'. See Russell, *Constitutional Odyssey*, 74–6 and 206, footnote 8.
51 Eric Black, *Our Constitution: The Myth That Binds Us* (Boulder: Westview Press, 1988).
52 Michael Foley, *Laws, Men and Machines: Modern American Government and the Appeal of Newtonian Mechanics* (New York: Routledge, 1990); *American Political Ideas: Traditions and Usages* (Manchester: Manchester University Press, 1991).
53 Foley, *Laws, Men and Machines*, 62–3.
54 Foley, *American Political Ideas*, 220.
55 Ibid. See 214–30. He does not mention Canada, but one cannot help making comparisons between the rich tapestry of America's ideological struggles, and the various explanations of and for their peculiarities, with Canada's traditions and experience.
56 Herman Pritchett makes this point in his *Constitutional Law of the Federal System* (New Jersey: Prentice Hall, 1984).
57 The Court has long held that it is not empowered to deal with 'political questions'. What constitutes such questions may well be those cases that the judges decide not to decide.
58 F.L. Morton, 'Judicial Politics Canadian-Style', in *Constitutional Predicament: Canada After the Referendum of 1992*, ed. Curtis Cook (Montreal and Kingston: McGill-Queen's University Press, 1994), 132–48.
59 Janet Ajzenstat, 'Reconciling Parliament and Rights: A.V. Dicey Reads the Canadian Charter of Rights and Freedoms', paper presented at the annual meeting of the Canadian Political Science Association (St Catharines, 1996), 2.

2

The Term and the Temperament

It would be an error, however, to imagine that the prudent man will of necessity be devoid of political principles.[1]

If distinctions between written and unwritten constitutions, or between conventions and positive law, do not provide the keys to an understanding of abeyances, might it still not be objected that we are already adequately served by our use of such terms as *compromises, instrumentalities, myths, fictions, taboos, keywords,* and even *common sense,* and do not really need to add abeyances to our constitutional vocabulary? Furthermore, is Foley not writing in the Oakeshott tradition of a disdain for rationalism and a defence of a deep-seated conservatism in which 'getting to know' things is what counts? Certainly, any discussion of the need for constitutional caution inevitably brings to mind not only Michael Oakeshott's work but also the writings of Edmund Burke.

In discussing Burke we move from the largely theoretical to the overtly practical. We find, perhaps not surprisingly, that Burke's approach to politics exemplifies the outlook necessary for an acceptance of the need for constitutional irresolution. Such views were as much the product of imagination and empathy as of prudence and distaste for speculative theory, and Burke's political wisdom accords rather well with Foley's views on the temperament needed to sustain abeyances. In addition, Burke's writings and speeches provided a good deal of inspiration for the political creed of Sir John A. Macdonald, and Burke's views therefore provide an appropriate backdrop to a discussion of the 1867 settlement and its associated abeyances. Before we get to Burke we must, however, deal with the problems of our constitutional vocabulary.

Might it not be objected that abeyances are really a form of *compromise*? Is the Foleyan disclaimer that abeyances 'are not, in any sense, truces between two or more defined positions' or 'a notional compromise between definite positions'[2] an adequate defence? One could make a strong case that the essence of politics is the ability to strike lasting bargains based upon the respective power of the participants, and upon the ability to accept that one cannot achieve all one wants. This is certainly true of politics as usual, but an abeyance is not politics of this type. Constitutional abeyances deal with very deep disjunctions that can go to the heart of what a state represents, who should 'run' it, or even who should be a citizen and what the rights of citizens are to be, especially if they feel themselves to be part of a separate nation. Abeyances are usually indeed macro- or mega-constitutional politics of the Russell kind. Any attempt to resolve them conclusively will lead to winners and losers, to a resolve to fight another day and to never forget, or perhaps to 'think of it always, speak of it never'. This is not the stuff of compromise: compromise assumes a conscious agreement. You surrender this, I surrender that. All are assumed to be modest winners. Abeyances are not compromises precisely because not only are they too difficult to put into print, their utility 'depends upon them not being subjected to definition, or even to the prospect of being definable'.[3] It is difficult to compromise when one does not even want to raise the issue, when there has to be 'complicity in delusion'.

These points are particularly important to bear in mind when considering the Canadian constitutional arrangements arrived at in 1867. Simeon and Robinson summarize the Canadian situation in 1865–7 in these terms:

> The common ground made a political deal possible, but it was a far cry from a shared vision of the common good and the corresponding purposes of a state. Without more extensive agreement on the purposes of the new nation, detailed questions of institutional design could not be fully resolved. The result was a constitutional document which remained deeply ambiguous with respect to the relative priority of national and sub-national political communities in the event that their interests came into conflict with one another.[4]

John Whyte has made the same point and it too reinforces the view that 1867 was indeed a compromise and that abeyances were avoided. He argues that the visions were:

> in sharp conflict with each other. The idea of confederation turns out to be not a single idea, but, rather, a mere hope that somehow a nation will exist, will grow and will become politically and economically viable.[5]

The 1867 settlement was a compromise, to be voted on as a whole because to do otherwise might tear the arrangements apart; it was to be carried in one fell swoop. This was how our abeyances could be skirted.

Even if a relatively straightforward case can be made that abeyances are not merely a form of weak convention, are not unique to unwritten constitutions, and are not just compromises, there is yet another term that has been used to explain how federal systems in particular deal with deep diversity and conflicting visions. This is the Livingstonian idea of *instrumentalities*.

Livingston's thesis is that federalism is a function not of constitutions but of societies: 'Federal government is a device by which the federal qualities of a society are articulated and protected.'[6] In the past ten years this society-centred and society-driven view has taken rather a beating in the literature on Canadian federalism. Scholars, notably Alan Cairns and the late Donald Smiley, have stressed institutional roles and power, the growth of the entrenched state, and the inertia that sets in once powerful interests are created.[7] However, the last volume of the Macdonald Royal Commission series moves us back to a more sociological analysis.[8] Wherever one stands in this debate there is no doubt that social diversities produce federalism in the first place and that a federal government is supposed to be a mechanism for the resolution of territorially grouped differences. Livingston contends that the federal state and the federal society develop in order to cope with such diversity: 'An indefinable complex of psychological and sociological attitudes and values that determines, in whatever fashion, the kinds of instrumentalities that are required in that community.'[9]

These instrumentalities will not be a set of characteristics of all federal systems; they will and must vary enormously to deal with the peculiar complex of psychological and sociological determinants that constitute the society. Instrumentalities are:

> not only the constitutional forms but also the manner in which the forms are employed; it includes the way the constitution and its institutions are operated. Beyond this it includes many things that are far from constitutional in importance in the normal sense of the word. It includes such things as habits, attitudes, acceptances, concepts and theories.[10]

This typology would perhaps seem wide enough to include abeyances even though Livingston does not identify them as such: are they not also a complex, society-specific response to the problem of federal diversities and their expression? The difference between the two only becomes clear when we consider what happens to instrumentalities once developed. For here Livingston tells us that once instrumentalities are put into operation they 'become rigid and acquire a status of their own. . . . They become ends in themselves instead of merely means towards other ends.'[11] The nature of an abeyance is, however, such that grave difficulties arise when there is an attempt to subject one to 'corrosive scrutiny', for there is neither agreement as to what it is, nor consensus as to how it is to be handled either procedurally or substantively. I would thus argue that what Livingston calls our instrumentalities serve to protect and hide our abeyances; if the former start to break down, the latter are more likely to emerge.

If abeyances are not legal images, unwritten conventions, mere compromise, or workable instrumentalities, we are still left with other possibilities. They might be part and parcel of our political myths; they might be a form of constitutional fiction; they might be taboos—and finally we might argue that they are the product of straightforward common-sense avoidance of the intractable. (And if so, avoidance was easy in an age of élitism and deference and privilege.)

That *myths* exist and change and have political power and resonance is hard to deny. Myths offer explanations and interpretations. They may be purely fictitious narrative, but 'for the historian, the separation of "myth" and "reality" is less simple than it appears on the surface. . . . We are faced with the ineluctable if paradoxical truth that in history a myth may be, indeed often is, a fact, a reality, in its own right.'[12] To use the term political myth does not mean that what is involved is a belief that has no foundation in fact. We can usually tell that a given account is a myth 'not by the amount of truth it contains, but by the fact that it is believed to be true and, above all, by the dramatic form into which it is cast.'[13] This certainly does not mean that the values or incidents *are* factual, because what is important is the point that is being made to contemporaries. We discover what a myth means, or meant, by looking at the climate of opinion prevailing at the time of its use: a myth is the community's possession and is not seen as an individual's creation (although it might be). A political myth, argues Tudor, 'is one which tells the story of a political society. In many cases, it is the story of a political society that existed or was created in the past and which must now be restored or preserved.'[14]

Kenneth McNaught has identified three current myths that he finds dangerous and pervasive.[15] The first of these is the notion that Canada was and is a new young nation, born in 1867. The myths of youth and newness 'have the curious effect of synchronizing Canadian nationality with that of the United States' for they reinforce the idea that we were created eighty years after the US and diminish our continuous Anglo-European ties, so that we too are seen as a 'new' nation.[16] Secondly, we believe that our multicultural mosaic is inherently less assimilative than the US melting pot. We tolerate, they absorb is the assumption, and this too purports to describe a basic difference that puts us at a disadvantage. But in fact 'the assimilative power of the United States is in serious decline while that of Canada is reasserting itself'[17] and neither metaphor is helpful. In the last census 765,000 people refused to name their cultural ancestry, whilst only 69,000 refused in 1986.[18] Thirdly, 'and it may be the most alarming misconception of the three', there is our view of ourselves as non-violent and peaceable. McNaught argues that our primary concern has always been not non-violence but rather the preservation of order. Our views on liberty have been tempered by a strong suspicion of US-style licence and disorder and 'democracy'.[19] Canadian governments over the years since 1867 have been quick to deploy the police, the militia, and even the regular army to control disturbances within Canada, and we have also entered world conflicts with far more alacrity than the United States. (McNaught could have added that in this sense Quebec has always been far more North American than the rest of Canada; it has not seen its interests bound up with Europe. English Canada has seemed far more willing to tolerate American isolationism as understandable; Quebec isolationism is another matter.) The toleration of these state-sponsored, collective resorts to force is not a historical phenomenon from which we are now immune—not given the October crisis of 1970 and the Mohawk warrior stand-off and confrontation of 1990. McNaught goes so far as to say that: 'The myth of the non-violent/peaceable kingdom, if not more precisely and publicly analysed, could prove catalytic in Canada's joining the tragic ranks of deconstructed, postmodern states.'[20] McNaught's three myths do have a great deal of political relevance.

Another myth, or at least what may be a myth, is that in inheriting the loyalists Canada received a band of resolute Tories who have helped to shape our conservative, collectivist, élitist political culture. Constance MacRae-Buchanan attacks this 'standard mythical perception' and argues that 'The loyalists were not imperialists and they were not Tories: they were American democrats and nationalists.'[21] Their silence and obedience were due not to their beliefs but to the Royalist and hierarchical political culture of the day; given the chance, they were far more democratic, egalitarian, and populist. We now have a standard interpretation of the story of the loyalists; it serves to show how and why Canadian society has differed from the undisciplined, individualistic chaos that is embodied in American-style democracy. This myth justifies feelings of both difference and superiority and it covers up contradictions, ambiguities, and interpretive problems.

And, of course, there are myths that deal with the Conquest, the settlement of 1867, Louis Riel, and Western Canada, to mention but a few. (Riel's death, and the political questions that came with it, were particularly important, for 'martyrs haunt the conscience of a political order like Shakespeare's ghosts'.[22]) Paul Romney questions what we have taken to be the underlying assumptions of the settlement of 1867, and argues that: 'The centralist interpretation of Confederation is a nationalist myth, and the idea that the Judicial Committee subverted the Founders' intentions is the Canadian nationalist version of the *Dolchstoss*'[23] (the myth of the stab in the back given to Germany in 1918).

Before investigating further the connection between myths and abeyances it is advisable to take a closer look at examples of our myths and at the idea of myths and symbols in a more general way. This is the subject of a monograph by C.E.S. Franks entitled *The Myths and Symbols of the Constitutional Debate in Canada.*[24] He bases his analysis upon the four kinds of structured myths outlined by Northrop Frye: those involving romance, tragedy, comedy, and irony. These are all forms of a story that includes characters and events, and the most important type politically is the romantic myth of the state: 'The key myths of the state have the structure of romance' (a hero, a journey, perils, hardships, battles, and victory).[25] Romantic myths are optimistic; they show that things can change, that leaders matter, and that virtue is rewarded. A wonderfully detailed example of just such a myth is given in Michael Oliver's study of the social and political ideas of French Canadian nationalists and the emergence of the myth of Dollard.[26]

Dollard des Ormeaux and his compatriots became patriotic symbols 'of *French* Canada'. Their stand and sacrifice at the Long Sault was given all the hallmarks of a medieval crusade, and was perfect from the standpoint of myth-making: seventeen men setting out to their deaths after receiving the sacraments, and dying to preserve church and society from extinction at the hands of savages backed by English heretics. Oliver quotes at length from a patriotic chorus and concludes that 'Here is myth in its fullest expression' applied as a contemporary lesson. Whether or not Dollard deserves such unrestrained praise is, of course, entirely another matter—and is one that has created intense and vitriolic debate, as André Vachon's review of the evidence makes clear.[27] What is so Canadian and sad about this, is that Dollard des Ormeaux's exploits remain unknown outside Quebec: he is not seen as a Davy Crockett or a Jim Bowie at the Alamo fighting for freedom against tyranny (although their exploits too are the subject of revisionism). The historical debate is now sullied by arguments about such macabre questions as how many Iroquois were really killed (aboriginal sources put the number at around twenty, rather than the hundreds usually claimed).[28]

Canada's romantic myths, argues Franks, are tempered by notions of survival and of victimization, oppression, and even conspiracy.[29] English and French have, in different ways, stressed 'hanging on and staying alive' and their respective powerlessness. French Canada becomes a victim of English Canada, English Canada of the United States, the West of the East (or centre), the disadvantaged of the advantaged. The victim myth is sometimes hidden behind the assertion that the victim is no longer prepared to be victimized; this, says Franks, is its 'latent' form. The assertion that 'we won't take it any more' can be felt to apply even by those groups whose survival is hardly threatened, such as those outside Quebec who feel tyrannized and marginalized by the 'imposition' of French. Exploring the role of myths and symbols in the current Confederation debates, Franks argues that they are vital elements of Canadian politics and cultures, 'and, through emphasis and interpretation, have become part of the political landscape, and have contributed to the attitudes, perceptions and reasoning that cause Canada's constitutional difficulties.'[30]

Perhaps Franks has placed too much emphasis on myths and symbols as causes, rather than effects, because he has not thought in abeyance-like terms. Indeed, some would prefer that we not use 'myth' to describe national beliefs, even though such beliefs are stories people tell about themselves and their values (e.g., the Scots are egalitarian; the French Canadians are hardy). Writing about Scotland, Lindsay Paterson avoids using the term because:

> it retains an irreducibly pejorative tone, akin to the patronizing implications of Marxist false consciousness . . . successive generations of nationalists have been engaged in a conscious process of symbolically constructing a community . . . none of these activities are reasonably described as myth-making, in however subtly anthropological a way.[31]

In other words, in Scotland and in Quebec, leaders have known what they were doing and were not cynical about doing it: they were defending their nation's autonomy.

Even so, Canadians' views on key historical events differ dramatically, and so do the stories that result. Myths will therefore vary with the teller, the tale, and the audience. They operate in such a way that society is told the important things that it needs to know, often in a metaphorical way.[32] Myths impinge upon, and condition, our views on the ultimate metaphysical and moral underpinnings upon which a constitution rests. Our beliefs about progress, history, the nation, community, society, good, and evil are all linked into a collective narrative. Such ideas are obviously problematic for they are not dealing so much in truth as in belief and justification.[33] What, then, is the relationship of myths to abeyances?

Myths can help abeyances persist, for they disguise reality and obscure details and can therefore help build a respect for institutions that may be entirely unwarranted. This respect helps to perpetuate that state of suspended irresolution necessary to discourage undue scrutiny. On the other hand, a myth may also force an abeyance to the forefront if it is a myth that deals in justice and injustice, in grievance and anger and the need for action. The truth of the myth is not the issue here, only its effects. (Whether or not Quebec does better than the West matters not if the West believes that it is always on the short end of the stick.) For abeyances to remain undisturbed we need myths that bind: tales that are positive, unifying, and reassuring. As Eric Black has commented, apropos of the United States:

> By calling the Constitution 'The Myth that Binds Us', I haven't meant that the Constitution is a lie. A myth is not a lie. A myth is a story that may or may not be consistent with history but that gains its power from people's belief in it. The Constitution's power over us is the flip side of our power over it. It becomes what we believe it is, and we become what we believe it makes us.[34]

Myths are essential, and élites as well as ordinary citizens must subscribe to them and help to maintain them, but they are not abeyances, for they tell a story and often employ well-known symbols to embody their content.

It should be absolutely clear by now that when dealing with constitutions, particularly ones that are federal, things are never quite as they appear to be. In fact, things may not be at all what they seem. David Milne has made the point explicitly: 'the first obstacle to avoid is the simple notion that constitutions always tell the truth.'[35] This should not really surprise us. Images, conventions, instrumentalities, and myths all make the issues cloudy—and so, in particular, do the constitutional fictions upon which all constitutions rest. Canada is no exception, except in the sense that our fictions may have a distinctly Canadian spin to them. To talk of constitutional fictions is not to diminish the idea that abeyances may be necessary; it is rather to outline their last line of defence, and to link fictions to myths and symbols.

To illustrate the role of *fictions* we can do no better than to turn to Edmund S. Morgan's lucid analysis of two of liberal-democracy's most cherished notions, namely representation and the idea of popular sovereignty. He begins from the assumption that:

> Government requires make-believe. Make believe that the king is divine and can do no wrong or make believe that the voice of the people is the voice of God. Make believe that the people *have* a voice and that the representatives of the people *are* the people. Make believe that governors are the servants of the people. Make believe that all men are equal or make believe that they are not.[36]

In *Inventing the People: The Rise of Popular Sovereignty in England and America*, Morgan lays bare the fictions that governments require in order to govern. In so doing, he uses virtually Foleyan language—although his work was written earlier. In order to successfully obtain the consent of the many to be ruled by the few, 'The success of government (thus) requires the acceptance of fictions, requires the willing suspension of disbelief, requires us to believe that the emperor is clothed even though we can see that he is not.'[37] Morgan's fictions, it bears repeating, involve the '*willing* suspension of disbelief'. We must see, and do see, our constitutional fictions as self-evident propositions and, adds Morgan, 'self-evident propositions are not debatable, and to challenge these would rend the fabric of our society.'[38]

Here we have the vital clue to what distinguishes an abeyance from a fiction and why the latter protects the former. The fiction requires that you believe *in* something. You believe that a King is and must be the highest under God, or that a Parliament is absolutely sovereign, even if upon close examination these things are at variance with observable fact and social and political reality. A fiction can be used in ways that are startlingly different from its origin. The doctrine and fiction of the divine right of kings 'was sustained in England as an instrument that gave to the many a measure of control over the man to whom the fiction seemed to subject them so absolutely.'[39] The King could do no wrong, but his advisors could and, if things were amiss, his advisors must be called to account, in the King's name, by his loyal servants even if the King himself could not recognize how he had been misled.

A fiction exists in the public domain: it must remain visible, so to speak, but it must not be interpreted too literally. It is only upon the suspension of belief (or the suspension of the suspension of disbelief) that the abeyances which exist in the shadows behind the fictions come to light. Constitutional fictions conceal our abeyances in many but not all cases, for abeyances can take the form of unresolved points at issue that lie within the accepted fiction *or* they can exist in a sort of constitutional limbo—a nether world—without having a protecting fiction constructed around them. This may leave them dangerously exposed.

For example, Morgan traces how the problem of providing credence to the emerging idea of popular sovereignty had to be balanced with the maintenance of deeply rooted patterns of deference and power, patterns that imparted stability and which enabled the few to dominate the many.[40] This balancing act requires that the fiction takes root at the same time as it is tamed; it also requires that new devices are put in place to ensure that fact and fiction do not get too far apart. If they do, then belief in the fiction is itself suspended, and its contradictory components may be interpreted literally. If the people *really* take it into their heads that they are not sovereign then the system may change dramatically. Perhaps more likely, we will invent new mechanisms that allow us to preserve the fiction and social order. This is because we wish to continue to believe in something and, as long as we do, serious points of suspended irresolution will be preserved. Our belief in the fictions that rule us will be acquired as much unintentionally and unconsciously as consciously, but it is still a belief. As long as it exists it protects and preserves the illogicality of our constitutional arrangements and the abeyances that lie behind them.

To protect our fictions we generally, as Morgan notes, turn them into self-evident truths, a much more exalted status, 'and that designation is not inappropriate, for it implies our commitment to them and protects them from challenge'.[41] Myths, operating in a much more general and metaphorical and personal way, will help our fictions to survive. Such myths, with their focus on story and actors, are separable from whatever constitutional truths (i.e., fictions) we believe in, even though mythical events and actions and actors may be seen to have created the circumstances in which a constitutional fiction either takes root or comes to be challenged.

Constitutional fictions are therefore essential if a political system is to operate successfully; they commingle with the real world in strange ways. To say that fictions exist is not to be pejorative or to undervalue the constitutional sophistication of a populace, any more than the acceptance of abeyances marks a form of constitutional delusion and cowardice.[42] Both fictions and abeyances perform a vital sustaining role that does not threaten human values and political aspirations, even though they make it harder to see political reality: fictions may conflict or contain glaring contradictions, abeyances remain silent. The governing as well as the governed are dependent upon them. Fictions can collapse if they stray too far from reality or fact; when they do, our constitutional worlds can be turned upside down. And our deepest abeyances will emerge.[43]

There will always be enormous pressures exerted against those who do wish to turn things upside down: our climate of opinion will tolerate some, but not all, forms of critique. This is especially true of those matters we treat as taboo subjects, not to be mentioned in polite and intelligent company and certainly not to be written about. What is the relationship of such taboos to abeyances?

We can admit that—under certain circumstances—an abeyance can also be a *taboo*, but this will not normally be the case. Taboos involve questions of good taste and political correctness, of social acceptability and respectability. They are not usually Gordian political knots, to be avoided because of their intractability: taboos are rooted in, and linked to, shame and guilt as well as to fear and circumspection. Abeyances involve only some of these elements. An example of a taboo subject is provided by David Cameron in his 1974 study of nationalism and self-determination in Quebec.[44] He discusses the natural reluctance of the rest of the country to contemplate openly the consequences of the break-up of Confederation. Those who attempted to at least contemplate the problems of secession, like the joint Senate-House Committee in its Final Report, were roundly condemned for so doing even before the publication of their findings. To talk of secession and its problems was then thought to bring it closer, to give it legs, to legitimize the unthinkable. It was a form of disloyalty or even treason, and words might take on a life of their own. No matter that the question was in the open and that the issue might have to be faced. This is a taboo against discussing not something that has happened, but something that one is fearful might take place. Taboos more normally are not as future-oriented and are more likely to involve issues of unacceptable, offensive opinion. Any reference to, for example, the innate biological superiority of one 'race' over another is now in this category, although, as R.C. Lewontin points out, this taboo does not yet extend fully to biologically linked sexism: 'To admit publicly to outright biological racism is a strict taboo, but the avowal of biological sexism is tolerated as a minor foolishness, unlikely to bring serious consequences.'[45]

Alan Cairns, writing in 1989, added to the Canada-without-Quebec taboo the linked problem of the 'viability and potential' of aboriginal self-government.[46] These twin taboos he places firstly in the context of our procedural disputes and divergent first principles of constitution making, and secondly as topics seen by 'insiders' as their preserve. Only some are really qualified to speak, and this largely on the basis of ascribed status. Outsiders lack legitimacy, especially if they are critical. Taboos are therefore subjects we approach very carefully or try to avoid, unless we want to be perceived as intellectual and social malcontents (or philistines) out of tune with the spirit of the times. In the case of abeyances there is a somewhat similar reluctance to allow into public consciousness a problem incapable of resolution until such time as we are either ready to address it, or are forced to do so. However, this is not a matter of shame, or taste, or fashion. There is no taboo against examining the deep disjunctions that lie at the heart of the jury system, no shame involved in laying bare the extent to which all constitutions contain great gaps of settled unsettlement. But to advance the idea that aboriginal communities may have been irreparably damaged by foetal alcohol syndrome would be taboo, and would meet with enormous hostility. Unlike taboos, abeyances are often unrecognized or taken for granted, matters for debate only if they become central to a crisis—when their innate contradictions and intractability become all too apparent.

A final objection to the view that abeyances are a useful addition to our constitutional vocabulary has to do with the notion of abeyances in themselves being a version of the Emperor's new clothes. Do we not, in practice, recognize what is quite simply not worth debating and discussing, and just put it aside, in much the same way as we no longer argue about the existence of God? So is the idea of abeyances simply a fancy, duded-up, academic version of common sense? To use the example often given, don't we all know that Quebec is distinct but that it is a waste of time trying to deal with it? The problem is, this assumes we have identified our abeyances, and we may well not have done so. Even if we have, there is certainly little likelihood that our 'common sense' will provide readily acceptable and clear answers. It may well lead us away from compromise, empathy, and objectivity and be more like common 'non-sense', for it can blind us to things and makes us willing victims of a prevailing climate of opinion.[47] Like Lord North and his views on the revolution in the colonies, our minds may be 'programmed with unappraised metaphysical distinctions: he said that "sovereignty cannot be divided", and away went the last chance of conciliating the Americans."[48] We may realize—too late—that there are problems and consequences, causes and effects, we simply had not thought of, and that the conventional wisdom we take for granted is indeed just that. In other words, we are not likely to be self-consciously aware of the range and scope of an abeyance if disinterred. In British political and historical writing, more so than in American:

> There was a rich, broad, often vague but much-tilled middle ground of 'common sense', sir, from which we could 'refuse to be torn' to the excesses of either positivism and scientism, or of academic and vulgar idealism. But descriptivism or 'common sense' always reflected as calm and unthinking an acceptance of certain peculiar things as 'natural' as ever did American political science.[49]

When abeyances are identified and raised there will be many who will argue that it is possible and advisable to solve them one way or the other. Thus once the idea of distinct society (or anything else) as a political and *constitutional* concept and as an identifiable goal is brought to the fore, the problems start. The ideas and the words begin to take on a life of their own, and demand an examination of the contradictions upon which we have hitherto based our ability to avoid such fundamental problems. This point is made explicit by Berel Rodal:

> Canada then, is at a defining moment in its history, one turning on the potency of symbols and interests, but also *on the meanings that attach to terms and the consequences which attach to such meanings* (my emphasis).[50]

Common sense conventional avoidance of complex and irreconcilable issues may be an important part of a climate where abeyances can exist, but it is not in itself sufficient to ensure that they remain where they are: i.e., buried. Institutions, conventions, instrumentalities, myths, fictions, political culture, and the political process itself must do this. The words that we choose may, or may not, help us in this endeavour, and our common-sense use of particular terms as keywords may have far more to do with rhetoric, fashion, and political mobilization than with a well-considered attempt to obtain greater clarity.

Such *keywords*, which are a part of all political debate, differ from the terms in use in political theory and from the specialized jargon of the social sciences:[51]

> keywords can be seen as especially important words in a larger body of tropes of political rhetoric. They are words that have endured and have been used by very different groups in very different times for different ends. The rhetorical question is, where do they come from? If one looks at keywords in this rhetorical sense, then it seems that we are talking about a national phenomenon. Rhetorical keywords make little sense outside their home arena. This chauvinism of political rhetoric—which it does not share with its political theory brethren—indicates that a satisfying answer for their

hold on the mind of the body politic should be looked for in the particularities of national history.[52]

Canada's keywords are unique, and so are Quebec's; this Canada/Quebec distinction has been made deliberately, for the rhetorical vocabularies both use are not the same. The words in use have a ring to them; they convey—and were often born as—slogans. Our changing keywords are not, as we shall see, attempting to convey the same commonly held, self-evident, political truths. We now have, in English Canada, the rhetoric of rights, and in Quebec there is the legitimation of the vocabulary of nationhood.[53] In addition, according to Carolyn Tuohy, 'ambivalence is embedded in the very language of Canadian politics, a language replete with unique oxymorons.'[54] We are reluctant, she says, to make either/or choices, and our language reflects this.[55] It may also reflect a conscious use of rhetoric, and such use is not confined to politicians, the spokespersons for politically motivated groups, and radio talk-show hosts.

Members of the legal profession, including the Supreme Court of Canada, also have a rhetorical style and vocabulary. Rhetorical not in the Aristotelian sense of discovering the available means of persuasion but as 'rhetorical analysis (which is) based upon a conception of rhetoric as the way in which we constitute ourselves as a community through language.'[56] The rhetoric of the legal profession, and its judgments, thus convey to us a *political* vision of what we are as a community. Marc Gold, in 'The Rhetoric of Rights: The Supreme Court and the Charter' argues, much as Conklin does, that the legal meaning given to something has to engage the political values, experience, and prejudices of the interpreter, and that the meaning of the Charter 'is exclusively a function of its interpretation' based upon these tacit values and assumptions.[57] However, the Court *must* preserve its appearance of objectivity. Public perception that it plays a balanced role is crucial, and to achieve this the Court, says Gold, has invoked the rhetoric of individualism in conjunction with suspicion of the state. It chooses which 'facts' it will comment upon, thus rhetorically portraying something in a negative way.[58] The characterisation of the legislation under review is crucial (is it coercive, compulsive, constraining, and so forth) and so is the denigration of those who advance opposing arguments (ill-prepared, poorly constructed, unclear, deficient). Above all it is a question of the manner in which the issue is posed. We must remember to be aware of the range and power of rhetorical devices, and of the effects they have on our views of political questions. We will revisit Gold's rhetorical devices and categories when considering the exchange of views between Pierre Trudeau and Gordon Robertson.

All of this discussion of the ways in which we communicate has to be evaluated in the knowledge that the messages people think they are sending are frequently not what is received. Our language betrays us constantly, although it might also be argued that misunderstandings may, at times, be mutually acceptable and constitute a way of avoiding confrontation. There can also be a clear recognition that a key term does not mean the same thing and that agreement is unlikely. (In 1867 no one would have argued over the meaning of 'defence', but 'education' was a different matter.)

In sum, what has been considered thus far is the possibility that Foley's abeyance thesis, notwithstanding its seeming utility, is not a particularly distinctive contribution to the way we must see constitutions and their operation. But no other term captures what Foley has in mind. Even if one takes a fairly broad view of the nature of a constitution, the analysis still tends to be legally and judicially focused; not surprisingly, abeyances are rarely considered. The metaphysical underpinnings of a constitution are by nature teleological; abeyances are not. Conventions as generally used and understood may have the force of law and represent particular ways of doing things; abeyances are not means or agreed-upon methods. Compromise assumes give and take and debate about things that are definable, and instrumentalities are the means to an end; neither functions as abeyances must do. Where compromise is important is that a willingness to compromise on other matters, on the non-abeyances, is still essential. Indeed, if there are serious and numerous areas of abeyance, then compromise on normal political questions is a safety valve and a key avoidance mechanism. It will provide a form of face-saving and a tradition of complicity and cooperation can develop, along with the temperament that goes with it. Myths provide social coherence and undergird a political culture; they are indeed tied to the question of abeyances for they may or may not help to sustain them. Constitutional fictions are taken as self-evident until the 'facts' supporting them become too divorced from reality; they are notions that one believes and accepts. Taboos exist and change as the boundaries of acceptability and evidence alter. And common-sense avoidance of the intractable does not explain abeyances either, for those who believe in it may well have completely different views as to what our common sense is telling us. If we look at an abeyance in the light of common sense it will not look sensible at all—and we are not going to agree upon what should 'logically' be done about it. There will be absolutely no agreement on 'the well-known proven facts' (indeed, anyone who starts an argument with these words is almost invariably saying something controversial). Keywords become central to the rhetoric we use and to the rhetorical devices we employ. Such keywords change and mutate and form an essential part of our political discourse, but they are not hidden. Paradoxically, we may use them readily without even realizing that we are doing so.

Yet even if we recognize that the notion of abeyances is a potentially crucial contribution to our constitutional vocabulary, and that other terms in current use do not deal adequately with the idea that mature constitutions have 'great yawning gaps' in them that are kept in place by implicit understandings and by 'settled unsettlement', there is still an obvious criticism to be made. Can it not be argued that there is nothing other than fear and a desire for order and stability that keeps abeyances in place? Are they not, by this measure, simply reactionary forces? Is Foley not writing in the Oakeshott tradition of a deep disdain for politics and for rationalism: a sort of modern

Burkean conservatism that stresses the risks of change, the need for deference and restraint, and the impossibility of proceeding 'as the crow flies'?[59] Oakeshott's views may be summarized by saying that he too believes that 'To interrogate political beliefs too closely calls into question the presuppositions on which politics rests and moves to a different level of inquiry altogether.'[60] Along with this defence of prevailing conduct Oakeshott has emphasized the limited character of political activity and its parasitic intent.[61] Oakeshott sees politics as 'a second rate activity, neither an art nor a science, at once corrupting to the soul and fatiguing to the mind, the activity of those who cannot live without the illusion of affairs, or those so fearful of being ruled by others that they will pay with their lives to prevent it.'[62] Is there not a danger that a defence of the need for abeyances is merely another way of maintaining the existing arrangements and that, as such, it is anti-reformist or even anti-political? Much as Foley wishes to defend the idea of liberal constitutionalism, has he, as Janet Ajzenstat argues, abandoned the idea that there are natural rights or universal principles of behaviour to be defended?

> Foley says, in effect, that the liberal-democratic edifice rests on sand, but all will be well if we close our minds, hold our tongues and carry on with politics as usual. There are no natural rights, but it is necessary to pretend that there are, and that liberal constitutionalism embodies them.[63]

The pretence that all is well can therefore easily become a defence of the *status quo* and a shield behind which governing élites take shelter.

The idea of abeyances, however, is not a disguised attack upon change. Indeed it can be argued that abeyance maintenance will have precisely the opposite effects, for it will help ensure that emotionally draining and ultimately dangerous or fruitless debate is avoided. The political system will be left with more time, resources, and inclination to turn its energies toward other less intractable but still challenging problems. This is not to argue that this is in itself a good or bad thing; one's answer to this depends upon ideological belief.

Richard Nutbrown has made the point that politics can be seen as a matter of consent through dialogue. When we talk about politics:

> we appeal to beliefs, attitudes, and word-images that give a narrative structure to such experiences. . . . Political science, by extension, is a specialized kind of story telling . . . *language structures what we say—and what we omit—from political conversation.*[64]

Our treatment of abeyances will help form this language, and therefore contributes to our political keywords and to our ideology, or at least to the ways in which we define and perceive meaning, function, structure, action—and politics.[65]

There is, however, one aspect of Oakeshott's philosophy that should give us pause. Even if abeyance maintenance is not necessarily innately conservative in its social and political results, does it not still depend upon the applicability of traditional modes of reasoning as a way of understanding society? Do we require traditions of behaviour where a great deal is unacknowledged and unstated, and where we 'get to know' things by being around them, and part of them, and living within the knowledge we so gradually acquire?[66]

Unsuspecting Confidence
This is, quite clearly, also the terrain of Edmund Burke: when one thinks of the temperament and viewpoint needed to sustain abeyances, one is inevitably drawn to his work. It is not, of course, that he used the term abeyances in the manner that Foley does, it is rather that his whole approach to politics illustrates, time and again, that during crises he thought of the problems in a way calculated to *preserve* abeyances:

> Burke approaches politics in a hardheaded and present-minded fashion, as well as with that quality of imagination which might be called romantic and historical; he turns upon hard fact, wherever it is to be met, a contemplative subtlety and concrete appreciativeness. He is committed to a practical approach to politics. . . .[67]

It is therefore appropriate to study Burke in both a Foleyan and a Canadian context. Our history is replete with references to Burke's wisdom, prudence, reverence for society and its traditions, and belief in the need for moderation.[68] Burke saw the need to find a reasonable middle way through things, was reluctant to go to extremes, and had an enormous respect for historical traditions. These days, Burke seems to suffer from a reputation for inconsistency.[69] He is portrayed as 'a natural law Burke; a historicist Burke; a liberal Burke; Burke the sceptic; a crusader for capitalism; and—surprisingly convincingly—even a Burke with resonances of post-modernism.'[70] This is, in itself, an indication that he was never rigidly doctrinaire.[71]

To see how great a practising theoretician Burke was, and to appreciate how much he thought in abeyance-like terms, there is no better way to approach the subject than to simply read him; to go back to his great speeches and causes and to his defence of principles he held to be so vital. When one does, and when one does so bearing Foley's ideas and Canada's constitutional problems and origins in mind, sentence after sentence, paragraph after paragraph convey points worth pondering. If we are to see ourselves as living according to the true tradition of Burke, we have a great deal to live up to, for he was no mere trimmer, though trim he would.

He faced questions just as divisive as those that confronted Canadians in 1867 or those which confront us now. He had to wrestle with such problems as the taxation and rebellion of the Colonies; the use of force; the Irish question; the impeachment of Warren Hastings and the treatment of India; constitutional reform; and the French Revolution. He used his extraordinary talents to try and preserve the existing order (not necessarily the government itself) whilst reforming it when it was necessary to do so. Burke did not inhabit a philosophical high ground; nevertheless his political life was built upon principled themes. What Burke would *not* do was pick one principle over another or over all others, and carry it through to its seemingly logical conclusion. His famous lines on liberty illustrate this clearly:

> Far from any resemblance to those propositions in geometry and metaphysics which admit no medium, but must be true or false in all their latitude, social and civil freedom, like all other things in common life, are variously mixed and modified, enjoyed in very different degrees, and shaped into an infinite diversity of forms, according to the temper and circumstances of every community. The *extreme* of liberty (which is its abstract perfection, but its real fault) obtains nowhere, nor ought to obtain anywhere; because extremes, as we all know, in every point which relates either to our duties or satisfactions in life, are destructive both to virtue and enjoyment.[72]

He argued always from a deep, detailed, historical knowledge that was not used merely for rhetorical purposes. As he said, his method was to wind himself into his subject, and then to deduce what should be done, bearing in mind that the ends of government were to secure the well-being of the governed. Politics was morality enlarged, and was an unending struggle to preserve that which had been won, and to build upon it without tearing down the organic traditions of the society: 'We are but too apt to consider things in the state in which we find them, without sufficiently adverting to the causes by which they have been produced, and possibly may be upheld.'[73] Burke's intense dislike of abstract speculation is evident throughout his work: 'since the wisdom embodied in institutions was based on experience and nothing but experience, it could not be completely rationalized: that is, it could not be reduced to first principles which might be clearly enunciated.'[74]

He opposed, even hated, the idea of rapid and ill-considered schemes of reform. But he nonetheless recognized that even though the bulk of mankind are 'not excessively curious concerning any theories whilst they are really happy', there are times 'when subjects, by a long course of ill conduct, at once thoroughly inflamed, and the state itself violently distempered, the people must have some satisfaction to their feelings more solid than a sophistical speculation on law and government.'[75] When matters come to such a pass, then satisfaction must be given, and the problem, the essence of a crisis, will be the nature of this satisfaction. And here only *wisdom* would suffice. Therefore in assessing whether our responses and our temperament have been (or are) Burkean in spirit and in practice—and in wisdom—we will always be forced to ask what principles we were applying and reconciling as they passed through the refracting medium of actual events. The prudent person is therefore *not* devoid of political principles.

Burke had a reverence for the past and was a true conservative, but Burke's political world was extremely complex, rooted in religion and family, in history, in 'manners', and 'acquaintance', in generosity, friendship and patriotism.[76] Yet it was not devoid of an appeal to reason, even though there will be occasions when 'our feelings contradict our theories; and when this is the case, our feelings are true, and the theory is false.'[77] This sounds reactionary in the extreme; what must be remembered is that Burke's feelings were steeped in his historical knowledge and his breadth of vision, whereas the feelings of most of us are more likely to be far more parochial. We are therefore more likely to be guilty of committing the great sin, in Burke's eyes, of taking the part for the whole, of pushing one over-simplified truth, ignoring circumstantial detail, reflecting on concepts in the abstract, and thus corrupting political discourse and adversely affecting political action:

> Circumstances (which with some gentlemen pass for nothing) give in reality to every political principle its distinguishing colour, and discriminating effect. The circumstances are what render every civil and political scheme beneficial or noxious to mankind.[78]

Burke was writing in the shadow of two traditions, as David Cameron has persuasively argued: the tradition of rationalism, with its belief in individualism and natural rights, and the tradition of empiricism, with its emphasis on hard facts, on will and on 'artifice'. Burke's idealism was 'an attempt to resolve some of the difficulties of the two major traditions of political thought and to move beyond the limitations of traditional dialogue.'[79] In an important sense Burke was operating in the territory that lies between political thought and political action. Essential to this world is the recognition that meaning does not inhere in ideas as such, without regard for person and context. Ideas may seem unchanging, but their meaning and applicability alter as the questions *behind* them change, and as the available alternatives also become more or less accessible 'alongside' them, as it were. His organizing concept was society and his human being is a creature of great complexity, living in, and not apart from, history and its vicissitudes:

> The nature of man is intricate; the objects of society are of the greatest possible complexity ... when I hear simplicity of contrivance aimed at and boasted of in any new political constitutions, I am at no loss to decide that the artificers are grossly ignorant of their trade. ....[80]

Burke's government is not a necessary evil, for civil order is a socializing force and governments have an improving and creative role. Burke welcomes governing from beyond the grave, and his traditional, developmental, organic, collectivist views are heartening to those who see Canada's constitution unfolding along such lines. Peace, order, and good government may seem a wiser choice than the pursuit of happiness. What we must bear in mind is that the political wisdom so accumulated must still 'match in subtlety the political "reality" that it is designed to cope with and consider',[81] and that political 'temperaments' were what counted.[82] Thus, in Burke, the relationship between concepts and reality was problematical. There existed a shadowy, porous domain much like Foley's, in between the metaphysical and teleological underpinnings of the state and the empirical and legal facts of active constitutional life. Certainly for Burke there were no simple explanations of relationships suitable for all times and circumstances: 'Political reason is a computing principle: adding, subtracting, multiplying and dividing, morally and not metaphysically or mathematically, true moral denominations.'[83]

I have let Burke's words speak for themselves, even if briefly, because rewriting what he said is to lose its tone and essence. Bearing the general points made above in mind, it still remains to be shown that Burke really thought in abeyance-like terms. His acceptance of the need for irresolution, for settled unsettlement, is nowhere more apparent than in his attitude to the taxation of the American colonies. In 'Observations on the Late State of the Nation' (written in February, 1769), Burke argued that the powers which each side possessed in theory had never been pressed to extremes, and that, if they were, the results would be disastrous. In the midst of their 'happy enjoyment' of an inexact middle ground:

> They [the colonists] never thought of critically settling the exact limits of power, which was necessary to their union, their safety, their equality, and even their liberty. Thus the two very difficult points, superiority in the presiding state, and freedom in the subordinate, were on the whole sufficiently, that is, practically, reconciled; without agitating those vexatious questions, which in truth rather belong to metaphysics than politicks, and which can never be moved without shaking the foundations of the best governments that have ever been constituted by human wisdom. By this measure was let loose that dangerous spirit of disquisition, not in the coolness of philosophical enquiry, but enflamed with all the passions of an haughty resentful people, who thought themselves deeply injured, and that they were contending for everything that was valuable in the world.[84]

Burke did not question the legal competence or the unlimited scope of parliamentary authority. The problem was, such abstract powers could not in fact be exercised in an absolute way:

> many things indubitably included in the abstract idea of that power, and which carry no absolute injustice in themselves, yet being contrary to the opinions and feelings of the people, can as little be exercised as if Parliament in that case had been possessed of no right at all.[85]

This is vintage abeyance terrain, when theoretically unlimited power is refracted through the prism of political life and political culture, along with other principles. What comes out the other side is not what goes in. Burke had absolutely no trouble in recognizing that some questions were irresolvable and that not even compromise would suffice. One had to act as if the dilemma had been resolved even if it had not. Thus, pushing a principle like sovereignty would mean 'you sophisticate and poison the very source of government, by urging subtle deductions, and consequences odious to those you govern, from the unlimited and illimitable nature of supreme sovereignty, you will teach them by these means to call that sovereignty into question.'[86]

Burke also, and it is an important point, speaks of 'unsuspecting confidence' as essential to political stability. It may be unmerited, it may be based on self-deception or fiction and myth: what matters is that it is retained. In his *Letter to the Sheriffs of Bristol* Burke put it thus:

> This unsuspecting confidence is the true centre of gravity among mankind, about which all parts are at rest. It is this unsuspecting confidence that removes all difficulties, and reconciles all the contradictions which occur in the complexity of all ancient puzzled political establishments. Happy are the rulers which have the secret of preserving it.[87]

There is about this and numerous similar examples a sense of the desirability of non-exposure, strategic oversight, and studied inattention, and of the temperament necessary to sustain those things which only seem incompatible once the veils are removed. Burke's world is just as equivocal as Foley's: when an irresistible force meets an immovable object, you act as if it has not, and find a way around it. Burke was fond of vivid metaphors linked to biological organisms or the family. In this he was not merely being rhetorical and striving for effect: his view of human institutions was indeed that they had, in some ways, a life of their own, and were constantly self-regenerating. They were like families in the relationships between their parts and, as we know, there are silences in families just as there are in politics writ large.

Yet while these connections among Burke, abeyances, and Canada's situation may seem (mildly) academically interesting, are they of importance now? Have we not marched forward into the sunlight of a far more egalitarian, democratic, and pluralistic world, free of the humbug of 'understandings' amongst élites who know better, a world in which our political culture is capable of accommodating deep differences and in which we allow meaningful dialogue on virtually any subject? Many scholars find it difficult to be this optimistic. From the start there have been unremitting tensions within the state, and a fundamental cleavage between French and English. This cleavage may have affected our modes of behaviour in such a way that, even for our élites, the roots of political accommodations are not that deep, and our 'conversations' have often lacked the shared understandings so necessary for success. Our traditional modes of political behaviour may have developed in such a way that we have never learned to simply inhabit and accept our principles and beliefs, and have taken instead to declaring them. Thus although one might expect that over a period of 130 years a more organic, and Burkean, view would take hold even in a binational and multicultural society, we have to ask ourselves whether or not this has taken place, and if it has not, how are our abeyances to be maintained?[88]

Furthermore, we are hardly at a point, either in Canada or in any other state, where we should not look backwards for guidance. This is not advocacy of a rose-tinted view of a previous state of supposed communal harmony (as is often the case); it is a recognition that modern nationalisms are a curious amalgam of old and new.[89] They are all rooted in historical experience and identity, yet they are all constantly adjusting to the pressures of the late twentieth century, and often do so from within existing 'host' states and in conjunction with, or in opposition to, the deliberate strategies of nation-building undertaken by governments. The political, economic, and social demands placed upon modern states, and until relatively recently, the ability of state bureaucracies to grow, have meant that nationalists have had to grapple with policy problems that make the enterprise of building a new civil society exceedingly complex. As they do so, they must use the tools at hand to support historic goals, goals that must now be defended using the new vocabulary of internationalism, globalization, and civic citizenship, as well as the old appeals to ethnicity and history.[90] In spite of a spate of books on the end of things (e.g., work, affluence, innocence, liberalism, education, reform, the nation-state, and the world), matters are usually rather more complicated. Reading Burke reminds us of this, and can be salutary.

For what are now offered as solutions to the problem of Quebec (i.e., ways to 'end' the Quebec question) are often not courses of action Burke would consider prudent, reasonable, or effective. In his view any polity, if it wished to succeed, had to reconcile the 'descriptions' within it, and had to deal with changes in the power and composition of these descriptions (which correspond to what we now call interests). Certainly, not all interests could actually be represented in parliament; for some interests 'virtual' representation would suffice (one commercial centre could, for example, speak on behalf of others). But to leave an important 'description' out altogether was asking for trouble.[91] Even worse was a situation where some presumed to know what was best for others, but in fact had little or no real sympathy of feelings towards them. English Protestants speaking on behalf of Irish Catholics was a case in point. Power here is in the hands of 'an adverse description'. In such cases, where a powerful interest is subordinated or feels oppressed, Burke advocated giving it a constitutional role, usually via representation. The alternative of using force to suppress it was anathema to Burke: this would be expensive, totally counterproductive, and would undermine the constitution. When it came to conciliating interests, a state *could* therefore change the rules of the contract; prudence, morality, expediency, history, and justice would march hand in hand as long as the peculiar circumstances of each case were understood, and as long as the *objective* interests of the nation were paramount.

But how are we to know when an interest/description is merely being obstreperous and cranky, and when it does not have a legitimate case? It is easy to blame King George in hindsight, but far more difficult to see the colonists' case at the time. What relevance does Burke's advice on how to deal with an aggrieved description hold for us when it comes to what many now see as Quebec's never-ending demands and the fact that Quebec has been, if anything, over-represented at the federal level, at least since the 1960s?

To pose or see the question in such terms is to violate the whole spirit of the approach that I believe is embodied by Burke. He would ask whether or not there was something peculiar to this 'distemperature' that made it unique and deserving of special consideration, something in our history and in the political realities and make-up of the nation. Opposition to an interest could be economic (and, if so, could usually be worked out), but it might be 'a product of mean-spirited bigotry and a natural desire to dominate others' and put them in their place.[92] This Burke would see as extremely dangerous.

He would have little faith in purely legalistic responses, which stress uniformity and process rather than results. For Burke, arguing that all provinces should be treated equally would not get at the real problems we face in terms of the future of the Canada/Quebec relationship (and to put it in these terms is not to deny that one is a part of the other). Melissa Williams has cogently argued that Burke's views on representation can help put in perspective the simplistic procedural notion that, because all citizens have an equal right to vote, all are fairly and adequately represented.[93] Burke points us towards far deeper questions, in particular in this case whether or not, for example, we can argue that aboriginals *are* adequately represented either in an actual or in a virtual sense, and if not, what are we to do about it? They may be represented by an 'adverse description', just as were the Irish. Our current mantra of equality (of citizens, provinces, and rights) would, I suspect, reflect to Burke our lack of political imagination and our inability to work out mutually advantageous solutions that are prudent and reasonable in the circumstances. Instead we turn to law and procedures, and often do so in a distinctly mean-spirited and declaratory fashion.

Rational mutual advantage, combined with making the best of things in a magnanimous way, keeps Burke's society together. When a society begins to fall apart its leaders must, within the constraints of history, set about renewing the partnership(s) upon which it must be based, a partnership which will have been 'largely invisible until it has begun to break apart, at which point we must make some explicit choices about its terms.'[94] Burke, although obviously élitist and possessed of a faith that our representatives in Parliament, in exercising their superior powers of reason, will discover the common good, still provides the soundest of advice. He advises us—admonishes us—to be imaginative, generous, and pragmatic.

If we apply some of his dictums to our situation, we can see that there are many outside Quebec who believe that Quebec should not be seen as a 'description' with legitimate grievances. Opposition is often couched in less than magnanimous terms and seems devoid of much 'sympathy of feelings'. Are our responses now grounded in a prudent and historically realistic image of a nation that rests upon mutual advantage? Of course there are those in Quebec who are just as unBurkean in their view of reality. Yet it seems to me that the majority of Quebec's population are not, and that they still search for a prudent and mutually advantageous outcome. They have not wished to make hard choices; they want to retain their multiple identities, and who can blame them?[95] The wording of the latest Quebec referendum question illustrates this not merely because of the obvious wish to avoid a toughly worded question, but also because, as Louis Balthazar has noted, the phrasing:

... reflected the deep-seated ambivalence of most about the sovereignist project. I would even go so far as saying that most Quebeckers would have felt terribly cheated by a question like: 'Do you want to separate from Canada?' For good reason.[96]

Sadly, Quebeckers are now blamed for their ambivalence, and for their belief that even sovereignty could be limited by a form of Canadian union: this is seen as Quebeckers wanting to 'have their cake and eat it too'. This attitude will not lead us to redevelop a view of the nation that reflects the historical forces that created us, and our need to creatively reconfigure our political arangements:

> Burke's image of the nation as a broad compact among a slowly shifting constellation of groups is of urgent relevance to contemporary liberal democracies, so many of which are being torn asunder by conflicts over group identity and group interest. . . . Burke urges us to see it as a project of redescription—and therefore of political creativity—which is partially constrained by the identity of the different 'descriptions' of citizens which history has made salient in our time.[97]

As a part of this process of rethinking the nation we will also have to take into account what our abeyances have been and how we are now to treat them. In the past, our democracy was built upon forms of power-sharing that were frequently dualist in practice. This essentially conservative approach accorded with the attitudes so necessary for abeyance maintenance, and represents one conception of democracy. It accepts anomalies and identities, protects group rights, believes in accommodation and incrementalism and a 'politics of security'.[98] Now we have moved towards the idea that democracy is based upon majority rule, American-style individual rights, and the politics of principle. This approach makes abeyance maintenance far more difficult, and if we cannot maintain them there will be serious consequences, for Foley also makes the important point, particularly powerful in Canada's case, that:

> The theory of abeyances, however, brings to light a deeper set of guarantees that keeps liberties intact and governments in their place through an unwritten code of deterrence, by which the volatile properties of constitutional settlements are kept safely buried to the mutual satisfaction of conflicting political interests.[99]

The willingness to defer indefinitely the consideration of abeyances/deep constitutional anomalies represents, to Foley, 'the core of a constitutional culture', as does the instinctive inhibition to questioning that which is persistently left off the constitutional agenda.[100] If such abeyances or gaps of unsettlement do become the subject of conflict, they are the essence of a real crisis, for the very foundations and interior supports of the constitution are 'exposed to corrosive scrutiny, thereby unleashing the reality of their internal contradictions'.[101] The greatest danger to a constitution and a political community will arise when these deep-seated constitutional disjunctions become aligned with specific political forces. This is made particularly clear in a federal system when such forces are often territorially based. This, as we shall see, is the Canadian condition.

When abeyances are exposed, internal contradictions thus become apparent. Intolerable ambiguities appear, and the ensuing debate will unleash 'the full force of disillusionment and frustration' because people's (misconceived) expectations will be challenged or seen as thwarted.[102] What we *thought* we had, we hadn't; what was created was built on sand, and what protected us from the truth were our abeyances, and our willingness to evade and defer indefinitely any attempts at resolution. We know when one has been found when we sense its force and intractability, and we do so by observing the reactions that it begins to generate. If we can, we should retreat: in the Canadian case *this may simply not have been possible.* Thus although we may recognize that their existence is not a sign of weakness, and the temperament needed to sustain them is likewise a virtue not a vice, there will come times when certain abeyances can no longer be maintained.

Even Burke did not treat moral questions as ones which could always be avoided or placed in abeyance; in our case keeping things as they are is unlikely to suffice, for we have not made a generous peace, though try we did. Our shared political understandings, and the kind of political conversations we have held, have broken down. In large measure, our conversation seems to me to have not so much been *with* as *about* Quebec, and the terms of the debate are often disparaging.[103]

None the less, we managed to keep our greatest abeyance at bay for almost a century.

Notes

1 Rod Preece, 'The Political Wisdom of Sir John A. Macdonald', *Canadian Journal of Political Science* 17, 3 (September 1984), 459–86.

2 Michael Foley, *The Silence of Constitutions: Gaps, 'abeyances' and political temperament in the maintenance of government* (New York: Routledge, 1989), 98.

3 Ibid., 9.

4 Richard Simeon and Ian Robinson, *State, Society, and the Development of Canadian Federalism,* Research Studies of the Royal Commission on the Economic Union and Development Prospects for Canada (Toronto: University of Toronto Press, 1990), vol. 71, 23.

5 John Whyte cited in Simeon and Robinson, *State, Society, and the Development of Canadian Federalism,* 23.

6 William S. Livingston, *Federalism and Constitutional Change* (Oxford: Clarendon Press, 1956), 2.

7 The list of contributors to this debate is a long and distinguished one; Smiley and Cairns are chosen as particularly important and representative because their work has spanned such a long period and has contributed so much to the way we think about the Canadian polity.

8   See Simeon and Robinson, *State, Society, and the Development of Canadian Federalism*.

9   Livingston, *Federalism and Constitutional Change*, 5.

10 Ibid., 7.

11 Ibid.

12 Ian R. Christie, *Myth and Reality in Late-Eighteenth-Century British Politics* (Berkeley: University of California Press, 1970), 27.

13 Henry Tudor, *Political Myth* (London: Macmillan, 1972), 17.

14 Ibid., 138.

15 Kenneth McNaught, 'Three Myths and the Canadian Continuum', *The Round Table* 327 (1993), 315–22. For a brief and stimulating review of a number of dangerous myths 'we carry around in our heads' see Sylvia Bashevkin, 'Myths and Rebuttals' in John E. Trent, Robert Young, and Guy Lachapelle, eds, *Québec-Canada. What is the Path Ahead?* (Ottawa: University of Ottawa Press, 1996), 35–9.

16 Ibid., 316.

17 Ibid., 317.

18 Tamara Palmer Seiler has presented an interesting reappraisal of the myths of melting pot and mosaic. See 'Melting Pot and Mosaic: Images and Realities' in *Canada and the United States: Differences that Count*, ed. David M. Thomas (Peterborough: Broadview Press, 1993), 303–25. Note also Allan Smith's earlier discussion entitled 'Metaphor and Nationality in North America', *Canadian Historical Review* 51, 3 (1970), 247–75, and his essay 'National Images and National Maintenance: The Ascendancy of the Ethnic Idea in North America', *Canadian Journal of Political Science* 14, 2 (June 1981), 227–57.

19 The sources for such a view are legion. See, for example, S. F. Wise and Robert Craig Brown, *Canada Views the United States* (Macmillan, Toronto, 1967), 122. 'Canadian views . . . were not really derived from actual use of observation, they were arrived at . . . by a psychological necessity to believe that the principles of the Canadian system were better than those of the United States.'

20 McNaught, 'Three Myths and the Canadian Continuum', 320.

21 Constance MacRae-Buchanan, 'American Influence on Canadian Constitutionalism' in *Canadian Constitutionalism 1791–1991*, ed. Janet Ajzenstat (Ottawa: Canadian Study of Parliament Group, 1992), 148.

22 Patrick J. Dobel, *Compromise and Political Action: Political Morality in Liberal and Democratic Life* (Savage, Md.: Rowman and Littlefield, 1990), 20.

23 Paul Romney, 'Why Lord Watson Was Right' in *Canadian Constitutionalism 1791–1991*, ed. Janet Ajzenstat, 178.

24 C.E.S. Franks, *The Myths and Symbols of the Constitutional Debate in Canada* (Kingston: Institute of Intergovernmental Relations, 1993).

25 Ibid.

26 Michael Oliver, *The Passionate Debate: The Social and Political Ideas of Quebec Nationalism 1920–1945* (Montreal: Véhicule Press, 1991), 95–9.

27 André Vachon, 'Dollard des Ormeaux', *Dictionnaire Biographique du Canada* vol. 1, 277–8. He notes that 'il arrive de plus que certains prennent le chemin glissant de l'histoire "engagée"'(277). Recruiting posters in Quebec during World War One urged men to follow the example of Dollard des Ormeaux and go to face the enemy. See Sandra Gwyn, *Tapestry of War* (Toronto: HarperCollins, 1992), 317.

28 Vachon, ibid.

29 Barry Cooper takes issue with this 'eastern' view of our myths and its focus on survival, the garrison mentality, and loyalism. He argues that the West's myths have been different, and assigns a central place to the 'the myth of Red River'. In over twenty years of teaching political science to Western Canadian students, it would be my conclusion that they have never even heard of the Red River settlement and its history, let alone understood its mythic significance. See Barry Cooper, 'Eastern Political Consciousness' in *Political Thought in Canada*, ed. Stephen Brooks (Toronto: Irwin Publishing, 1984), 214–38. The point remains, none the less, that the tale told by Western myths is different: it is a story of neglect, domination, adversity, individualism, and triumph.

30 Franks, *The Myths and Symbols of the Constitutional Debate in Canada*, 7.

31 Lindsay Paterson, *The Autonomy of Modern Scotland* (Edinburgh, 1994), 25.

32 The importance of such explanations is stressed by both Donald Smiley and Peter Russell. Smiley, in *The Canadian Political Nationality* (Toronto: Methuen, 1967), 30, uses MacIver's definition of myth: 'By myth we mean the value-impregnated beliefs and notions that men hold, that they live by or live for.' See R.M. MacIver, *The Web of Government* (Toronto: Macmillan of Canada, 1947), 4. Russell follows suit in *Constitutional Odyssey* (Toronto: University of Toronto Press, 1992), 49. Smiley discusses in particular the need for a compact myth as an expression of the Canadian political community: 'The appeal to community is of more significance than the violence which compact theories do to the historical record' (30).

33 See Max Nemni, 'Canada in Crisis and the Destructive Power of Myth', *Queen's Quarterly* 99, 1 (Spring 1992). For an extensive discussion of nationalism and myths see Anthony D. Smith, *National Identity* (Harmondsworth: Penguin Books, 1991), ch. 2. He argues that 'myths of ethnic chosenness go to the heart of the modes of ethnic self-renewal and hence survival' (36). Societies can harbour grudges for rather a long time. This phenomenon, and the amazing power of myth, can be seen during the English Civil War. Nearly 600 years after the Norman Conquest, Cromwell's Ironsides saw themselves as reversing the results of the Battle of Hastings, and as acting out the culminating episode of the saga of the English people: 'a wave of anti-Norman feeling swept the ranks.' Plain russet-coated troopers were going to root out William the Bastard's successors, including those in the House of Lords, and restore the rights of Englishmen, 'for who were the Lords but William the Conqueror's colonels?' See Tudor, *Political Myth*, 101–2.

34 Eric Black, *Our Constitution: The Myth That Binds Us* (Boulder: Westview Press, 1988), 172. Songs can also shape our interpretations of events and can help create identities. The late Stan Rogers, in 'Northwest Passage', gives us a wonderful evocation of who we are and what we have accomplished, 'tracing one warm line through a land so wild and savage'. See Nick Baxter-Moore, 'The Songs of Stan Rogers', *British Journal of Canadian Studies*, 10, 2 (1995) 306–29.

35 David Milne, 'Politics and the Constitution' in *Canadian Politics: an introduction to the discipline*, eds Alain-G. Gagnon and James P. Bickerton (Peterborough: Broadview Press, 1990), 207–8. Milne notes that 'it is this rationalist idea of constitutions and their importance in political life that has preoccupied Canadians' and asks whether this is not 'naive'. Constitutions, he says, rarely tell the truth; they mean 'no more and no less than what their interpreters *say* they mean' (208).

36 Edmund S. Morgan, *Inventing the People: The Rise of Popular Sovereignty in England and America* (New York: W.W. Norton, 1988), 13.

37 Ibid.

38 Morgan charts how old fictions and old self-evident truths give way to new: 'The search begins with the old fiction, the divine right of Kings. Since we have long given up suspending our disbelief in this one, we should have no difficulty perceiving its fictional qualities.' The problem for us will be the recognition of the true nature of our current fictions without, at the same time, undermining them. For it has to be remembered that fictions affect the governing few as well as the governed many, and that the former may be restrained by such fictions in ways that are 'deviously' vital to liberty and individual security. See Morgan, *Inventing the People*, 14–15.

39 Ibid. See Chapter One for a discussion of the divine right of kings, and how the elevation of the king prepared the way for his destruction—and the rise of new fictions that were not at all what men in power had intended.

40 Ibid., 152. Just as the House of Commons had developed the means to restrain the king first by exalting him and then by inventing the sovereign people, so also, argues Morgan, did the exaltation of the people provide the means for controlling and directing their power and for sustaining the new fictions so contrary to fact.

41 Ibid., 14.

42 When using the idea that abeyances are a form of 'irresolution' I do not wish to imply that this means weakness or mere vacillation. In both French and English to say that someone is 'irresolute' does imply a criticism and is usually taken as a form of character defect. The idea of irresolution, as applied to constitutional questions, is not meant in the same way.

43 The fiction of popular sovereignty continues to unfold, surrounded and buttressed by new protecting fictions. The notion of the independent yeoman-farmer or the English country gentleman as the democratic bulwark against despotism from above or below, may have been replaced by the majesty of the law and its objective guardians and the view that under it all are equal. In Canada these particular fictions create unusual difficulties, tied as they are to our deepest problems, including the status of Quebec and how to keep it in abeyance.

44 See David Cameron, *Nationalism, Self-Determination and the Quebec Question* (Toronto: Macmillan of Canada, 1974), 8.

45 R.C. Lewontin, 'Women Versus the Biologists', *The New York Review of Books* 41 (7 April 1994), 31–5. See 32.

46 Alan C. Cairns, 'Ritual, Taboo, and Bias in Constitutional Controversies in Canada, or Constitutional Talk Canadian Style' in *Disruptions: Constitutional Struggles from the Charter to Meech Lake*, ed. Douglas E. Williams (Toronto: McClelland and Stewart, 1991).

47 R.D. Laing's essay 'Family Scenarios' begins as follows: 'The most common situation I encounter in families is when what *I* think is going on bears almost no resemblance to what anyone in the family experiences or thinks is happening, whether or not this coincides with common sense . . . there are complicated strategies to keep everyone in the dark.' See *The Politics of the Family and other Essays* (New York: Pantheon Books, 1971), 77.

48 Bernard Crick, 'The English and the British' in *National Identities: The Constitution of the United Kingdom*, ed. Bernard Crick (Oxford: Basil Blackwell, 1991), 101.

49 Bernard Crick, 'A Footnote to Rally the Academic Defenders of Politics' in Bernard Crick, *In Defence of Politics*, 4th edn (London: Weidenfeld and Nicholson, 1992), 190.

50 Berel Rodal, 'State and Nation in Conflict', in *Boundaries of Identity: A Quebec Reader*, ed. William Dodge (Toronto: Lester Publishing Ltd, 1992), xviii.

51 Academic and legal terminology becomes more widespread with the involvement of academics in public debate, but even in this case the words remain fuzzy or reflect particular specializations.

52 See Daniel T. Rodgers, *Contested Truths: Keywords in American Politics* (New York: Basic Books, 1987). The quotation is taken from a review of Rodger's book by Michael Pollak entitled 'Politics and Rhetoric', *Telos* 76 (Summer 1988), 186–91.

53 See Lysiane Gagnon, 'How the word "nationalist" changed its meaning in the Quebec lexicon', *The Globe and Mail*, 23 April 1994, D3. She discusses the changing use in Quebec of such terms as sovereignty, national, separatist, province, French Canadian, Québécois, federalist, and even Canada. She concludes that 'words can be more effective than guns—especially if they are used by bright people with prominent jobs'. One could add, as a further illustration, the way in which two stock expressions are taken to mean the very opposite of what was intended. We use 'good fences make good neighbours' to mean that we should build fences—when in fact Frost meant that we should not. We refer to 'the two solitudes' implying that never the twain shall meet. The Rilke quotation with which MacLennan introduces his book speaks of love consisting of two solitudes which 'protect, and touch, and greet each other'. For a more extended discussion of this point, and of its relationship to nationalism and patriotism, see Jeremy Webber, *Reimagining Canada. Language, Culture, Community, and the Canadian Constitution* (Montreal and Kingston: McGill-Queen's University Press, 1994), 190–3.

54 Carolyn J. Tuohy, *Policy and Politics in Canada: Institutionalized Ambivalence* (Philadelphia: Temple University Press, 1992), 4.

55 Ibid., 'One of two major political parties calls itself "Progressive Conservative". The term "Red Tory" is well recognized in Canadian political parlance. A major referendum was held on the question of whether Quebec should establish a new form of "sovereignty-association" with the rest of Canada. The same province underwent what is commonly referred to as a "Quiet Revolution" of social and political change. This language reflects the Canadian aversion to either-or choices, the *tendency to find distinctive ways of reconciling divergent concepts.*' (My emphasis.)

56 See Marc Gold, 'The Rhetoric of Rights: The Supreme Court and the Charter' in *Making the Laws: The Courts and the Constitution*, eds John Saywell and G. Vegh (Toronto: Copp Clark Pitman, 1991), 365.

57 Ibid., 367.

58 Gold uses the example of *Big M Drug Mart* in which Chief Justice Dickson wrote that the police had witnessed the Sunday sale of such items as 'groceries, plastic cups and a bicycle lock'. Gold's point is that the banality of these transactions is a rhetorical device which would not have been used if the stores had been selling pornographic materials. 'Would the Court have been so quick to specify the nature of the transactions in such a case?'

59 I am indebted to Dr David Cameron for his penetrating insights into the abeyances/Oakeshott/Burke connections.

60 Jeremy Rayner, 'The Legend of Oakeshott's Sceptical Philosophy and Limited Politics', *Canadian Journal of Political Science* 18, 2 (June 1985), 313–52. This quotation is to be found on page 333.

61 Ibid., 315.

62 Michael Oakeshott, introduction to Thomas Hobbes, *Leviathan* ([Oxford: Basil and Blackwell, 1946], 1xiv) cited in Jeremy Raynor, 'The Legend of Oakeshott's Sceptical Philosophy and Limited Politics', 324, footnote 27. Bernard Crick has argued, in no uncertain terms, that Oakeshott and others are guilty of a 'spinsterish concept of "objectivity"' which causes them to turn their backs 'on the whole tendency of Western civilization to be an improving, reformist, ameliorative, not simply a contemplative, culture.... Britain has the distinction of possessing some academic doctrinaire anti-doctrinaires to whom all theoretical knowledge is either a fallacy—"rationalism"—or else a threat to the working of those unconscious intimations and habits on which political order depends, etc., etc.' See 'A Footnote to Rally the Academic Professors of Politics', 188–91. Oakeshott does admit that the acceptance of 'Rationalism' in politics—which he despises—was 'tacitly resisted and retarded by, for example, the informality of English politics (which enabled us to escape, for a long time, putting too high a value on political action and placing too high a hope in political achievement ...)'. See his *Rationalism in Politics and Other Essays* (New York: Barnes and Noble, 1974), 21.

63 Janet Ajzenstat, 'Reconciling Parliament and Rights', 5.

64 Richard Nutbrown, 'State Images and the Writing of English Canadian Political Science', in *Canadian Politics*, eds Alain-G. Gagnon and James P. Bickerton, 63–4. See also Mallory's comment that 'There must be a collective will to survive, and a collective understanding of what the important values of the community are which are important to preserve.... To the extent that our political values and institutions, created with anxious care by our forebears, are failing us, the failure must to a degree be because our political language has failed us. We cannot find the right words, and we have forgotten the meaning of old ones.' See J.R. Mallory, 'The Continuing Evolution of Canadian Constitutionalism' in *Constitutionalism, Citizenship and Society in Canada*, eds Alan Cairns and Cynthia Williams, Royal Commission on the Economic Union and Development Prospects for Canada (Toronto: University of Toronto Press, 1985), vol. 33, 60. David Milne writes that 'it is not at all uncommon to find in academic works on federalism literally hundreds of images and modifiers ... federalism metaphors include, for example, an awesome variety of cakes ... and fences, as well as a barrage of value-laden terms.' To which I am adding graveyards, black holes, and wreckage-strewn constitutional highways. See *Tug of War:*

Ottawa and the Provinces Under Trudeau and Mulroney (Toronto: James Lorimer and Co., 1986), 7. Oakeshott too reminds us that 'The language of politics is the language of desire and aversion, of preference and choice, of approval and disapproval, of praise and blame, of persuasion, injunction, accusation, and threat.' See *Rationalism in Politics*, 321. J.G.A. Pocock has argued that the reason that political scientists study political theory is not to reveal the character of a past society but, more abstractly, to 'study the rise and the role of an organizing political language in a society's political activity'. See 'Machiavelli, Harrington and English Political Ideas in the Eighteenth Century' in his *Politics, Language and Time: Essays on Political Theory and History* (New York: Atheneum, 1971), 104.

65 Kenneth Dewar has made the point that Trudeau has attempted, with some success 'to transcend politics altogether' and to replace it with an anti-politics. The rhetoric of 'rights and freedoms' has, he thinks, turned us away from our traditions of civic politics and we have not yet come to terms with the consequences of so doing. Ideological terms like liberal democracy have replaced institutional terms. He sees this as similar to the flight from politics in the 1920s, 'when the cult of efficiency and expertise seized the minds of progressive reformers'. 'The flight from politics', *The Chronicle-Herald*, 2 July 1991, A7. The relationship between anti-political attitudes and abeyances is explored at greater length in Chapter Six.

66 Oakeshott, in his extremely élitist way, argues that 'we may look forward to the time when the professions will be stocked with clever men, but men whose skill is limited and who have never had a proper opportunity of learning the nuances which compose the tradition and standards of behaviour which belong to a great profession.' We do not have to accept his generational deference to take the point that unacknowledged premises and traditions are socially derived and are not merely learned from books. *Rationalism in Politics*, 34. What is written into a constitution in a seemingly clear way may not be true. According to the Constitution of the Irish Republic, Irish is 'the first official language'. Yet it obviously is not. See Colm Toibin, 'On Not Saying What You Mean', *London Review of Books*, Nov. 30, 1995, 3–6.

67 Gerald W. Chapman, *Edmund Burke: The Practical Imagination* (Cambridge: Harvard University Press, 1967), 4–5.

68 See Rod Preece, 'The Political Wisdom of Sir John A. Macdonald'.

69 For example, Crick's comment that he 'tried to prove that the French Revolution was impossible in the same breath as he berated the iniquities of its success'. See his 'footnote' to this effect in 'To Rally Those Who Grudge the Price' in Bernard Crick, *In Defence of Politics*, 268. Burke faced a barrage of criticism in his own day for his views on the Revolution (including, of course, the writings of Thomas Paine and Mary Wollstonecraft); recent criticism includes comments on its 'gendered semiotic code'. See Linda K. Zerilli's comments in 'No Thrust, No Swell, No Subject?' and Stephen K. White's reply in *Political Theory* 22, 2 (May 1994).

70 Melissa S. Williams, 'Burkean "Descriptions" and Political Representation: A Reappraisal', *Canadian Journal of Political Science* 29, 1 (March 1996), 23. Full footnotes for these judgments are provided by Dr Williams, whose article I found particularly helpful. See also Gerald W. Chapman, *Edmund Burke: The Practical Imagination*, ch. 1.

71 See Conor Cruise O'Brien, *The Great Melody: A Thematic Biography of Edmund Burke* (Chicago: University of Chicago Press, 1992). He makes a concerted effort to rescue Burke from his detractors. For a useful review of O'Brien's work see J.G.A. Pocock, *London Review of Books,* Feb. 24, 1994, 9–11.

72 Edmund Burke, *A Letter to the Sheriffs of Bristol*, in *Edmund Burke on Government, Politics and Society*, ed. B.W. Hill (New York: Fontana Books, 1976), 199.

73 Edmund Burke, *Reflections on the Revolution in France*, in *Edmund Burke on Government, Politics and Society*, ed. B.W. Hill, 345.

74 J.G.A. Pocock, 'Burke and the Ancient Constitution: A Problem in the History of Ideas' in his *Politics, Language and Time,* 203.

75 Edmund Burke, *A Letter to the Sheriffs of Bristol*, 200.

76 Burke's ideas on 'acquaintance' are particularly interesting in a Canadian context, because we have suffered from far too little 'acquaintance' between French and English, and 'Where men are not acquainted with each other's principles, nor experienced in each other's talents, nor at all practised in their mutual habits and dispositions by joint efforts in business; no personal confidence, no friendship, no common interest, subsisting among them; it is evidently impossible that they can act a public part with uniformity, perseverance, or efficacy.' See James T. Boulton, *The Language of Politics, in the Age of Wilkes and Burke* (Toronto: Routledge and Kegan Paul, 1963), 65.

77 See David Cameron, *The Social Thought of Rousseau and Burke* (Birkenhead: Willmer Brothers, 1973), 139.

78 Edmund Burke, *Reflections on the Revolution in France*, in Conor Cruise O'Brien, *The Great Melody,* 404.

79 David Cameron, *The Social Thought of Rousseau and Burke*, 25.

80 Edmund Burke, *Reflections on the Revolution in France*, in *Edmund Burke on Government, Politics and Society*, ed. B.W. Hill, 327–8.

81 David Cameron, *The Social Thought of Rousseau and Burke*, 139–40. Cameron adds that for Burke: 'Political thought and thought related to political action, are matters of detail, of time and occasion, and of experience. Simplicity, in these circumstances, is not a virtue, but an ignorant failing; it is "the offspring of cold hearts and muddy understanding".'

82 In *Reflections on the Revolution in France*, Burke notes that 'opposed and conflicting interests . . . make all change a subject of *compromise*, which naturally begets moderation; they produce *temperaments.*' See *Edmund Burke on Government, Politics and Society,* ed. B.W. Hill, 300.

83 Ibid., 328.

84 Edmund Burke,*The Writings and Speeches of Edmund Burke, vol. 2: Party, Parliament and the English Crisis, 1766–1774*, ed. Paul Langford (Oxford: Clarendon Press, 1981), 187–8.

85 Edmund Burke, *A Letter to the Sheriffs of Bristol*, 196.

86 Edmund Burke, *The Writings and Speeches of Edmund Burke, vol. 2,* ed. Paul Langford, 458.

87 Edmund Burke, *A Letter to the Sheriffs of Bristol*, 203. This 'Letter' of 1777 completes a quartet of major writings on America that are particularly relevant to the idea of acceptable irresolution. The others are speeches on the *Declaratory Act* (1766), *On American Taxation* (1774), and *On Conciliation with America* (1775).

88 It should be remembered that Britain has never been able to successfully apply its accumulated constitutional wisdom and practice to Ireland, and its track record *vis-à-vis* Wales and Scotland leaves much to be desired. Burke placed a considerable emphasis on 'association' and on deep social links, developed over time.

89 Many critics of today's social arrangements look back to the ideals supposedly entrenched in earlier communities. For a critique of this kind of communitarianism see Derek L. Philips, *Looking Backward: A Critical Appraisal of Communitarian Thought* (Princeton: Princeton University Press, 1993). He concludes that, although he shares much of the critics' disenchantment with modern life, 'If those were the good times, Lord protect us against the bad'.

90 See Michael Keating, *Nations Against The State: The New Politics of Nationalism in Quebec, Catalonia and Scotland* (New York: St. Martin's Press, 1996). Keating's book is an important work. He argues, amongst other things, that nationalist politics is not only about demanding a nation-state, it is now about 'preserving social cohesion in a world of weakened states'. As such, it is about new forms of civic society as much as it is about ethnic particularism. Keating's conclusions are discussed at greater length in Chapter Six.

91 For a full discussion of 'descriptions' and representation, and Burke's contractarian views, see Melissa S. Williams, 'Burkean "Descriptions" and Political Representation'.

92 Ibid., 42–3.

93 Ibid.

94 Ibid.

95 As I write, the latest Léger and Léger poll shows that a sizeable majority (59.4%) wants Quebec to be sovereign but an even larger majority (65.3%) wants Quebec to remain a part of Canada.

96 Louis Balthazar, 'Within the Black Box: Reflections from a French Quebec Vantage Point', *The American Review of Canadian Studies* 25, 4 (Winter 1995), 526. David Milne makes the important related point—as do others—that complaining about the vagueness of the referendum question merely hides the fact that both sides increasingly concurred that a 'yes' vote really meant a new country and that 'for the first time a majority of Quebec Francophones have voted for sovereignty'. David Milne, 'Past and Future: Reflections After the Referendum' in Trent, Young, and Lachapelle, eds, *Québec–Canada*, 81–2.

97 Melissa S. Williams, 45.

98 See S.J.R. Noel, 'Canadian Responses to Ethnic Conflict. Consociationalism, federalism and control', in *The Politics of Ethnic Conflict Regulation*, eds John McGarry and Brendan O'Leary (New York: Routledge, 1993), 41–61. Noel provides a very clear overview of our conflict management strategies, in particular consociational approaches.

99 Michael Foley, *The Silence of Constitutions*, 129. Consistently leaving things off the agenda was a Canadian strategy, as we shall see.
100 Ibid., 10.
101 Ibid., 11.
102 Ibid.
103 The conversation metaphor has obvious problems associated with it. We might assume that all are party to this conversation, when in fact they are not. See Dobel, *Compromise and Political Action*, 17.

3

Settled Unsettlements

A federal constitution shall not include too many silences.[1]

The situation that existed in 1860s British North America, and the constitutional settlement that emerged, illustrate what could well be a classic case where the conditions for the circumvention of abeyances were propitious. At the same time, paradoxically, this has meant that certain problems left as abeyances have surfaced over the past thirty-odd years, and we have not been able, as yet, to lay them to rest.

That the agreement of 1867 left plenty of scope for strategic evasion and complicity in delusion is evident from a close reading of the settlement itself—the legal text—for we acquire from it some very broad clues about what our abeyances were and what they would become. And, as one would expect, we discern them by their absence, not their presence. Before examining them, however, it is appropriate to remind ourselves of Carl Becker's dictum that 'whether arguments command assent or not depends less upon the logic that sustains them than upon the climate of opinion in which they are sustained.'[2] We are as susceptible to what Becker called our 'specious present', and its attendant use of history, as were our predecessors.[3] Current constitutional assumptions may well, in future, look as jarring as those of our nineteenth-century forebears now, perhaps, appear to us. If the arrangements made in 1867 are approached in this spirit of caution, leaving so many matters in abeyance may take on a different, and more positive, complexion.

In the debate and discussions prior to Confederation, principles were as much negative as positive; we were discussing what we did not want to be—the United States—as much as what we were. Temperament, personality, chance, and Machiavellian *fortuna* also played a considerable part in the successful creation of the new Confederation. Sir John A. Macdonald was an adroit and wonderful politician, surrounded as he was on all sides by suspicious allies who watched him 'as eager dogs watch a rat hole'. Johnson and Waite put it thus: 'Macdonald's protean mind, his resourcefulness, his reserves of doggedness when the going was really rough—all gave him tremendous depth and resilience.'[4] One could write of George-Étienne Cartier's crucial role in exactly the same vein. We must, however, also recognize that the scene was set for abeyance circumvention not only by the views and talents of those involved but by the overall, interdependent, circumstances of the time:

- The contending parties were powerful, but no single group was strong enough to 'win' outright. Each was powerful in that it had the ability to prevent a settlement, or to ensure that an imposed settlement would be far too costly. Each was threatened by external forces sufficient to cause serious economic and military fears.[5] All were under British pressure to arrive at workable new arrangements that would lessen the imperial burden.
- There was an acceptable, even an appealing, way out. It was both a retreat and an advance. It retreated into the already established vagueness of a system to be run according to British principles of government: thus many matters could be left unstated, whilst others could acquire a veneer of specificity. At the same time, it advanced into the unknown terrain of federalism and, ultimately, one could assume, to the achievement of the goal of complete national autonomy.[6] The resolutions were voted upon en bloc, so that they had to be treated as a seamless web. And, at the same time, it promised considerable economic benefits, if not for all at least for many.
- A triumph could be proclaimed. The participants could walk away from the table with their own differing constitutional images and, shortly thereafter, their own constitutional myths and fictions. It assumed away, or postponed, the need for clarification of the deepest disjunctions that lay at the heart of the debate. Everyone lived to fight another day. This was precisely the objective, at a time when external pressures were threatening to destroy the country unless it acted in unison.[7]

In order to establish, therefore, what our abeyances were and are, we need to examine the settlement more closely and see how power, constitutional ambiguity, and wishful thinking overcame the pull of our existing and embryonic constitutional black holes, and enabled us to develop new fictions and satisfying myths, although neither have the force and power one would expect after over two centuries of constitutional development.

'Circumstances'

When the Union of Upper and Lower Canada was established in 1841, Lower Canada had 697,000 inhabitants and Upper Canada 432,000.[8] By 1852 the population of Upper Canada had surpassed that of Lower Canada, and agitation for representation by population grew apace. Even so, it is vital to remember that at the Quebec conference in 1864 the four French-Canadian delegates (Cartier, Langevin, Taché, and Chapais) of the 33 present, represented a Lower Canada that still contained one third of the population of the proposed Confederation, and of this one third (of approximately 1 million people) 75% were French Canadian. Montreal might have been 50% anglophone, and Quebec City almost 40%, but there could be no denying the sheer weight of French-Canadian numbers as well as sentiments.[9]

This was why Macdonald was conscious that a forced union and simple representation by population would not work:

> It would have left the Lower Province with a sullen feeling of injury and injustice. The Lower Canadians would not have worked cheerfully under such a change of system, but would have ceased to be what they are now—a nationality with representatives in Parliament, governed by general principles and divided according to their political opinions—and would have been in great danger of becoming a faction, forgetful of their national obligations, and only activated by a desire to defend their own sectional interests, their own laws, and their own institutions.[10]

Macdonald's own political and partisan position was such that, to survive, he had to have the support of Cartier and French-Canadian representatives. This has to be added to the total unacceptability of assimilation to French Canada, which in this case meant Lower Canada. Assimilation would, it was thought by many outside Quebec, arrive later.

Ged Martin has provided a skilful and interesting reappraisal of Macdonald's options.[11] He attacks the view of Confederation as a golden age, 'when Canada's politicians sank rancorous personal disagreements and rose above sectional selfishness to lay the foundation stone of a transcontinental and bicultural nation.'[12] In addition to taking on the conventional wisdom that the Province of Canada had been an abject, deadlocked failure, he shows how Macdonald 'was in reality walking a desperately insecure tightrope'[13] and how close-run a thing it was. Macdonald's power depended upon the Confederation gamble coming off; if it failed, his great rival Brown would win. The fact that Macdonald was always able, as he himself said, 'to look a little ahead, while he [Brown] could on no occasion forego the temptation of a temporary triumph'[14] does nothing to lessen the fact that Macdonald depended on Cartier.

Rod Preece in particular has emphasized Sir John's political wisdom rather than his political ideas, 'not to deny Macdonald a political philosophy but to reflect its pragmatic and non-rationalist character.'[15] Preece strongly objects to the view that there is a separation possible between theory and practice such that it is possible to put someone, like Macdonald, into one or the other camp, as either theorist or pragmatist. To do so is to create a false dichotomy.[16] Macdonald, says Preece, may not have been a man of theoretical bent, but he did more than merely take up ideas just like spare parts. The fact was, he 'lived in an age of philosophical complexity'. He was well aware of the contributions of a great many British figures, and referred to them often.[17] Macdonald thus did defend his principles even though the *test* of a principle was its result. And, asks Preece:

> Why should a concern with consequence not be based upon precept? Was it not Burke's dictum? And was Burke not the philosopher who claimed that abstract ideas, ideas not grounded in experience, would cause the

'conflagration of Europe'? . . . Did not Burke explicitly, and Macdonald implicitly, recognize that the ends of one question were the means of some other question? . . . Macdonald's apparent inconsistencies are in fact consistent with Burke's doctrine of 'circumstances'.[18]

Preece emphasizes throughout that Macdonald was prudent in the Burkean mould: possessed of a sophisticated political philosophy circumscribed by devotion to the Crown, to British institutions in general, and to the belief that change should be minimal. He sees him as a liberal-conservative in the Canning-Pitt-Peel tradition.[19] It was a world not of abstraction but of belief in order, tradition, the rule of law, constitutional monarchy, the national interest, and experience. In this sense it was anti-rationalist in spirit and outlook. Freedom was inseparable from restraint and loyalty and obligation; true politicians were also good patriots, who used to the full the materials to hand, and avoided fruitless theoretical debate. Given these beliefs, Preece concludes that 'Burke's political disposition had become Macdonald's political disposition.'[20]

Loyalty to Britain, and to British principles, was Macdonald's best available antidote against distance, provincialism, economic pressures, and the different traditions and needs of Quebec. Even economics had to be subservient to politics and to national needs. Confederation in 1867 therefore represented a cautious political settlement that maintained the virtues of the British connection and which, given the political beliefs of its chief architect, avoided, wherever possible, tackling problems best left, in his view, well alone.[21] Thus it was 'that the philosophy of the trimmer—and Macdonald was, indeed, a trimmer, became the founding philosophy of Canada.'[22]

If Burke's world is to be seen as just as equivocal as Foley's, so may Sir John's. Phrases such as 'strategic oversight', or 'studied inattention', or 'conventions of non-exposure', all seem tailor-made for Macdonald's approach to the complexities of change. He was forced to act, and the others were forced to compromise or equivocate.

Macdonald's reliance on Lower Canada's support has already been noted. French Canada's readiness to embrace Confederation was certainly due as much to negative as to positive factors. Quebec was faced with a range of options of which a federal system was the only one to hold out any real promise: it could offer the prospect of the *minimal* degree of unification combined with the *maximum* amount of local autonomy. In the circumstances facing French Canada, what is surprising perhaps is that so many French-Canadian members still voted against Confederation:

> It was a huge vote. Of a house of 130 members, 124 responded. Of the 62 members from Canada West that were present, 54 voted for Confederation; of 62 from Canada East 37 did so. Of the 48 French-Canadian members present, 27 voted for, 21 against.[23]

Quebec had already lost 50,000 of its population to the United States in the decade between 1850–1860.[24] The threat of annexation to the United States and the likely fate that would then befall the French language, culture, and religion was ever-present. Confederation promised access to new markets. It restricted the impact of representation by population. It kept Quebec as part of the British Empire and therefore within the more conservative, orderly framework of responsible government. Tensions between the liberal traditions of parliamentarism and a multi-national empire, and the jingoistic demands of sacrifice for the mother country, would come later. For the moment, to men such as Cartier a British connection was decidedly preferable to an American one.[25] Confederation built upon the guarantees put in place in 1774 and 1791; Mason Wade in fact argues that the Quebec Act 'conceded that the French Canadians could be British without being English' (and that the Commonwealth was an eventual outgrowth of the Act).[26] Respect for British traditions of governance is exemplified in the oft-quoted remark of Colonel Taché in 1846: "Be satisfied we will never forget our allegiance till the last cannon which is shot on this continent in defence of Great Britain is fired by the hand of a French Canadian" (loud cheers in the assembly).'[27] Respect for things British—perhaps more accurately things English—thus predated Confederation and was to last well into the next century.

British political influence of a positive kind had made the Conquest palatable; it had demonstrated the attractiveness and superiority of British institutions and political culture over American, and even made of the Empire a cult of service and adventure, of civilization and belonging to something that mattered:

> This is a delicate subject that embarrasses some historians, but the facts are incontestable. During this period the Canadiens were more or less seduced by their conquerors. The historian Burt's expression for this period implies something terrible: 'the moral conquest'.[28]

Yet there was more to it than this, and perhaps it is to be found in the appeal of British political tolerance, Lord Durham notwithstanding. In the eighteenth century British politics had taken a decided turn towards greater accommodation.[29] As George Savile said in *The Character of A Trimmer*, 'Fundamentals are dangerous: there are some issues in life which are better left sleeping, we will raise only the issues on which we may disagree without imperiling our country; and even on them we will disagree with buttons on the foils.'[30] This was a sentiment that resonated in Quebec after the events of 1837. It also represents precisely the kind of thinking one associates with abeyances, and, as we have seen, with the beliefs held by Macdonald.

It could also perhaps be argued that some of the cult of the English country gentleman may well have had its appeal, including, as it did, not only a love of sport and a distrust of ideas and any great intellectuality, but also 'a cult of good manners—which after all, has implications for the parliament house not simply the private house; a social tolerance of the upwardly mobile from trade or industry, but aversion to any obsessive commitment to making money; . . . a belief that the good life moves back and forth from town to country, country to town.'[31] This 'British' emphasis on style, on property, on personal rights and on toleration of eccentricity and difference, even though it may have stemmed from complacency, self-assurance, anti-intellectualism, and even arrogance was nevertheless probably far more attractive than either the narrow bigotry of the Orange order or the Protestant, democratic, unruly, materialistic sentiments found to the south. Lest this be seen as too speculative, we must remember that 'Cartier all his life had an almost morbid fear of the United States, and was always strongly opposed to its republican institutions.'[32] Consider also the things that Henri Bourassa disliked about Americans: 'The list was formidable: accent, dress, yellow journalism, intolerant patriotism, political corruption, business corruption, professional corruption, snobbish worship of titles and money.'[33] The British might not be entrepreneurs in the American sense, but this was to the good, and British institutions, if modified, could suit a conservative French Canada very well indeed.

Taché and Cartier were thus well aware that they were not negotiating from a position of particular strength even though they could count on the intensity of French-Canadian sentiments. Lower Canada was seen by its French-speaking inhabitants as a national homeland; 'even the word Canada, as they used it, usually referred to the Lower province or, even more specifically, to the valley of the St Lawrence.'[34] The petitions drawn up in 1822 to oppose the proposed union had expressed the belief that 'this province had to be set aside for all time as a homeland for their nationality, a territory to be characterized by their laws, their institutions, and their language.'[35] What was at stake in 1867 was the future of the French-Canadian 'race', a race chastened and rendered a great deal more conservative after 1822 by the defeat of the Patriotes in 1838.[36] And this had been followed by the writing of the infamous *Report* of Lord Durham. French Canada could prevent change, but mere prevention was no guarantee that worse was not to come, and options were very limited indeed.[37] The population was numerous enough for cultural survival but too few to encourage any dreams of an independent state.[38] The Union of the Canadas in 1841 had reduced the French to a permanent minority; Durham's remedy had been to so reduce their political power that they would abandon their 'vain hope of nationality'. But what had happened was that political opinion split not along ethno-linguistic lines (important though these were) but along a reform-conservative axis involving questions of legislative control.

The move to federalism therefore represented a break with dualism, and what Macdonald and Cartier and the others therefore had to contrive was a settlement that avoided dealing with the central abeyance: Quebec's desire for separate and distinct-society status which, if carried to its logical conclusions, was either a claim to the rights of an equal founding partner or was a claim to national independence and statehood. The compromise that was 1867 sidestepped the problem and buried it under a new constitution. It made no statements about such matters as partnership, equality, or distinctiveness. French-Canadian claims to nationhood cannot be found.

The arrangements of 1867 were in some ways only a readjustment, not a new departure, for French Canada. The preceding period of the union between the Canadas had in many ways set up the expectation that there was an acceptance of dualism that would persist. There had been dual leadership, with two first ministers; dual capitals at Toronto and Quebec City with the government moving first to one, then, four years later, to the other; two systems of public administration; two religious 'establishments'; and equal representation in the legislature.[39] What emerged were power-sharing agreements, shared patronage, and local autonomy. In this system, 'the principle of duality served as a useful guideline, but it was rarely invoked as a doctrine' and what had emerged 'was arguably the world's first consociational democracy'.[40] This could not continue, but it was argued that the marriage of flexible British political institutions—the Crown and responsible government—with the new notion of federalism, was the best, indeed the only, way to reconcile the country's perceived need for union with Quebec's need for assurance, whilst at the same time preserving both notions of dualism and the imperial connection. French Canada's view was, in so many ways, an unemotional and rational loyalty rooted in self-interest, 'indeed, this is (was) its strength.'[41] Moreover, this readjustment was, to French Canada, only one in a line of 'regime' changes, and was not necessarily the last.[42]

But what enabled Cartier and his colleagues to obtain the support of French Canada was not mere loyalty to British institutions, conservatism, the support of the church, and the aftermath of 1837, it was also the clear understanding that the settlement provided guarantees that would enable French Canada to preserve itself. French Canada's understanding of the 'federal principle' was that, when applied, it would mean that matters of a general nature, like defence, would be under federal control, but that the rest would be local. The dominant image of a federation in the minds of those in Quebec was undoubtedly that 'all questions affecting the French-Canadian nationality as such would be dealt with at Quebec City.'[43] The French had given up a broad range of powers in return for 'territorial autonomy in Quebec over a narrow range of powers.'[44]

There was still considerable fear, evinced by A.A. Dorion and others, that the settlement would benefit English Canada and was a risk not worth taking. French Canada had been forced to compromise: it did so over such issues as the Senate, language guarantees for the English in Quebec, the absence of bilingualism in Ontario, the granting of the great subjects of state to Ottawa, the allocation of concurrent powers, and the additional special powers that Ottawa assumed, such as disallowance and the declaratory power contained in Section 92 (10c).[45] At the same time, A.I. Silver's seminal study of French-Canadian views of Confederation makes it abundantly clear that French Canadians still saw Confederation as a chance to be 'a majority in their own land, with absolute control over a wide range of jurisdictions, and each government sovereign and untouchable—receiving its powers from the Imperial parliament.'[46] Silver argues that French Canadians' desire to protect their homeland meant that they were prepared to ignore, at least initially, the existence of French minorities outside their borders. As with so much else surrounding questions of original intent, this view can be questioned. Minority rights involve both religion and language, and so when French prelates defended other minorities (Métis, Acadians, Irish, Scots) it was because any attack on Catholicism 'was an attack on what they regarded as the fundamental characteristic of a major protagonist of Confederation.'[47] There is thus a long-standing debate as to whether or not minority rights were historically opposed to provincial rights, and were seen as such. Silver (and others) have been charged with relying too heavily on political documentation taken from speeches and a highly partisan press, and the case has been made for a more nuanced view which pays greater attention to religion, and less to language.[48]

Two other objections, both important, might be raised at this point. One is that there are considerable difficulties to be faced when using words like sovereign, sovereignty, nation, nationalism, and nationhood. Meanings can change dramatically, and there is the added complication of translating nineteenth-century French into twentieth-century English. (For example, 'quite' now usually means 'partially', whereas in the nineteenth century it meant 'absolutely'.) We must be very careful not to ascribe current usage to our forebears. 'The further back one goes the more obvious it is that "nation" and nationhood had a different meaning from what we understand today. . . .'[49] It can also be argued that Cartier and the federalists did not really have to be as worried about such nationalistic rhetoric, and the related long-term political questions, as we might think. These were issues raised by political minorities, like the Rouges, who were relatively weak.

Yet even though we do have to recognize that there will be ongoing debates surrounding causes and effects, and what was really meant and intended, one can still argue that the leaders of Lower Canada did see matters in terms of the *long-term status* of Quebec as an autonomous and viable community. A recent important work by Ralph Heintzman has cast a good deal of light on this question.

Heintzman argues, in 'Political Space and Economic Space: Quebec and the Empire of the St Lawrence', that there has always been a close relationship 'between the French Canadians' perceptions of economic space and their definitions of political space'.[50] He charts the emergence of a new outlook in Lower Canada, one that switched from opposing the development of the St Lawrence system, with Montreal as its hub, to one that embraced it: 'It was this growing conviction—that the fate of French Canada depended on its insertion into a broader economic "space"—which induced politicians like Cartier, Cauchon and Langevin to look with growing favour on an even wider political union.'[51] And, argues Heintzman, this outward-looking economic vision necessitated an outward view of *political* space, destiny, and empire. This meant abandoning older projects, in particular independence and close economic ties with the United States (or even annexation); these were 'held in abeyance while the Laurentian project occupied such a monopoly of public discourse'.[52] But they never disappeared, and could resurface as circumstances changed. Heintzman makes the vital point that:

> The nationalist and separatist impulse had always been present. Neither the Union of 1841 nor the Confederation of 1867 had obliterated it, and many (perhaps most?) of those who supported both had done so only provisionally, believing that they were necessary to protect and develop French Canada until the distant day appointed by Providence when she would be strong enough to take her independent place in the world. This view was still very much alive in the age of Laurier.[53]

Such feelings had to contend, by the early twentieth century, with other emerging bicultural, pan-Canadian impulses. But in 1867 there existed (if we accept Heintzman's and Silver's evidence) a strong feeling of support for what might be called 'providential independence'. It seems reasonable to argue, therefore, that Quebec's claims to either recognized equality with English Canada or to any kind of associate statehood, or separation, are to be seen as being in a state of abeyance.

They were about to be buried in a rather shallow federal grave, but they did exist, and are not merely the creation of later generations. For it should be remembered that while nationalist intellectuals may invent a tradition, 'they cannot invent just any tradition'—it must be based upon some 'recognizable continuum' of memory and in almost all cases of nationalism 'it was the memory of conquest at the hands of others, or of the successful rebuff' that is so important.[54] Quebec was not a nation-state, it was not an associate state, and it was not an equal partner; it could not be, but it *was* concerned with its independence, its power, and its future potential as a state—and as a nation. Fernand Dumont in *Genèse de La Société Québécoise*, sums up the situation in the first half of the nineteenth century in these words: 'la nation était présente; elle n'avait pas la prédominance.'[55] Étienne Parent had phrased it clearly (in 1852) in the following terms: 'Lorsque dans un mouvement, dans une démarche quelconque, il y aura clairement à gagner pour notre nationalité, ne nous inquiétons du reste que secondairement.' Dumont asks rhetorically, when commenting on Parent's statement, 'N'est-ce pas une parfaite définition du nationalisme? La première, à ma connaissance, qui soit énoncée en des termes aussi nets.'[56]

The mention made above of the Imperial Parliament is a reminder that there was another problem to be faced. Constitutional rearrangements could not be contemplated in a vacuum, for British concurrence could not be taken for granted, even if Canadians themselves were in agreement and even though the Colonial Office was pushing and prodding the colonies to unite for defensive and economic reasons. We should not forget that in the great patriation debate one hundred and fourteen years later, British MPs moved numerous amendments (58 in all); peers rose and spoke in the House of Lords, and provinces and interest groups lobbied British politicians. If this could happen in 1982, reactions in 1867 were clearly more unpredictable. In 1867 British ministries did not control back-benchers. Previous Canadian constitutional questions, notably the Constitution Act of 1791, had created deep divisions within British parties, and representation by population was still an undecided and highly volatile question in Britain. All in all there was no guarantee that anything would pass unless it had widespread, almost unanimous, support in the British house. Only a federal union met this test.[57] French Canada could not seriously contemplate negotiating its equality or its independence, only its federal autonomy and its future greatness. Macdonald could not obtain his legislative union and was reliant on French-Canadian support of a federal settlement. All the provinces were under social, economic, and political pressures; none could impose a settlement no matter how deeply held were their beliefs and feelings.

If the first ingredient for abeyance maintenance is an effective balance of power, a second element is the availability of an acceptable way out. Acceptability in this case meant combining very divergent elements.

Ambiguities

The British model was supposedly firmly centred on the sovereign and indivisible power of government, and found its focus and its home in Crown-in-parliament.[58] This was, in turn, tied to the belief that popular sovereignty was encapsulated and expressed through representation in the House of Commons. This fiction, and the notion of indivisible, absolute sovereignty itself, were put to the test whenever confronted with demands that involved national claims (as was the case with Ireland), or challenges to the fictions of representation (as was the case with the American colonies or with the franchise), or claims that would limit the powers of the sovereign state (in the name of something else, like the people, or a higher law, or national sub-units). The American model, on the other hand, commenced with 'we the people' (without settling who the people were), established divided sovereignty in a federal system (avoiding the issues of secession and ultimate loyalty), created the separation of powers and checks and balances (with the attendant dangers of paralysis and fragmentation), and entrenched the idea that citizens had individual rights that transcended those of the community (but under what circumstances?). Neither of these models seemed to provide the answer Canada needed, yet both had a strong appeal.

It is hardly surprising that the final *mélange* of the existing (British) with the new (American) produced such a strange hybrid. In addition, and perhaps even more importantly, theoretical considerations were mixed also with very practical, partisan, and personal needs, and with the demands of business. Gordon T. Stewart has concisely contrasted the profound differences between the pre-Confederation political culture that had developed in the Canadas with developments in Britain and America. Canada was a peculiar hybrid, with a record of persistent political violence that had 'no parallel anywhere else in the post-1783 British Empire'[59] and with political traditions that were fundamentally different even from Britain's. 'Court' and 'Country' rivalries were not settled in the same way or with the same results.

And, always, there lurked on the sidelines the shadow of the American Civil War, its 600,000 dead, with a triumphant North and its vast military power. Even so, when one examines the Canadian settlement what is praiseworthy is that, given this range of ideological choice, agreement was reached at all. Is it now fair to argue that this agreement meant that visions were blurred and contradictory, principles confused, and the resulting amalgam an unwieldy mix of the desire for central control and the principles of federalism; a refusal to settle the deeper questions of inter-state and intra-state power? The division of powers was in fact comprehensive; it seemed clear and this may well be one reason why a domestic amending formula was not included in the provisions of the Act.[60] In addition, much of the vagueness in the document—its archaic and stilted style and its superficially incoherent description of such things as the power of the Governor-General—was merely an expression of British parliamentary tradition and constitutional practice, understood by all. In this context, it is important to note that what was understood by all was the effect of the advent of responsible government in the 1840s.

Twenty years later it was an integral part of the 'constitution' of the British Empire, which 'by binding convention could not legislate on the domestic affairs of a self-governing colony—including constitutional matters—without the colony's consent.'[61] In Paul Romney's view, this understanding and these limits are extremely important when assessing the presumed post-1867 rules of the political game. He contends that the received wisdom on Confederation, as related by such luminaries as F.R. Scott, Donald Creighton, Norman Rogers, and Arthur Lower, has a misguided central(ist) thesis. They assumed that Ottawa possessed 'imperial' powers (such as disallowance), plus the general residual powers, and was itself the creation 'of the sovereign imperial power, not of the provinces'. Therefore, so their line of reasoning went, the provinces were meant to be subordinate, the centre was meant to be dominant, and the compact theory of Confederation could be discredited. But what in fact was intended, says Romney, was the adoption, by the Fathers of Confederation, 'of the practice of the imperial constitution along with the letter'.[62] This practice enshrined the idea of provincial rights as an integral part of responsible government; each level of government was given its own general residual category, and powers were divided as fully as possible. Thus, argues Romney, 'we can conclude that they [the Fathers] designed Canada on the principle of coordinate sovereignty' and did not feel the need to spell out all of the implications.[63]

So seeming specificity and the attendant references to existing practice hide some extremely significant omissions, and many would argue that there were indeed, as Foley would say, great yawning gaps of unsettlement that were based on unstated assumptions, assumptions which quickly became common, if disputed, political currency. For example:

> Confederation clearly assumed a spirit of Anglo-French amity; this spirit was supposed to well up as soon as the 'ethnic' issues which divided Canadians—cultural, religious and linguistic issues—were removed from

the federal forum to the provinces. The survival of French Canadian culture under Quebec's protection was thought by nearly everyone to be 'une chose donnée'. But the BNA Act itself gives little hint of such an implied agreement.[64]

A list of the unsettled problems, constitutional matters to be arranged at some future date, will therefore usually include the following:

- the future constitutional relationship with the United Kingdom;
- the status of French speakers and Catholics outside Quebec;
- the uses to which certain key federal powers could be put;
- whether or not provinces were equal;
- the future process of constitutional amendment;
- the role of the upper house;
- the locus of sovereign powers;
- the question of judicial supremacy;
- the contradiction between parliamentary sovereignty and federalism;
- the special status of Quebec;
- the right of secession;
- constitutional equality between the centre and constituent units;
- provincial participation in central institutions;
- the protection of rights.

This constitutes an impressive list. Most, if not all, have come back to haunt us. Even more might be added.

One is bound to ask why so much was left unclear. The usual and most straightforward explanation is that this was pure pragmatism in action. As one member put it in the debates of 1865, 'I fully believe that all the faults to which I now object to in the plan of Confederation will, like the diseases incident to childhood, grow out of our system as we advance in political strength and stature.'[65] Black, Waite, Smiley, and Johnson all argue that Sir John embodied a 'plain no-nonsense practical approach' and that Confederation was an empirical rather than a speculative exercise.[66] It was also seen as driven by the desire to avoid repeating and duplicating American mistakes and by an outright hostility to federalism as embodied in the American experience. As previously noted, Rod Preece has summarized the Macdonald approach in just such prudential terms, without assuming that it implied a lack of over-arching principles.[67]

This standard interpretation has been challenged by recent scholarship which reveals a far more complex situation, reinforcing the picture of ideological as well as practical disagreement sketched briefly above, and helping us understand why highly intelligent, pragmatic personalities still left so much unresolved.

Peter J. Smith 'directly challenges a commonly held belief that Canadian Confederation was the product of a purely pragmatic exercise.'[68] He sees it also as a product of an ideological debate, 'a debate between the defenders of classical republican values and the proponents of a rising commercial ideology'.[69] At the heart of the debate was a struggle, says Smith, between wealth and virtue, Reformer and Tory, democracy and élitism, independence and patronage. This was therefore a battle over citizenship and civic virtue, influenced by philosophical ideas from Europe and the United States. He casts a new light on the struggle between Tories—who wished to strengthen the Crown's position, provide national outlets for ambition and patronage, and undertake national economic development—and Reformers, with their version of agrarian democracy and the need for a government amenable to local interests and free of corruption.[70] According to Smith, centralization and commercialism triumphed and localist attachments would have to be satisfied, 'particularly in French Canada . . . with the greatly inferior provincial governments they were given'.[71] As already noted and explored in more detail below, this was not to be French Canada's understanding!

Confederation also involved a debate, not surprisingly, about federalism and sovereignty in which the Blackstonian notion that sovereignty could not be divided was, in Robert Vipond's view, challenged successfully.[72] Even in Britain itself, where lip service was regularly paid to the idea that there must in all governments reside somewhere an absolute despotic power, theory and practice were far removed, and such powers were only intended to be used in states of extreme, Hobbesian crisis. To use it in any unlimited way would call into question its illimitable nature. The mistake of confusing sovereignty with power was far easier to avoid in federal systems, with, admittedly, the proviso that in an emergency settled and separate jurisdictions would temporarily collapse. Vipond's contention is that we did borrow heavily from the American experience in a positive as well as a negative way, but, in typical fashion, did not acknowledge the debt: 'The creation of the Canadian federal constitution thus provides another example of one of the deepest habits of Canadian political culture: the habit of accepting things American whilst claiming to reject them.'[73] Those who negotiated the settlement did agree, implicitly, that federalism meant reconsidering sovereignty, but they wished to avoid being trapped by any Calhoun-like notion of states' rights.[74] The Americans ultimately located sovereignty, or at least its fiction, in the people at large outside of government itself. Canadians did not go this far, nor did they give such general propositions clarity. On the contrary, this was a constitution that recognized linguistic and denominational minorities, and entrenched a form of pluralism into the constitution. There was, says Vipond, 'strategic circumspection'. How 'local' and 'general' were to be distinguished was not clear; the preservation of minority rights was similarly vague, and:

> most supporters of the Confederation did their best to avoid giving these general propositions substance. Most speakers were little inclined to explain how precisely the local was to be distinguished from the general; how conflicts of jurisdiction were to be resolved; and whether federalism was

compatible with the protection of minority rights, or other crucial matters of substance in a federation. . . . The text of the proposal seemed to contradict the very federal principles that it was meant to embody.[75]

Devising genuinely clear answers to such questions would have meant tackling abeyances head-on. Far better to leave matters as general as possible, and to claim that all conflicts of jurisdiction and authority had been avoided, even though it was obvious that this was not so. And here we must bear Romney's important point in mind: responsible government had been a mechanism for establishing local control, and Confederation similarly was a mechanism for extending this, for preserving provincial autonomy, and for ensuring co-ordinate sovereignty. This makes the whole enterprise look far more like a compact of the provinces than is often argued.[76]

Thus, what did triumph was the federal idea that each province had 'exclusive' power to legislate and that the federal government would not be fully sovereign; both would be beholden to the Imperial Parliament, and so power and sovereignty could be distinguished in ways not possible in the United Kingdom. But even though they *could* be distinguished, it was not clear how they would be wielded and what might happen in the event of conflict.

Jennifer Smith, in an essay entitled 'Canadian Confederation and the Influence of American Federalism', in part supports Vipond's argument that the distribution of legislative powers could not itself be altered, and she notes that this was precisely the understanding of Taché and Cartier.[77] She too paints a more enigmatic picture of the influence of federalist ideas and of the results of the hostility towards federalism so evident in the debates. The Senate that emerged was a Canadian version of the British House of Lords, not an effective second chamber in a federal sense. Although there was a lengthy debate over its composition, this was not an early confrontation over the mechanisms of interstate as opposed to intrastate federalism, for 'the wrangle on the proposed Senate was over patronage'.[78] The result of the failure to create a powerful Senate is now often seen, paradoxically, as a cause of weakness at the centre.[79] Overall, the settlement gave to the central government an arsenal of intrusive powers but this was played down, especially the matter of disallowance:

> the politic Macdonald declined to mention it at all, while his close colleague from Montreal East, George-Étienne Cartier, only alluded to it when seeking to placate the fears of the British minority in Canada East that the French-speaking majority in the local assembly would injure it through laws adversely affecting the rights of property.[80]

Analyses such as these reappraisals of Confederation reveal a world of constitutional debate that was more sophisticated, more ideological, and less pragmatic than has been thought. This could, presumably, mean that as principles became clearer it was far more difficult for abeyances to exist, but this does not seem to have been the case. Greater complexity offers not less but more evidence as to why ambiguity was so apparent and why abeyances were left unresolved. There was the evident appeal of Madisonian principles—but there was the horrible and terrifying reality of the American experience. Federalism was clearly a two-edged sword, especially when it would be tied to questions of race and religion, buttressed by geography. This was why there was such fear. Advocating an American-style senate raised deeper questions about the nation than the 'nation' could handle. Severing the Imperial tie, even had it been deemed desirable, would have meant tackling the fundamental problem of sovereignty rather than the division of sovereign powers. Canadians, to use Peter Russell's central theme, were still to be loyal subjects and not a sovereign people.[81] The invisible Crown, with its prerogative powers, was to have profound effects upon political and constitutional developments. Thinking in terms of patronage, capitalism, and economic development was in fact easier than delving any deeper than was absolutely necessary into philosophical issues such as rights. And above all there was the question of Quebec's status, and how to avoid giving a clear answer as to what it really was.

Canada was founded on allegiance, not a covenant, unless, that is, it was an *assumed* covenant between Quebec and the rest of the country, and an *assumed* covenant between Ottawa and the provinces based upon the normal expectations of representative government, and the specific educational and religious requirements that had been entrenched. Confederation was thus a formal obliteration of the English conquest and, even though there were few specific clauses delineating legal rights specific to Quebec, French Canada could feel that these were, in A.R.M. Lower's telling phrase, 'but the evidence of things unseen, the crystallization into law of understandings', the kind of understandings (added Lower) that are like those in a marriage, which create a reasonable degree of equality.[82] Richard Verney has developed at some length the idea that there has been what he calls 'philosophical federalism' in action throughout Canada's history. It is, he says, rooted in a deeply historical approach, in a toleration and accommodation of a broad range of views, in the natural inclination to accept less than perfect, and less than clear, answers. We have, he says, shied away from the intellectual pursuit of arguments to their logical conclusions. Verney's whole theory is built upon the notion that Canadians have been willing to accept contradictions:

> (Canada) seemed almost to thrive on the contradictions underlying much of its conflict. These contradictions appeared capable of continuing indefinitely, being submerged and then reemerging, with one part or another of the contradiction dominant. Canada's philosophers had long been aware of the contradictions in their environment, and had been reluctant to press arguments to their conclusions, because they knew that the contradictions could not be resolved.[83]

The problem with such an approach, and its unwillingness to pursue arguments to their 'logical' conclusions, is that it ignored the fact that contradictions may get worse, not better. The dialectic of change does not necessarily lead to an acceptable synthesis. For the moment, the point to be made is that many of the contradictions were not clear in 1867, and it was perhaps thought that the mere division of powers *in itself* would solve our problems. For these were powers to be wielded by governments who in themselves inherited all the authority and privileges that came with being the agents of the Crown.[84]

I therefore contend that, behind the list of matters left ambiguous, we find key abeyances rather than clarity. Matters were indeed fudged in a variety of ways that ranged from partial to total avoidance. For example, a matter that was not discussed and was partially avoided was the volatile question of an established religion. In the United States, thanks to Madison and others, there was separation of church and state, whereas in the United Kingdom there was an established state religion and religious observances in schools. In Canada disputes over religion were always linked to language as well as to Catholicism and schooling.[85] But church establishment was not a battle that preoccupied the Fathers of Confederation in their debates. They put it largely into abeyance. In an article entitled 'Debates and Silences—Reflections of a Politician', Monique Bégin uses the example of religion to illustrate the larger point:

> A politician, in fact any public figure, learns by intuition and by observation what can and should be discussed as well as what cannot and should not be spoken. The issues that require silent accommodation, however, are often less clear than the fact of their existence. To understand Canada's debates and silences one must study the social fabric of the country and the type of democracy it has developed.[86]

She then goes on to discuss examples of such silences, and her first choice involves religion. Surrounding it she finds a 'wise silence', for Canada never established 'even at the constitutional level' the place and status of religion. She sees our silences as varying in intensity, with some being rooted in social psychology 'like the silences about divisive issues and the debates that enhance shared experience'.[87]

Another thorny issue in 1867 was the matter of divorce. Divorce was one of the powers to be given to the new central government. Not surprisingly, this caused serious problems within Quebec, for it would mean the public recognition of a practice that was deeply opposed, even if tolerated to some extent. It also meant transferring a provincial power to Ottawa, where it would be wielded by a Protestant majority which could allow the dissolution of Catholic marriages. Those politicians in Quebec who argued in favour of this change could, however, point to the fact that divorce was already allowed in the Canadas, and that transferring the power exercised by a province to the federal government might make divorce more, not less, difficult.[88] The solution arrived at illustrates rather neatly how either a confrontation or the necessity to place the matter entirely in abeyance was avoided, even though the compromise reached was exceedingly awkward. The general assumption governing laws in effect was to be that those British laws already in place would continue after Confederation, and each province would therefore have its own laws depending upon when they had been 'received' from Britain. So the laws relating to divorce varied from province to province, and the date of the laws' reception was therefore extremely important.[89] Quebec had its own Civil Code, but to leave it unaltered left as a problem the plight of the non-Catholics and anyone else in Quebec who might want a divorce. Their needs, as well as the concerns of Quebec's Catholics, were met by the eventual agreement that, because divorce was a federal matter under section 91, those who wanted a divorce would, in the absence of a general federal law, require a specific federal statute to obtain one. 'In Newfoundland and Quebec, and in Ontario until 1930, there was no judicial procedure to obtain a divorce, and a federal statute was necessary in every case.'[90] The federal government's powers to make laws in relation to divorce therefore lay dormant until 1968, by which time Quebec itself was desirous of change, although it still wanted control over marriage, divorce, and family courts to be within Quebec's jurisdiction.[91] In the meantime, thousands of expensive divorce acts went through the Senate, and most of the laws concerning marriage were in fact enacted by the provinces. Sometimes, if a problem is left alone long enough it can solve itself.

And sometimes it cannot, for another and more important example of a major issue that was also partially discussed, but then left well alone, was the question of constitutional amendment. In Paul Gérin-Lajoie's opinion we have to recall that:

> the framers of the constitution had many delicate problems to tackle before they could reach agreement. The determination of a process of amendment would have undoubtedly proved to be crucial. The Fathers may have set this aside to avoid a further difficulty. . . . The procedure in Canada for requesting the enactment of such amendments was a problem which could be faced later.[92]

This was to become one of the most difficult of all our abeyances because it encapsulated so many different problems and was, in Frank Scott's words, 'fraught with the dangers of race conflict'.[93] This conflict would be inseparable from the great abeyance, namely how to avoid spelling out Quebec's 'real' status without creating impossible difficulties.

Before we examine the text of the Constitution Act of 1867 for further evidence that a large number of abeyances existed, let us consider something that was not treated as an abeyance even though, given its importance, we might expect that it too would have been exceptionally difficult to handle. This is the question of aboriginal rights, a matter today as fraught with constitutional problems as anything we can think of.

In 1867 this was not the case. The issue was certainly powerful enough, legally and morally. Treaties existed, there was the Royal Proclamation of 1763: tribes and confederacies had been valued allies in earlier trading partnerships and in major wars.[94] But the relationships had changed. Native peoples were now subservient. Assimilation was presumed to be the only desirable and laudable liberal goal and Sir John stated this unequivocally. Native rights—and any form of inherent rights—were not an abeyance because they were not seen as problematic. The fictions of the Crown as the concerned and benevolent guardian and the North West Mounted Police as the stern but fair agents of justice, law, and peace were to be unchallenged for a considerable time. Indians and Eskimos were denied the right to vote until 1960 precisely because they were wards of the Crown.[95] Now, in an era when there is far greater awareness of the suffering and injustice native peoples have suffered, and when Armalite rifles, plastic explosives, and world-wide communications have altered the balance of power, relations have changed yet again. But in 1867 the native populations in the original provinces of Canada were relatively powerless and were outside the political frame of reference. French Canadians and the English-speaking minority in Lower Canada, Catholics and Protestants, Maritimers and Upper Canadians, none of them could be ignored in the same way. Our abeyances at this time clearly did not include matters involving the powerless. The provision in the Act itself bears testimony to this. The federal government was given legislative authority over 'Indians, and the lands reserved for the Indians', and that was to be that (even though it is still true that there was, and is, an assumed special relationship between the Crown and aboriginal peoples).[96]

Nothing like this was possible with regard to French Canada. Here the problems had to be resolved or sidestepped. What then was in fact said about the great issue of French-English equality? In fact, precious little.

> The Constitution Act, 1867 created a federal state rather than a unitary state primarily because of the concern of French-Canadians to protect a distinct society in the territory of Quebec. That is an historical fact never explicitly acknowledged in the language of the Constitution Act, 1867.[97]

What the Act contained were specific provisions encompassing a guarantee of the right to use English and French in federal courts and in both houses of the federal parliament, as well as in Quebec courts and the Quebec Legislature. Records, debates, proceedings, and Acts emanating from these bodies were to be in both languages. Recognized also was Quebec's right to its own civil law, including the right of the Catholic church to tithe its members. Under section 93, Quebec and the other provinces received the right to control their educational systems; there were guarantees of a fixed number of Quebec seats in the House of Commons, upon which the representation of the other provinces would be proportionately based, and, in addition, a fixed number of seats for Quebec in the Senate. Section 93 also dealt with the extremely contentious matter of religious schooling and, in so doing, limited provincial power, specifically in Quebec, by guaranteeing the rights of denominational schools in existence at the union and by extending this right to 'the dissentient schools of the Queen's Protestant and Roman Catholic subjects in Quebec'. Several of the key provisions which made Quebec 'different' were guarantees to Quebec's powerful English minority; these could be taken as statements about dualism, but not in the sense in which it was used by Quebec nationalists. Additionally, section 94 contemplates uniform laws over property and civil rights in only three of the four provinces, with obvious implications for Quebec, and Quebec alone 'cannot divest itself of its power over property and civil rights'.[98]

There is widespread agreement that the debate over Confederation was therefore not *framed* as an agreement between two founding peoples, and that the details reflect this. (The agreement to allow the use of French in the House of Commons and the Senate, and to have statutes in both languages, was only taken on third reading after fierce debate.) That it may have been *perceived* as such is a different matter. The focus was on specific questions, particularly educational and religious rights; the state that emerged was not binational in structure; and the assumptions and conventions that would drive the institutions were taken as understood.[99] Adequate French-Canadian representation in the federal cabinet was therefore assumed. But of course to emphasize the specific terms of the agreement is to lose sight of the woods for the trees, and is to see only the narrowly constitutional rather than the essentially political and historical:

> It was clear that any new political order in the 1860s would have to address the insistence of the French community that its ethnic, linguistic and religious distinctiveness be accorded an absolute guarantee. . . . Without using terminology like 'federal society' the political leaders of Upper Canada had essentially, though not without reluctance, accepted its existence. . . . During the debates there were few real defenders of federalism as a theoretical basis of government. It was about contemporary issues and 'who was selling out whom'.[100]

The quotation above is taken from an interesting study by Wagenberg, Soderland, Nelson, and Briggs in which they attempt to apply Deutsch's interaction model to Confederation, but find that the data do not support it, nor does the evidence point to the utility of a neo-functionalist economic model. Their conclusion is unequivocal: 'In terms of Deutsch's formulation, then, Canada must be viewed essentially as a political unit that had been amalgamated without necessarily achieving integration.'[101]

If there was no statement of French-English equality or dualism as such, no mention of Quebec as a distinct society or homeland, no references to founding peoples with collective rights, to pacts, or to bilingualism and biculturalism as the basis for the state, no recognition of linguistic rights for French-speaking minorities outside Quebec, was there a clear declaration that, at the very least, the provinces were equal? This too remained elusive. Each of the provisions mentioned above regarding Quebec also constitutes an argument that there were distinct differences. David Milne, in a discussion of Canada's current dilemmas entitled *Equality or Asymmetry: Why Choose?* has set out the ways in which the settlement of 1867 was clearly asymmetrical. The most striking example was probably unequal representation in the Senate. Added to this were differences in law: section 129 continued in force those laws existing in each province at the time of union, and only three provinces were expected, as noted above, to create uniform laws under section 94. Judicial qualifications in Quebec also differ (section 98), as do the qualifications for senators from Quebec. And, of course, there was Quebec's bilingual legislative regime, plus the educational rights guaranteed Protestant schools under section 93 (2). Provinces entered under different terms of Union. This was true with respect to subsidies, commitments to such things as the Prince Edward Island steamship and telegraph service, and even to the rights to natural resources in the case of the prairie provinces in the next century. Asymmetrical arrangements have grown even as the arguments that the provinces are equal have also gained force. But this is to rush ahead once again, when the point being made is a simple one: in 1867 there was no ringing declaration of equality and the institutional arrangements reflected faithfully the absence of such a principle.[102] The idea of the equality of the provinces was to reappear much later as a mutated form of the compact theory. However, we should not exaggerate the importance of the asymmetrical arrangements that were made; what has kept the country together has little to do with any formal asymmetry.[103]

There was likewise no clear definition of citizenship and of what it meant to be a Canadian. Citizenship was 'so awkward a problem that those who drafted the confederation largely avoided it'.[104] The result of the arrangements of 1867 would be the continuation and the emergence of two 'distinct, if intertwined, political citizenships one provincial, the other national'.[105] Rather than two intertwined citizenships, it may be better to think of three, or at least to see the unique place of francophone Quebec as constituting its own separate strand. As we shall see, this strand became more not less complicated after Confederation; to it was added the debate over pan-Canadianism and the equality of cultures. The irony is that Macdonald's very Britishness, Cartier's and Quebec's acceptance of British institutions, and the success of a court-statist patronage approach sowed the seeds for one of our now most problematic questions, the lack of an overarching agreement on national identity and community.[106]

The absence of a bill of rights setting out restrictions on the state was indicative that responsible government, not individual citizens, was the focus of the arrangements.[107] There was an acceptance of the British view of parliamentary sovereignty—to be tempered and curtailed by federalism. However, as we have seen, in practice the exercise of sovereignty, even in Britain, was a very different thing from contemplating it while reading Hobbes. In Canada this became starkly apparent in the years immediately following Confederation and in the interpretations put upon the agreement and discussed below, including those of the Judicial Committee of the Privy Council. The way out was a curious combination of detail and avoidance: some key problems were tackled, others were left murky. There was a degree of asymmetry. There was an absence of clear statements on many of the new nation's most intractable issues. This was all to lead to the eventual reemergence of our deepest abeyances, yet it also enabled us to engage in interpretations that suited the political needs of élites and that also represented an important form of wishful thinking, including the question as to what, if anything, could be regarded as entrenched and who had the right to change the rules of the game. In 1867 we were true to Burke, but have we been so since?

Triumphs

What has been discussed thus far constitutes, in part, a lengthy reminder that the settlement's ambiguities were crucial to its success. Although recent analysis has revealed a more complex picture, it has not altered the fact that the circumstances lent themselves to abeyance maintenance. If anything, the unstated ideological underpinnings, the debts to Madison, the power of patronage, and the ideological conflict that lurked behind a pragmatic front, can all be seen as further evidence of a willingness to disguise reality and rein in confrontation. Confirmation of the settlement's essential ambiguity is to be found in the views of Confederation that were proclaimed in the years immediately following. It must not be forgotten that in addition to, first, the absence of the power to enforce a settlement and, second, the availability of an acceptable way out, there is a third requirement if abeyances are to remain unexamined. This third requirement is wishful thinking.

In Ontario, Confederation was rightly hailed as a national triumph; it was spoken of in terms of the creation of a great new nation that would stretch from sea to sea. There were glorious phrases in abundance. For the purposes of my argument it is essential to avoid being taken in by all the euphoria, heartfelt though much of it was. As Ged Martin has noted, we tend to use the arguments of the winners, and base our expectations on 'an affectation of scientific proof with the literary technique of assembling pungent illustrative quotation from contemporary sources'.[108] We must remember that the Fathers had no intention of putting the settlement to the test of elections and spoke against so doing because it was simply too risky. In the Maritimes—even though economic considerations were pressing and the appeal of the intercolonial railway loomed large—there was widespread opposition led, in Nova Scotia, by Joseph Howe. 'Indeed, the first time that Nova Scotians had an opportunity to give a popular verdict on Confederation they left no doubt where they stood. In September 1867, in the first Canadian general election, the anti-Confederates took 18 out of 19 Nova Scotia seats. . . . By then, however, Confederation was a *fait accompli*.'[109] Newfoundland and Prince Edward Island rejected the Quebec resolutions, and New Brunswick eventually came to agree in large part because Fenians were massing along its border. Nova Scotia was later pacified by arrangements to restructure its debt, and Prince Edward Island did not join until 1873. Maritime delegates had occupied a good deal of the debate and had been 'far from being yesmen or nodders' signing on the dotted line as they were told.[110] Distance was also a factor: 'poor communications help to explain how contemporaries identified themselves. The term "Canadian" referred to people living in the province of Canada.

Maritimers were a different breed....'[111] All of this is merely by way of illustrating the tenuous nature of the agreement between loosely linked communities that *all* viewed themselves as distinctive socially and politically.

And if this was the case in the Maritimes it was certainly so in Quebec. Quebec's provisional and qualified understanding of federalism has already been noted. The Rouges led the opposition and saw the arrangements as a sell-out of Quebec's interests. Cartier's great Canadian political nationality speech, so often quoted—'if union were attained, we would form a political nationality with which neither the national origin, nor the religion of any individual, would interfere.... Look, for instance, at the United Kingdom, inhabited as it was by three great races'[112]—also contained a passage, less often noted, in which he emphasized that:

> We could not do away with the distinctions of race. We could not legislate for the disappearance of the French Canadians from American soil, but British and French Canadians alike could appreciate and understand their position relative to each other. They were placed like great families beside each other, and their contact produced a healthy spirit of emulation.[113]

Even those in favour of the union—let alone those who were not—came away with differing interpretations, made possible by the settlement itself, by the expectations brought to it, and by the necessity to believe that what had been accomplished accorded with the political, economic, and cultural interests that had to be defended. Not surprisingly, every politician wanted to go home to his own legislature to sell quite different things to that which was being sold in the other colonial houses. It may well be that in some senses the Fathers were rather too clever in their attempts to hide their real beliefs about the arrangements made.[114] Yet it would not be fair to suggest that it is easy to disentangle calculated, self-conscious awareness from the simple necessity to strike bargains and make reasonable deals. Constitution-making, seemingly inevitably, simultaneously involves the highest and lowest forms of political arrangement and accommodation.

Macdonald could see the settlement providing 'the strength of a legislative and administrative union' but this was not, in spite of the evidence in its favour, to be French Canada's understanding and was 'hotly rejected by French Canadians of both parties'.[115] In the words of *La Minerve*, French Canadians 'form a state within the state. We enjoy the full exercise of our rights and the formal recognition of our national independence.'[116] French Canadians would be, it was argued, a majority in their own land; it was assumed that each level of government would be autonomous and separate. National questions would be debated in Ottawa along party lines, but such questions would not involve 'race' or culture or local affairs as these matters were now in the hands of the provinces. This was wishful, even naive, thinking.

Therefore, at the one extreme were those who saw Confederation as the triumph of British principles and as the eventual death-knell for French Canada: a classic example of this is to be found in a letter from George Brown

Settled Unsettlements 73

to his wife after the Quebec conference: 'Is it not wonderful? French Canadianism entirely extinguished!'[117] (To be fair, he did mean extinguished initially in Upper, not Lower, Canada.) Brown could see the national government becoming majoritarian and hegemonic; there had indeed been a repudiation of dualism. Sir John himself is reported to have said that, 'if confederation goes on, you, if spared the ordinary age of man, will see both Local Parliaments and Governments absorbed in the General Power. This is as plain to me as if I saw it accomplished, but of course it does not do to adopt that point of view in discussing the subject in Lower Canada.'[118] At the other extreme were those who believed either in the compact theory or in the state-within-a-state assumption noted above.

In such a climate of self-congratulation and delusion, of élite consensus over an agreement that was a seamless web, and of popular misgiving about its contents, it is little wonder that all portrayed themselves as winners and that differing interpretations immediately took root:

> the critics of Canadian confederation proved to be embarrassingly good losers. Sandfield Macdonald became Sir John's Ontario lieutenant in 1867; Joseph Howe joined his cabinet in 1868; Christopher Dunkin followed the next year. This may prove only that they were hypocritical in their opposition to the new system, but it is probably fairer to conclude that in coming aboard, they helped in practice to shape it to meet their concerns. In contrast to countries in which major constitutional change left a legacy of bitterness, the distinction between those who had argued for or against Confederation quickly blurred.[119]

Oliver Mowat, a Father of Confederation, became a staunch opponent of central power; Sir Wilfrid Laurier, a determined and spirited opponent, became a revered Prime Minister.

It is not surprising that Edwin R. Black introduced his study *Divided Loyalties: Canadian Concepts of Federalism* with a chapter on 'Confederation's Competing Images: Sorting them out'.[120] This he follows with a discussion of five concepts and their evolution: centralist, administrative, co-ordinate, compact, and dual. Black's opening sentence strikes home to remind us what this seemingly academic and semantic argument is all about: 'For the Canadian State the politics of federalism are the politics of survival.'

Black stresses the pragmatic side of the settlement: the need for self-government, defence against annexation, and the settlement of the West before the Americans. This purely pragmatic, essentially 'Canada as an un-American activity' approach has been questioned. What has not been disputed is Black's conclusion that 'Canadians were seldom if ever impelled during their country's first century to debate what it was they sought in terms of a state.'[121] It was this fact, combined with differing interpretations of the nature of the agreement, that kept our abeyances under control.

What is particularly striking is the immediate appearance after 1867 of radically differing interpretations that are, at face value, incompatible and that one might assume would create major crises. Macdonald's centralist vision, in which a sovereign national government—and the English majority—would reign supreme in economic affairs (a government that is the agency of nation building beloved of both conservatives and non-Quebec socialists) clearly runs completely counter to the assumption of dualism. A poignant current restatement of the dualist view that illustrates its historic roots is provided by Guy Laforest in his recent study *Trudeau et la fin d'un rêve canadien*:

> French Canadians . . . the majority of whom since the Quiet Revolution, recognize themselves as Québécois, have invested a great deal in the dream of dualistic equality. This was the project of Étienne Parent, of Louis-Hippolyte LaFontaine and of George-Étienne Cartier, of Henri Bourassa and of André Laurendeau, of Daniel Johnson and of Claude Ryan. Duality has not always meant the same thing for each of these great personages of our history. Except that, in these different versions it was always necessary to adhere to a certain type of Canadian patriotism. This patriotism was possible as long as it permitted French Canada, Quebec, to remain itself, as long as it did not require of Québécois a pure and simple renunciation of their primary allegiance towards their society of origin.[122]

It matters not whether the agreement of 1867, upon close examination, reveals the constitutional weakness of the two founding peoples argument. In Quebec this assumption has been there from the start. Quebec was not driven by dreams of a bilingual Canada; the Acadians might as well not have existed (indeed, few in Quebec appeared to realize that Acadians in any numbers had survived eviction and transportation by the British); the status of the French language and of Catholicism in the West was not yet an issue. French Canada was, in the main, turned inward and its new status as a 'partner' was complemented by the compact theory.

Almost from the outset, the provinces, notably Ontario, argued that provincial consent was necessary prior to any substantial constitutional changes, and that the federal government itself had been the product of an agreement between the independent colonies/provinces and was therefore the creature and creation of the provinces. This case has been argued back and forth over the years, and is still a matter for reappraisal, even though 'it is probably fair to say that a majority of those who have studied the evidence seriously have concluded that there are just too many evidentiary problems to make the compact theory stick.'[123] For most of Canada's history, dualism and the compact theory could support and sustain each other; both saw the provinces as the constituent and constituting power, thus giving to Quebec—as a province—considerable authority. In its 'strong' form the theory would have had the effect of excluding the federal government from a central role in the amending process, and this was obviously unrealistic, unacceptable, and totally at odds with the amending process in place, which assumed away any difficulties and was formally reliant entirely upon the cooperation of the Parliament of the United Kingdom. In its weak form, it was an argument for including the provinces and obtaining their consent.[124] This too was potentially to Quebec's advantage, or so it was thought until 1981 and the Patriation Reference case.

What was not immediately clear with the idea of the compact, or with a defence of the assumed principles of federalism versus the central government's incursions, was that the 'principle' of the absolute equality of each province within a federal system would prove to be so injurious to the strength of Quebec's view of itself as a founding partner. The compact theory had been developed to protect provincial communities from federal intrusion and control. Its Quebec version was limited to the idea of a racial compact; its appeal outside Quebec was as a way in which both Ontario and the periphery could influence the centre.[125] Over the years, the compact theory weakened, and the dualist version grew. But dualism was not to dominate the settlement finally arrived at in the Trudeau years, for there was a resurgence of the idea of formal provincial equality, led not by Ontario but by a burgeoning West. This came at a time when Quebec had moved away from federalism as its sole defence, and was demanding a more asymmetrical relationship, with special powers and rights. The dialectical relationship of equality and distinctiveness took over a century to unfold, and we have not arrived at a synthesis.

What the compact theory certainly *did* do was make the provinces feel more comfortable with the settlement. It gave them a founding myth, albeit a weak one, and a form of reassurance. It did, to some degree, tackle the ongoing question of sovereignty at least in terms of who could wield which powers, and under what rules powers could formally be changed. It was a mainstay of the debate between Ottawa and the provinces, and 'criticism of the doctrine centred on its validity rather than on its existence.'[126] Even Macdonald himself had spoken of a treaty, the provinces had voted at London, Quebec, and Charlottetown as equal units, and French Canada, as already noted, also saw 1867 as a form of compact.

None of the implicit or explicit claims made for the success of 1867 could be made unequivocally. The 'ideologies' of centralism or duality, or provincial equality and autonomy, were all ambiguous. Proponents had to remain positive about the results or, alternatively, had to claim that the other side was violating the spirit of the settlement. There was thus a great deal of wishful thinking about what had been accomplished, as well as perhaps more subtlety than we might expect. Certainly there were many outside Quebec who saw that province's future as assimilation into English Canada and domination by Ottawa. And there were certainly those in Quebec who saw the arrangements as a temporary expedient, as a way-station on the road to ultimate independence, negotiated at a time when Quebec was too young, too inexperienced, and too weak. When asked why Quebec did not demand independence, 'The Confederationists answered this, not by saying that Quebec's independence was an undesirable goal, not by saying that French Canadians wanted to join together with English Canadians to form a Canadian nation, but by claiming that complete independence was simply not practicable.'[127] Independence would arrive providentially, like the millennium, at some future date.

Therefore many of the constitutional assumptions we now hold so dear were not clearly a part of the 1867 settlement. Quebec was *not* treated as an equal of British Canada or as a founding nation in any clear constitutional sense.[128] The settlement did not create anything like a bilingual country: it created a bilingual parliament in which Quebec MPs were a significant minority and an Upper house where Quebec held one third of the seats (and even less in future). The provinces, it must be noted, were not treated as equals in federal institutions; special arrangements were made and deals struck, and in this respect Quebec could certainly claim to see itself as a province unlike the others, given its legal, linguistic, and educational differences and the treatment of its English minority. This justifiably reinforced the idea that Confederation had been a bargain between French and English Canada, but it does not constitute an equal partnership. Although the belief that 1867 was a nationalist and centralist triumph perhaps has the most to support it (and certainly most historians on its side), in key ways the arsenal of federal powers was undermined from the start by the strength of local forces, by the genuinely federal nature of the country, by the ability of Quebec and Ontario to each build a rival provincial state apparatus, by the very existence of differing interpretations of what had been accomplished, and, paradoxically, by the strength of the connection to Britain and Empire and the assumptions of Imperial federalism, responsible government, and the royal prerogative. The fiction of popular sovereignty as a self-evident constitutional feature was also therefore weak.

Thus, in terms of abeyances, 1867 was a feat of legerdemain, constitutional sleight of hand. Edward McWhinney in his study *Quebec and the Constitution 1960–1978* introduces his analysis with the argument that a constitutional system must rest upon fundamental compromises that come *before* a written settlement:

> Another key aspect of a constitutional system is that it rests—and must rest, if it is to be seen as workable—upon certain political presuppositions. Fundamental societal compromises must precede and accompany the act of constituent power involved in the enactment of a constitutional charter and the setting up of the constitutional system itself. This is a demonstration of the symbiotic relation between law and society. In technical terms, these fundamental compromises constitute a pre-legal, meta-legal basis—the constitutional *Grundnorm* as Kelsen has called it, the necessary starting-point for a constitutional system.[129]

This sounds eminently reasonable and logical. In 1867 there were indeed compromises made, and the lengthy debate over the Senate illustrates this clearly. Yet some key matters became or remained constitutional abeyances right from the start. Every time they were raised, it was to the growing realization that they were intractable, volatile, injurious to our constitutional health, and better left alone. These questions stemmed both from what had been decided upon and what had been left to be allowed to unfold.

It bears repeating that the 1867 arrangement did not deal directly with Quebec's claim to distinct status and powers. It did not proclaim that Canada was an independent nation. It did not contain a declaration that citizens had rights as individuals. It assumed away any problems with future amendments.[130] It dodged the question of the rights of French speakers outside Quebec. It created an upper house that was a vehicle for patronage, not governance. It may have weakened the idea of federalism to the point where many claim that the settlement deserves the designation 'quasi-federal'.[131] It avoided any clear statement that provinces were—or were not—equal. It accepted the traditions of British responsible government without, perhaps, understanding fully what abeyances these traditions contained (particularly those surrounding the exercise of 'sovereign' powers).

Confederation does not therefore look like a set of fundamental *societal* compromises.[132] It looks like what it was, a patchwork quilt of élite agreement, driven by the centralizing vision of Sir John, the defensive power of Quebec, the financial needs of the Maritimes, the end of Reciprocity, the economic opportunities which union (and a railroad) would provide to central Canada's business élites, and Great Britain's determination to see a new arrangement in place as a counter to the United States. Though driven by the exigencies of the time, it was not devoid of vision and ideas: the problem is that these were not shared. To argue this is not to lay blame, and who would want to do so, given our own track record? In 1867 Confederation was a pragmatic triumph, even if more subtle and nuanced than we have realized. But it meant that in addition to the usual pressures placed upon a constitution as it evolves, pressures from such things as changing social circumstance, technology, legal precedents, and the exercise of political power, later generations were bequeathed a set of problems that would need to be kept as abeyances.

Irresolution, and abeyance maintenance, rather than a constitutional *Grundnorm*, therefore seem to be a better description of much of what we got. Out of the old intractibilities of Canada's political history the Constitution Act, 1867, created a new set of rules that repackaged matters in such a way that most could have faith in differing versions of the implications of what had been agreed upon. Over the next century or so the whole edifice survived and grew. Some constitutional fictions were strengthened, others were weakened. Instrumentalities were devised. Further compromises were made. Conventions became the basis for much of what took place. Taboos arose. And still our abeyances remained *relatively* undisturbed, and we did our best to avoid those 'no-go' areas we knew to be fraught with problems. Unarticulated understandings, élite consensus and accommodation, asymmetry, and political power and patronage were amongst the substitutes for constitutional clarity.

These factors are discussed in greater detail as the analysis now moves to the consideration of how, after 1867, we were able to keep our abeyances interred and manageable and why, despite these efforts, we found that the constitution itself was more and more exposed to corrosive scrutiny. The suggestion in Chapter Three has been that, if we accept Foley's premise that the existence of abeyances is a sign of constitutional health and maturity, then leaving so much in abeyance in 1867 had a great deal to be said for it. In any event, what other more palatable choices did the founding Fathers have? But how many silences can a federal constitution contain?

Notes

1 Gérald-A. Beaudoin, 'Devolution, Delegation, Centralization and Decentralization of Powers as Seen by the Pepin-Robarts Commission' in *The Cambridge Lectures, 1979*, ed. Derek Mendes da Costa (Toronto: Butterworths, 1981), 91.

2 Carl L. Becker, *The Heavenly City of the Eighteenth Century Philosophers* (New Haven: Yale University Press, 1969), 5.

3 Ibid., 119. Becker discusses the 'specious present' in these terms: 'Past and future are two time regions which we commonly separate by a third which we call the present. But strictly speaking the present does not exist.... Nevertheless we must have a present; and so we get one by robbing the past, by holding on to the most recent events and pretending that they all belong to our immediate perceptions.'

4 J.K. Johnson and P.B. Waite, 'Macdonald, John Alexander' in *Dictionary of Canadian Biography*, vol. 12 (Toronto: University of Toronto Press, 1990); see 601 and 611.

5 Note the conclusion reached by Banting and Simeon in their study of comparative constitution-making that 'the evidence seems to suggest that successful constitutional innovation will take place when the pressures are strong enough to make the risk of failure seem greater than the inevitable attachment of incumbent élites to institutions, or when successful revolution or major catastrophe destroys these institutions and the legitimacy of the leaders....' See Keith G. Banting and Richard Simeon, 'Introduction: The Politics of Constitutional Change' in *Redesigning the State: The Politics of Constitutional Change in Industrial Nations*, eds Keith G. Banting and Richard Simeon (Toronto: University of Toronto Press, 1985), 20. Note also Lower Canada's economic situation. David Gauthier comments that 'It then seems reasonable to identify ... three interests. The first I shall call the capitalist interest ... the second the French interest ... the third I shall call the Imperial interest.... The payoffs from Confederation corresponded roughly to what might reasonably have been expected.' See 'Confederation, Contract and Constitution' in *Philosophers Look at Canadian Confederation*, ed. Stanley G. French (Montreal: The Canadian Philosophical Association, 1979), 193–4.

6 For an interesting discussion of how ill-conceived and misunderstood the 'federal principle' was, see P.B. Waite, *The Life and Times of Confederation 1864–1867: Politics, Newspapers, and the Union of British North America* (Toronto: University of Toronto Press, 1962), ch. 8. In addition to Waite's, major acounts of the settlement remain D.G. Creighton, *The Road to Confederation: The Emergence of Canada 1963–1867*; and W.L. Morton, *The Critical Years: The Union of British North America 1857–1873*.

7 Ged Martin notes that, perhaps, 'Confederation was not a logical deduction from the circumstances of 1864 at all, but a panic response to what C.P. Stacey has called

"the atmosphere of crisis" in the closing phases of the American Civil War. . . . .' See *The Causes of Canadian Confederation*, ed. Ged Martin (Fredericton: Acadiensis Press, 1990), 20. Note also his discussion of the opposition to Confederation. Ged Martin, 'The Case Against Canadian Confederation 1864–1867' in Thomas J. Barron, Owen D. Edwards, and Patricia J. Storey, eds, *Constitutions and National Identity* (Edinburgh: Quadriga, 1993).

8 Population figures vary somewhat. These are taken from Mason Wade, *The French Canadians: 1760–1911* (Toronto: Macmillan of Canada, 1968), vol. 1, 388. Ged Martin puts the figure at 1.1 million for Lower Canada, with just under 900,000 being French-speaking. See his *Britain and the Origins of Canadian Confederation, 1837–67* (Vancouver: University of British Columbia Press, 1995), 8.

9 In the rural areas there were nine French speakers for every anglophone, or 494,000 francophones out of a total rural population of 550,000. See Fernand Dumont, *Genèse de la Société Québécoise* (Montreal: Boréal, 1993), 365. For further details see Ronald Rudin, *The Forgotten Quebecers* (Quebec: Institut québécois de recherche sur la culture, 1985).

10 P.B. Waite, ed., *The Confederation Debates in the Province of Canada* (Toronto: McClelland and Stewart, 1963), 40. Macdonald voiced similar sentiments when he said 'Treat them as a nation and they will comport themselves as, generally, a free people do: with generosity. Treat them as a faction and they will behave as one.'

11 Ged Martin, 'What We Know and What We Think We Know: The Great Coalition of 1864 in The Province Of Canada', paper presented at the Annual Meeting of the British Association of Canadian Studies (Nottingham, 1991). Note also Ged Martin, *Britain and the Origins of Canadian Confederation, 1837–67*.

12 Martin, 'What We Know', 2. D.J. Hall makes the same point: 'The golden age never existed. The roots of conflict have always been present, the spirit of toleration, all too rarely. . . . The diverse interpretations of the meaning of Confederation were honestly held, based upon past experience, existing convictions and particular hopes—however vague—for the future.' See 'The Spirit of Confederation: Ralph Heintzman, Professor Creighton, and the bicultural compact theory', *Journal of Canadian Studies* 9, 4 (1974), 24–43.

13 Martin, 'What We Know', 26.

14 Ibid., see footnote 108.

15 Rod Preece, 'The Political Wisdom of Sir John A. Macdonald', *Canadian Journal of Political Science* 17, 3 (September 1984), 459–86 at 459.

16 Ibid., 460.

17 Ibid. These figures included 'Macaulay, Bentham, Acton, Mill, Cobden, Bright, Coleridge, Disraeli and Gladstone' and he often quoted from Burke, Pitt, Chatham, Fox, and others.

18 Ibid., 462–3.

19 Between 1851–4 the old Reform Party broke up and initially was replaced by the newly styled Liberal-Conservative Party, which soon became the Conservative Party.

20 Preece, 'The Political Wisdom of Sir John A. Macdonald', 468.

21 Gordon T. Stewart notes that by 1867 Macdonald had already spent 25 years labouring in the pre-Confederation political world and that his 'most basic political values and assumptions' were already set. Insofar, says Stewart, 'as he looked for vantage points outside Canada, he turned not to the England of Gladstone and Disraeli but to the constitutional world of Pitt the Younger and Edmund Burke.' *The Origins of Canadian Politics: A Comparative Approach* (Vancouver: University of Vancouver Press, 1986), 9.

22 Preece, 'The Political Wisdom of Sir John A. Macdonald', 463.

23 P.B. Waite, *The Confederation Debates in the Province of Canada*, xviii.

24 Mason Wade, *The French Canadians: 1760–1911*, 388–9.

25 For a clear, brief discussion of the appeal of interstate federalism and of parliamentary over republican government see Jennifer Smith, 'Intrastate Federalism and Confederation' in *Political Thought in Canada*, ed. Stephen Brooks (Toronto: Irwin Publishing, 1984). She points out that Cartier saw democracy as mob rule and wished to maintain the 'monarchical principle'. The Senate was to be a restraint on democracy.

26 Mason Wade, *The French Canadians: 1760–1911*, 67.

27 Jacques Monet, *The Last Cannon Shot: A Study of French-Canadian Nationalism 1837–1850* (Toronto: University of Toronto Press, 1969). Taché was, as previously noted, present at the Quebec Conference in 1864.

28 Christian Dufour, *A Canadian Challenge/Le défi québécois* (Lantzville: Oolichan Books, 1990), 28. Even in the Boer War there was pride in the record of the French-Canadian voyageurs who served, in 1885, as volunteer boatmen on the Nile in the expedition to rescue Gordon.

29 See Bernard Crick, 'The English and the British' in *National Identities: The Constitution of the United Kingdom* (Oxford: Blackwell, 1991), 93.

30 Ibid.

31 Ibid., 95.

32 See J.C. Bonenfant, 'Cartier', in *Dictionary of Canadian Biography*, vol. 10, 143–51.

33 See Michael Oliver, *The Passionate Debate: The Social and Political Ideas of Quebec Nationalism 1920–1945* (Montreal: Véhicule Press, 1991), 25–6.

34 A.I. Silver, *The French-Canadian Idea of Confederation* (Toronto: University of Toronto Press, 1982), 33.

35 Ibid., 15.

36 See Denis Monière, *Ideologies in Quebec: The Historical Development* (Toronto: University of Toronto Press, 1981). He notes that the failure of the rebellion was crucial because a 'dynamic and liberating resistance, based on the aspiration to build a politically independent and economically autonomous French-Canadian society on the shores of the St Lawrence, was succeeded by conservative and defensive resistance. The struggle for survival replaced the struggle for independence' (164–5). The use of the term 'race' is misleading but widespread. In the nineteenth and early

twentieth centuries, references to the 'race' question in Canada, as in André Siegfried's famous work with this title, were taken to mean 'races' such as the French, the English, the Irish, and the Scots. It was a reference to nationality and culture, not genetic difference.

37 For a reappraisal of Durham, see Janet Ajzenstat, *The Political Thought of Lord Durham* (Montreal and Kingston: McGill-Queen's University Press, 1988).

38 Martin, *Britain and the Origins of Canadian Confederation*, 8.

39 For an extensive discussion of these arrangements see Douglas V. Verney, *Three Civilizations, Two Cultures, One State: Canada's Political Traditions* (Durham: Duke University Press, 1986).

40 S.J.R. Noel, 'Canadian Responses to Ethnic Conflict. Consociationalism, federalism and control' in *The Politics of Ethnic Conflict Regulation*, eds John McGarry and Brendan O'Leary (New York: Routledge, 1993), 41–6.

41 Monet, *The Last Cannon Shot*, 399. Monet quotes Buller's memorandum (of September 1841) to Peel arguing that 'The governor that would raise them up to a social equality by mere justice and kindness would make them the instruments instead of the enemies of government. The French Canadians, if rightly managed, are the natural instrument by which the Government could keep in check the democratic and American tendencies of Upper Canada' (90).

42 See Verney, *Three Civilizations, Two Cultures, One State*, for a thorough discussion of the idea of 'regimes'. For an extended and extensive discussion of the Meech Lake Accord and the ways in which it was tied to the traditional forces that have shaped the country, and its regimes, see also Roderick A. Macdonald, 'Meech Lake to the Contrary Nothwithstanding', *Osgoode Hall Law Journal* 29, 2 (1991), 253-328 and 29, 3 (1991), 483-572. Macdonald makes the important point that Canada's constitutional 'grand constructions' have tended to come in pairs (particularly the pairings of 1774 and 1791; 1840 and 1867; and 1982 and 1987). First comes an effort to centralize, followed by some efforts at decentralization. See 'Meech Lake to the Contrary' (Part II) 508-9.

43 A.I. Silver, *The French-Canadian Idea of Confederation*, 40–1.

44 Noel, 47.

45 See Edmond Orban, 'Quebec Alienation and the Trend Toward Centralization', *Quebec: State and Society*, ed. Alain-G. Gagnon (Toronto: Methuen, 1984).

46 Silver, *The French-Canadian Idea of Confederation*, 42–3.

47 Roberto Perrin, 'Clerics and the Constitution: The Quebec Church and Minority Rights in Canada,' in *Constitutions and National Identity*, ed. Barron et al., 166.

48 See Perrin, 'Clerics and the Constitution,' 162–80.

49 See the discussion of nationalism and recent works on the subject by Tony Judt, 'The New Old Nationalism', *The New York Review of Books* (26 May 1994), 46. It is also important to note that in French there is always a clear distinction made between 'état' and 'nation', whereas in English there is a greater tendency to use these terms interchangeably. Macdonald in 'Meech Lake to the Contrary' makes the

point that 'twice since 1967, English-speaking Canadians have appropriated the term by which French-speaking Canadians identified themselves', thus confusing matters even more. See pp. 299-301.

50 Ralph Heintzman, 'Political Space and Economic Space: Quebec and the Empire of the St Lawrence', *Journal of Canadian Studies* 29, 2, 19–63. I would like to express my thanks to Dr Heintzman for allowing me access to, and use of, an earlier draft of this work.

51 Ibid., 26.

52 Ibid., 34.

53 Ibid., 37.

54 Judt, 'The New Old Nationalism', 46.

55 See Dumont, *Genèse de la Société Québécoise*, 276. '[T]he nation was present; it was not uppermost.'

56 Ibid. 'When, in any move, in any kind of initiative, our nationality clearly stands to gain, let us not concern ourselves with anything else except secondarily.' 'Isn't that a perfect definition of nationalism? The first one I know of to be expressed in such precise terms.'

57 For a full discussion of this point see Ged Martin, *Britain and the Origins of Canadian Confederation, 1837–67*.

58 Vincent Di Norcia comments apropos of contract theory that 'Canada's constitution is based on the authority of the Crown and the sovereignty of parliament and the Crown, but not of the people', that if 1867 was a contract 'it was a very statist one indeed', and that if contract means what it should, 'a mutually binding voluntary pact, listing specific mutually known and agreed-to conditions and modes of amending', this did not exist either. See 'The Empire Structures of the Canadian State' in *Philosophers Look at Canadian Confederation*, ed. Stanley G. French, 223. Di Norcia of course wrote this before the Supreme Court assumed its present interpretive role. For a full discussion of the role of the Crown see David E. Smith, *The Invisible Crown: The First Principle of Canadian Government* (Toronto: University of Toronto Press, 1995.)

59 Gordon T. Stewart, *The Origins of Canadian Politics*, 5. This work provides an excellent comparative discussion of court versus country issues in the three countries, and discusses Canada's reliance on a 'court' approach before and after 1867.

60 For a brief discussion of the reasons why it was given short shrift see Eugene Forsey, *Freedom and Order: Collected Essays* (Toronto: McClelland and Stewart, 1974), 227.

61 Paul Romney, 'Confederation: The True Story', paper presented at the biennial meeting of the Association for Canadian Studies in the United States (Seattle, 1995), 8. I would like to thank Dr Romney for sending me a copy of this paper.

62 Ibid., 2.

63 Ibid., 14.

64 David V.J. Bell, *The Roots of Disunity: A Study of Canadian Political Culture*, rev. edn (Toronto: Oxford University Press, 1992), 103. The British North America Act of 1867 (the BNA Act) has now been confusingly renamed The Constitution Act, 1867.

65 P.B. Waite, ed., *The Confederation Debates in the Province of Canada*, 154.

66 See Peter J. Smith, 'The Ideological Origins of Canadian Federalism', *Canadian Journal of Political Science* 20, 1 (March 1987), 3–29, esp. footnote 1. Also note E.R. Black, *Divided Loyalties: Canadian Concepts of Federalism* (Montreal and Kingston: McGill-Queen's University Press, 1975), 4. Black argues that 'Confederation was born in pragmatism without the attendance of a readily definable political philosophy.' Donald Smiley follows this line of reasoning in his *Canada in Question: Federalism in the 80s*, 3rd edn (Toronto: McGraw-Hill Ryerson, 1980).

67 It is important to remember that the pragmatism we are talking about is not of the kind that took root in the United States. US-style philosophical pragmatism became equated with the single school of empiricism and its 'scientific' methods. Canadians were indifferent to philosophical pragmatism in this sense, and utilized a far more historical approach. See Verney, *Three Civilizations, Two Cultures, One State*, ch. 2.

68 Smith, 'The Ideological Origins of Canadian Federalism'.

69 Ibid.

70 Ibid. Smith quotes Sir John's comment that 'for twenty long years I have been dragging myself through the dreary wastelands of Colonial politics. I thought there was no end, nothing worthy of ambition, but now I see something which is worthy of all I have suffered.'

71 Ibid., 28.

72 See the argument presented in Robert C. Vipond, '1767 and 1867: The Federal Principle and Canadian Confederation Reconsidered', *Canadian Journal of Political Science* 22, 1 (March 1989), 3–25.

73 Ibid., 5.

74 The delegates at Philadelphia were preoccupied with the problems of state sovereignty and the residual powers problem, and even West Point cadets were to swear allegiance to their states, not to the United States, until the Civil War.

75 Vipond, '1767 and 1867', 7–8.

76 Romney, 'Confederation: The True Story', 17.

77 Jennifer Smith, 'Canadian Confederation and the Influence of American Federalism', *Canadian Journal of Political Science* 21, 3 (September 1988), 443–63. See 453.

78 Jennifer Smith, 'Intrastate Federalism and Confederation', 262.

79 See, for example, Smith, 'Canadian Confederation and the Influence of American Federalism', 462. Smith makes the point that many now argue that 'the decision to deny serious institutional expression to local concerns within the central government has served to weaken rather than to strengthen it.'

80 Ibid., 451.

81 See Peter H. Russell, *Constitutional Odyssey: Can Canadians Become a Sovereign People?* (Toronto: University of Toronto Press, 1992).

82 Lower's views, along with those of numerous other historians, are quoted in Richard Arès, *Dossier sur le Pacte Fédératif de 1867. La Confédération: pacte ou loi?* (Montreal: Bellarmin, 1967), 237. Arès mounts a vigorous, and detailed, defence of the two-nations theory. Confederation was, and is, in his view, an agreement, a pact, or an entente based upon an acceptance of cultural duality. For a recent extended discussion and defence of this view see Macdonald, 'Meech Lake to the Contrary', 279-307. Macdonald's thesis is that there have been two co-existing thematic understandings of Canadian federalism, a 'centralist, unitary conception known conventionally as the statute (loi) theory, and a decentralist, pluralist conception usually labelled the pact or compact (pacte) theory'. There are other thematic explanations too, but these capture, for Macdonald, the heart of the debate over the Meech Lake Accord.

83 Verney, *Three Civilizations, Two Cultures, One State*, 333. The contradictions theme appears frequently: for an earlier version of the economic contradictions question see Herschel Hardin, *A Nation Unaware* (Vancouver: J.J. Douglas, 1973).

84 David Smith has provided a detailed discussion of the key role of the royal prerogative. See *The Invisible Crown: The First Principle of Canadian Government* (Toronto: University of Toronto Press, 1995).

85 Public schools continued to be Protestant in spirit but those who later pushed for the 'restoration' of the Church to its rightful position after the battles over the Jesuit Estates and Clergy Reserve problems, were ignored. When the religious question did recur—as it did over Mercier's compromise in the case of the Jesuits (in 1887)—reactions were especially fierce in Ontario.

86 Monique Bégin, 'Debates and Silences: Reflections of a Politician', *Daedalus* 117, 4 (Winter 1988), 335–62 at 335.

87 Ibid., 359. She also notes that, even in Quebec, only once in recent history has a religious reference been made by a politician, and he was 'almost assassinated' by the cartoonists.

88 See Perrin, 'Clerics and the Constitution', 169–71.

89 See Peter Hogg, *Constitutional Law of Canada* (Toronto: Carswell, 1985), ch. 2.

90 Ibid., 537.

91 Gouvernement du Québec, declaration by Jean-Jacques Bertrand, Federal-Provincial Conference of Ministers of Finance, Ottawa, 4-5 Nov. 1968, 16.

92 Paul Gérin-Lajoie, *Constitutional Amendment in Canada* (Toronto: University of Toronto Press, 1950), 37–8. He also notes that it is 'very plausible' that John A. Macdonald thought that this approach would leave amendment initiation in the hands of the federal parliament. He also rejects outright the suggestion that the problem was set aside on the grounds that the pact was unalterable save by unanimous consent. See p. 40.

93 F.R. Scott, 'Areas of Conflict in the Field of Public Policy and Law' in his *Essays on the Constitution* (Toronto: University of Toronto Press, 1977), 324.

94 Dr Edwin Black commented to me that the concept of inter-nation treaties has changed markedly over the years and to speak of treaties signed at different times as

if they are the same is to ignore the different notions that were in play. We may well be prepared now to ignore historical data and act as if all treaties have the same force and status, because to do otherwise is to violate a taboo and to stir up a hornet's nest.

95 See R. Kenneth Carty and W. Peter Ward, 'The Making of a Canadian Political Citizenship' in *National Politics and Political Community in Canada*, eds R. Kenneth Carty and W. Peter Ward (Vancouver: University of Vancouver Press, 1986), 73. They explore the 'very late development of a distinctive sense of citizenship' and the fact that Canadian nativism meant the exclusion or impeding of rights for all of non-British descent. J.R. Mallory makes the same point: 'the place of native peoples in the constitutional order, remained a non issue for another century because the group was politically invisible.' See J.R. Mallory, 'The Continuing Evolution of Canadian Constitutionalism' in *Constitutionalism, Citizenship and Society in Canada*, eds Alan Cairns and Cynthia Williams (Toronto: University of Toronto Press, 1985), 84.

96 See David E. Smith, *The Invisible Crown* (Toronto: University of Toronto Press, 1995), 177. In focusing on dualism and federalism, and on interpretations of 1867, I should perhaps reemphasize that arguing for recognition of Quebec's distinctiveness within the federation is not in itself an argument against other forms of recognition for other groups.

97 Peter Hogg, *Meech Lake Constitutional Accord Annotated* (Toronto: Carswell, 1988), 14.

98 Forsey, *Freedom and Order*, 280.

99 See Mallory, 'The Continuing Evolution of Canadian Constitutionalism', 51–97. Note Mallory's view that economic issues were not dominant. He argues that the most serious problem was education and the turmoil it produced. Education meant language and religious problems; feelings (and abuses) ran high. Pride of place therefore went to arrangements to protect minority rights in these two areas. 'By contrast, the arrangements to diffuse conflict between the French and English were slight and ambiguous' (84).

100 Ronald Wagenberg, et al., 'Federal Societies and the founding of federal states: an examination of the origins of Canadian Confederation' in *Canadian Federalism: Past, Present and Future*, ed. Michael Burgess (Leicester: Leicester University Press, 1990), 8–9.

101 Ibid., 32. Note the tables used to provide an analysis of the attitudes of the participants.

102 Note also the 1915 amendment governing the creation of a floor for provinces in the House of Commons to be 'not less than the number of senators representing such province'.

103 See the discussion of this point by Kenneth McRoberts in F. Leslie Seidle, ed. *Seeking a New Canadian Partnership: Asymmetrical and Confederal Options* (Ottawa: Institute for Research on Public Policy, 1994), 153–8.

104 Carty and Ward, 'The Making of a Canadian Political Citizenship', 67. They provide a very useful summary and discussion of the evolution of the definitions of citizenship.

105 Ibid., 70.

106 Charles Taylor, 'Legitimacy, Identity and Alienation in Late Twentieth Century Canada' in *Constitutionalism, Citizenship and Society in Canada*, eds Cairns and Williams, 183–229. 'Up to this day there has never been a commonly understood formula of national identity in Canada. Various political arrangements have been negotiated, and something like common understanding of what these involve has existed among those political élites who negotiated them, but no common formula has ever been accepted across Canada by the population at large. In French Canada, the traditional interpretation of the Confederation was as a pact between "two nations". In this understanding, Canada was a bi-national state and allegiance to the whole was via allegiance to the part—one adhered to the larger entity because this was the political home which the nation had chosen for itself. The rest of Canada was seen as making up another "nation", which would similarly be the primary focus of allegiance for its members. . . . But that has never been the way the rest of Canada sees the country' (217).

107 See the Alan Cairns argument that constitutions establish 'parameters' for orderly change, and that in 1867 the individual citizen was not seen as 'the source of political legitimacy'. Alan Cairns and Cynthia Williams, 'Constitutionalism, Citizenship and Society in Canada: An Overview' in *Constitutionalism, Citizenship and Society in Canada*, eds Cairns and Williams, 35.

108 Martin, *Britain and the Origins of Canadian Confederation*, 31.

109 See Russell, *Constitutional Odyssey*, 30.

110 Eugene Forsey, *A Life on the Fringe* (Toronto: Oxford University Press, 1990), 209.

111 Martin, *The Causes of Canadian Confederation*, 11.

112 P.B. Waite, ed., *The Confederation Debates in the Province of Canada*, 50. It should be noted that the 'three great races' of Britain presumably excluded the Welsh. This is borne out if one visits the Quebec National Assembly building. On the walls are the coats of arms and emblems of France, England, Ireland, and Scotland. This is ironical given the remarkable survival of the Welsh language.

113 Ibid., 51. Hector Langevin voiced similar sentiments in the debates: 'Ce que nous désirons et voulons c'est défendre les intérêts généraux d'un grand pays. . . . D'un autre côté, nous ne voulions faire disparaître nos différentes coutumes, nos lois: au contraire. . . .' See Dumont, *Genèse de la Société Québécoise*, 208.

114 Martin asks: 'how far they (the arguments) were designed to convince, and how far merely to mobilize?' See *The Causes of Canadian Confederation*, 21.

115 Silver, *The French-Canadian Idea of Confederation*, 41.

116 Ibid. *La Minerve* was, in Dumont's words, 'in the service' of Cartier and Confederation and although exaggeration was to be expected, Dumont adds that 'Voilà qui contredit singulièrement l'idée de "nation nouvelle".' See Dumont, *Genèse de la Société Québécoise*, 208.

117 J.M.S. Careless, *Brown of the Globe* (Toronto: Macmillan and Company, 1963), vol. 2, 171. Preece does not see him as such a strong centralist. See 'The Political Wisdom of Sir John A. Macdonald', 480. He argues that 'the evidence seems to support the view that Macdonald was rather less centralist than is sometimes imagined.' He did respect French Canada, and defended Quebec's right to its own civil law.

118 December 1864 to Dr Matthew Crooks Cameron. See Johnson and Waite, 'Macdonald, John Alexander,' 598.

119 Martin, *The Causes of Canadian Confederation*, 20–1. Dunkin had, in his speeches to the House, 'showed Confederation as a shambling, illogical mixture of compromises and rule-of-thumb methods.' See Waite, *The Life and Times of Confederation*, 153.

120 Black, *Divided Loyalties*, 'For the Canadian state the politics of federalism are the politics of survival. . . . In no other mature country does it seem likely that political figures concentrate so much on the geographical distribution of power to the apparent neglect of debate over ends and purposes toward which authority is organized.'

121 Ibid., 5.

122 Guy Laforest, *Trudeau et la fin d'un rêve canadien* (Montreal: Septentrion, 1992), 13.

123 Robert C. Vipond, 'Whatever Became of the Compact Theory? Meech Lake and the New Politics of Constitutional Amendment in Canada', *Queen's Quarterly* 4 (1989), 793–811 at 799. Paul Romney's work constitutes an important exception to this view.

124 Ibid., 802.

125 For an extensive discussion of Ontario's role see Christopher Armstrong, *The Politics of Federalism: Ontario's Relations with the Federal Government, 1867–1942* (Toronto: University of Toronto Press, 1981). Ontario's premiers have not lacked aggrandizing ambitions.

126 Black, *Divided Loyalties*, 151. In addition to Black and Vipond noted above, for extended discussions of the compact theory and its complexities see, for example, Ramsay Cook, *Provincial Autonomy, Minority Rights and the Compact Theory, 1867–1921*, Studies of the Royal Commission on Bilingualism and Biculturalism (Ottawa: Queen's Printer, 1969); Norman McLeod Rogers, 'The Compact Theory of Confederation' in *Proceedings of the Canadian Political Science Association* (1931), 205–30; Donald V. Smiley, *The Canadian Political Nationality* (Toronto: Methuen, 1967); Robert C. Vipond, *Liberty and Community: Canadian Federalism and the Failure of the Constitution* (Albany: State University of New York Press, 1991).

127 Silver, *The French-Canadian Idea of Confederation*, 45.

128 As Ged Martin comments, 'the common thread of identity shared by the anglophone population of the provinces was to define themselves as "British"; by and large, the label "colonial" sat uncomfortably on them.' *The Causes of Canadian Confederation*, 11.

129 Edward McWhinney, *Quebec and the Constitution 1960–1978* (Toronto: University of Toronto Press, 1979), 4. See also his 1981 study of the rules for successful constitution-making in his *Constitution Making: Principles, Processes, Practice* (Toronto: University of Toronto Press, 1981). Rule 7 is 'prior political consensus'.

130 Johnson and Waite argue that 'Macdonald's omission from the BNA Act of a formula for amending the structures and powers of the central government was probably not, as is often suggested, an oversight. Having seen to it that the local legislatures could amend their own constitutional arrangements within the tight constraints of

section 92, Macdonald would not have neglected something analogous in section 91, on the powers of parliament, had he thought he needed it.' 'Macdonald, John Alexander', 598.

131 Most notably, of course, in the work of K.C. Wheare. See his *Federal Government* (London: Oxford University Press, 1963).

132 Such agreement is rare: 'Seldom indeed is there agreement on a fundamental set of premises—what McWhinney calls the "prior political question" or *Grundnorm*— which "progressively unfolds or concretises itself" in constitutional provisions.' See Keith G. Banting and Richard Simeon, 'Introduction: The Politics of Constitutional Change' in *Redesigning the State*, eds Banting and Simeon, 18. Richard Arès, although he sees the Confederation settlement as a Pact, notes that because it was colonial in its origins, incomplete in its arrangements, and complex in its founding principles, it lacks the clarity and force of a formal constitutional declaration of the principles upon which the Pact was based. See *Dossier sur le Pacte Fédératif*, 244–50.

4

The Way We Were: Abeyance Maintenance

Psychologically the two founding peoples lived in different constitutional worlds and had different constitutional identities.[1]

Neither the United States nor the United Kingdom were able, at a certain stage, to keep abeyances under control. Conventions were inadequate, appropriate instrumentalities did not exist, myths and symbols became counterproductive, taboos were broken, and fictions and compromise became unacceptable in the face of the inexorable logic of contradictory assumptions and the pressures of partisan debate. Circumstance and personalities played a key part. In the United Kingdom Charles I had strict legality on his side, had little regard for the House of Commons, was not prepared to let sleeping issues lie, and was convinced of the logic and righteousness of his cause. He could also not be trusted and was anything but a shrewd politician. In the United States Calhoun advanced the doctrine of states' rights and argued that the amending formula had not settled the ultimate question of sovereignty.[2] Changing ideas and changing socio-economic conditions also played their complex and interrelated roles. Everything in Stuart England, including economic beliefs, was touched by the religious outlook of the times: the world was seen through a religious prism and 'the culture was from top to bottom biblical.'[3] Support for Cromwell and his New Model Army was class linked, and territorial particularisms played a part, even in Britain. But nowhere was the ferocity of territorial strife shown to more horrible effect than in the United States, for federalism lends itself to such cleavages, even though the decision as to which side to choose was agonizing for many (including even General Robert E. Lee). The miscalculations of Jefferson Davies played their Charles I-like part along with the deeper forces at work.

Unlike the divine right of kings and the beliefs which had for so long surrounded it, slavery had never really become either a constitutional fiction or an acceptable abeyance, and even though 'slavery did not enter national politics as an issue in any significant way until 1819' it was still clearly an extremely volatile topic.[4] Thomas Jefferson 'would have included a statement against slavery in the Declaration of Independence had not other members of Congress ruled it out.'[5] It was always to be 'America's haunting original sin'.[6] Nevertheless, in 1787 the Northwest Ordinance had, under the Articles of Confederation, banned slavery in the territories without, apparently, much dispute. At the constitutional convention there was a good deal of discussion and it produced two compromises: navigation acts were not prohibited but the importation of slaves was banned after 1808; the issue of representation was settled by counting slaves as 3/5 of a person for the purposes of apportionment of representatives. Partisan interests had also buried the slavery issue in the first place with the triumph of the 'country' mentality and its attendant results: 'rampant individualism, stunted institutional development, and a glorification of self-interest'.[7] David Brion Davis sees in the defeat and collapse of the Federalists the reason why the South's peculiar institution remained untouched for so long.[8]

William Riker argues that the battle over slavery in Missouri, when it erupted in 1819, thirty years after the framers of the Constitution had accepted the existing arrangements, was due to political forces emanating from the ambitions of political losers.[9] (He does add that by his attribution of the issue to ambition, he does not wish to imply that the motives were cheap or cynical, for 'in a democracy, the function of a politician is to find an issue on which he or she can win, for thereby a politician expresses some part of the values of the electorate.'[10] This is a somewhat disturbing point of view.) As the century and the struggle wore on, through the Missouri compromise, the gag rules, the Dred Scott case and other incidents, powerful forces outside the political system (like technological change and British abolition of slavery) came to play their part, but partisan political advantage, not mere moral outrage, had brought it to the surface in the first place. What is frightening about Riker's thesis is that he sees manipulation occurring 'on the grand scale of national politics' and then combining with an issue that splits the factions along territorial lines.

Thus in spite of a recognition of the volatility of the issue, and notwithstanding the expedients to buy peace in the hope that the problems would be solved by time and changing circumstance, compromise and the party system had failed. Between 1830 and 1860 there was a profound transformation of public opinion in the North. Even if they weren't abolitionists, most Northerners had 'run out of tolerance for the Southerners' mad efforts not only to push their system into the unsettled territories but to cut off the least discussion of it, whether in their own home communities or in the US Congress.'[11] This conversion of opinion thus came about indirectly, via a defence of the rights of petition and freedom of speech and civil liberties in general, not by direct anti-abolitionist arguments.[12] When a problem of this magnitude and complexity did re-emerge, other *genuine* abeyances, such as the right to secede, the role of the court, the power of the President, and the sovereignty of the people, all became linked and the inner fury of opposing and contradictory assumptions was unleashed. And, at the end of it all, in both the British and American cases, many of the problems which had driven these two nations into civil war were not really resolved, yet they were no longer the subject of debate in anything like the same way.

Both states have since proven themselves capable of developing complex systems of issue avoidance and of leaving some questions in abeyance. They could do so on the basis of powerful new myths, revitalized symbols, modified constitutions, flexible conventions, changing taboos, reinforced fictions, and alterations to political rhetoric and keywords. In both cases a people in arms had triumphed; in England it could be seen as the victory of sturdy independent yeomen over centralized tyranny. This was more difficult to believe in the United States, for Southern officers and gentlemen had been vanquished by an urbanized North. But this made it more of a democratic victory, and so in both cases the people could be seen as having won, notwithstanding the regrettable role of the Major-Generals and the return of the King to Britain, and the carpet-bagging of the South and the continued repression of black Americans. These were aberrations in the march of history and progress.

This briefly sketched background is intended to be a contrast, a counterpoint, to the Canadian experience. It reminds us of the weight of historical circumstance and experience that sat atop the coffin lids of the constitutional undead of the two countries to which Canada owes so much of its political thought. It is not only that—in very different ways—there came to exist in Britain and the United States the constitutional temperament needed to keep matters under control. It can be argued that in the United States this temperament may be wearing thin, and even in Britain there are signs that the impact of the European Community on British institutions will be significant, and that British temperament may be changing too.[13] It is also the case that such a complex thing as temperament must be buttressed by accepted myths, believable fictions, the complex and subtle mechanisms of avoidance, legitimized institutions, and the fear of a return to a pre-Hobbesian world where Lockean contracts take a back seat to violence. The spirit of a trimmer is, as already noted, derived from experience, and it was not for nothing that the writings of Hobbes had, for a century and a half, 'lain like a brooding spirit behind much of European political culture'.[14]

It is not my intent to provide a potted history of Quebec and Canada, or to trace in great detail the development of such things as notions of dualism, or the conflict between changing concepts of federalism and parliamentary sovereignty. This has already been done in such compelling works as Douglas Verney's *Three Civilizations, Two Cultures, One State*, and in the writings of Smiley, Simeon, Black, Russell, Milne, Dumont, Dufour, McRoberts, Dion, Gagnon and so many others—works that often took years to write and represent a lifetime of thought. Nor is it the intention to present and deal with historical evidence in a patronizing way, as mere background.[15] My approach, as was the case in Chapter Three, is and must be thematic. The theme is that we in many ways set ourselves up for failure, because our abeyance maintenance mechanisms were based too much upon pragmatism and politics, and upon circumstances beyond our control, and too little upon *principled* and *timely* accommodation. This is ironical, in that it suggests rather too much avoidance as opposed to too little. We may have been so determined to whistle past the graveyard of our shallowly buried abeyances, that we did not realize that some of them had to be disinterred sooner rather than later. They may also have rested too little upon 'temperament' and too much upon élite accommodation, but this is speculative, interesting though it may be, for it does raise the question of how wise we really were, as opposed to merely rather lucky. While we must remember how much sheer luck played a part, it is also necessary to examine the maintenance mechanisms in somewhat more detail, to see how succeeding crises made questions if not more difficult to handle, certainly more complex, and how our abeyances were not buried ever more deeply as one might have expected. What were the major factors that allowed us to maintain fictions, taboos, and abeyances themselves without agreeing on unifying myths, keywords, and symbols? How, paradoxically, did the seeming success of the approaches taken, and the instrumentalities and conventions used, perhaps illustrate what Edward McWhinney has called the lesson of the Sibylline Books and allow us to postpone significant change, but in so doing perhaps forsake opportunities to act more decisively? And when and why did our abeyances start to come unravelled?

This chapter will emphasize that our responses and institutional arrangements had serious drawbacks as well as advantages—and owed a great deal to political patronage, both inside and outside Quebec. It will then show, using key examples, how succeeding crises served to weaken the abeyances surrounding amicable French-English relations and made them ever more difficult to maintain. In particular the Tremblay Report of 1956 revealed the gap between French-Canadian views and the new federalism of the post-war world, and it was, in fact, prepared to debate the roots of our differences. It did not shy away from what was identified in Chapter Three as our most intractable abeyance: Quebec's claims to be, minimally, something other than a province. This was translated into claims to be an equal partner, and to a desire to see its founding status recognized. The conservative approach embodied in Tremblay then gave way to far more activist notions regarding the constitutionalisation of differences—and to a federal response via the Royal Commission on Bilingualism and Biculturalism. The changing constitutional demands made by Quebec are noted, as is the highly illustrative failure to reach agreement over an amending formula; in this case the demise of the 1971 Victoria formula nicely encapsulates our dilemma. These, in turn, help set the scene for the triumph of the Parti Québécois and the discussion, in Chapter Five, of the *Report of the Task Force on Canadian Unity*.

What is particularly intriguing about Canada is that although the settlement of 1867 in itself created new areas of irresolution, and further compounded some problems whilst it seemed to solve others, the constitutional arrangements were to remain, formally, in a relatively undisturbed state until 1982. Writing in 1982, Donald Smiley could comment that 'I can find only two major and important sets of suggestions for basic constitutional change prior to the 1960s: the report emanating from the interprovincial conferences of 1887, and the highly structuralist thrust of the proposals of the League for Social Reconstruction in 1935.'[16] This is really quite extraordinary, given the wishful thinking that went into the settlement and the very different expectations it had generated.

The usual reasons given for this absence of philosophical and constitutional conflict range from natural pragmatism and philosophical federalism to the operations of the party system. Before these and other factors are investigated further, it is important to note that our *successful* efforts at abeyance maintenance may, paradoxically, have sown the seeds for the depth and intensity of current problems. The reasonably accommodating, practical, and élitist approaches used in governing worked quite well under normal circumstances, and abstract principles did not get in the way of sensible deal-making and special arrangements. Some of the asymmetries that were accepted were quite startling, as David Milne has noted. (He argues that Parliament's decision to withhold powers over lands and natural resources from the three prairie provinces was 'the most dramatic constitutional expression of asymmetry in our history'.[17]) Seven provinces entered confederation as former colonies, and, in a sense, as equals under the Crown; three were, for a time, internal colonies subject to the federal government. Yet much of what was agreed to was what might be called non-constitutional asymmetry, particularly as it applied to Quebec, and while its very practicality helped keep things patched together, we were no closer to agreement on mega-constitutional questions. Therefore, while progress was being made in the march from colony to nation, or to alienation, as some might have it, succeeding political crises deepened many of the cracks papered over in 1867 and have worked against the development of national heroes, unifying myths, appropriate symbols, and acceptable fictions.

How was it that a constitution that left unresolved and constitutionally unrecognized such matters as Quebec's claims to distinct status, provincial claims to equality, the citizenry's need for entrenched rights, the relationship between the judiciary and parliament, and the nation's need to settle the locus (or loci) of sovereignty and the means for changing the rules of the game, managed to survive at all, let alone flourish? On an *a priori* basis we might well answer that the Canadian political culture and character would readily incorporate both fictions and abeyances. Are Canadians not 'by nature' cautious, conservative, orderly, deferential, and reasonably tolerant; unconvinced that there are absolutes; joined in collective ventures by the struggle against distance, isolation, and the climate; lacking in a sense of moral righteousness except when it comes to judging America and Americans; missing a proselytizing or imperial vision, and above all aware that our political history and roots are firmly bilingual and bicultural and loyalist? Has all this not led to political pragmatism, élite accommodation, asymmetry, forms of consociationalism, and even to anti-intellectualism and a distrust of theory?

In the third edition of *Canada in Question: Federalism in the Eighties*, Donald Smiley entitled his last chapter 'Is There a Basis for Political Community in Canada?'[18] He starts from the assumption that:

> Canadians have been loath to raise first order, broadly philosophical questions—questions of freedom and equality, of the basis of human rights, of political obligation and of the standards by which political regimes are to be judged. Unlike Americans and Frenchmen in the eighteenth century—and Englishmen in the seventeenth—Canadians have never experienced the kind of decisive break with their political past which would have impelled them to debate and resolve fundamental political questions. Our tradition of discourse is pervasively conservative and legitimist.[19]

While some in Canada may have thought that John Locke and contract theory were politically relevant to our situation, it was clear that this was not a major concern, especially in the West.[20] Our external political heroes (philosophical or partisan) surely were British liberals and Tories of the Fox, Pitt, Disraeli, Bentham, Gladstone, Acton, Mill, Cobden, Bright, and Hobhouse type.[21] Our leaders saw themselves in these traditions. Our conservatism was supposedly Burkean and, later on, as conservatism waned, our ideological debates were strongly influenced by ideas from the British left: the left of the union movement, of the Fabians, of the Parliamentary Labour Party, of academic socialists, and of politicians such as Bevin, Bevan, and Attlee. And our economics became essentially Keynesian.[22] This was, until at least 1945, a British political world, even for French-Canadian leaders who saw in Britain, and in the British parliament, the light of liberalism and the practice of responsible government.[23] It was a world based upon a British constitution that was itself rife with gaps and ambiguities, and which contained agreed-upon fictions involving crown, government, parliament, and people; it was a world that readily accepted British political thought and parliamentary practice. Whether or not French-Canadian leaders really saw Britain in the same way that English Canadians did is not of course certain. Although both might use some of the same vocabulary of praise, English leaders hearing eloquent statements about loyalty to empire might have profoundly misconstrued what was implied. They heard what Quebec was saying, but did they realize what was meant?[24] The British connection was *defensive* for Quebec. It provided protection against majority rule; it had guaranteed responsible government within Quebec, provided an external judicial umpire, and constituted a bulwark against assimilation by the United States. The extent of such loyalties depends upon the questions being asked.

If we accept this line of argument—and there is a good deal to support it—it could perhaps account for our willingness to tolerate abeyances and suspend disbelief, for we felt reasonably comfortable with our constitutional furniture and with our pragmatic evolution from colony to full self-government. Frank Underhill put it thus: 'We never make issues clear to ourselves. We never define our differences so that they can be understood clearly or resolved.'[25] However, there is less cause for satisfaction if one examines the picture more closely, and takes note of the actual mechanisms of abeyance maintenance and the real world of politics. In particular, highly unusual circumstances continued to keep the great abeyance, namely Quebec's claims to equal partnership or nation-statehood, under control.

The first of these circumstances is what had been settled for by Quebec's leaders. Donald Smiley has set out what he takes to have been Cartier's assumptions in 1867. He is not claiming him as an original political thinker, nor does he read more than is warranted into the Cartier vision of Canada and the new political nationality. He sees it as having three components: the belief that being a Canadian was a political matter and that 'neither religion nor language should influence a citizen's rights'; that the powers necessary for the survival of Quebec society were in provincial hands; the assumption that whatever cleavages emerged in Canada regarding federal matters, the divisions would not be along ethnic/linguistic lines.[26] As we shall see, this vision was undermined in a series of crises in which loyalty was associated with Britishness; the linguistic rights of French-Canadian minorities were ignored or rescinded; and federal powers expanded and moved into cultural and other areas.[27]

Secondly, to the usual political culture explanations for our stability, to the academic conventional wisdom involving innate political pragmatism and a respect for our history, is often added the appealing idea of consociationalism first developed by Arend Lijphart.[28] But a consociational approach has a price and may run counter to the nationalizing goals of pan-Canadian policies, for 'consociational mechanisms involve broad bargaining among élites representing the most important groups in society, with groups choosing their own representatives.'[29] Therefore in the idea of consociationalism lie the seeds of some particularly difficult problems, and it is important to bear in mind what consociationalism is supposed to entail, and what our other key maintenance mechanisms were.[30]

Consociationalism is not merely élite accommodation, important though this linkage may be.[31] It in fact 'implies a specific set of decision-making rules, most important of which is a veto by sub-culture representatives.'[32] Co-operation between deeply divided groups, groups that do not share a common historical understanding or common expectations, is arrived at by élite agreement *and* by arrangements that guarantee segmental autonomy at the level of the sub-units. The mass of the population(s) do not have to become involved, nor is it wise if they are. The assumption is that the masses are likely to be less understanding, less forgiving, and more reactionary than their better educated, more refined leaders. In Lijphart's world, territorially based pluralism goes hand in hand with balance, stability, and accommodation. It is widely held that 'Consociational agreements have from Confederation until the present represented accommodations between élites speaking for territorially organized populations.'[33] Canada thus seems a good example of consociationalism in action, for, so it is argued, it is—or at least was—driven to deal with

French/English questions in consociational terms. Segmental balance and élite agreement have been at the heart of Canadian affairs. Élites have tried to counter disintegrative tendencies. There have been a variety of formal and informal agreements to share power, including the emergence of rotation (the Governor-General), tacit proportionality in some appointments, and other practical arrangements. There has also been segmental isolation and hence reliance on élite negotiation; traditions of deference; historical precedents for accommodation; strong governments at provincial and national levels, empowered by the political resources bequeathed by the Crown; and an external threat (the United States).[34]

At the same time it must be remembered that Lijphart's formulation has been criticized as being 'based on little more than crude empiricism'. It is seen as open to circular or tautological reasoning, as lacking predictive power, as having a 'weak conceptualization of basic concepts'.[35] Additionally, Canada may lack some of the necessary characteristics for successful consociationalism.[36] Consociationalism in Canada raises such thorny questions as whether or not it is workable where ethnicity or language is the basis of the divisions and where leaders cannot bind followers. It may also enhance élite autonomy, and it requires a degree of secrecy which may have been possible in the nineteenth and early twentieth centuries but is clearly not acceptable now.[37] This is not to argue that accommodative practices have been lacking, or that Canada has not displayed many of the characteristics of what Lijphart calls 'a power-sharing democracy', but whether it has been truly consociational in the Lijphart sense is to be doubted.[38] It has rarely been the preferred option.[39] Quebec's members of the federal cabinet did not, and do not, exercise a veto power. Our consociational arrangements have broken down over language and education in Manitoba, Ontario, and the West, as well as over conscription and taxation, and whatever consociational arrangements we had they certainly did not include the indigenous peoples or the Acadians. Majoritarianism always lurked around the corner.

> Thus, despite the claim of some students of 'consociationalism', Canadian political life has not been organized on the basis of equality between the representatives of the Francophone and Anglophone 'subcultures'. In particular, there is no evidence of adherence to the 'consociational' decision-making rules that require more than a simple majority in order to afford adequate protection to 'subcultures'.[40]

What élite accommodation did do was make it possible to exclude matters from debate. It was not that, upon close examination, our constitutional world was simple. Verney and others make it clear that it was not. What was simpler were the ways in which we could treat this world, for the politics of élite accommodation was exclusionary and was procedurally focused.[41] It was a case of the powerful being able to ignore the weak, as well as the English being able to dominate the French. Our constitutional world, as we have seen, excluded Canada's native populations. It also left out ethnic and racial minorities and women in general. Our predecessors were able to avoid the problems that now beset us.[42]

Thirdly, Douglas Verney has discussed, in considerable detail, the development of what he calls 'philosophical federalism' and the extent to which first principles have remained unstated or unclear. His perspective, and it is one that seems particularly useful, is that insofar as Quebec was concerned, 1867 was yet another 'regime', yet another set of arrangements, made by élites, under which Quebeckers would live. The term is not meant to be critical. Previous regimes had set up an accommodative framework, starting with the Royal Proclamation of 1763, followed by the Quebec Act (1774), the Constitution Act (1791), and the Act of Union (1840). These arrangements were driven not so much by principles as by political realities, such as the relationship between the Quebec Act and the incipient American Revolution. Thus it was that Daniel Johnson (whose son of the same name was to succeed Robert Bourassa as premier), in 1966 referred to the constitution adopted in 1867, the BNA Act, as Quebec's fifth constitution. Verney's description of the regime immediately prior to Confederation lays considerable stress on its genuinely dualistic characteristics.[43] Rather than emphasizing its capacity for deadlock and the picture this conjures up of French and English inability to agree, he notes instead the considerable accommodation that went on and which was briefly reviewed, along with philosophical federalism, in Chapter Three.

Therefore to the list of the key abeyance maintenance prerequisites stressed in Chapter Three, we should now add another, and it is this: in 1867 none of the parties felt aggrieved or dishonoured. Pride was at stake, but it was not grievously wounded pride, and there were prizes worth getting. Macdonald, Cartier, and the others did not let a single principle divide them or carry the day. 'Representation by population' was not an absolute demand, to triumph above all. The very fact of federalism had meant compromise and the recognition, implicitly, of alternatives to British practice. Our élites were not radicalized or driven by revolutionary zeal; they were indeed prepared to put order and stability at the top of their list of institutional requirements.

Fourthly, élite accommodation was backed up by patronage, and patronage was the lubricant of the whole machine. There are two facets to the patronage question: it has a national, partisan dimension and particular provincial applications, especially in Quebec. Canadian society was rural and local; there was a narrower range of occupations than could be found in the United States, and fewer of them were non-governmental. In Canada, industrial capitalism did not dominate the state in the same way that it did in the United States. Gordon Stewart has therefore argued not only that patronage 'played a dominant role in job distribution'[44] but that these were dignified and respected jobs.[45] So the basic political and economic realities of the new nation gave parties great power. Nearly every important position in society was available only through the two political parties, making the political élite 'the top power élite'.[46] Élite accommodation took place within parties and not simply between separate ethnic and linguistic blocs:

> There was then a fundamental convergence in how English- and French-Canadians regarded politics and political parties and the social ramifications of politics. In particular both major ethnic groups shared the same expectations and derived the same kind of rewards from the system of political patronage. On patronage English- and French-Canadians spoke the same language.[47]

But there is a paradox, for although this created agreement, it did not help to produce pan-Canadian leaders of the Diefenbaker or Trudeau type, or pan-Canadian policies that were other than economic.[48] Issues were compartmentalized, and there was no real communication on even such matters as language in the public service. Patronage stifled ideological and principled debate and 'helped to entrench a political culture which because of its nature pushed problems concerning the nature of Confederation to the background', which has meant that the national parties were ill-suited to the task of finding solutions to issues long avoided when they did come to the fore.[49] No subsequent Quebec lieutenant enjoyed Cartier's place and influence and French-Canadian ministers rarely held (in the nineteenth century) the portfolios 'that had the greatest impact on federal-provincial relations'.[50] However, Quebec was usually governed by the same party that held power in Ottawa and so 'the same factional intrigues took place within the Bleu organization at both levels.'[51]

And if for French Canada 1867 was the fifth regime, for English Canada it rapidly became the first and only regime. As Canadians came to terms with the implications of Confederation and with the federal system it had created, the system itself underwent considerable change. Even so, 'the main constitutional paradigm from the 1860s to the 1950s successfully kept many of the big issues at bay, an unwelcome gift for future generations.'[52] What helped keep matters under control was this uniquely Canadian mixture of Quebec's understanding of the settlement, a weak but important type of consociationalism, the assumptions of philosophical federalism, the linkages between parties and patronage, and the able leadership of first Macdonald—and then Laurier. Laurier was the great conciliator; a man of 'steady civility' to use Barbara Robertson's words.[53] Laurier epitomized, and made explicit, the need for compromise between French-speaking and English-speaking Canadians. Like David Lloyd George, he was an orator who could charm the proverbial birds out of the trees. Anyone who wishes to understand Canada's, and Quebec's, ability to stay together must acknowledge his amazing contribution and the price that he was often called upon to pay:

> I am branded in Quebec as a traitor to the French and in Ontario as a traitor to the English. In Quebec I am branded as a jingo and in Ontario as a separatist. In Quebec I am attacked as an imperialist and in Ontario as an anti-imperialist. I am neither. I am a Canadian. Canada has been the inspiration of my life. I have had before me as a pillar of fire by night and as a pillar of cloud by day a policy of true Canadianism, of moderation, of conciliation.[54]

What is remarkable is that these are the words of someone who had opposed the constitutional settlement of 1867 in favour of a government 'libre et séparé'.[55] Yet he spent the rest of his life trying to ensure harmony between the two races. This view was implicit rather than explicit, and manifested itself in pragmatism, but on occasion it revealed itsef clearly. Writing of Laurier's actions in 1916, Réal Bélanger concludes that 'Laurier believed at this moment that Confederation was an agreement between the two founding races . . . his whole life was based on the harmony of the two races, the two people of Canada . . . he never wrote explicitly that it was an agreement. . . .'[56]

The man who eventually emerged as Laurier's heir, someone who could sweep the parliamentary seats in Quebec for the Liberals, was of course Mackenzie King. Prime Minister for over twenty-two years, King's natural caution made him particularly sensitive about how Quebec would react, especially on any issues that had implications for national unity. He certainly did not want to preside over any discussion of divisive first principles, and neither did his Quebec lieutenant, Ernest Lapointe. Robert Bothwell summarizes King's task as being 'not only to make French-Canadian opinions count in politics again, but to make them appear to count, and to do it without arousing the sleeping demons of English-Canadian political sensitivities.'[57] King was the perfect politician to ensure that our abeyances remained intact.

To these factors that helped maintain political accord should be added those things that helped change the *balance* of the system, in particular the role of the Judicial Committee of the Privy Council, federal-provincial rivalry, and provincial leadership.[58] And always there were those issues that reinforced the need to hang together economically and culturally in the looming presence of the United States. Finally, and *above all,* there was Quebec's relative passivity, isolation, and conservatism, plus the ability of Quebec's federal ministers to maintain harmonious relations in Ottawa—no mean achievement.

Different Worlds
In some respects, Quebec went to sleep for a century, and the country as a whole could ignore the problem of constitutional change.[59] Although Fernand Dumont rightly takes exception to the idea that Quebec society was immobile and was then brusquely woken up ('cette societé n'a jamais cessé d'être soumise au changement'[60]) even he then asks 'Pourquoi une si longue hibernation?'[61] Hard to imagine as it is, the constitution was not the focal point for a change agenda before 1967 (with the exception of the two incidents cited by Smiley and the abortive initial discussions on an amending formula, discussed below):

> Until the 1960s, the constitution was neither discussed nor considered relevant to public debate, if the personal and official papers of Canada's politicians are to be believed. James J. Gardiner, the West's proconsul in the Mackenzie King and St Laurent governments and holder of every possible party post but that of national leader, never referred in his voluminous papers (66,000 pages) to constitutional or institutional reform.[62]

Quebec was in the grip of a traditionalist Catholicism.[63] Its economic structure was dominated by Montreal anglophones; English speakers ran the world of commerce and the French could dominate law, medicine, the church, education—and politics. As Alan Cairns has succinctly observed, 'psychologically the two founding peoples lived in different constitutional worlds and had different constitutional identities.'[64]

This reluctance to engage in constitutional debate, and attitudes within Quebec towards the provincial state, were intimately linked to patronage, and to political culture, within as well as outside the province. There are numerous approaches taken to the task of explaining Quebec's social and economic development. In order to account for Quebec's political culture—its isolation and backwardness—scholars have pursued what in general could be termed ideological/modernization themes or socio-economic/dependency explanations.[65] Such theories use a broad range of evidence: anglophone domination, resource and capital dependency, the class-linked division of labour, the absence of countervailing élites, contagion effects from abroad, the gap between culture and economic change, the ideological hold of the church, the suffocating power of political corruption, the effects of a rapidly changing birthrate, and the centralising powers of the British North America (BNA) Act. All such theories have flaws or are in some respect incomplete, especially if one adds the influence of personalities and world events:

> Modernization theories raise many pivotal issues: the importance of industrialization in throwing previously isolated groups into contact, the disruption of traditional institutions, which leaves modernizing groups culturally suspended, the significance of modern communication vehicles for forging collective identity and mobilizing groups, the crucial role of intellectuals, and the independent effect of ideology. But there is, as numerous critics have pointed out, a teleological bias to modernization models.[66]

Dependency and conflict models rightly stress the plight of subordinated ethnic groups who attempt to control their own economic and political institutions, but it will often 'draw a picture of ethnic group solidarity which is historically inaccurate'.[67] Neo-Marxist approaches, which stress such things as uneven development and split labour markets, have a tendency to reduce everything, including ethnicity, to a problem of economic relations.[68] The point is, development and change are complex processes and no single explanation suffices—but to understand Quebec's position on constitutional matters, and why it changed, one must set it against this background of social evolution. At first glance the situation seems clear enough: Quebec's political culture was such that for almost a century major demands for change were not made and then, when Quebec 'woke up', new constitutional goals were set. When Quebec claimed more, the other provinces were not far behind; some were more than willing to ride the Quebec wave as far as they could.[69] This in turn forced Ottawa to take a stand, which culminated in the patriation battles of 1980–1, and in the showdown at the Union station, when Trudeau and the premiers made their historic deal, sans Québec.

Even so, in the same way that 'it is not really plausible to think that a society which welcomed the role of government after 1960 was deeply hostile to it before,'[70] it is not plausible either to think that Quebec dreamed up a whole new set of constitutional concerns and demands that came out of nowhere and were constantly changing. Nor is it reasonable to think that there was only one realistic solution to the impasse of 1981. Certainly French Canadians' views on the role of the state—both provincial and federal—were central to their ideas on the constitution. As confidence in 'their' state grew, and as Quebec's culture underwent a profound change, this was bound to become entangled with the traditional desire to stick to what was perceived as the spirit and the letter of the bargain struck in 1867.[71] Attitudes towards politics within Quebec were certainly as crucial as events and crises in the broader federal arena, and until the 1960s what drove much of this internal debate was what Ralph Heintzman has called 'the dialectic of patronage'.[72]

Heintzman's thesis is extremely helpful because he is able to 'illuminate links between phenomena which have hitherto been considered—often deliberately—in isolation from each other'.[73] It shows that attitudes to politics in Quebec, and to political thought in general, involved a confusing mix of contradictory elements, and that 'the traditional attitude to politics and the state was a dialectical one, because while the twin impulses of enthusiasm and distrust were contradictory, they were inseparable.'[74] Quebec life was deeply politicized, civic morality was in short supply, corruption went hand in hand with partisan zeal. It was not that attitudes to patronage were any different in the rest of Canada. It simply seemed more pervasive and important in Quebec. Heintzman shows how it was linked to the socio-economic condition in which the franco-Québécois found themselves: 'Many French Canadians assumed that the only way they could secure a fair share for *their* nationality and religion was through *political* influence.'[75] English speakers in Quebec could avoid direct participation in the political fray; their influence was powerful but indirect. Patronage was a key, probably *the* key, mechanism for the personal advancement of francophones at a time of continuing economic hardship, and its scope was enormous: 'L'éventail du patronage est vaste.... Le politicien est omniprésente, mais l'État est absent.'[76]

The paradox of this network of influence, the antithesis of patronage in Heintzman's dialectic, was a deep distrust of the state and of the politicization of all that the parties touched.[77] There was an anti-political side and temper to attitudes in Quebec, one that moves Quebec closer to other North American anti-party manifestations. Those who ran the state could not be trusted; they would exploit any additional powers for their own benefit. A love-hate relationship to politics was therefore unavoidable in Quebec. Patronage was the best way of forcing the economic system 'to deliver up some of its benefits'[78] but it was not the best way to run the province. What, however, was the alternative?[79] Heintzman notes that when, in 1918, federal civil service hiring was removed from political control and was delegated to the Civil Service Commission the proportion of francophones dropped (as the Royal Commission on Bilingualism and Biculturalism was to note) from 22% in 1918 to a mere 13% by 1945, thus reinforcing the view that only *political* influence counted, either inside or outside Quebec.

But patronage and power are not *constitutional* problems, and the graft, corruption, electoral fraud, and gerrymandering that were the accompaniment to political life in Quebec served to mask the growing need to reconcile the twentieth-century growth of the state with the dilemma over how it would be controlled, and who would run it. In Quebec these decisions were postponed. Quebec's constitutional demands prior to the 1960s were straightforward. José Woehrling has charted the evolution of Quebec's position from 1867 until 1993.[80] It is indicative of the debate that he allocates a mere 15 pages to the pre-Quiet Revolution questions and issues, and 148 pages to events after 1960.

He emphasizes that what Quebec thought it obtained in 1867 were the powers necessary to preserve its distinct character, notably competence over education, agriculture, hospitals, municipal institutions, marriage, property and civil rights, civil law, indirect taxation, and matters of a local or private nature. He discusses the importance of section 93 and the expectation that it would protect not only religious educational rights but also linguistic ones. He makes the important point that section 133, which guaranteed a certain level of bilingualism to Quebec and Ottawa, also contained gaps and inadequacies, 'des lacunes et des insuffisances' that guaranteed serious difficulties between Quebec and English Canada after 1867. It did not deal with the use of French in schools or in the civil service, but it was the first constitutional text since 1760 that truly recognized the official use of the French language.[81] Woehrling emphasizes, as do so many others, that for Quebec 1867 'constituait une sorte d'entente politique (un "Pacte") entre deux peuples' and that this dualist interpretation remained the essence of Quebec's view, although it was subject to serious strain by events outside Quebec itself. Quebec's constitutional claims were defensive and traditional and conservative, and were rooted in the internal dynamics of a small and close society. Because of the dialectic of patronage Quebec was even less autonomy-minded than certain other provinces, notably Ontario. 'L'objectif des gouvernements québécois de cette époque n'était pas d'étendre leurs pouvoirs, ni même de les utiliser dans leur pleine mesure, mais simplement de les préserver de toute diminution.'[82]

Thus those areas left so unclear in the British North America Act *remained* unclear, and successive Quebec governments had no intention of opening up for full discussion the questions the existing arrangements concealed. The history of the debate over the amendment problem discussed below illustrates this perfectly. What did change the tenor of the debate, and helped set the scene for later and lasting distrust, were crises outside Quebec. It is these significant events that deepened the gulf between the two cultures, and prevented even war itself from being the crucible within which the nation could come together. It affected our consciousness of our abeyances; if there had been a mutual willingness to set matters aside we would expect to find very strong and muscular defensive mechanisms. There would be ways of making statements that would deny the existence of gaps of unsettlement and constitutional black holes, whilst at the same time acknowledging, subtly, their existence and their effects on our behaviour.

Britain handled its internal challenges in different ways. The Irish question was never resolved, except to the extent that Ireland was placed outside the constitution. Scotland had signed a Treaty of Union, and although sovereign power was supposed to reside in Westminster, the Scots retained their distinctive civic culture, and the *symbols* of nationalism were encouraged. The Welsh were too weak numerically and politically to pose a threat, and had been conquered. Welsh concerns came to focus on the preservation of the Welsh language. And so the myths and fictions surrounding parliamentary sovereignty lived on, and the British constitution could be seen as an organic, evolving Burkean partnership across generations, a partnership 'between those who are living, those who are dead, and those who are to be born'. Thus what could be emphasized was not only the civic side of things, where all had rights as citizens, but also the more metaphysical linkages between state and nation, even though, in the British case, nation had an 's' on the end of it. The ideals of state and nation could fuse; individual liberties and legal rights could be imbued with national spirit: the British 'nation' had a historic role and a constitution that embodied the wisdom of history. Fundamental questions about state and nation, individuals and rights, the Crown and popular sovereignty, could be buried and ignored.

Canada inherited many of these traditions, but they were, and became, intertwined with other questions born of federalism and, in a sense, of confederalism. Just how strong should the centre be; should the constituent units be a genuine counterbalance to Ottawa; was Canada really a binational state comprising two founding peoples (plus aboriginals with special rights)? We could not, therefore, develop our constitutional world in such a way that our habits of mind—and of the heart—meant an acceptance of constitutional fictions as self-evident truths. And when we did not like the way things had developed, we had others to blame, in particular the Judicial Committee of the Privy Council. This left our abeyances dangerously close to the surface and, periodically, crises arose which revealed how deeply divided we were on fundamental questions, questions which involved what Canada was as a country, and what it could expect of its citizens.

The renewed crisis which erupted over Riel in 1885 was symptomatic of a much larger question: the relationship of Quebec to French speakers outside the province. It is agreed that, initially, inside Quebec there was neither much knowledge of, nor interest in, the other French-speaking communities such as the Acadians. There was ambivalence about minority rights outside Quebec as these might at some stage undermine and endanger the character and autonomy of Quebec itself.[83] The privileges and prerogatives of Quebec's large anglophone minority were seen as a threat. At the same time, there was deep resentment that franco-Ontarians had not received the same treatment. Succeeding language/education crises (in the Maritimes, Ontario, and Manitoba) forced French Canadians to take an interest in the plight of their 'fellows'. Initially there was little support for Riel or what he stood for. Many in Quebec were embarrassed by him, and French-speaking troops were part of the forces dispatched against him. But the later treatment of Riel, as with other incidents, became a matter of Quebec pride and patriotism. It reinforced a growing distrust of perfidious English-speakers: the rejection of educational and linguistic duality, and the execution of Riel, were seen as affronts to Quebec and to Catholicism. In Silver's opinion (and others'), these external events led some Quebeckers to a new view of Confederation, in which Canada had to become a nation founded on cultural and linguistic duality across the country as a whole.[84]

This view finds perhaps its clearest expression in the life and work of Henri Bourassa. For Quebec, as well as for the rest of the country, there has been no resolution to the problem of pan-Canadian bilingualism, francophone minorities, and Quebec's concerns over linguistic control. Laurier had always to walk a delicate line between defending local, i.e. provincial, autonomy, and defending the right of francophones to separate schools.[85] Any Quebec insistence upon special status and/or special privileges for a dualistic minority outside Quebec caused an inevitable reaction in English Canada. Even in the nineteenth century it was seen as a threat to national unity. It would have to be countered, it was argued, by a single (unhyphenated) Canadianism, or it could tear Confederation apart. Thus the expectations put in place in 1867 were undermined almost immediately by something that had not been foreseen—the plight and needs of non-Quebec francophones and the reaction this would cause inside and outside Quebec. Paradoxically, the same events also helped to create the dream of Henri Bourassa, which was to represent an ongoing, and powerful, moral claim and ideal, taken up especially by Pierre Trudeau and working its way eventually to the heart of the debates over the Meech Lake and Charlottetown Accords. Bourassa's views helped to keep separatist impulses in check, and created an attachment—at least to some degree—to Canada as a whole.

Apart from ongoing political troubles over education, religion, language, Riel, free trade, and control over the navy, one other crisis served to widen the gulf between English and French Canada: the First World War.[86] (Followed of course by yet another conscription crisis in World War Two, culminating in the 1942 referendum in which 71% of the Quebec electorate voted 'no' to conscription while in the rest of Canada 80% voted 'yes'. Even so, this crisis was not as serious as the events of 1917.)[87] There had certainly been disputes over previous Imperial involvements, especially the Boer War, but these were insignificant when compared to the conscription crisis of 1917. Although there were French-Canadian volunteers, and distinguished service by regiments such as the Royal 22nd, it was a war in which the inter-cultural goodwill built up by Laurier, and the pan-Canadian dreams of Bourassa, ran headlong into jingoism and British patriotism. The debate within Quebec is exemplified by the very moving and bitter exchange of public correspondence between Captain Talbot Papineau (a great-grandson of Louis-Joseph of 1837 fame) and Henri Bourassa himself. Papineau, who was Bourassa's cousin, argued national sacrifice would knit the country together: 'At this moment, as I write, French and English Canadians are fighting and dying side by side. Is their sacrifice to go for nothing, or will it cement a foundation for a true Canadian nation?'[88] Bourassa replied by analysing the reasons why Quebec opposed the war and why the idea of 'fighting for the preservation of the French civilization in France while endeavouring to destroy it in America'[89] seemed absurd. Had Papineau survived (he died at Passchendaele in 1917) he was clearly destined for political prominence. Sandra Gwyn sees him as having been a possible future Prime Minister: 'Tread softly at Passchendaele, because you tread upon a dream of what we might have become.'[90] Even if this is to minimize the damage done to his reputation in Quebec by his attack on Bourassa, the point is well taken that a Talbot Papineau, a decorated veteran of impressive talents and pedigree, could have been a truly national hero. Out of World War I came a generation of anglo-Canadians committed to the public service, to the building of a nation, and to an effective federal government. No such mission fell upon Quebec's leaders. The war had opened up an enormous gulf. Each side was seen as having let the other down. And for some French Canadians, it was the war years that helped turn French Canada into Quebec, and which revealed the enormous cultural gap between Canada's two 'peoples', who so obviously disagreed over imperialism, North Americanism, nationalism, education, and even feminism.[91]

There were few common heroes: war did not play its normal unifying role, in spite of its contribution to national independence by way of Vimy Ridge and the enormous sacrifices made.[92] Not that Canadians themselves came out of the war more anglophile in nature; there had been far too much British arrogance and bungling for that. But French Canadians had not stood willingly alongside their fellow English Canadians and been slaughtered like them, and English Canadians had not seen the war for what French Canadians thought it was, a European tragedy fuelled by imperialism, in which French Canadians would often not even have their own units and in which Canadian troops came under British control. Requests for distinctive uniforms for French-Canadian regiments were denied, in sharp contrast to the deliberate creation, by the British government, of the regiments of Scotland, with their distinctive national dress. The conscription crisis in Quebec had led to deaths, bombings, and serious rioting all across the province, and to the unfortunate dispatch of a Toronto battalion to quell the disturbances. At the beginning of 1918 there was a protracted debate in the Quebec National Assembly over the motion that Quebec 'would be disposed to accept the breaking of the Confederation pact of 1867 if, in the other provinces, it is believed that she is an obstacle to the union, progress and development of Canada.' The motion was withdrawn once honour and emotions had been satisfied.[93]

The country had demonstrated an inability to agree on amicable solutions to serious political problems with clear constitutional implications, and had been lucky that economic nation building—the opening of the West and the national policies of the federal government—had served as substitutes for introspection. So had Quebec's conservatism and political culture. Yet nation-building schemes, the history of francophone defeats outside Quebec, and economic change always contained the possibility of further discord if Quebec ever came out of hibernation.

Special Status

Was there a precise moment when the idea that Quebec's 'distinctiveness' should be constitutionalised became a fact of our overt constitutional life and debate? The answer would appear to be both 'no' and 'yes'. It is 'no' because the idea itself—in general—appears in so many ways and in so many places. It was, as we have seen, always part of the general 'dream of a nation', as Susan Mann Trofimenkoff has put it. It is eloquently and clearly expressed in the Report of the Tremblay Commission, published in 1956 and discussed below in more detail. In the 1960s it was the guiding principle of André Laurendeau's work for the Royal Commission on Bilingualism and Biculturalism. Yet the idea of Quebec wishing to radically alter the constitution to *entrench* this recognition, and desiring to alter the assumed rules of the game, did not begin to coalesce until the mid-1960s, did not emerge full-blown and in tangible form until the mid-1970s, and did not take the specific form of the demand for a distinct society clause until the mid-1980s.[94]

After 1867 Quebec retreated into a defensive nationalism that was always rooted in a discourse on identity and in the lived experience of being a francophone. It was always in reference to a *culture* that Quebec assessed itself.[95] And even though, in the aftermath of World War II, Quebec was changing rapidly, its constitutional position remained traditional. The first Duplessis government (1936–9) rested its constitutional demands upon the claim that there should be no constitutional change without the consent of all the provinces: 'Participant de la nature des conventions, le pacte fédératif ne peut être ni amendé, ni modifié, sans l'assentiment de toutes les parties, c'est-à-dire de toutes les provinces.'[96] The provinces are 'sovereign states' in their own sphere and powers do not 'flow' from the centre; on the contrary the central government was 'born of the common will of the provinces' ('de volonté des provinces').[97]

The Godbout government (1939–44) wanted a clarification of powers 'pour préciser la compétence des gouvernements' but the war got in the way. In these circumstances 'no province of the dominion, nor any group of its population' would stand in the way of Ottawa's use of its wartime powers, but after the war Ottawa should restore provincial prerogatives and should revise the text and spirit of the BNA Act 'to specify provincial powers or even to increase them'.[98] The second Duplessis administration (1944–59) repeated its views that Confederation was a pact, but there was an important alteration in phraseology when it came to constitutional change. The pact 'ne saurait ni ne devrait être modifié sans le consentement de toutes les parties contractantes, ou de moins sans *le consentement des quatres provinces pionnières*'[99] (my emphasis). Here we have the germ of a veto proposal that would be two-tiered or regionalized. In other respects, Quebec wanted Ottawa out of provincial fields, it wanted greater control over taxing powers, and the position taken by the Tremblay Report reflects this line of reasoning. In 1950 Duplessis had proposed a new division of powers, reorganization of spending powers, limitations on Ottawa's use of its existing powers, and a revised procedure for Supreme Court appointments. Confederation was 'a pact of union between two great races'.[100]

In order to understand the immediate post-war view from Quebec there may well be no better starting place than the *Report of the Royal Commission of Inquiry on Constitutional Problems* established by the government of Quebec in February 1953.[101] Known as the Tremblay Commission, after its chair, Judge Thomas Tremblay, it completed its work in 1956. It is an extraordinary document, well worth re-reading, especially now that the dominant vision of federalism that it challenged is itself no longer nearly so unassailable, and we are seeking a replacement.

The Report is nothing less than a philosophical defence of Quebec as the homeland of a nation. As a key part of this defence it offers a view of what it calls the essential spirit that should animate a federation. Reading this section one cannot fail to be struck by how far apart French Canada's defence of 'classical' federalism has been from the centralizing proclivities of the Keynesian, Ottawa-focused, Canadian state. Tremblay was intended to be a counter to the Rowell-Sirois Report in particular, and also to the work of the Royal Commission on National Development in the Arts, Letters and Sciences (the Massey Commission).[102] During the 1930s, an impressive generation of civil servants and academics moved easily into, and back and forth between, jobs in the federal civil service, in law, in education, and in politics. This was the era of Brooke Claxton, Norman Rogers, Frank Underhill, Eugene Forsey, Clifford Clark, Graham Spry, and others. They were outspoken critics of capitalism, often despised the provincial governments, and were predominantly nationalists and centralists. But, as Louis Balthazar has noted, they had very little communication with French-speaking Canadians, especially during the crucial pre-war decade, and after the war the authoritarian hand of Duplessis again lay over Quebec.[103] This assertion of nationalism and left-liberalism in English Canada was not therefore seen as a defence of *federalism*—and defend federalism was what the Tremblay Commission set out to do.

But the approach taken is not at all what one would expect given its primary mandate, which was to examine the *fiscal* relations between the government of Canada and the provincial governments, and to recommend changes that would restore fiscal balance. David Kwavnick, in his introduction to the abridged English translation of the Report, puts the matter thus:

> What is unique about the Tremblay Commission is that it undertook to expound the unarticulated major premises of society's existence and to justify those premises by reference to what it believed to be absolute and immutable standards of eternal verity. The Tremblay Commission raised questions the answers to which most people simply take for granted. The surgeon about to enter the operating theatre does not engage in a philosophical debate on the value of human life or attempt to find in absolute morality a basis for saving the life of his patient. But this, by analogy, is precisely what the Tremblay Commission did.[104]

Note Kwavnick's choice of terms: 'unarticulated' premises; answers people 'take for granted'; 'philosophical' debate. The Commission, in other words, did not avoid our abeyances. It attempted a totally different strategy: it went to the very heart of what it saw as our deep and fundamental differences and *attempted to put them on paper*. The premises of the Report are as vital—indeed more vital—than its conclusions.

In innumerable ways the Report was a defence of conservative Catholic nationalism but it also embodied progressive ideas from such philosophers as Jacques Maritain. It was rooted, of course, in the compact theory, emphasizing that the Federal Parliament should have no legislative powers that were not expressly granted under section 91; if matters were of a local nature these were clearly provincial, and this power is seen as constituting a sort of residual provincial power in general.[105] Canada is seen as a nation in a *political* sense, but 'if on the other hand the word "nation" is understood in its true sense, as designating a sociological unit formed through practice in common of a single culture, the Province of Quebec, in view of its historical experiences, may well ask what is meant.'[106] In other words, Canada was not a 'true' nation like Quebec, and claiming that it was could not change the fact that French Canadians could be part only of a political nationality that united two 'particularities' through federalism. Federalism was seen by the Commissioners as designed from the outset to separate, preserve, and protect, to be a system based first and foremost upon cultural, sociological, and philosophical diversity:

> What then, after all, is federalism? We have said it is a system of association as opposed to the system of singleness . . . it appears as a system which, in simultaneous reaction against unitarianism and individualism, proclaims association between individuals and social groups as a central organizing principle of society.[107]

The Report argued that the federal government with support from the other provinces had been, and was, encroaching upon Quebec's powers, powers rightfully given as part of the federal bargain. Ottawa was seen as ignoring the general principles upon which federalism should be based. These were: (1) The principle of 'subsidiarity' which meant 'in all cases the higher authority should limit its activities to those matters with which the lower are incapable of dealing.'[108] The state should stay out of 'men's lives' as much as possible, leaving local, voluntary, or professional associations to flourish. (2) The 'suppletory' principle. The state supplements; it 'is not the creator of the common good; it is its guardian.'[109] It co-ordinates but takes direct action only in cases where no other remedy can be found. (3) The constitution should be written, rigid, not easy to modify, and 'neither of the two orders of government should have the right to modify the constitution by themselves, at least insofar as the distribution of powers and the status of each is concerned.'[110] (4) Powers are to be divided so that each level of government is master within its own house, even though co-operation will be necessary. (5) A completely independent tribunal is needed to act as the referee in case of disputes. (6) Cultures must be given security.[111]

These are the sorts of federal conditions laid down by Dicey and Wheare (who are cited), buttressed by a deep set of religious convictions, for Quebec's culture was seen as Catholic, communal, and humanist. According to the Commission's Report, Quebec should not—could not—support the individualism, scientism, positivism, materialism, rationalism, and technocratic imperatives to be found in both liberalism and socialism. They all ignore a Christian solution 'which by its attachment to liberty, responsibility and human dignity, lies at the heart of every truly humanist political and social economy.'[112] Quebec was therefore arguing that federal encroachments were undermining French Canada's culture, and federalism, in an alarming way. Ottawa had invaded the tax field and had seriously limited the ability of the provinces to raise revenues. It was bureaucratically centralizing powers in a way incompatible with federalism. It had taken upon itself the right to make major amendments to the constitution, and in the 1949 amendment 'it even had London admit its claims of being able, alone, to amend the constitution of Canada in matters wherein it considered itself the only interested party.'[113] It was encroaching into social and cultural fields, and making plans for national schemes, that violated the division of powers in their 'interest and substance'. Ottawa saw its taxing and spending powers as omnipotent and unlimited and, in the Tremblay commission's view, the *Report of the Royal Commission on Dominion-Provincial Relations* (the Rowell-Sirois Report) merely confirms this.[114] And Ottawa had made a Canadian court—its court—the final forum of appeal.

Quebec therefore had to become, perforce, 'the champion of Canadian federalism, a federalism which is neither so obsolete or out-of-date as some have tried to describe it.'[115] The 'new Canadian Federalism' was unacceptable to Quebec and the federal government's spending claims must be rejected if true federalism were to survive.

In many ways the Report is a plea for a return to lost values. It reflects an élitism and a conservatism at variance with the changing North American world. Nonetheless, it was also an eloquent and passionate plea for a purer federalism and for a return to what the Commission perceived as the classical federal bargain of 1867: 'In our opinion, only a frank return to the

Constitution can conciliate the principles enumerated above.'[116] And at the heart of it all was the duality of *cultures*. If the idea of 'nation' meant one community with similar values, this was not what they thought Confederation had intended or promised.

In Tremblay, we see the equal partner abeyance come to the surface. It had raised fundamental questions about federalism, many of which would probably have a greater appeal now. But it was a report that was little known in the country as a whole, and it received scant attention in the English-language press.[117] Within Quebec, new forms of secular nationalism were emerging, and energies would be channelled into state building. The Tremblay Report's religious version of the roots of Quebec's distinctiveness and cultural identity gave way to pride in a technocratic and newly dynamic society. What did not alter was the belief that Ottawa was rigging federal rules in its own favour, that English Canada was implacably centralist, that culture was central to survival, and that 1867 had been a bargain between two peoples. Dualism lived on as a central tenet of federalism, and federalism itself was suspect if it did not live up to the original 'federal spirit'. Whether or not that spirit had really been there is, of course, a very different matter. Perceived continuities are important, and the idea of the values supposedly inherent in federalism is, without question, of ongoing and particular significance.

To ask deep questions about federalism as the Tremblay Commission did, is to ask questions about our values and about the meaning of our social and political lives. Should the majority rule? What is the purpose of government? How are we to define culture? Can we have a national identity not based upon a single nationalism? What role can concurrent majorities play? How are we to change the fundamental rules of the game? What protection does the citizen need from the state? What protection does a *society* and a culture need? What is a society? What is civic duty? What is a nation? How were liberalism, nationalism, and Catholicism to co-exist? The Commission did try to answer such questions and so, in its own way, did the Pepin-Roberts Report a quarter of a century later.

After Tremblay the pent-up forces of change burst forth. Political opponents became powerful enough to tackle the entrenched power of patronage, the rurally gerrymandered electoral system, and the hold of the church. New élites became more vocal and increasing political activism came to fruition in 1960 with the election of Jean Lesage's Liberals. Inspired, still, by the Tremblay Report:

> the Quebec government elaborated a doctrine of provincial responsibility that went further than anything envisaged by previous provincial administrations. This approach, known as the Gérin-Lajoie doctrine . . . proposed allowing Quebec to assume exclusive sovereign powers in areas of exclusive provincial jurisdiction. The Gérin-Lajoie doctrine *constitutes the first serious attempt to give meaning to Quebec's special status within Confederation* (my emphasis).[118]

By 1965 Quebec's constitutional demands *had* changed. Lesage was talking of Quebec's need for equality of the two founding 'groupes ethniques' (which in itself was nothing new) and a status 'qui respecte ses caractères particuliers', regardless of the views of the other provinces. Quebec was heading towards 'un statut particulier qui tiendra compte à la fois des caractéristiques propres de sa population et du rôle plus étendu qu'elle veut conférer à son gouvernement.'[119] Such a particular status might be applicable in principle to other provinces, but 'in practice would only apply to Quebec for reasons of its own'.[120]

The Lesage position was dominated by the idea of a resurgent, modern Quebec, and the natural desire to both reclaim and augment its constitutional power. Passive became active. 'En matière constitutionelle, la "Révolution Tranquille" a fait passer le Québec d'une attitude passive de simple défense des pouvoirs acquis à une attitude active—voir agressive—de revendication de nouveaux pouvoirs.'[121] This involved, or would involve, a decentralization of powers; it therefore might also mean either giving all the provinces additional powers or creating a special status for Quebec alone.[122] This was to become known in English Canada as the asymmetrical option: long recognized in practice, long avoided symbolically or in any clearly declared way; far easier to implement in the case of minuscule principalities such as a Monaco or a San Marino, but problematic in the case of a very large constituent unit in a transcontinental state.[123] Quebec also wanted the Supreme Court replaced by a constitutional tribunal on which the majority of the judges would be directly nominated by the provinces.[124] The Quebec government also indicated that it would be preferable if senators were provincial nominees: they should be term appointments and the Senate should have merely a suspensive veto. In terms of the idea of 'patriating' the constitution, Quebec held to two views. Patriation should take place after the distribution of powers question was resolved, and should involve a right of veto on change for Quebec.[125] This too could be extended to all. But, even so: 'Le Québec ne défend pas le principe de l'autonomie des provinces seulement parce qu'il s'agit d'un principe, mais bien plus que l'autonomie est pour lui la condition concrète non pas de survivance qui est désormais assurée, mais de son affirmation comme peuple.'[126]

In 1966, the Union Nationale came back into power, with Daniel Johnson as Premier. There was a dramatic change in tone and purpose. The theme was now 'égalité ou indépendance', not 'maîtres chez nous' or even 'affirmation as a people'. The Johnson administration position called for a *new* constitution, conceived in such a way that Canada:

> was not solely a federation of ten provinces, but a federation of two nations equal in law and in fact. From an institutional standpoint, a truly binational order should be established, where the agents of the two cultural communities could work together, on an equal footing, to manage their common interests.[127]

This would not be obtained merely by the territorial extension of bilingualism by the federal government. This was to be an association of 'two founding peoples, two societies, two nations in the sociological sense of the term'.[128] Quebec demanded additional powers especially in health, taxation, social security, education, broadcasting, finance, immigration, and culture. It also wanted a whole range of areas to be under exclusive provincial jurisdiction, as well as the authority to sign agreements with foreign governments on matters that came within the province's 'internal' authority. These, along with other suggestions for increased provincial power, were a far more extensive set of demands than those of Lesage. It seems likely that Johnson's position was essentially a political and strategic one, staking out the maximum claims as one does so often in collective bargaining.[129] The real question would be how much less Quebec would settle for.[130]

Johnson was succeeded by Jean-Jacques Bertrand (in October, 1968). His government demanded a constitution flexible enough to be adaptable 'to the needs of each province'. French Canadians must be able 'collectively, to live in French, to build a society in their own image'.[131] Any recognition of rights via a new federal charter was not to modify the division of powers, and collective and provincial rights were as important to Quebec as the individual rights to be protected by Ottawa: 'the most important constitutional problem is the distribution of powers between the two orders of government'.[132] This view was supported by a lengthy list of those areas over which Quebec wanted jurisdiction.

Whilst Quebec's demands were escalating whether they looked backward as in Tremblay, or forward, as with Lesage, Johnson, and Bertrand, Ottawa had not stood idly by. In response to Tremblay, and to these later developments, the government of Lester Pearson had come reluctantly to the conclusion that linguistic and cultural questions would have to be tackled; by 1968 the federal-provincial conference approach would be used, as it had been in the past, to commence the task of constitutional renewal.

Quebec's and Bertrand's concerns began to reflect in part the federal government's growing counteroffensive and its effects. At this point in the narrative it is therefore probably advisable, and helpful, to turn to the federal reaction to Quebec nationalism, and to provide greater detail on the debate over the amending formula that loomed so large in federal thinking.[133]

All of the federal parties ran into very heavy weather on the Quebec question. In the case of the Conservatives it was to lead to the two nations controversy that so bedevilled Stanfield.[134] John Diefenbaker, ousted as leader by Stanfield in 1967, was adamantly opposed to any idea of 'two nations'. Even so, at the Montmorency policy conference of 1967, the general assembly of the conference adopted a resolution stating that: 'Canada is composed of two founding peoples (deux nations) with historic rights, who have been joined by people from many lands.' The two-word French translation was only placed there to ensure that there was no misunderstanding!'[135] This phrase was to be used and misused by many, including, particularly, Diefenbaker and the Liberals. (Pierre Trudeau was to refer to it in 1990 as he campaigned against the Meech Lake Accord.[136]) Stanfield endorsed special status, and the Montmorency resolution was adopted by the Conservative Party conference later in the year. Diefenbaker, whose knowledge of French was close to non-existent, claimed 'nation' meant 'state'. He wanted no part of a two-nation Canada because, he said, it made of others second-class citizens. Diefenbaker's own government had, in Alan Cairns's words, 'been a vanguard government presiding over a transition' and he had anticipated the challenge to dualism that was to come from the 'third force' of multiculturalism.[137] In this he paved the way for Trudeau, and for a new view of rights which ran counter to Quebec's 'collectivist' concerns.

The New Democratic Party (NDP) was always suspicious of any weakening of the centre even though it formally put a two-nations policy in place in 1967, and had recognized at its founding convention in 1961 that Canada had been created by the association of two nations.[138] The 1967 decision and resolution, and its defence of special status, was to cause Eugene Forsey and others, such as Ramsay Cook and Kenneth McNaught, to leave the party in disgust. The party was caught between the demands of Canadian nationalism versus the United States, and the desirability of a strong welfare state, with the need to be sympathetic towards Quebec's aspirations, particularly when expressed by left-of-centre Quebec governments.[139] Charles Taylor and Tommy Douglas and others in the NDP took the position, in 1968, that there would be a far better chance of a strong central government if there were special powers for Quebec but not for all. Douglas 'bitterly decried' the Trudeau contention that any talk of special status was a sell-out to separatism. Kenneth McRoberts has noted that, in all three federal parties, 'at least the "two nations" thesis and special status for Quebec were viewed as legitimate positions for discussion, and had strong advocates in English Canada.'[140] But not nearly strong enough, as it turned out.

In 1963 the Liberals had decided to launch a Royal Commission on Bilingualism and Biculturalism—this, however, did not mean that Pearson was prepared to open up the division of powers question even though an amending formula was under intermittent debate from 1955 on:

> Mr Pearson came into power in 1963 and I became the Secretary to the Cabinet in 1963. Jean Lesage was in power in Quebec . . . we spent five years trying to work out arrangements that would satisfy Quebec without getting into the constitution, because we were convinced (we didn't know the word abeyance) that the constitution was a can of worms. It was only after trying for nearly five years to get something worked out that finally Mr Pearson decided that it just wouldn't work, and that like it or not—and he didn't like it—there had to be discussion on the constitution.[141]

Pearson was, however, prepared to do something on the very dangerous linguistic front. Diefenbaker's late 1950s unhyphenated Canadianism had not reassured Quebec that its case was being strengthened. The noted—and later revered—Quebec journalist, playwright, and politician André Laurendeau had suggested 'the creation of an exploratory commission on bilingualism and the participation of French Canadians in the federal civil service'.[142] Diefenbaker (in power from 1957 until 1963) refused. Pearson, eventually, did not, and in 1963 Laurendeau became co-chair of the commission (with A. Davidson Dunton, former chairman of the CBC, a noted academic, and President of Carleton University).[143]

Others have charted the Commission's role and impact. The key aspects of its life and work that must be noted are, first, that in terms of dealing with our abeyances it was at best a partial success; second, it illustrates rather dramatically a key abeyance maintenance mechanism in action; third, it may, paradoxically, have increased the difficulties we have had with Quebec's unrecognized constitutional claims to distinct and equal status not as a province but as a founding culture and equal 'partner'. Patricia Smart notes that 'the Royal Commission on Bilingualism and Biculturalism was arguably the most important—also the most lengthy, the most expensive, and the most controversial—commission of inquiry in Canadian history.'[144]

It was a partial success in that, while it did have a significant impact on Canada's constitutional thought and practice—as Michael Oliver has argued—it did not deal with institutional reform and change in a way that reflected an equal partnership, as Laurendeau had, above all, hoped it would.[145] From the beginning, he envisioned a decentralized Canada in which cultural duality would be enshrined. But his experience on the Commission radicalized his vision, leading him to the conclusion that 'bilingualism can only work if it is supported by two unilingualisms', and that the Constitution must be amended to allow special status for Quebec.[146]

The commission began its work in 1963 and finished the last report in 1970. It held, as later did Pepin-Robarts, hearings across the country. The Official Languages Act of 1969 'embodies the substance of what the B & B Commission had recommended'[147] as the basis of bilingualism. In this part of its endeavours, backed by Pierre Trudeau, it had a considerable effect. Where it failed was in turning the concept of an 'equal partnership between the two founding races' into something clear, acceptable, and meaningful. This was supposedly the Commission's 'mainspring', yet it was to fade from view.[148] It did not lead to what francophones (a term the Commission itself popularized) in Quebec desired: new powers for Quebec, asymmetry, special or associate status, and greater protection for the French language within Quebec. Laurendeau's work, and his view of Quebec's needs, echoes in some important ways the views of the Tremblay Report. It was Quebec's needs in terms of the division of powers that were vital to Laurendeau, not only because French Canadians could claim to be a founding people but because they constituted a viable society 'with a complex of organizations and institutions sufficiently rich to permit people to lead a full life in their own language'.[149] Seen in this light, only the English and French had 'distinct societies'. Other groups were culturally different and certainly had many of the attributes of distinctiveness (indeed, most of them). But societies they were not.

Distinct society as a developed concept can therefore clearly be seen in the Commission's work, but its corollary, an equal partnership, was not accepted. Michael Oliver asks why such a concept was not more developed:

> A literature *could* have developed, one speculates, around the trade-offs between power and recognition for Francophones across Canada and recognition for Quebec . . . whatever the reason may have been, the fact of the near disappearance of the concept of equal partnership by the late 1980s can readily be documented.[150]

The problem was, and remains, that federal politicians and others were willing to accept asymmetrical arrangements in practice (including Pierre Trudeau on such matters as immigration) but not on any symbolic or constitutional level. Pearson, thought Laurendeau, 'believes in a Canada based on the notion of Québécois specificity'[151] but Laurendeau himself put it thus, in terms which clearly echo the theme of this chapter:

> Don't they see [he said in reply to Pearson] that systematic silence, the solution adopted by Diefenbaker or King, is no longer possible. It only puts off the problems until later. You asked earlier: why today, why has Quebec been moving for the last five years? Not easy to answer. But it's moving even more so because the *wall of silence* (my emphasis) has been so dense and so thick for so long. The idea 'never to mention it' is in opposition to the existence of the Commission, its mandate and its activity: and we're coming up against this opposition everywhere we turn.[152]

The wall of silence was there to preserve our greatest abeyance: the claim of Quebec that it was far more than a province and, if so, what then was it to be?[153]

The actual way in which the Commission did its work is also an important illustration of abeyance maintenance mechanisms in action. 'To begin with, it may be suggested that the Royal Commission, rather than functioning primarily as a knowledge *gathering* body, actually operated principally as a knowledge *legitimating* body.'[154] This legitimation function was performed primarily through the presentation of briefs to the Commission (404 in total) and these briefs became, argues Richard Heyman, 'part of the Commission's construction of a reality in which knowledge is created through the process of being collected'.[155] We never knew, of course, how the information provided was used, or evaluated. The mere collection of vast amounts of material gave the whole thing a pseudo-scientific air, as did testimony in private hearings and meetings and the enormous amount of research into the facts. The causal links between such 'facts' and the Commissioners' values is obviously tenuous.

What was at stake is knowledge which was 'problematic'—'its continued legitimacy cannot be taken for granted and the Commission's job is to redefine or to reestablish its legitimacy through the process of assertion and negotiation with reference to *a priori* "truths" of the social order.'[156] These are important points for they mean that the Commission represented, in a sense, a way in which dominant groups, mainly French and English, could retain power without the exercise of coercion. The Commission was attempting to renegotiate an aspect of social reality—but within limits. Dealing with one abeyance was quite enough; they did not wish to raise others, nor did they wish to face even one abeyance head on.

Even the groups testifying realized this. There was a 'tacit social order' they crossed at their own risk. The brief from the Netherlands Cultural Council said that they would 'attempt to avoid returning into these fields (bilingualism and biculturalism) lest we violate the constitutional limitations which the Netherlands Cultural Council has set itself. This submission will, perforce, be superficial and incomplete.' We could speak about it, but we won't. However, Ukrainian groups did not back down. They did 'challenge the basic premises of the Commission and the definition of reality it espoused.'[157] They held that there 'was no real basis for the assumption that in Canada the overall tendency is towards a British-French biculturalism,' and argued that all cultural groups must be 'equal'.[158] This was the Canadian 'reality'. Yet even having said this, and raising an issue not capable of resolution, the act of participation in the hearings, says Heyman, 'allows confrontation to take place at the symbolic level without necessarily escalating to physical violence over apparently differing perceptions of reality.'[159] Royal Commissions—and participation in them—are therefore a mechanism for *legitimizing* a disinterred abeyance and, at the same time, for burying others. The problem was, the Commission could and did get away with legitimizing bilingualism outside Quebec (not without difficulty) but could not go further, because 'Canadians who did not come from the "two founding races" choked on the concept of equal partnership'.[160] Equal partnership ran headlong into Pierre Trudeau, Western provincialism and populism, and multiculturalism. The problem—and the abeyance—did not go away. It resurfaced in 1980–1, in Meech and in Charlottetown, and in all that went on in between these watersheds. (In fact, in Meech, according to Guy Laforest, we see a renewal of the battle that had been waged on the Commission between Laurendeau and F.R. Scott.[161])

What the B & B Commission may have done was set up a backlash in the rest of the country to the very idea of equal partnership. People thought that Quebec had now 'got what it wanted'; that bilingualism was really a bloody nuisance, and expensive to boot, and was tolerable only if Quebec were now satisfied. People believed that Quebec would and did have too much power in Ottawa with bilingualism being required at the higher levels of the civil service. The fact that all of this was only a *part* of what Quebec wanted was not understood or appreciated. It was not that bilingualism was symbolically unimportant: Henri Bourassa's dream was still alive. This was heartening, but it was clearly not the core of the matter. One of the ironies of the whole Trudeau approach, discussed in greater detail in Chapter Six, is that these policies designed to placate or outflank Quebec nationalism may have backfired. And to the three opponents of special status noted above (the federal government, certain provinces, multicultural groups) we later have to add the claims of other interest groups, indigenous peoples, and even the women's movement.

In 1969 this was yet to come. The B & B Commission did not lay our abeyances to rest and it may, as noted, have helped, in fact, to make a resolution of the Quebec abeyance even more difficult. Failure to agree on an amending formula in the 1960s, combined with the federal government's refusal to open up the division of powers issue, and the Official Languages Act itself all, in their way, made matters worse and sidestepped the central problems. The pre-Quiet Revolution period had marginalized Quebec. English Canada's strategy had been to let sleeping issues lie in the reasonable expectation that they would disappear as Quebec became more assimilated and 'modern'.[162] By 1970 this hope should have been, if not gone, then at best highly questionable, and the failure to reach agreement over the Victoria Charter in 1971 illustrates rather nicely how another ingenious attempt at a compromise that refused to spell out the real questions it was trying to answer, failed.

The Robert Bourassa government, elected in 1970, wanted a *precise* definition of Quebec's place in Confederation; 'le problème d'une définition précise de la société Québécoise dans l'ensemble fédéral canadien demeure fondamental pour le Québec.'[163] Federal structures were to respect the 'distinct character' of Quebec society. Quebec wanted to revise and renew federalism, but a new Canadian constitution 'qui ne reconnaîtrait pas clairement et de façon concrète le fait que les Québécois constituent un groupe différent et forment une société distincte qui désire ardemment maintenir son identité sociale et culturelle, serait inacceptable.'[164] Quebec wanted an equal partnership, significant decentralization, and a veto over major change. Ottawa, English Canada, and multicultural Canada did not agree.

Formal Change

The closest Quebec came to reaching a settlement (until the Meech Lake Accord) that met at least some of its deepest concerns came in 1971 with the initial agreement over the Victoria Charter. The entire tortuous history of the debate over an amending formula that would take the formal power away from Britain and entrench it in Canada has been well described in such earlier works as W.S. Livingston's comparative study of federalism and constitutional change, and Paul Gérin-Lajoie's account of Canada's search for an amending formula.[165] Peter Russell's *Constitutional Odyssey* is a current overview of the development of the amending question(s), and is likely to remain the classic account of our abortive attempts to find a compromise and a formula both acceptable and workable.[166]

Quebec's ultimate refusal of the formula negotiated at Victoria between the provinces and Ottawa is fascinating in that it reveals firstly how far Quebec had moved in its constitutional odyssey and, secondly, that it may have been a blunder on Quebec's part to have refused it—as some would now argue. Russell says, apropos of Victoria, that:

> all of its items would appear again in some form or other in subsequent stages of the constitutional debate. The charter serves also as a benchmark

of the constitutional thinking of Canada's political élites at the end of the first round of the mega constitutional struggle.[167]

How far we had come by 1971, and how the climate had changed, is perfectly illustrated by contrasting the televised drama of Victoria with the situation prevailing 44 years earlier. At the 1927 federal-provincial conference, the only real discussion revolved around the issue of constitutional amendment. This was because in 1925 Parliament had passed a resolution calling for Senate reform, to be discussed at a Dominion-Provincial conference, and Lapointe had concluded, as federal justice minister, that the BNA Act should be patriated with an amending formula. 'The federal cabinet concluded, however, that this was too dangerous an issue to raise, since it was likely to unite in opposition the imperialistic Ferguson with Taschereau, who considered that Britain could still provide significant protection for French-Canadian rights.'[168] Nevertheless, a plan was presented, and in response Taschereau said:

> The Fathers of Confederation have stated that changes should be made not by a majority but by consent of all. . . . Quebec is composed of French people with a different code. Even with a fixed constitution rights have been infringed upon, so we must be very careful to open the door for other changes. Why not let it remain? Quebec is unanimously against a change. If the majority can decide on an amendment there is no security in our charter. If, on the other hand, we request unanimity there are difficulties ahead. On some questions Quebec would be alone and would be pointed out as a barrier to the progress of other provinces. I do not want my province to be in such a position.[169]

At this conference Lapointe had 'formally conceded the claims which proponents of the compact theory had been making for so long about the right of the provinces to be consulted on changes in the constitution.'[170] Thus, even though Ernest Lapointe wanted to bring the constitution home, the governments of Ontario and Quebec did not. Quebec's leaders were obviously in a defensive and very wary mood. It is particularly interesting that they did not want Quebec blamed if in future it had to stand alone, as it might if the formula required unanimity. This seems prescient in view of later events! Quebec was content to let sleeping mega-issues lie; it preferred to rely on conventions and usage, on a British backstop in the shape of the Judicial Committee of the Privy Council, and on its claim that what was needed was respect for the original division of powers, and the original spirit of federalism.[171]

By 1971 what was on offer was a combination of new federal priorities and some important concessions to Quebec and the provinces. There was to be a mini charter of rights, plus the entrenchment of the Supreme Court in the Constitution, with some provincial input into judicial selection. Three justices would still come from Quebec, and they would form a majority in any Quebec civil law cases. There would be an expansion and admission of federal jurisdiction over some areas of social policy (family, youth, and occupational training) although provincial paramountcy would be maintained. There were brief pledges regarding equality for individuals and the need to reduce regional disparities, and Ottawa offered to give up its powers of reservation and disallowance. Last—but not least—there would be a new all-Canadian amending formula. It remains a benchmark, and was revived in large measure by the Beaudoin-Edwards Committee as it searched for an amending formula in 1991.[172] The Victoria formula involved not unanimity but approval by:

- the House of Commons (the Senate would have only a 90-day suspensive veto)
- the legislature of any province that had, or had ever had, 25% of the population
- at least two Atlantic provinces
- at least two Western provinces that had 50% of the Western population.

This was an ingenious approach. It got around the problem of 'equality'—either of Quebec with the rest of Canada or of Quebec with the other provinces—by moving to a two-tier system disguised as regionalism. There was and is a lot to be said for this. It avoided unanimity. It gave Canada's two largest provinces each a veto but certainly not a preponderance of power. British Columbia and Saskatchewan combined could, for example, defeat any proposal. The formula had therefore neatly sidestepped two traps. It did not require a declaration that the provinces were equal,[173] and it could thus avoid inflaming Quebec pride and fear. Secondly it did not place Quebec, as such, on a separate pedestal. (It also preserved Maritime pride, especially Prince Edward Island's.) It would also, one can argue, have been possible to graft onto this arrangement regional referendums, four in total. This too has considerable advantages over the provincialized referendum problem we now face.

Robert Bourassa agreed to the Victoria provisions and took them back to Quebec City and to his cabinet. All the premiers were to do this prior to submitting the plan to their legislatures for approval. (This was not, as Peter Russell has noted, to be a requirement in 1981, and only Alberta and Quebec were to put the Trudeau package of 1981 to a legislative vote.) In 1971 the Victoria Charter did not go to the National Assembly: the Quebec cabinet turned it down. The official reason was the social policy clause but behind it—as one would expect—lay the obvious problem of the division of powers. Quebec now wanted a federal restructuring before, not after, the amending formula had been carved into constitutional stone. What might have worked in 1961 would not work in 1971. 'The Victoria Charter only responded partially to the needs expressed by Quebec.... First of all, the Victoria Charter removed completely all references to notions of nation, community or the Quebec people ... in addition, in social policy only federal competence was recognized.'[174] It did, however, also contain other French language provisions, now often forgotten. For example, it guaranteed the use of French in the legislatures of Ontario, Manitoba, New Brunswick, Newfoundland, and Prince Edward Island; it provided for French and English statutes in Quebec, New Brunswick, and Newfoundland, and also for trials in French and English; it allowed individuals in New Brunswick, Ontario, Newfoundland, and PEI to communicate with the federal government in French. (Section 23 of the Manitoba Act already dealt with most of these matters, but Manitoba was not mentioned.)[175]

This failure was, one suspects, a serious blow to Ottawa. It helped to convince the federal government that agreement with Quebec was unlikely. The Charter's demise was followed by a lengthy hiatus in First Ministers' Meetings on the constitution, which did not resume until the late 1970s. Gordon Robertson considers that this was one of those moments of constitutional truth when the wrong decision was made:

> Our constitutional history would have been very, very different if Mr Bourassa had not backed out . . . this was a cruel blow to Mr Trudeau. He had tried very hard and gone a long distance to meet Mr Bourassa and Quebec. And we had worked very hard with the other provinces, got apparent agreement, and then failed.[176]

After Victoria, attitudes hardened. Even so, the federal government certainly did not expect the Parti Québécois, and René Lévesque, to win the election of 1976, and set the scene for the confrontation with Ottawa and Trudeau. It was the Parti Québécois's surprising victory that put in motion the creation of the Task Force on National Unity to which we turn in the next chapter.

The argument presented in this chapter has been that the mechanisms of élite accommodation and patronage, Quebec's defensiveness and isolation, the unpredictable ways in which federalism unfolded, the structure and operation of the parties, and the political leadership of politicians, notably Laurier, are the kinds of things that kept the country together. To these can be added other well-known factors: Mackenzie King's studious avoidance of controversy and his incredible caution; the successes of the federal government and the Canadian state during World War II; the creation of a federal welfare state as a new form of national policy, modelled on British and Keynesian lines; the continued success of French-Canadian politicians at the federal level, notably Lapointe and Louis St Laurent. If we look at the unfolding of Canada's constitution it is relatively easy to take the view that Canadians have been pragmatic and prudent: the Conquest was not really a conquest; the arrangements of 1867 were deliberately vague at key points; theory was noticeably absent but practical politics and paternalism prevailed; French Canadians would be free to vote one way provincially and another federally; at times of crisis, the contending parties backed down or retreated; consociationalism worked; Canadian nationalism grew; the federal state expanded; some asymmetries were allowed.

Even so, what can also be noted is that the legacy of the Conquest was not exorcised; Quebec, unlike Scotland, could not look back on a long history of independence, on a union of two crowns, and then on a formal legislative Treaty of Union. Quebec had passed from one colonial status straight to another. The arrangements of 1867, pragmatic though they were, were in themselves responsible for on-going conflict and confusion, the constitutional images we carried in our heads were never settled, and practical politics were often the politics of dominance and exclusion. In times of crisis we did not retreat into the safety of renewed 'unsuspecting confidence'. Each time there was a crisis, philosophical federalism and pragmatism did not work. The results were usually a stand-off that revealed how far apart were the views of francophones and anglophones. Charles Taylor concludes that 'when faced with the demands of a French Canada for some recognition of its rights as a nation . . . the rest of Canada has been generally hostile and uncomprehending.'[177] The crises surrounding minority language, religion, and education; Louis Riel; conscription in 1917 and 1942; and pan-Canadian dualism were *never* satisfactorily resolved or forgotten. The Manitoba Act was altered, Riel hanged, and conscription imposed. Our symbols, our myths, our fictions, and our constitution did not coalesce, and the stage was being set for the emergence of full-blown Quebec nationalism, for 'When any community is subordinately connected with another, the great danger of the connections is the extreme pride and self-complacency of the superior, which in all manners of controversy will probably decide in its own favour.'[178]

Each crisis revealed profound misunderstanding. By the end of World War II federal predominance, especially in fiscal matters, threatened the federal-provincial balance, and the Tremblay Report reflected the apogee of a philosophical, religiously rooted, conservative, and nationalist Quebec vision of federalism. Even at this stage, crises and circumstances notwithstanding, the Quebec abeyance was under control because it had not emerged as a demand for anything *new*; it was an argument for a reassertion of the old, and the British connection still provided some protection. Couched in such terms, it was acceptable. Given Quebec's power, or rather the lack thereof, it could also largely be ignored (and federal programs also increased support for Ottawa, even as they brought about a negative reaction from the governments of Quebec).

But when the old combined with the new, then the assertion that Quebec was—or should be—an 'equal' partner, and that this meant a different kind of status, brought the abeyance to the cave door. It had waked from its hibernation and was lumbering slowly into the daylight. How could the beast be forced to go back to sleep? It could not. The debate in the B & B Commission, and André Laurendeau's anguished concern that in obtaining the Official Languages Act there was nothing in it that addressed Quebec's needs, reveals that by the mid-1960s things had changed. So too do the constitutional positions taken by successive Quebec governments from the 1960s on. Each crisis, and each failure to agree, made things more difficult (and so too, paradoxically, did the partial success of the B & B Commission). The irresolution at the heart of the constitution moved from being in a state of settled unsettlement (we had not really settled it, and we did not need to do so) to a state of 'unsettled unsettlement' that was to last until 1982. We could not even agree on the appropriate location of formal amending power. But to say 'even' is to be unfair; amendment was, as so many had foreseen, fraught with all the deep questions that we had kept in abeyance. It went to the heart of what we were—and that was something upon which we could not agree.

The clash of deeply opposing principles developed its own vocabulary, words which meant what one wanted them to mean. There was statut particulier, société distincte, pacte fédératif, véritable société, deux communautés culturelles, dualité Québec-Canada, caractère distinct, deux nations and, finally, sovereignty-association, separatism, associate-statehood, and independence. The ideas such terms expressed were constitutional dynamite because they are sufficiently powerful, when exposed and debated, to bring other intractable problems (in other words, other abeyances) to light. They revived a mutated version of the compact theory that Quebec could not accept, namely the absolute equality of all provinces in a federal system, *as well as* the right of all to consent to major change. They raised the problems of popular and parliamentary sovereignty, and called into question executive federalism as an appropriate mechanism, at the same time as they elevated the visibility and role of First Ministers' Conferences. The problems of constitutional inclusion and exclusion grew apace; which groups were to get 'their' particular rights entrenched, and why. The mechanisms of intrastate federalism, in particular the Senate, had failed. Quebec was wedded to a view of federalism that saw it in terms of a classical balance in the distribution of powers, as advocated by K.C. Wheare. The workings of responsible government concentrated and centralised powers federally and provincially and this suited, at least in some ways, Quebec's needs. Quebec did not, however, see federalism as a system of government which by definition 'entrenches the representation of territorial units in the central government'.[179] Provincial equality was not the goal.

Quebec's aggressive resurgence, its determination to settle for something more than mere *survivance*, and the final emergence of the 'providential separatism' discussed in Chapter Three, came at a time when the federal government was deeply worried that federal powers, national will, and national programs were being eroded. By the mid-1970s the West was booming and was clearly a new threat to Ottawa's hegemony, but Pierre Trudeau was seen as the best antidote to Quebec's nationalism even by those westerners who distrusted his economic agenda.

There is much that is paradoxical in all of this. In Quebec, distrust of politics did not necessarily mean anti-statism, as is often assumed. The acceptance of the recommendations of Volume I of the B & B Commission may have created a deep misunderstanding in the rest of the country about Quebec's claims and intentions, even as they helped to legitimize the Canadian state in the eyes of French Canadians. Symbolic recognition, which may have meant little, was opposed. *De facto* changes, which could mean a lot, were not. The Canadian public itself seemed split in its distrust of its provincial governments and in its distrust also of Ottawa: Canada's multiple political personalities were beginning to multiply even further. Survey data showed and still show, counter-intuitively, that as affection for one's province increased, so could one's feelings of national identity.[180] It is not really surprising that, as Resnick has noted, 'ambiguity is the hallmark of minority national sentiment within multinational federations.'[181] And then there came the Parti Québécois victory of October 1976.

By the time that the Unity Task Force was created in 1977 it could already look back on a road littered with constitutional wreckage. Each failure meant that it was more, not less, difficult to deal with the Quebec 'partnership' problem. The Task Force had enemies on all sides. It was wrestling with historical dreams and assumptions few knew or appreciated. Deference, pragmatism, patronage, and philosophical federalism mattered less and less. Informal asymmetry was not enough and could only go so far. Intrastate federalism threatened 'responsible' government. The Prime Minister was bent on using Canadian nationalism to counter Quebec nationalism, and was not prepared to give an inch. His view was not Laurendeau's. The West was not in a docile mood, either; provinces that had hitherto stayed out of the fray (Manitoba for example) had themselves become constitutionalized since the late 1960s, and modest but sensible schemes for reform, like the Victoria package, had been rejected by Quebec even without the presence in power of a separatist government.

In order to try and find a way through this labyrinth the Unity Task Force Commissioners, as we shall see, tried to be radical in a conservative way. This may not have been a bad choice, given their other options.

Notes

1 Alan C. Cairns, 'The Constitutional World We Have Lost' in Douglas E. Williams, ed., *Reconfigurations: Canadian Citizenship and Constitutional Change* (Toronto: McClelland and Stewart, 1995), 111. I am greatly indebted to Professor Cairns for having made available to me an earlier unpublished version of this essay.

2 See Walter H. Bennett, *American Theories of Federalism* (Alabama Press, 1964), esp. 128–51. Note also the recent outpouring of literature on 'Southern' history. See Susan Bishay, 'Conformist Federalism', *Telos* 95 (Spring 1993), 77–108. She discusses some of the current literature on Calhoun and states' rights, in the context of an overall attack on the views of federalism held by, amongst others, Daniel J. Elazar and Samuel Beer. She thinks that they conflate federalism with pluralism.

3 Frank Kermode, 'The Old New Age', *The New York Review of Books* (24 March 1994), 49.

4 William H. Riker, *Liberalism Against Populism* (Prospect Heights: Waveland Press, 1982), 215. There is an enormous literature on slavery and the civil war, still growing apace, and my intent is to be illustrative only. Generalizations about America and slavery are risky because of the complexity of public and private actions: as early as 1782 Virginia allowed manumission, and over the next eight years, 10,000 slaves were voluntarily freed.

5 Edmund S. Morgan, *The Birth of the Republic, 1763–89,* 3rd edn (Chicago: University of Chicago Press, 1992), 97.

6 See David Brion Davis's review of Stanley Elkins and Eric McKitrick, *The Age of Federalism* (Oxford: Oxford University Press, 1993), 'The Triumph of the Country', *The New York Review of Books* (12 May 1994), 26. For a comparative discussion of 'court' versus 'country' see Gordon T. Stewart, *The Origins of Canadian Politics* (Vancouver: University of British Columbia Press, 1986).

7 Davis, 'The Triumph of the Country', 26.

8 Ibid., 28.

9 Riker, *Liberalism Against Populism*, 214. He comments that the *status quo* 'persisted for a generation without significant challenge, and during that time slavery was not a salient political issue. Then the political losers raised it, presumably as a way to generate disequilibrium from which they might improve their position. . . .'

10 Ibid., 216.

11 See Eric L. McKitrick, 'A Hero of Antislavery', *The New York Review of Books* (14 November 1966), 46.

12 Ibid., 49.

13 See, for example, the concluding chapter of Michael Burgess's *The British Tradition of Federalism* (London: Leicester University Press, 1995).

14 David Cameron, *The Social Thought of Rousseau and Burke: A Comparative Study* (London: Weidenfeld and Nicholson, 1973), 63.

15 I am mindful of Oakeshott's scathing comment that the relationship between political science and history is often corrupting to the latter: '"History" appears, not as a mode of explanation but merely as some conclusions . . . believed to account for the present structure . . . [it] is patronizingly admitted as long as it remains in the background.' See 'The Study of Politics in a University' in *Rationalism in Politics and Other Essays* (New York: Barnes and Noble, 1974), 330. My only defence lies, perhaps, in the historians used and the overall clarity of the theme.

16 This comment is attached as a footnote to 'A Dangerous Deed: The Constitution Act, 1982' in *And No-One Cheered: Federalism, Democracy and the Constitution Act*, eds Keith G. Banting and Richard Simeon (Toronto: Methuen, 1983), 94. For an extensive review of the Quebec position on the division of powers question from 1900 until 1976, see *Les positions traditionnelles du Québec sur les partages des pouvoirs 1900–1976* (Quebec: Secrétariat aux affaires intergouvernementales canadiennes, document de travail, 1991). A very useful collection and summary, *Les positions traditionnelles du Québec en matière constitutionnelle 1936–1990*, is also produced by the Secrétariat. This document is cited hereafter as *Matière Constitutionnelle*. (An English version of this document is also available.)

17 David Milne, 'Exposed to the Glare: Constitutional Camouflage and the Fate of Canada's Confederation' in F. Leslie Seidle, ed., *Seeking a New Canadian Partnership: Asymmetrical and Confederal Options* (Ottawa: Institute for Research on Public Policy, 1994), 109.

18 Donald V. Smiley, *Canada in Question: Federalism in the Eighties* (Toronto: McGraw-Hill Ryerson, 1980). For a recent discussion of some of the political cul-

ture questions see Ian Stewart, 'Putting Humpty Dumpty Together: The Study of Canadian Political Culture' in *Canadian Politics: An introduction to the discipline*, eds Alain-G. Gagnon and James P. Bickerton (Peterborough: Broadview Press, 1990).

19 Smiley, *Canada in Question*, 284.

20 Guy Laforest does develop a Lockean argument against the settlement of 1982. See *Trudeau et la fin d'un rêve canadien* (Montreal: Septentrion, 1992), ch. 2.

21 At least until the appearance of the New Deal and Roosevelt's reforms.

22 A key factor has been our inability to come to terms with Quebec in part *because* of Keynesianism. There are a number of ironies in the present situation: Keynesianism may still be alive in Quebec at a time when it is under savage attack in the rest of Canada.

23 Sir Wilfrid Laurier represents a clear example of this type of admiration, notwithstanding his suspicions of Imperial foreign policy.

24 Jeremy Webber makes a similar point about the 'tendency towards autonomy in our political debates' because of the versions that occur in two different public languages. See *Reimagining Canada. Language, Culture, Community, and the Canadian Constitution* (Montreal and Kingston: McGill-Queen's University Press, 1994), 204–5.

25 Frank Underhill, *In Search of Canadian Liberalism* (Toronto: Macmillan of Canada, 1960), 118.

26 Smiley, *Canada in Question*, 291.

27 See John F. Conway, *Debts to Pay: English Canada and Quebec from the Conquest to the Referendum* (Toronto: James Lorimer and Company, 1992).

28 Arend Lijphart, *The Politics of Accommodation: Pluralism and Democracy in the Netherlands* (Berkeley: University of California Press, 1968); *Democracy in Plural Societies: A Comparative Exploration* (New Haven: Yale University Press, 1977); *Democracies: Patterns of Majoritarian and Consensus Government in Twenty-One Countries* (New Haven: Yale University Press, 1984).

29 R. Kent Weaver, 'Political Institutions and Canada's Constitutional Crisis' in *The Collapse of Canada?* ed. R. Kent Weaver (Washington: The Brookings Institution, 1992), 12.

30 Ibid. Weaver provides a brief review of the pros and cons of consociationalism.

31 See J.T. Stevenson's essay 'Consociationalist Models For Canada' in *Philosophers Look at Canadian Confederation,* ed. Stanley G. French (Montreal: The Canadian Philosophical Association, 1979), 245–53. He notes that 'élite accommodation is taken as a hallmark of consociationalism' and provides a critique of the model's applicability to Canada, whilst noting, however, that Canada does have many consociational characteristics.

32 Kenneth McRoberts, in Seidle, ed., *Seeking a New Canadian Partnership*, 154.

33 Ronald Wagenberg et al., 'Federal Societies and the founding of federal states: an examination of the origins of Canadian Confederation' in *Canadian Federalism: Past, Present and Future*, ed. Michael Burgess (Leicester: Leicester University Press, 1990). Note the essays by S.J.R. Noel and Arend Lijphart in *Consociational*

Democracy: Political Accommodation in Segmented Societies, ed. Kenneth D. McRae (Toronto: McClelland and Stewart, 1974). Note also Robert Presthus, *Élite Accommodation in Canada* (Toronto: Macmillan of Canada, 1973).

34 There was also a sense of superiority. As late as 1943 Lester Pearson commented that Congress had 'a level of intelligence somewhat below that of the Upper House in Haiti'! Quoted in Robert Bothwell's *Canada and the United States: The Politics of Partnership* (Toronto: University of Toronto Press, 1992), 164. Bothwell adds that 'Pearson's comment is a classic example of Canadian anti-Americanism intended for domestic and private consumption only.' For an extensive discussion of the ways in which the Crown has empowered governments, see David E. Smith, *The Invisible Crown* (Toronto: University of Toronto Press, 1995).

35 Rupert Taylor, 'South Africa: Consociation or Democracy', *Telos* 85 (Fall 1993), 17–32 at 26.

36 For a still useful summary and critique of consociationalism and its applicability to Canada see Herman Bakvis, *Federalism and the Organization of Political Life: Canada in Comparative Perspective* (Kingston: Institute of Intergovernmental Relations, 1981).

37 Ibid., 83–5.

38 See his short essay 'Self-Determination Versus Pre-Determination of Ethnic Minorities in Power-Sharing Systems,' in *Language and the State: The Law and Politics of Identity*, ed. David Schneiderman (Cowansville: Yvon Blais Inc., 1989), 153. For a discussion of the politics of consociationalism in ethnic organizations, see Henry F. Srebrnik, 'Multiculturalism and the Politics of Ethnicity: Jews and the Charlottetown Accord' in Howard Adelman and John H. Simpson, eds, *Multiculturalism, Jews and Identities in Canada* (Jerusalem: The Magnes Press, 1996).

39 See S.J.R. Noel's conclusions in 'Canadian Responses to Ethnic Conflict: Consociationalism, Federalism and Control' in John McGarry and Brendan O'Leary, eds, *The Politics of Ethnic Conflict Regulation: Case Studies of Protracted Ethnic Conflicts* (New York: Routledge, 1993). Noel argues that it has 'rarely if ever' been a first choice; it has been seen as a poor second choice or the 'default option'.

40 Kenneth McRoberts, *Quebec: Social Change and Political Crisis*, 3rd edn (Toronto: McClelland and Stewart, 1993), 35.

41 This emphasis may even have affected our approach to international relations. Thomas Hockin argues that the ineffectuality of Canadian action in international affairs was less a result of our middle power status than of 'our *domestic* habits of mind, our Canadian political style . . . the diversity of the federal systems components may compel its political leaders to avoid ultimate questions of purpose in order to maintain a minimal common denominator of consensus.' Thomas Hockin, 'Federalist Style in International Politics' in *An Independent Foreign Policy for Canada*, ed. Stephen Clarkson (Toronto: McClelland and Stewart, 1968), 19–20.

42 This is the thesis of Alan C. Cairns's essay 'The Constitutional World We Have Lost', *Configurations*, 97–118.

43 This included allowing reform candidates from Lower Canada to run in Upper Canada constituencies, and vice versa.

44 Gordon T. Stewart, 'Political Patronage Under Macdonald and Laurier 1878–1911' in *Canadian Political Party Systems*, ed. R.K. Carty (Peterborough: Broadview Press, 1992), 60. For an overview of the whole patronage question, commencing in the years before Confederation, see Stewart's *The Origins of Canadian Politics*.

45 See also Reg Whitaker, 'Between Patronage and Bureaucracy: Democratic Politics in Transition' in *A Sovereign Idea: Essays on Canada as a Democratic Community*, ed. Reg Whitaker (Montreal and Kingston: McGill-Queen's University Press, 1992). Whitaker notes that patronage penetrated much farther down into society than it does now.

46 Stewart, 'Political Patronage Under Macdonald and Laurier 1878–1911' in *Canadian Political Party Systems*, 65.

47 Ibid.

48 See David E. Smith, 'Party Government, Representation and National Integration in Canada' in *Party Government and Regional Representation in Canada*, ed. Peter Aucoin, Research Studies of the Royal Commission on the Economic Union and Development Prospects for Canada (Toronto: University of Toronto Press, 1985), vol. 36.

49 Stewart, 'Political Patronage under Macdonald and Laurier', 65.

50 Garth Stevenson, 'Intrastate Federalism in Nineteenth Century Canada', paper presented at the Annual Meeting of the Canadian Political Science Association (Charlottetown, 1992), 15.

51 Ibid.

52 Cairns, 'The Constitutional World We Have Lost', 25.

53 Barbara Robertson, *Sir Wilfrid Laurier: The Great Conciliator* (Kingston: The Quarry Press, 1991).

54 Ibid., 120.

55 See Réal Bélanger, *Wilfrid Laurier: quand la politique devient passion* (Quebec: l'Université Laval, 1986), 57–8.

56 Réal Bélanger in Robert Bothwell, ed., *Canada and Quebec: One Country Two Histories* (Vancouver: University of British Columbia Press, 1995), 56.

57 Bothwell, *Canada and Quebec*, 63.

58 The idea that the country has always been run by either an English-Canadian Prime Minister with a French-Canadian Lieutenant, or vice versa, must be treated with a great deal of caution. See John English, 'The "French Lieutenant" in Ottawa' in *National Politics and Community in Canada*, eds R.K. Carty and W. Peter Ward (Vancouver: University of British Columbia Press, 1986), 112–50. He argues that the only successful 'lieutenants' have been Cartier and Ernest Lapointe.

59 Ralph Heintzman notes that the customary view of Quebec in the decades after Confederation has been to see it as 'sunk in a dark fog of religious controversy, ultramontane reaction, theocratic obscurantism, and a utopian anti-industrial, anti-urban, anti-modern, back to the land movement'. He and other historians now chal-

lenge these assumptions, emphasizing in particular the importance of 'railway politics'. See 'Political Space and Economic Space: Quebec and the Empire of the St Lawrence', *Journal of Canadian Studies* 29, 2 (Summer 1994), 19–63.

60 Fernand Dumont, *Genèse de la Société Québécoise* (Montreal: Boréal, 1993), 332. Léon Dion argues that 'modern Quebec dates from at least as long ago as 1920. It was not until the 1950s and especially the 1960s that this crucial change began to be fully recognized.' See 'The Mystery of Quebec', *Daedalus* 117, 4 (Fall 1988), 283–318 at 297. '[T]his society has never ceased to be subject to change'.

61 Dumont, *Genèse de la Société Québécoise*, 336. 'Why so long a hibernation?'

62 David E. Smith, 'Perennial alienation: the prairie west in the Canadian federation' in *Canadian Federalism*, ed. Michael Burgess, 92. Nelson Wiseman makes the same point. See 'In Search of Manitoba's Constitutional Position, 1950–1990', *Journal of Canadian Studies* 29, 3 (Fall 1994). Until the 1980s there was no Department of Intergovernmental Affairs, and such discussion as there was focused on fiscal issues.

63 Even if we accept the importance of secular questions, and the effects of the enormous debts incurred in the building of the railways, the power of the church remains a crucial political factor.

64 C. Cairns, 'The Constitutional World We have Lost', *Configurations*, 111. Also note David R. Cameron's comment that 'the effort to secure and maintain a settlement between French and English in Canada depended for more than a century on the existence of what might be called mutually compatible solitudes.' This was because the 'character and values' of the two societies were so different that the scope for direct conflict and competition was diminished. See 'Lord Durham Then and Now', *Journal of Canadian Studies* 25, 1 (1990), 5–23 at 11.

65 This does not mean that the constitution was not a topic in the background, ever-present and omnipresent in some ways, but not on the formal political agenda in another. In the 1930s, Lionel Groulx had spoken of 'notre état français, nous l'aurons'. Between 1939 (October) and March 1940 Richard Arès wrote a series of articles on the federal practice of 1864–7, and his work still forms an important part of the ongoing compact theory debates. See, in particular, *Dossier sur le Pacte Fédératif de 1867. La Confédération: pacte ou loi?* (Les éditions Bellarmin, 1967).

66 Katherine O'Sullivan See, *First World Nationalisms: Class and Ethnic Politics in Northern Ireland and Quebec* (Chicago: University of Chicago Press, 1986), 8.

67 Ibid., 10.

68 Ibid., 15.

69 See David Milne, *Tug of War: Ottawa and the Provinces Under Trudeau and Mulroney* (Toronto: James Lorimer, 1986), 21.

70 Ralph Heintzman, 'The Political Culture of Quebec, 1840–1960', *Canadian Journal of Political Science* 16, 1 (March 1983), 3–60. See 50, footnote 156, for a reference to this issue.

71 Note Léon Dion's view that 'In essence, the change that most radically altered the face of Quebec was cultural.' See 'The Mystery of Quebec', 299. World War II in Dion's view is also a watershed, changing profoundly, as it did, the ways in which people lived and worked.

72 Ralph Heintzman, 'The Political Culture of Quebec, 1840–1960'.

73 Ibid., 47.

74 Ibid., 41.

75 Ibid., 37.

76 See Dumont, *Genèse de la Société Québécoise*, 217–20, for a discussion of patronage. 'The extent of patronage is immense. . . . Politicians are everywhere, the State nowhere to be seen.'

77 Ronald Rudin has argued that Heintzman's argument 'makes sense as far as it goes' but 'hardly warrants Heintzman's categorical conclusion that there was no experience of any "atypical cultural or ideological inhibition which would distinguish it from other societies"' for there was—the Catholic church. See 'Revisionism and the Search for a Normal Society: A Critique of Recent Quebec Historical Writing', *Canadian Historical Review* 43, 1 (1992), 30–61 at 53.

78 Heintzman, 'The Political Culture of Quebec, 1840–1960', 36.

79 Dumont also makes this point. See *Genèse de la Société Québécoise*, ch. 3 ('L'aménagement de la survivance').

80 José Woehrling, 'La Constitution canadienne et l'évolution des rapports entre le Québec et le Canada anglais, de 1867 à nos jours', *Points of View* 4 (1993). As have many others. For a useful summary see François Rocher, ed., *Bilan québécois du fédéralisme canadien* (Montreal: VLB éditeur, 1992). Rocher's essay 'Le Québec et la Constitution: une valse à mille temps' in this volume provides an excellent starting point. Also in this volume is a new analysis of francophones in Ottawa that suggests that 'equality' is far from achieved. See Michel Sarra-Bournet, 'French Power, Québec Power: La place des francophones québécois à Ottawa', 199–225.

81 Woehrling, 'La Constitution canadienne et l'évolution des rapports', 11.

82 Ibid., 16–17. 'The goal of Quebec's governments in this period was not to expand their powers, or even to use them to the fullest extent, but simply to preserve them for any diminishment.'

83 This ambivalence is reflected as late as 1956 in the Tremblay Report. See David Kwavnick, ed., *The Tremblay Report: Report of the Royal Commission of Inquiry on Constitutional Problems* (Toronto: McClelland and Stewart, 1973), 56: 'It must, however, be admitted that the Province of Quebec's attachment to its autonomy risks putting it into contradiction, if not with itself, at least with that part of French-Canada which historical hazards have dispersed throughout the country.'

84 Silver may overstate this argument and underestimate the support of French-Canadian élites for the expansion of French rights. This is Heintzman's view. See 'Political Space and Economic Space', footnote 30.

85 Robertson, *Sir Wilfrid Laurier*, 68.

86 Jean H. Guay and François Rocher also select these events, although they stress the referendum as the key factor. See 'De la difficile reconnaisance de la spécificité québécoise' in *Bilan québécois du fédéralisme canadien*, ed. François Rocher, 58–78.

87 See J.L. Granatstein, 'The "Hard" Obligations of Citizenship: The Second World War in Canada' in *Belonging: The Meaning and the Future of Canadian Citizenship*, ed. William Kaplan (Montreal and Kingston: McGill-Queen's University Press, 1994).

88 Mason Wade, *The French Canadians: 1911–1967* (Toronto: Macmillan, 1986), vol. 2, 713.

89 Ibid., 714.

90 Papineau is the central hero of Gwyn's book *Tapestry of War: A Private View of Canadians in the Great War* (Toronto: HarperCollins, 1992). Chapter 18 details the exchange of views. Gwyn relies upon Wade for Bourassa's words, but utilizes in addition the private papers of Talbot Papineau, especially his letters.

91 See Susan Mann Trofimenkoff, *The Dream of a Nation: A Social and Intellectual History of Quebec* (Toronto: Macmillan, 1982), 201–17.

92 Out of a population of almost eight million, approximately half a million men volunteered. Manitoba had the highest rate of enlistment and 'contributed anywhere from 40% to 61% of its eligible men . . . an astonishingly high level'. Canadian voluntary enlistment overall was 31.4%. See C.A. Sharpe, 'Enlistment in the Canadian Expeditionary Force 1914–1918: A Regional Analysis', *Journal of Canadian Studies* 16, 4 (Winter 1983–4), 15–29.

93 See Mason Wade, *The French Canadians: 1911–1967*, ch. xii.

94 A comprehensive overview of the changing nature of the constitutional debate and the role and work of the various federal and Quebec commissions of inquiry is provided in Alain-G. Gagnon and Daniel Latouche (avec la collaboration de Guy Falardeau), *Allaire, Bélanger, Campeau et les autres: Les Québécois s'interrogent sur leur avenir* (Montreal: Éditions Québec, 1991). This work provides a Quebec perspective on dualism and its disappearance as a key constitutional concept. A very useful review of the predecessors of both the 'distinct society' clause in Meech and the 'Canada clause' in the Charlottetown Accord is provided in F.L. Morton's essay 'Judicial Politics Canadian Style' in *Constitutional Predicament: Canada After the Referendum of 1992*, ed. Curtis Cook (Montreal and Kingston: McGill-Queen's University Press, 1994). Morton makes the important point that prior to Meech such preambles were intended as guides to '*political* development of the constitution, *not judicial* development' (134).

95 And culture was based, of course, upon language, language which was itself held to be a representation of a collective mental structure, and the particularity of a culture. See Léon Dion, 'The Mystery of Quebec', 289.

96 Brief submitted by the Government of Quebec to the Royal Commission on Dominion-Provincial Relations (1938). See *Matière Constitutionnelle*, 3. 'It is in the nature of constitutional conventions that the federative pact can be neither amended nor modified without the assent of all the parties, that is, all the provinces.'

97 Ibid.

98 See Claude Morin, *Le Combat québécois* (Montreal: Boréal, 1973), 68.

99 Declaration by Duplessis, Federal-Provincial Conference, 1946. See *Matière Constitutionnelle*, 6–7. '. . . cannot and must not be changed without the consent of the four original provinces.'

100 These are all points made at various conferences and in various briefs. The last quotation is taken from Duplessis's opening declaration at the federal-provincial conference of 1946. We had moved from three (races) plus one to two only!

101 Quebec: Éditeur officiel, 1956.

102 Ottawa: The King's Printer, 1951.

103 Louis Balthazar, 'The Liberal Idea of the Canadian Nation-State', paper presented at the Biennial Conference of the Association for Canadian Studies in the United States (Seattle, 1995). I wish to thank Professor Balthazar for sending me a copy of his paper.

104 David Kwavnick, ed., *The Tremblay Report: Report of the Royal Commission of Inquiry on Constitutional Problems* (Toronto: McClelland and Stewart, 1973), viii.

105 Ibid., x.

106 Ibid., 55. See also 14.

107 Ibid., 87.

108 Ibid., 95. Interestingly, such statements now reappear as tenets of the new variant of neo-conservatism prevalent in the West.

109 Ibid., 69.

110 Ibid., 84.

111 Ibid., 51. According to provincial rights theorists, including the influential work of Quebec Justice Thomas J.J. Loranger, the rights of individuals and the protection of communities were not in opposition, but built upon each other. Alain-G. Gagnon argues that Loranger's influence is to be seen in the Commission's report and in many other documents. According to the Loranger thesis, provincial powers are 'the residue of the former colonial powers', and 'the political arrangements that preceded Confederation remain relevant to the settlement of ongoing differences.' Remain relevant, that is, to Quebec (and to aboriginal peoples). See Alain-G. Gagnon, 'Quebec: Variations on a Theme,' in *Canadian Politics,* eds Alain-G. Gagnon and James P. Bickerton, 452–4.

112 David Kwavnick, ed., *The Tremblay Report*, 55. The Report also noted that 'French-Canadian culture differs from American culture in its religious inspirations, its language and its great social and legal traditions' (47).

113 Ibid., 118. In many ways 1949 may have been the high-water mark of federal power.

114 Ibid., 173.

115 Ibid., 166.

116 Ibid., 214.

117 This is noted by Edwin R. Black, who comments that 'apart from a few isolated comments, the English language press devoted little attention to the most scholarly exposition of dualism, that of the *Tremblay Report.*' See *Divided Loyalties* (Montreal and Kingston: McGill-Queen's University Press, 1975), 196.

118 Alain-G. Gagnon, 'Variations on a Theme', 456. It was followed by the Quebec Liberal Party's document, 'Québec, une société distincte'. For a full discussion of the doctrine itself, and its links to the Tremblay Commission, and to the other key reports, see Gagnon and Latouche, *Allaire, Bélanger, Campeau et les autres*, 71–87.

119 Jean Lesage, speech to the Empire Club, Toronto, 1964, in *Matière Constitutionnelle*, 13. '. . . a distinctive status recognizing both the particular features of its people and the expanded role it envisions for its government'. The key term 'statut particulier' is difficult to translate. 'Particulier' could be translated as 'specific', or 'distinctive'. Translations thus become politicized as these words (and there are others that could be used) take on different connotations in English. In this case 'distinctive' has been chosen rather than 'special' or 'specific'.

120 Jean Lesage, speech to the Vancouver Club, 1965, in *Matière Constitutionnelle*.

121 Woehrling, 'La Constitution canadienne et l'évolution des rapports', 26. 'In constitutional affairs, the "Quiet Revolution" took Quebec from the passive stance of defending existing powers to the active—even aggressive—stance of claiming new powers.'

122 Ibid. '. . . la création d'un statut particulier pour le Québec.'

123 See Stéphane Dion, 'Le Fédéralisme Fortement Asymétrique: Improbable et Indésirable' in F. Leslie Seidle, ed., *Seeking a New Canadian Partnership*, 133–52. Dion discusses the considerable difficulties facing those who argue for a stronger dose of asymmetry.

124 Woehrling, 'La Constitution canadienne', 27.

125 Ibid., 28.

126 Opening speech by Jean Lesage, Federal-Provincial Conference, 1963. 'Quebec defends the principle of autonomy for the provinces not simply because it is a matter of principle but much more because for Quebeckers autonomy is the concrete precondition not for survival, which is henceforth assured, but for affirmation as a people.' In December, 1965, Jean Lesage confided to André Patry that he was 'absolutely resolved to obtain for Quebec special status inside the Canadian federation', and when Patry asked what this meant specifically, he was told it comprised, notably: 'the nomination by Quebec of its lieutenant-governor, the choice by Quebeckers of their senators, the creation of a constitutional court, the exercise of a certain individual competence'. . . . See André Patry, 'Temoignage' in Robert Comeau, ed., *Jean Lesage et l'éveil d'une nation* (Sillery: Université du Québec, 1989), 137–9.

127 See Daniel Johnson, *Égalité ou indépendance, 25 ans plus tard* (Montreal: VLB éditeur, 1990), esp. part 3.

128 Opening speech by Daniel Johnson, Federal-Provincial Conference, Ottawa, February, 1968.

129 For a review of the events of this period see the introductory essay 'Le Québec et la Constitution: une valse à mille temps' in *Bilan québécois du fédéralisme canadien*, ed. François Rocher.

130 The Quebec government accepted the idea of a federal Charter of Rights but announced the intention to also create one of its own. The point was made that if there were to be a declaration of rights used by the 'highest' court, then the creation of a special, new, 'genuine constitutional court' should be examined.

131 Opening declaration by Jean-Jacques Bertrand, Constitutional Conference, Ottawa, February, 1969.

132 Ibid.

133 It is not necessary to explore all the proposals made over the years: the Victoria formula provides a sufficiently illustrative example in itself.

134 See Edwin R. Black, *Divided Loyalties,* 205–7.

135 Ibid.

136 The first photograph in Donald Johnston, ed., *Pierre Trudeau Speaks Out on Meech Lake* (Toronto: General Paperbacks, 1990) is of Stanfield who, it is noted, 'endorsed the concept of "two nations"'. That he did so with great reservation and with specific provisos is not mentioned.

137 Cairns, 'The Constitutional World We Have Lost', 112.

138 Black, *Divided Loyalties,* 189–92.

139 See Serge Denis, *Le Long Malentendu: Le Québec vu par les intellectuels progressistes au Canada anglais 1970–1991* (Montreal: Boréal, 1992). Denis discusses the dilemmas thus created for anglophone scholars.

140 See Kenneth McRoberts, *English Canada and Quebec: Avoiding the Issue* (York University: Robarts Centre for Constitutional Studies, 1991), 8.

141 Gordon Robertson interview.

142 André Laurendeau, *The Diary of André Laurendeau* (written during the Royal Commission on Bilingualism and Biculturalism 1964–7), ed. Patricia Smart (Toronto: James Lorimer and Co, 1991), 19.

143 See Donald J. Horton, *André Laurendeau: French Canadian Nationalist* (Toronto: Oxford University Press, 1992).

144 Patricia Smart, introduction to *The Diary of André Laurendeau,* 7. It may be neither, now that we have had the Report of the Royal Commission on Reproductive Technology (certainly controversial), and the Report of the Royal Commission on Aboriginal Peoples (the most expensive).

145 See Michael Oliver, *The Passionate Debate: The Social and Political Ideas of Quebec Nationalism 1920–1945* (Montreal: Véhicule Press, 1991); Michael Oliver, 'Laurendeau et Trudeau: leurs opinions sur le Canada' in *L'engagement intellectuel* (Sainte-Foy: Les Presses de l'Université Laval, 1991); Michael Oliver, 'The Impact of the Royal Commission on Bilingualism and Biculturalism on Constitutional Thought and Practice in Canada', *International Journal of Canadian Studies* 7–8 (Spring-Fall 1993), 315–32. Michael Oliver was the Research Director for the Commission. Laurendeau had wanted the first volume to be a synthesis of the overall report. Others argued for a series of special studies with the final, broad view appearing last. By the time it appeared Laurendeau was dead, killed by an aneurism (probably exacerbated by overwork) at the age of 54. His broad vision never came to pass. (He was able to insert into the first report the so-called 'blue pages' which defined the overall structural problems for the French majority in Quebec.) However, both the Pepin-Robarts Report and the *Livre beige* forcefully echoed the need to treat Quebec as a distinct society, just as Laurendeau had done.

146 Patricia Smart, introduction to *The Diary of André Laurendeau*, 7. See also the discussion of Trudeau's opposition to this whole line of Laurendeau's reasoning in Alain-G. Gagnon and Daniel Latouche, *Allaire, Bélanger, Campeau et les autres*, 60–3.

147 Oliver, 'The Impact of the Royal Commission on Bilingualism and Biculturalism on Constitutional Thought and Practice in Canada', 316.

148 Ibid., 317.

149 Ibid., 320.

150 Ibid., 321–2.

151 Laurendeau, *The Diary of André Laurendeau*, ed. Patricia Smart, 115.

152 Laurendeau, in words that would be echoed by his successors on Pepin-Robarts and Spicer, lamented the ignorance he found: 'there is little understanding of cultural nationalism, and attempts to discuss it always fall back into talk about multiculturalism. . . .' See *The Diary of André Laurendeau*, 116. Opinions on Quebec were 'almost all of them cursory and ill-informed'. In all of anglo-Canadian society 'there is an astonishing lack of self-criticism' and 'there is a fatigue which comes from being Canadian.' See 46–9.

153 Laurendeau was sick at heart even when after four years of effort the first volume on 'The Official Languages' was presented to parliament. It represented gains for French speakers across Canada, but when asked why he looked so depressed as they went to the debate, Laurendeau said to a colleague 'But Neil, it does nothing for Quebec.' See Patricia Smart, introduction to *The Diary of André Laurendeau*, 8.

154 Richard Heyman, 'A Political Economy of Minority Group Knowledge Demands', *Compare* 8, 1 (1978), 3–13 at 4.

155 Ibid., 5.

156 Ibid., 6.

157 Ibid., 10.

158 Ibid.

159 Ibid., 11.

160 Oliver, 'The Impact of the Royal Commission on Bilingualism and Biculturalism on Constitutional Thought and Practice in Canada', 323. See also Webber, *Reimagining Canada*, 62–6.

161 See Guy Laforest, *Trudeau et la fin d'un rêve canadien*, ch. iii.

162 See Cairns, 'The Constitutional World We Have Lost', 102.

163 Declaration by Robert Bourassa, Standing Commission on the Constitution, Victoria Conference, May 1971, in *Matière Constitutionnelle*, 34. '[T]he problem of a precise definition of Quebec society within the Canadian federation as a whole remains fundamental for Quebec.'

164 Speech by Claude Castonguay, Minister of Social Affairs, January 1971, in *Matière Constitutionnelle*, 35. '. . . that did not recognize clearly and concretely the fact that Québécois constitute a different group and form a distinct society, which fervently wishes to maintain its social and cultural identity, would be unacceptable.'

165 William S. Livingston, *Federalism and Constitutional Change* (Oxford: Clarendon Press, 1956); Paul Gérin-Lajoie, *Constitutional Amendment in Canada* (Toronto: University of Toronto Press, 1950). Gérin-Lajoie was the Minister of Education for the province of Quebec.

166 Peter H. Russell, *Constitutional Odyssey: Can Canadians Become a Sovereign People?* (Toronto: University of Toronto Press, 1992).

167 Ibid., 87. The reasons for Quebec's refusal are discussed, briefly, in Chapter Six and below (see note 174).

168 Christopher Armstrong, 'Ceremonial Politics: Federal Provincial Meetings Before the Second World War' in *National Politics and Community in Canada*, eds R. Kenneth Carty and W. Peter Ward, 112–50 at 123.

169 Ibid., 124. The three Maritime provinces were also opposed.

170 Ibid.

171 See Christopher Armstrong, 'Provincial Rights and Dominion-Provincial Relations' in J.M. Bumsted, ed., *Interpreting Canada's Past* (vol. 2) 2nd edn (Toronto: Oxford University Press, 1993), 43–63.

172 See *The Report of the Special Joint Committee of the Senate and the House of Commons on the Process for Amending the Constitution of Canada* (Ottawa, 20 June 1991). The Committee explicitly endorsed a regionally based amending formula of the Victoria type, to replace sections 38, 42, and 41 of the current formula. See 26. The predecessor to the Victoria Charter had been the Fulton-Favreau formula, debated between 1960 and 1966. In 1966, Lesage declared it dead and buried. For a chronology of these events see Jacques-Yvan Morin, 'Jean Lesage et le rapatriement de la constitution,' in Robert Comeau, ed., *Jean Lesage et l'éveil d'une nation*, 116–36.

173 It should be noted that even under the later 1982 formula they are not, for most amendments would require seven out of ten provinces containing 50% of the population, giving a *de facto* advantage to Ontario, and allowing an amendment to pass even if it were opposed by BC, Alberta, and Saskatchewan or Manitoba. In this sense the 1982 arrangements weaken the influence of the West and the Maritimes and offer less power than Victoria, a point Westerners often seem to miss.

174 Rocher, ed., *Bilan québécois du fédéralisme canadien*, 267. Claude Ryan agrees with this view. In his opinion, Quebec was first and foremost seeking a new distribution of powers, and needed a concrete sign that there was going to be change in this area. The failures of the other governments to respond to the requests for change in the social jurisdictional areas were crucial. Overall, Ottawa's goals at Victoria were not, in Ryan's opinion, those of the Quebec government. Quebec's aim was a redefinition of its constitutional status and an improved distribution of powers (private correspondence). Thus Quebec, in his opinion, did not miss the constitutional train in 1971. See also Jeremy Webber's discussion of Quebec's twin-track approach in *Reimagining Canada*, 92–106.

175 For these and other details see Nelson Wiseman, 'In Search of Manitoba's Constitutional Position, 1950–1990', *Journal of Canadian Studies*.

176 Gordon Robertson interview.

177 Charles Taylor, 'Why Do Nations Have to Become States?' in *Philosophers Look At Confederation*, ed. Stanley G. French, 32.

178 Edmund Burke, *A Letter to the Sheriffs of Bristol* in *Edmund Burke on Government, Politics and Society*, ed. B.W. Hill (New York: International Publications Service, 1976), 189.

179 See Garth Stevenson, 'Intrastate Federalism in Nineteenth Century Canada', 1. Note also that this is the key to Preston King's definition. See his *Federalism and Federation* (Baltimore: Johns Hopkins Press, 1982).

180 See André Blais and Richard Nadeau, 'To Be or Not To Be Sovereigntist? Quebeckers' Perennial Dilemma', *Canadian Public Policy* 18, 1 (1992), 89–103.

181 Philip Resnick, *Thinking English Canada* (Toronto: Stoddart, 1994), 18.

5

Unsettlement

The question is not whether their spirit deserves praise or blame, but— what in the name of God, shall we do with it?[1]

The past is, as we know, a foreign country, and when discussing it we have to come to terms with its essential strangeness.[2] This is true not only of the investigation of times long past, as is the case with early medieval Europe. It applies even to recent events. Political priorities and fashions change. Not long ago resource rents and a Bundesrat type senate were the topics of the year. Now they have been replaced by the furore over individual *versus* collective rights and by concerns about what constitutes 'deep' diversity, and how it is to be recognized and treated.[3] The constitutional battles of the late 1980s over daycare, a social charter, or the supposed threats to gender equality in Quebec posed by the Meech Lake Accord will probably seem, in retrospect, even more arcane and parochial than previous concerns.[4] For a dramatic illustration of how fast our fashions change our constitutional clothes, we should remember rabid provincial opposition in 1978 to all previous federal proposals to have a national referendum as part of the process of ratification of formal constitutional change, even if such a referendum were regionalized. A little more than a decade later, the western provinces demanded and put in place referendum legislation of their own, forcing the federal government's hand on the issue.[5]

Constitutions, and constitutional arrangements, are not supposed to be deeply affected by the ebb and flow of issues and what one might call epiphenomena, as concerns and ideological positions (and parties) alter. However, if one is forced into major constitutional change at a particular time, then one is always open to the charge that what is written is a tract for the times. Thus it was that the *Unity Task Force Report* released on January 25, 1979 was immediately seen as vulnerable on this account, as, in their turn, were the Constitution Act (1982), the Meech Lake Accord (1990), and the Charlottetown Accord (1992). Pandering to current tastes is a serious constitutional charge, and the Pepin-Robarts Report may well have been guilty of it. Yet even if this charge turns out to have some—or a good deal—of substance, and even though the Report can be seen as having 'failed', for it was immediately put into cold storage, the case will be made that it is still well worth revisiting.

By 1979 the strategies for the avoidance of constitutional abeyances and our deeper problems seemed to have run their course. There began to be a discernible difference in negotiations. Rather than being tactical, with strategies of postponement from one round to the next, the differences over underlying principles became apparent. It was not merely that formal constitutional change is never easy, and that this in itself makes it likely that it is in the constitutional arena that abeyances will be found. Content and symbolism were linked to process, and it is not really surprising that attempts at constitutional change which had focused on the amending problem had all been thwarted, most notably at Victoria in 1971.[6] Even so, in 1979 the old constitutional mechanisms for change were still the only game in town, and the constitutional shopping list had not yet grown to its later proportions. Not all groups had decided that their rights had to be protected by entrenchment and that judges had to be given very specific guidelines, even instructions, to follow. Pepin-Robarts was thus a report at a nodal point, dealing with the old, grappling with the new, where the rules for change were still unclear, and with an unprecedented referendum on sovereignty-association looming.

Although timing may have made its appearance seem pivotal, has it not now been dissected and discussed and cast on the rubbish heap of constitutional history? What appeal can it possibly have after all we have been through since? A number of answers can be suggested:

(1) The Report represented a head-on collision with the views of Pierre Trudeau, for it embodied a different philosophy of federalism. It was a clash between his Lockean liberalism, and a collectivist/communitarian approach with different roots.[7] Bill C-60 and Canadian nationalism represented Trudeau's agenda, Pepin-Robarts and dualism did not.
(2) The Report was the work of individuals who really did represent our best and brightest, and their failure illustrates the difficulties of the task. Many of those involved with the Report have, however, continued to play important constitutional roles and the ongoing influence of the Report may have been important.
(3) The Report marked the end of philosophical federalism and abeyance avoidance, and attempted to provide an overarching new framework for the Canadian state, within which Quebec would have a unique place and our key abeyances would be confronted—and therefore, it was hoped, laid to rest.
(4) The Report was attacked as a tract for the times, in particular by Alan Cairns (but his critique, devastating though it was, reveals his own difficulties when dealing with the central problem of Quebec's place in Canada).
(5) The Report illustrates the workings of the political system, especially the federal parties and the role of a Prime Minister. Its demise brings us back to the ongoing appeal of counterfactual history, and to the unresolved questions of paths not taken. The Trudeau assumptions were to 'win', but we can clearly see that they did not go unchallenged, and that the more

we understand about our choices, the less sure we may become about the outcome. One of the most interesting things about the Report was, as noted, that it represented a direct clash with the views of Pierre Elliott Trudeau. Two entirely different approaches as to how to tackle the Quebec abeyance came to the forefront, and have remained in the spotlight ever since.

It is no secret that Trudeau, like Pearson, was convinced that opening up the Constitution for debate was a can of worms. On the federal side in the late 1960s and early 1970s:

> We did everything possible to sidetrack and postpone any discussion of the distribution of powers. . . . I don't mean that it didn't come up, it came up in 1973 after the first Organization of Petroleum Exporting Countries (OPEC) oil crisis, when the federal government moved (on oil pricing and taxation) and that awakened the government of Alberta to the fact that the distribution of powers was important. . . . It was a tactical device but it was also an attempt to hold this thing in abeyance because we were convinced that if we got into the distribution of powers we would never escape.[8]

In 1964 Trudeau had argued that he would be surprised if 'real statesmen' would reach the conclusion that 'our constitution needs drastic revision'.[9] Writing in 1991 he stated that he was 'on record since the mid-sixties as having pointed out the dangers of embarking on a constitutional voyage when the virus of constitutionitis had begun to infect the ship of state. But the provinces took matters into their own hands in 1967. . . surely the federal government had no choice but to accept the challenge and sail on?'[10] Like scurvy, the virus would spread, but the ship's captain at least knew where he wanted to go, even if many of the officers and crew did not agree with his choice of destination.

H.D. Forbes has offered a provocative and very useful analysis of the Trudeau 'moral vision'.[11] Forbes notes that many have argued that Trudeau had an unusually lucid and reflective set of coherent political ideas, based upon a lifetime of reflection and study.[12] One could, for example, see in his views of the need for balanced federalism and equilibrium a well-developed theory of counterweights. There was a need for a new federalism to counter the provincializing swing underway in the late 1970s, and Canada needed 'nationalist glue'. The time had come 'to assert that Canada was one country'; there needed to be a new national policy and a more decisive stand against endless provincial demands being spearheaded by Quebec.[13] There had to be a 'preponderant power' at the centre.[14]

Trudeau's views were also rooted in a set of presuppositions about nationalism. Nationalists were reactionaries; they were tribalistic, atavistic, and dangerous.[15] They 'want the whole tribe to return to the wigwams.'[16] In place of ethnic nationalism, which he detested, Trudeau opted for what Samuel LaSelva calls 'moral universalism'.[17] All citizens were to be equal under the law and a charter of entrenched rights. Quebec nationalism would be outflanked by federal policies which stressed Canadian nationalism, bilingualism, a national commitment to multiculturalism, a charter, and the assumption of a uniform federalism in which all provinces are equal.[18] In the Trudeau approach there is little recognition for 'liberal nationalism' of the kind so ably defended by Yael Tamir, and discussed in more detail in Chapter Six. She presents a sustained and detailed defence of the need for a communitarian context, in which the moral responsibilities and associative obligations that develop when one resides in a 'constitutive community' can develop in harmony with liberal values. For her, the notion that there is a conflict between liberalism and nationalism, because the former represents reason and the latter passion, is 'simplistic and misleading'.[19]

This extremely brief summary is intended only to make the important point that Trudeau's views look like a very coherent philosophy based upon procedural liberalism, federalism, and individual rights.[20] Forbes, however, argues that although it may look coherent, it was, in fact, not a very well-argued case:

> Judging from his earlier writings, Trudeau is a liberal (or a socialist) without any clear theory of rights of any kind.... Trudeau's early writings leave the impression that there is nothing controversial among men of good will about either the nature or the definition of rights. Rights exist; they are a good thing; the more the better.[21]

Trudeau's *writings* are, by this measure, of limited value both intellectually and as a guide to action, whereas his *ideas*—and their effects—have had a considerable impact (particularly where they involve constitutional questions).[22] His emphasis on the Charter, bilingualism, and multiculturalism has been exceedingly important, and Forbes emphasizes that the multicultural policies:

> were not just a short-sighted bit of electoral politicking. They did far more than sprinkle a few million dollars on folk dances in church basements. They clarified the Canadian identity, provided a framework for a new immigration policy, and marked an important step in developing a new technology of tolerance.[23]

Trudeau's ideas on Canadian political nationality, on pluralism, and on federalism are still being worked out in the real world of politics. He has, says Forbes, launched the country on an experiment based not upon a coherent, well articulated, closely argued philosophy but upon a moral vision. Whether or not polyethnic individualistic pluralism will hold the nation together is a matter that goes well beyond the scope of this analysis. Nevertheless, it is important to bear these key aspects of Trudeau's ideas in mind as the Unity Task Force's Report is discussed because, whatever one thinks of them, one thing is clear: Trudeau systematically and deliberately avoids any recognition of Quebec's claims to collective recognition and special status. There was not, and never would be, a two-nations policy or strategy.[24] Not for him an acceptance of the *need* for Quebec nationalism or any sustained appreciation of its positive aspects. His was not an argument that federalism required what Peter

Hogg has referred to as a 'margin of appreciation' as used by the European Court of Human Rights which is, in effect, a margin of discretion allowing the Court to 'permit different treatment of civil libertarian issues by the member states'.[25] Trudeau's 'moral vision' was and is pluralistic, not dualistic: it challenged Canadians to reinvent themselves.

Trudeau's approach to the great abeyance was twofold. The question of Quebec's status could be *outflanked* by new policies, institutions, and symbols, and it could be *countered* by emphasizing, in particular, that all the provinces in a federal system were *equal*, and that Canada already had the world's most decentralized federal system. This therefore meant recognizing another problem that had long lain in abeyance—the question as to whether the provinces were indeed equal and what this meant. The compact theory had mutated. As is almost always the case in politics, Trudeau's arguments bordered on simplistic hyperbole. Richard Bird has commented, apropos of Trudeau's views on decentralization, that the figures he used were 'misleading and generally useless';[26] Milne notes that the conclusions that Trudeau drew made all sorts of assumptions about actual decision-making power that were extremely contentious;[27] Ronald Watts has questioned Trudeau's use and knowledge of other federal examples.[28] Miriam Smith and François Rocher have outlined recent changes in the types of federalism we espouse, and how this is linked to notions of identity and power.[29] They discuss how far apart our differing notions of federalism have been, and how Trudeau's centralist ideas clashed with these other interpretations. Trudeau's views were now unabashedly centralist and fundamentally opposed to any recognition of Quebec as different; 'every time Quebec asked our government for special status or for recognition of its distinct society or sovereignty association we would resist . . . it could only be a fight for more power for the provincial politicians.'[30] Not all his cabinet ministers necessarily shared his views on the state of Canadian federalism and federal power. Jean-Luc Pepin was one who did not:

> Some people think that the federal government of Canada is a weak institution. Having been Minister of Industry, Trade and Commerce I have a totally different view. The federal government of Canada is a powerful organization. When it decides that something is going to take place, the chances are great that it will.[31]

Such optimism did not fit well with the view that the centre had to be strengthened. Trudeau could and did counter the principle of the recognition of Quebec with other principles he argued were more defensible: the pre-eminence of the Charter, provincial equality, federal balance, individual rights, bilingualism and multiculturalism.[32] This was a powerful armoury.

But if this was to be his approach, why did he decide to create a Task Force in the first place? What did it recommend that was so anathema to him? Why was its approach to our abeyances so different? The Task Force was different because of who had been chosen and what they immediately set out to do: it turned out to be a most unusual commission, and Trudeau got both more and less than he had bargained for.

Well-known Entities

The federal government had not anticipated a Parti Québécois victory. Trudeau had confidently, only a few months before, predicted that the separatist threat was over. In the wake of the trauma following the Quebec election of October 1976, the federal government hurriedly began the creation of an appropriate defensive infrastructure. Paul Tellier became the head of a new bureau in the Federal-Provincial Relations Office, its job being to plan and co-ordinate all of the studies and activities that the federal government's departments would be taking to combat separatism, and to produce a viable constitutional plan as an alternative. Marc Lalonde was to head another group and be the 'super-minister' of the national unity campaign; he later became the Minister of State for Federal-Provincial Relations. (His group included cabinet ministers who knew Quebec, in particular John Roberts and Monique Bégin.) A Canadian Unity Information Office was established in 1977 to run a counter-propaganda campaign, and finally there was also another group of key senior officials under Donald Thorson, who had been appointed Constitutional Advisor to the Prime Minister, who reported directly to Trudeau on constitutional matters. This was an impressive array of bureaucratic talent, and the key figures, such as Lalonde and Tellier, had direct access to Trudeau, as did Gordon Robertson, who became Secretary to the Cabinet for federal-provincial relations. The Tellier group began work immediately on a set of federal proposals for change.[33]

In spite of these moves, by 1977 there were calls for another kind of group, one that would be highly visible and would be *seen* to be doing something. Trudeau was not enamoured of the idea of a public debate of this type: it could prove politically dangerous, his views were well known, the Tellier Group was at work, and Gordon Robertson could sound out the provincial Premiers on their views. But the pressures to act mounted. Individuals such as Professor Léon Dion, Jean Marchand, and Mme Solange Chaput-Rolland were urging the need for a different approach, as were members of the opposition, and so by July of 1977 Trudeau gave in:

> The Commission was set up by the Prime Minister to allow the public to air its views on national unity and the government to buy some time. The government wanted to proceed cautiously in light of the PQ victory, to reassure the Canadian public that it was not on the edge of a precipice and to give the impression that the national unity issue was being prudently managed.[34]

It was set up under section 11 of the Inquiries Act—normally used to establish Royal Commissions—but John Robarts had insisted that the group be called something other than a commission, and settled on the more action-oriented title of 'Task Force' with its military overtones of decisiveness.[35] Trudeau, who may have signed the empowering documents in haste, wanted the Task Force to report within the year, and did not have substantive proposals in mind. If this was his intention, the first two mistakes he made were in choosing Jean-Luc Pepin and John Parmenter Robarts to be the co-chairs.

Jean-Luc Pepin was a former Liberal MP and cabinet Minister, serving first as Minister without Portfolio in 1965 and shortly thereafter as Minister of Mines, Energy and Resources. In 1968 he became the Minister of Industry, Trade and Commerce, but was not re-elected in 1972. In 1976 he had been made the Chairman of the Anti-Inflation Board (AIB) where, starting from scratch, he had rapidly built up an impressive organization.[36] During this period he 'never saw Trudeau; I made it a matter of principle never to see him.'[37] (There had been some open disagreements with the Prime Minister.) This was intended to be a short-term post and when Pepin decided it was time to leave, a meeting was arranged with the Prime Minister, who asked the obvious question, 'And what will we do now?' Pepin recalls replying that he could stay on at the AIB with a changed educative role regarding inflation and controls, or he could go to Industry, Trade and Commerce (which he very much wanted, interested as he was in economic restructuring and Japanese development models), or he could do something on the unity front:

> To this day, I really do not know why he appointed me and I don't know why he appointed Robarts, . . . the record is there, to tell you who I was and who Robarts was. Robarts had organized the Confederation of Tomorrow conference and insulted Pearson. . . . He was a well-known entity. And I was a well-known entity. So he appointed two eccentrics to lead his commission. I don't know how to explain that. It's probably Trudeau's basic concept—looking for counter-balance all the time . . . or he may have had nobody else of sufficient stature to run a creditable institution.

The latter is certainly likely. Robarts and Pepin were almost stereotypically representative of the two cultures: Robarts 'stolid, slow moving, careful'; Pepin 'dynamic, bubbling with enthusiasm, full of ideas, wanting to get things done'. 'Robarts', said Pepin in an eloquent and moving tribute to him delivered at the opening of the Robarts Centre for Canadian Studies, 'was a peaceful man. He did not like conflict, at least not for the sake of conflict, the so-called "creative confrontation" . . . he was at ease with his ego, his identity, his roots as an Ontarian and as a Canadian . . . he was essentially a generous man.'[38]

It turned out to be a fortuitous match.[39] Robarts proved to be sensitive and caring; he listened, he helped steady the team, he provided essential balance and leadership. Pepin made sure things got done, and took on the whole organizational burden of the enterprise. Pepin ran the show, Robarts gave it ballast. Pepin was not told by Trudeau how to organize the commission, or even how much to spend. He 'did not talk to Trudeau between 1977–1979, not even to discuss my political future.' He chose as research director Dr David R. Cameron.

He was not sure, at the outset, whether or not Cameron had the necessary drive for such a job, and worried that he might be too diffident, too much a quiet academic: all such fears were to become unalloyed admiration. The choice he now regards as an inspired one, as do others. It is also interesting to remember that in 1974 Cameron had published a book on Quebec nationalism in which, while he challenged many assumptions held in Quebec on the self-determination question, he also took Trudeau to task for some of his views on nationalism. (Pepin had read the book and this was a key factor in his choice.) Another member of the steering committee who was to become a key figure was Dr Ralph Heintzman. He could provide the kind of historical depth the Commissioners needed, and, once again, his was a personality that brought a quiet, reflective, and careful judgment to bear on key issues, and which helped build the team. It was a team of which Pepin was and is rightfully proud.

Other distinguished names on the ten-person Research Steering Committee included Robert Décary, Ghislain Fortin, Allan Robbins, and Michael Stein. The Executive Director (until May 1978) responsible for such things as salaries and budget was Reed Scowen, who had served under Pepin at the AIB. He played a vital role as the chief administrator and commented on the report as it was being prepared. The research staff numbered another twenty-one and once again included names that were or would become well known. Added to this were staff members, tour organizers, translators, and executive assistants. Starting a Commission is, in other words, an enormous bureaucratic undertaking. Pepin was a self-confessed slave driver and authoritarian, at least in the organizational sense, and it took someone like this to kick-start things into action, to get the thing going so that order and efficiency became the norm. Based upon his experiences with Pepin-Robarts and other Commissions, David Cameron has recently suggested that 'Given that there are Royal Commissions in operation in Ottawa all the time, it seems to me that there is a good case for the establishment of a generic unit within the federal government which would provide the basic administrative and financial support necessary to allow the commission to get up and running faster....'[40] Nothing had been set up for the Task Force; it had a very tight reporting deadline (one year); it could easily have foundered. But it did not, because Pepin was given a free hand to organize the enterprise, and his formidable energy proved equal to the task.

Appointed as Commissioners at the same time as the co-chairs were announced were Muriel Kovitz of Calgary, Ross Marks from British Columbia, Richard Cashin of Newfoundland, and Dr John Evans. Kovitz, Marks, and Cashin were seen as the regional appointments. Dr Evans, who was an Ontario representative, was soon (in March, 1978) to drop out unannounced and unexpectedly, as he had decided to run as a Liberal candidate in the next federal election. His place was then taken by Dr Ronald Watts, who moved over from the advisory side. This was another crucial adjustment. Anyone who has seen Professor Watts in action as either lecturer or expert witness knows how intellectually formidable he is. He too would not hesitate to contradict even the Prime Minister if he thought that he was wrong. (As he did when the Report was finally presented!) But this list of appointees did not initially include representation from Quebec, and there was an embarrassing period of six weeks during which time the search for acceptable Quebec members who were willing to take the posts went on. This choice, once made, was also important: Gérald A. Beaudoin was and still is a distinguished constitutional scholar, 'dedicated, profoundly nice, obsessed by the law . . . he reads decisions of the Supreme Court for amusement.'[41] Solange Chaput-Rolland was a broadcaster, author, and journalist who brought passion and an extremely powerful personality to bear on issues such as language. She provided a perspective that made an audience realize that real feelings, and real lives, were at stake. She too was not afraid to challenge Trudeau—and did not share his distrust of Quebec nationalism.[42]

These are all names that have figured prominently in the ongoing constitutional debates, and their experiences with each other and with the intense work of the Task Force cannot but have had an abiding effect. To take only a few examples: David Cameron went on to work on the federal proposals during the period leading up to patriation as Assistant Secretary to the Cabinet, Strategic and Constitutional Planning (and was one of the primary authors of the famous/infamous Kirby memorandum). From 1987 until 1989 he was the Ontario Deputy Minister for Intergovernmental Affairs, and then became Ontario representative to the Government of Quebec and Special Constitutional Advisor on Constitutional Reform to the Premier of Ontario (1989–90 and 1991–3). Ronald Watts became a consultant to the Federal Provincial Relations Office in 1980, and, after a distinguished academic and administrative career, became Assistant Secretary to the Federal-Provincial Relations Office during the crucial period leading up to the Charlottetown Accord (1990–2). Gérald-A. Beaudoin was appointed to the Senate in 1988. He was the co-chair of the Special Joint Committee of the Senate and House of Commons on the Process for Amending the Constitution of Canada as well as the *Report of the Special Joint Committee on a Renewed Canada* (Beaudoin-Dobbie), and was also the chair of the Senate's Permanent Committee on Constitutional and Judicial Affairs. Solange Chaput-Rolland was also appointed to the Senate, and has continued an active involvement in constitutional affairs. Ralph Heintzman, in addition to continued academic work, was heavily involved in the writing of the *Report of the Special Joint Committee on a Renewed Canada* (Beaudoin-Dobbie) and is currently the Vice-Principal, Research, of the Canadian Centre for Management Development.

And then there were the co-chairs themselves, between whom there was 'a real balance' for which, to be fair, the Prime Minister is entitled to some credit for his choice in the first place. As a former, and popular, Premier of Ontario (1962–71) Robarts had a wealth of political experience. He had all the qualifications for political office: he had been a good athlete, had a distinguished war record (he volunteered for the navy and served throughout the war), took post-war legal training at Osgoode Hall, and had looks that were a publicist's dream. If central casting had to find someone who looked like a Prime Minister, Robarts would be the model. His ideas on federalism could be summed up as decentralist, with a belief in what would later be called a 'community of communities' view.[43]

He had fought against the 'arbitrary' introduction of medicare, had fought unsuccessfully for the introduction of a capital gains tax and some of the other recommendations of the Carter Commission, and argued that there was a failure to co-ordinate federal-provincial taxation.[44] He believed in recognizing duality and distinctiveness and had made commitments in Ontario to Catholic schools and to French education. By 1967, insofar as Ontario was concerned 'federal-provincial relations had all but collapsed.'[45] In late 1966, deeply worried by the state of the nation, he had broached the idea of a conference on Confederation. (He had already created an all-star Ontario Advisory Committee on Confederation.) This was resisted by Lester Pearson ('I can think of nothing more unproductive') who worried that it was premature and that the federal government was not prepared for such an event. Robarts did not back down. His biographer, A.K. McDougall, thinks that Expo '67 was pivotal in the development of Robarts's thinking, and that his speech at the opening of the Ontario pavilion on August 5 was an indication of his concerns and principles. 'He went out of his way to stress national unity and described his own province as a mosaic of ethnic communities, not a bastion of the British Empire.'[46] He hoped to translate some of the enthusiasm over Expo into the Confederation of Tomorrow conference then being organized. It went ahead regardless of Ottawa's grumbling reluctance and opened, at the top of Ontario's tallest building, on November 27, 1968. It was televised—the first conference of its type where this was done—and John Robarts chaired it. 'This was his finest hour as a national politician, an act of great service to his country.'[47] Robarts was a strong provincialist as well as a nationalist; he preferred piecemeal solutions, obtained via 'calm balance and common sense'.[48] He had always gone out of his way to maintain good relations with successive Quebec Premiers, and was regarded by them as someone who understood Quebec's problems better than most outside the province. He postponed his retirement so that he could lead a delegation of 150 Londoners to Quebec in December 1970 (just after the FLQ crisis, in which he had supported Trudeau's actions), and then on December 8, 1970 he announced his resignation.

When he was approached regarding service on the Task Force he was very reluctant to take up the post. He blamed the collapse of his first marriage on overwork and was determined that his second would not suffer the same fate. He had managed to get his diet, weight, drinking, and blood pressure under control. He disliked Ottawa, and was to make sure that he got home on weekends. But he took the job nevertheless, and insisted from the outset that a report be written, and that it had to be unanimous. Pepin speculates that it was Robarts's love of public service that in part brought him back, and that 'he could not find full satisfaction . . . in going to a law office, sitting on boards of companies and attending yacht clubs.'[49]

Jean-Luc Pepin's roots reveal a uniquely intercultural heritage.[50] His grandmother was a schoolteacher in Montreal, someone who believed above all in education and was a great anglophile ('not untypical in Quebec'). His grandfather had gone to search for gold in the Klondike rush and had been told not to come back. Bilingualism was stressed for all the children and five of his nine brothers and sisters went into educational careers. Education 'was a form of salvation'. He was educated by the Oblates of the Order of Mary Immaculate, the same Oblates who were so instrumental as missionaries in western Canada; 'I have national unity in my blood.' In many ways his career parallels Trudeau's, except that, as he recalls pointing out in a speech made in Vancouver: 'This guy [Trudeau] is imitating me. I go to study in France. He goes to study in France. I become a university professor. He becomes one. I go into politics. He joins the Liberal Party. . . . I marry a Vancouver girl. He marries a Vancouver girl. When will he stop?' Pepin entered federal politics in 1963 and was made a member of the Cabinet in 1965.

It was not therefore surprising that Pepin saw the Task Force's role as educational, and saw the chairs taking the same sort of approach that Macdonald and Cartier had done: a Liberal-Conservative compromise, in the Liberal-Conservative tradition.

The Commissioners were assisted by 'the three wise men': Professors Léon Dion, John Meisel, and Edward McWhinney, who offered periodic advice and counsel, and who represented also a formidable range of views.[51] A major part of the hearings was comprised of the testimony of a galaxy of academic and bureaucratic stars: 'it was the best constitutional seminar in town.' Prior to these intensive private seminars the Task Force had spent a gruelling eight months on the road, travelling *en masse*, unlike the B & B Commission which had split into groups. The public hearings were a shock. Some people were 'enraged'; they were 'vomiting' on French Canadians; there was a depth and strength to antagonisms that was profoundly unsettling, and there was lamentable, invincible, ignorance about the country's history.[52] Shades of the past (Laurendeau) and what was to come (Spicer). The Task Force was eventually to release three documents. Not surprisingly, one was a report on what the public had said, entitled *A Time to Speak*, which was largely prepared by Pepin himself with two assistants. There was also a glossary of key terms: words were weapons, and several of the commissioners were determined that at least a concerted effort should be made to avoid key words meaning whatever people thought they did. *Coming to Terms: The Words of the Debate* was the result. And then there were the recommendations themselves, some 75 in all, plus the 118-page rationale, entitled *A Future Together*.

To Pepin's regret these documents were not released in their logical order. Due to what were perceived to be vital deadlines, the final report came first. 'The responsibility for preparing a draft of an entirely new version of the report was entrusted to one Commissioner and one member of the research staff.'[53] In the amazingly short period of seven weeks the work, including revising, translating, and printing, was complete. David Cameron has provided an authoritative and succinct account of the reasons for haste, and the nature of the final process, and this need not be repeated here. What is important to remember is the nature of the intense effort that had gone into draft after draft, into the discussions, and into the research. There had been 'Searing conflicts . . . giddy exhilaration . . . matchless camaraderie'.[54]

Major Surgery

Pepin and Robarts were experienced politicians, both conservative in their own way. They knew that their views, and those of the rest of the Task Force, did not accord with Trudeau's. This was apparent from the moment that they announced, at the end of the very first week, that they were in search of a 'third option' and that the Task Force would write a report. But they could still hope that he could be influenced. Surely their appointment and work had not merely been an exercise in public relations? Pepin was not initially sure that a Report was necessary, but did not take a great deal of convincing. Nor did he stand in the Commissioners' way when it became apparent that their views would not please the Prime Minister or help Jean-Luc Pepin's future career. He threw himself into the job, and it is still apparent that he enjoyed himself. It really was a case of full speed ahead and damn the torpedoes. Pepin said, generously, that one should 'Give the benefit of the doubt to Trudeau . . . by thinking that he wasn't setting a trap for us, that he was quite genuinely interested in other sets of ideas. I think that this is a more generous interpretation.'

The Commissioners decided that the time had come to recommend major surgery on the body of Canadian federalism. The patient just might accept it. What was needed was a radical abeyancectomy. Robarts, in spite of his natural caution and innate conservatism wanted 'clarity, practicality, and finality'.[55] And the root of the country's problems, they said, was dualism, with regionalism/provincialism a close second. Robarts, with a lifetime of experience in Ontario politics, was prepared to be daring. Pepin, the closest of them all to Trudeau, was prepared to offer an alternative vision of the country. Why was it so different to the Trudeau vision, and what did it have to say about Quebec's claims to 'equality'?

Even its severest critics regarded the Report as 'well written, even eloquent'.[56] Its 118 pages of analysis and explanation opened by recognizing the importance of 'attitudes', but considered that mere exhortation would not change them, whereas institutional and policy reform could 'encourage the development of attitudes which support unity' at a time when the country was in the midst of a crisis and the populace expected reform via constitutional change.[57]

Immediate events should, the Report said, be taken as symbolizing the crisis rather than constituting its roots 'which are much deeper'. Since the B & B Commission, which 14 years earlier had faced the first serious challenge to the 1867 arrangements, there had been a number of important changes which had ameliorated some problems, but there was also a 'backlash' in English-speaking Canada, and things that the Commission had assumed could 'no longer be taken for granted'.[58] Modernization, and governmental growth, had taken place not only in Quebec but also in other provinces and regions. And the 'Canadian reality has become more complex', with increased multiculturalism and a 'new urgency' with regard to native peoples. Ottawa was often seen as a 'remote, shambling bureaucracy and people are asking fundamental questions about their country'.[59]

The Task Force then chose two key issues as the most pressing and profound. First—and foremost—was the problem of 'duality'; a close second was 'regionalism'. These two issues were at the heart of everything and would have to be dealt with before other urgent questions, such as native rights, could be tackled successfully. The Task Force made a concerted and deliberate decision to solve problems in stages. There was a clearly written explanation of the problem of duality and how to define it. Whatever emphasis one gave it (Pan-Canadian dualism, two-nations dualism, etc.), 'the essential condition in recognizing duality within Canada at the present time is to come to terms with modern Quebec . . . at once a society, a province, and the stronghold of the French Canadian people . . . the living heart of the French presence in North America.'[60] Regionalism likewise could be defined in various ways but its building blocks were the provinces (and territories) and these were 'the logical units on which to focus a discussion'.[61]

What they set out to do was secure a clearer expression of 'duality', the better accommodation of the forces of 'regionalism', and the recognition that the principle of 'sharing' was an 'operational value' of federalism. Following these points, in its remaining 70 pages the report sets out how these goals are to be achieved and how they were linked to other issues. The most contentious area, and the last to be settled, was language. It created serious problems in the discussions within the Task Force (especially among those from Quebec) and Pepin's views prevailed: each province was to be allowed to set its own language policies. As in Switzerland, the provinces could set out 'the languages in which their services will be provided and the language and languages of work'.[62] At the federal level bilingual services should be extended 'in circumstances where the demand is sufficient and it is feasible to do so'.[63] French language education should be improved across the country, but would remain a provincial matter. The Report did set out the guidelines for the linguistic rights which could and should be expressed in provincial statutes, but this was optional and they also supported 'the efforts of the Quebec government and of the people of Quebec to ensure the predominance of the French language and culture in that province'.[64] The Commissioners also noted, in passing, that although the federal government's language policies had accomplished much, on the negative side 'must go the costly, and relatively ineffective, attempt to provide adequate language skills to anglophone civil servants'.[65] In their use of comments such as these—and others—the Commissioners showed that the public criticisms they had heard had made a considerable impression.

These were bold and controversial language recommendations. They ran directly counter to Trudeau's views on the matter. Such an approach, it was argued, was far more pragmatic, less likely to antagonize English-speaking Canadians, and more realistic about what could be accomplished. It also, and most important of all, recognized that Quebec had the right to impose its own laws, thus removing the guarantees contained in section 133. The rights of the anglophone minority in Quebec were to be left up to the province and its own legislation:

> We are confident, however, we are convinced, that the removal of the constitutional obligations created by Section 133 will not undermine the will of French-speaking Quebecers and the Government of Quebec to maintain the rights of the English-speaking community freely, openly and with generosity, by ordinary legislation of the province.[66]

On the overall cultural front there should be more national prizes and programs, the national availability of French language radio and television, and tax policies to help cultural industries. At the same time the provinces would be given increased powers to undertake cultural initiatives.

In order to meet the demands of regionalism/provincialism, as well as those of dualism/Quebec, they proposed a 'substantially restructured' federalism and a revised constitution. These proposals were grouped under six headings involving the distribution of powers; a reformed senate and better federal-provincial co-ordination; a revamped and independent Supreme Court; provisions for constitutional amendment; electoral reform for the House of Commons; and constitutionally entrenched fundamental rights.

In the discussion of this restructuring, the Commissioners did not shrink from stating certain principles:

- They rejected the view that Ottawa was paramount: the provinces and Ottawa were to be recognized formally as equals (the Queen was to appoint each Lieutenant-Governor on provincial recommendation).
- They rejected the notion of provincial equality as an inviolable principle of federalism. 'Let us put our conviction strongly: Quebec is distinctive and should, within a viable Canada, have the powers necessary to protect and develop its distinctive character; any political solution short of this would lead to the rupture of Canada.'[67]
- They accepted Quebec's right to leave Confederation. 'We wish, however, to underline one thing unequivocally: if it turns out to be the clearly expressed and settled preference of Quebecers to assume a sovereign destiny, none of us on the Task Force would wish to see their right to do so denied.'[68]
- Federal-provincial powers should be *redistributed* so as to avoid concurrent jurisdiction as far as possible.
- The parliamentary system should be altered by the creation of a Council of the Federation in place of the Senate; it would consist of 60 members with seats being allocated to provincial delegations (12 for the largest, 2 for the smallest). Voting requirements would vary depending on the bill, and federal cabinet ministers would be *ex officio* non-voting members, able to speak to legislative proposals.
- Formal constitutional change would be democratized and would require passage by both federal houses, and a popular majority in all four regions via a referendum.
- Some key individual rights would be entrenched.

These are recommendations both radical and principled, and they do not even constitute all the major suggestions. They are, however, highly illustrative of the approach taken. They represent many of the Report's highlights (or lowlights, according to one's point of view). The Commissioners therefore came face to face with at least the following former abeyances:

- the constitutional recognition of dualism and Quebec's distinctiveness;
- the balance of federal-provincial power;
- the need for a democratic amending formula;
- Quebec's claim to a right of veto over formal change;
- the question of provincial equality and symmetry;
- the clash between federal and parliamentary principles;
- the recognition of individual and group rights;
- the need for judicial supremacy in some areas.
- Quebec's right to secede.

The recommendations were logically connected, comprehensive, and driven by an underlying philosophy of federalism. Even so, some issues were still left deliberately vague, including language (e.g., education wherever numbers warrant 'could be included' by the provinces; if all provinces agreed on 'these and other linguistic rights' they should be entrenched. Similarly a Declaration of Rights was to include 'the usual political, legal, economic and egalitarian rights'). Dupré and Weiler make the important and connected points that although the Commissioners had 'reached too often for the constitutional lever', the Task Force had, ironically, taken a reverse position on language: 'this is the one setting in which the Task Force displays reticence about the value of a constitutional approach.'[69]

The question that was still capable of causing extreme difficulty was not only the issue of Quebec's distinctiveness as such, but how it was to be linked to the problem of provincial equality. Here the Commissioners' nerve perhaps failed them. Robarts, certainly, felt uncomfortable with the idea of special status but could live with asymmetry. The fudge was in, because they recommended allotting:

> to all the provinces powers in the areas needed by Quebec to maintain its distinctive culture and heritage, but to do so in a manner which would enable the other provinces, if they so wished, not to exercise these responsibilities and instead leave them to Ottawa. There are two methods for achieving this: to place those matters under concurrent jurisdiction with provincial paramountcy, thus leaving provinces with the option whether to exercise their overriding power in these fields; and to provide in the constitution a procedure for the intergovernmental delegation of legislative powers. In our view both methods should be used.[70]

This, noted Alan Cairns pithily in a comprehensive and scathing critique, 'is capable of producing two antithetical outcomes at the opposite ends of the spectrum and anything in between.'[71]

The Report also skirted aboriginal issues. There was a three-page discussion of the need to tackle native issues, and five recommendations are made, but they are in the main general and declaratory. To be fair to the Commissioners, they did recognize the need to address the problems—but they had no one on the Commission with expertise in the area, and they made the conscious choice to play for time, knowing full well that native issues would constitute 'the next great problem'.[72] It is highly unlikely that, had they grappled with the question in detail, Pepin himself (and others) would have agreed that Quebec as a 'distinct society' and aboriginal communities were at all comparable. The latter were islets of cultural difference, not societies in the same full and complete sense; Quebec was a whole archipelago.

Vagueness can imply realism and adaptability; it provides room to grow and to manoeuvre. But it runs counter to the demand to know 'what things really mean' which has become so much a part of Canada's constitutional culture. The Report had a view of federalism that saw Canada as a community of communities, and allowed that one of these was very different from the rest. It tried to use the experiences of other federations and other federal mechanisms, notably Switzerland for language and Germany for a Bundesrat-style second chamber, in order to defuse the language issue and to strengthen a key mechanism of intrastate federalism. It made the provinces Ottawa's equal and redistributed powers, whilst trying hard to preserve the overtly symbolic aspects of national unity. It suggested entrenchment and major reforms of equalization payments, and made some moves to liberalizing interprovincial trade and promoting economic integration (not enough, in Pepin's opinion). It was democratic in its approach to constitutional change, noting that in a matter as important as constitutional change 'citizens should be involved', and that previous formulas involving the provinces 'would introduce a very high degree of rigidity'.[73] The provinces would, under the Report's formula, be involved via the restructured Senate. Individual and collective rights should be recognized, but this would have been limited to those on which the provinces and the federal government could agree, adding others later. The Supreme Court itself would be enlarged, and the Council of the Federation would have to ratify federal appointees.

Overall, the Report thus appeared to be strongly decentralist in tone and content, and herein lay a major part of its downfall, for *A Future Together* was immediately seen as 'an eloquent panegyric to provincialism'.[74] The press seized upon this aspect of the Report. Transferring powers, including the residual power, to the provinces; provincializing and empowering the Senate; giving the provinces the power to appoint all superior court judges,[75] as well as a role in selecting judges for an enlarged Supreme Court; undercutting national bilingualism and enhancing Quebec's control over language, communications, and culture in general—these were not the sort of things the Prime Minister had in mind for Canada, not even in his wildest dreams. What Trudeau had in mind had already appeared and been shot down, at least temporarily. This was Bill C-60 and the position papers that had preceded it and which accompanied it.

The timing of this bill is particularly interesting, because it came out as the Task Force was doing its work, and therefore before its report had been written. It clearly took the Commissioners by surprise. That the Tellier group was active was one thing; that it was going to present *A Time for Action* and C-60 was another. Apparently not even Liberal Senators such as Eugene Forsey knew what was coming.[76] It could be argued that it mattered not, as the Unity Task Force was engaged in producing a report and would not deviate from its task. It can also be argued that the federal government felt that it had to show that it was capable of responding flexibly to the challenge of separatism and that the system could change.[77] It can also be argued that this was a pre-emptive strike, designed to ensure that the key components of a Trudeau-inspired federal plan were made public. Senator Arthur Tremblay sees in C-60 the essence of Trudeau's vision: 'et là, c'est important, à mon avis, de poser la question: pourquoi Trudeau, a-t-il publié le Bill C-60 au mois de juin *sans attendre* [my emphasis] le Rapport Pepin-Robarts?'[78]

In June of 1978 the federal government released *A Time for Action: Toward the Renewal of the Canadian Federation*. Part one of this document comprised those questions on which the federal government thought that it could act alone, without provincial consent. It contained eleven categories covering a new preamble, a Charter of Rights and Freedoms, a new House of the Federation to replace the Senate, changes to the Supreme Court and its entrenchment, and a number of other clauses involving the monarchy/Governor General, the Cabinet, and First Ministers' Conferences. The documents stressed the need for national unity and a strong centre. Quebec did not have special status or a special role, and the centrepiece of the whole edifice was the Charter—shades of what was to come. When Trudeau spoke in 1980 of renewed federalism anyone who had read C-60 would know that a Charter plus an amending formula were the two key ingredients. What they could not guess was what kind of formula, for in its discussion paper on the subject of amendment the federal government had advocated a national/regional referendum approach. Bill C-60 was soon dropped because it got trapped by the investigations that took place in various committees and because, in a reference case, the Supreme Court ruled that Ottawa could not unilaterally change the Senate (the Senate proposal itself was an amazing mix of representational ideas). Federal strategy towards the great abeyance was still to ignore it, outflank it, and appeal to an overarching nationalism in which the centre was and would remain greater than the mere sum of its parts.

The Task Force's strategy was totally different, and was to get it into serious trouble as soon as the Report was released. Perhaps the most telling and scathing critique of all (in my estimation) was penned by Alan Cairns.[79] He opened his discussion by noting that the Report's 'great strength and profound weakness . . . both spring from the simplicity of its major organizing principles.'[80] He then seizes upon the Commissioners' willingness to 'hammer home one brutal, fundamental point', namely the role and place of Quebec. The Report, says Cairns, 'has declared a winner in the intense struggle between Ottawa and Quebec that has gone on for a decade and a half over the locus of a homeland for the Francophone community.'[81] The winner was Quebec. Abandoned was the Trudeau logic of a bilingual Canada from coast to coast. This can be seen as one of the Report's great strengths; it takes on Trudeau's linguistic vision and says it has few clothes. Cairns does in fact praise the Report's 'commendable realism' and its willingness to appeal to the 'intelligence and fairness' of provincial governments and majorities. Given the evidence amassed on linguistic survival and genuine bilingualism both before and after the Report (not merely passive bilingualism), it is hard to argue that the Commissioners' assessment was in any way less logical, or less compelling, than their rivals'.[82] It was a painful task: they could be accused of abandoning the approximately one million francophones outside Quebec to their old enemies, provincial governments. Above all, this choice has a profound effect on one's view of federalism and on the territorialization of difference, and it was, predictably, also seized upon as a profound weakness in the Report.

In spite of his willingness to give some credit to the Commissioners, and in spite of the presentation of no defence at all of the Trudeau linguistic model, one gets the impression that Cairns is himself trapped. He cannot help siding with those measures that would prevent Quebec from being the homeland of a nation in an acknowledged and entrenched way. He seems unwilling, at bottom, to recognize the need to have the boundaries of our political system coincide formally with the boundaries of an acknowledged national society. There are very good reasons for this, especially the pull of a transcending Canadianness, a need for a sense of national identity from coast to coast. This is precisely the point. When push comes to shove Cairns chooses a Canadian political nationality and favours the Trudeau ideal. This can be seen throughout his extensive writings on the constitution. In phrase after elegant phrase, he eviscerates rampant provincialism, highlights our contradictions, and pleads for a strong, democratic centre.[83] His concerns for Canada, at least Canada outside Quebec, are palpable and grow as the situation becomes more complex. Alan Cairns became, a decade after Pepin-Robarts, a strong critic of Meech.[84] He censures those political scientists who did not see the implications of Trudeau's Charter, saying that many in the profession were 'ill-prepared to sympathize with the political role that Trudeau assigned to the Charter" and that some anglophone political scientists suffered from a 'cultural lag'.[85] He wants a national vision, and it is not surprising that he did not find one in the Report of the Task Force.[86]

This is above all because he is unwilling to accept its initial dualist premise. When faced with our greatest abeyance Alan Cairns—perhaps our pre-eminent constitutionalist—is forced to take sides. He places himself with those who oppose the idea of a formal and recognized federal partnership with Quebec, based upon Quebec not being a province like the others. In his critique of Pepin-Robarts, he did not have to say this explicitly because there was so much else in the Report to attack, particularly its second major premise, 'regionalism'. Here he is on firmer ground, and the Report is weaker. It avoided using words like 'special status' or 'distinct society' and it got around the problem of separate legal recognition by allowing all provinces the same rights. Cairns is able to seize this particular provision by the throat, and one can hear the gasps for air as he does so.

The logic of his argument is rooted in the implications of dualism in practice, which, if carried out in the manner suggested in the Report, has obvious implications for federal institutions. It would be 'profoundly decentralizing': the avoidance of explicit legal recognition of special status for Quebec is achieved at the price of giving it to all if they want it, and this would mean 'the emasculation of the federal government'.[87]

He therefore takes the Commissioners and the Report to task for its views on the national dimension of the country's existence, which was:

> characterized by hesitation and embarrassment . . . the overriding stress on what divides us . . . undermines the occasional references to common interest, common purpose and common will and thus provides little sociological or psychological justification for a strong, autonomous central government role. The Task Force report lacks the subtlety necessary to handle the complexities of an identity which, earlier, for English Canadians could accommodate elements of Canadianness and Britishness and now allows the great majority of Canadians, even in Quebec, to live comfortably with both provincial and Canadian identities and loyalties.[88]

This is an argument for multiple loyalties, for complexity, for historical awareness, and for obfuscation; for not picking one principle over another. It does assume the existence of an acceptable and accepted overall national identity (and history) *within which* basic principles then diverge, and it accords priority to nation-building tools like a Charter of Rights.[89] Cairns is not picking provincial equality as his principle, nor is he a supporter of dualism either, for he does not seem to believe in the possibilities of federalism in Canada as a geographic arrangement in which separate cultures and national identities are protected and enhanced through the medium of a partnership. We are back to the never-ending problem of how to reconcile deep cultural differences (in this case Quebec and Canadian nationalism) within a larger state, even if it is federal. Writing in 1993 Alan Cairns was to reach the conclusion that 'Some significant recognition of distinctiveness, of special status, so that Quebec and its people will not be precise counterparts of other provinces and provincial populations, appears to be inevitable.'[90] By this time, such a position had become anathema to the majoritarian and egalitarian sentiments of many in the rest of the country. Yet as the Report itself noted, if the response to the problems facing federalism was 'a regionalism which submerges duality, or a pan-Canadian nationalism that denies both, then it will not serve.'[91] To put it another way, Quebec's spirit was not to be praised or blamed; the question was, what in the name of God were we going to do to accommodate Quebec whilst maintaining a balanced federation?

The Task Force report was attacked for being inconsistent and contradictory even though it tried to move logically from dualism/regionalism to ways in which to sustain national identity (via a Charter, economic integration, equalization, referenda, partial proportional representation, a revamped House of Commons, and strengthened intrastate institutions) and to a new division of powers. Again and again, Cairns and others accuse the Commissioners of aiding and abetting provincialism, and of advocating a revised version of the compact theory in which Ottawa is 'the creature of the provinces'.

Thus Cairns prefers the Trudeau approach even as exemplified in Bill C-60; the notion of an equal partnership of founding peoples is a non-starter. He is perspicacious enough to realize the difficulty. In the introductory essay to a new edition of his writings on the constitution, published in 1991, he rightly said, 'Readers of some of these essays will pick up additional evidence of bias founded on my sympathy for the Charter, that may inhibit the kind of appreciation of the nationalist realities of Quebec that is natural to Québécois political scientists.'[92] Exactly so. When an abeyance comes into full view, we choose sides or we temporize and hope for the best. In 1979 Alan Cairns did not exactly choose his side on the dualism and language issue. He gave grudging recognition to the Task Force for its common sense on this score, but this did not lead to the conclusion that Quebec had to be the winner and that Trudeau's pan-Canadian bilingualism came a clear second. Of course, because of linkages and the scope of the debate, there was far more to it than this, yet attitudes to the Quebec question and to Quebec's claims are fundamental to Alan Cairns's approach. Ten years later he chose sides again and opposed the Meech Lake Accord because, amongst other things, it lacked a national vision. Quebec's distinctiveness lost again. On both occasions he was a formidable adversary.

What If?

One can certainly say of the Report's reception that it highlighted some of the workings of the federal system, especially the parties and the federal parliament.[93] By 1979 the Trudeau administration was deeply unpopular, and the prospect of a Conservative electoral victory loomed. The deliberations of the Task Force do not seem to have been influenced by this at all in terms of what was decided.[94] There was no contact with the opposition parties outside the formal hearings; there was no sense that it was a report driven by the prospect that Trudeau would not be there for long.[95] At the same time the Commissioners and the research staff could not remain in a cocoon and must have realized that their views would find more support with Joe Clark, leader of the Conservative party. David Cameron puts things this way:

> We'd done our calculations beforehand, we knew Trudeau would hate it. We thought Clark, and several of the provincial premiers, could pick it up and really do something with it, and the PQ; you would start both to attract their interest and spike their guns, to some extent. . . . I still don't really understand it.[96]

Clark was indeed well disposed towards the document: 'as the leader of the Progressive Conservative Party, Pepin-Robarts was certainly acceptable to me'.[97] One would want to add, in fairness to Clark, that this acceptability was in terms of general principles rather than all the specific detail. None the less this is important, for these principles were so contrary to those held by the Prime Minister. In addition Clark, in the above quote, is not speaking for his party, a party he had to prevent from fracturing as it had done before under Stanfield.[98] There would be many Conservatives who might like decentralization but would resist special status for Quebec. Additionally, Clark notes that 'One of the things I regret was that the federal-provincial process did not allow for real participation by the opposition . . . we were always playing catch-up . . . the dynamics of opposition were in play.'[99] The opposition had to concentrate more upon what they opposed than what they wanted; this was true in 1979 before the election and in 1980 with Trudeau's return to power. The system does not encourage the real discussion of 'full blown alternatives'. If it did the country might have seen a serious debate about the approach taken to the language question and the presentation, by at least one federal party, of a Pepin-Robarts/Swiss type alternative. The NDP also 'did not pay much attention' to the Report and other battles soon took over, including the full-scale federal-provincial war over the National Energy Program. (In 1980 Trudeau even offered the New Democrats 'six or seven' Cabinet seats.[100]) Alberta and the West had their sights fixed on other matters; the immediate questions of federal taxing powers and resource rents were far more pressing than hypothetical wholesale reform of Confederation. Even the proposed Council of the Federation did not make much impact upon a Peter Lougheed, for whom Senate reform was not a priority.

In Quebec, the press coverage was largely favourable.[101] Editorialists gave it 'an enthusiastic reception'.[102] Outside Quebec, some, like William Johnson in *The Globe and Mail*, praised it in one column as having 'the ring of truth' but rejected it in another, largely because of its 'mistaken' language recommendations.[103] *The Globe and Mail*'s editorialists saw it as 'a very strange report' that smacked of 'anything-that-will-get-us-out-of-this-place', and as giving off a disconcerting 'pervasive scent. . . . A dog would sniff it and think: they are scared.'[104] For *La Presse* strangely it was not radical enough and had adopted 'la vision Trudeau'.[105] This is indicative of the fact that, in Robert Normand's words, the Report had 'caught the Parti Québécois with their pants down', especially after Trudeau came out so solidly against it. The PQ, thinks Normand, had no intention of settling: 'so Morin used the Pepin-Robarts Report to show Quebeckers what kind of chap Trudeau was . . . it was a political game.' Normand also argues that had Lévesque chosen to do so, he could have used Pepin-Robarts to achieve something.[106] In public, Lévesque admitted that it contained much that was positive, but he also made the observation that the Task Force proposals would just make Quebec 'hungry for more' and that the appetite grows with eating.[107] This was, of course, also Trudeau's view. Academic opinion in English Canada was lukewarm: Ramsay Cook was opposed and saw it as a sell-out to sovereignty-association all round.[108] However, Professor Dennis Smith suggested that, at the forthcoming

February meeting of the First Ministers, the agenda should be suspended and the Report endorsed as a starting point.[109] (This meeting was the deadline that the Commissioners had imposed upon themselves, seeing it as crucial.)

On January 25, 1979 Trudeau presented the Report to the House and said that he and his government accepted 'the broad lines' of its recommendations. He even called it 'a landmark contribution' and noted that it was unanimous and had been completed in a remarkably short period.[110] However, his summation of what he considered its four basic principles was a masterpiece of evasion and obfuscation, focusing on its treatment of diversity as a 'national resource', its attempts 'to encourage greater sensitivity to the Canadian dimension of our lives', and its efforts to 'understand the major forces operating in Canadian society'.[111] By the next day he was to tell a press conference that the Report was 'dead wrong' on language. It was apparent to all, including the Commissioners, that he saw it as incompatible with his views, and there were many in the Liberal party who supported him. The Report was not added to the agenda of the February meeting. Nor, despite requests, was it ever reprinted.

Probably the best chance that the Task Force ideas had of making an impact was during the nine-month Conservative reign from June to December 1979. Perhaps the Task Force members could have done more to influence the opposition before it came to power. 'I (Pepin) should have paid more attention to him (Clark) probably. I should have gone to brief him in relative depth. I was so non-partisan . . . if Joe had said why don't you come and talk to Maz (Don Mazankowski) and Jack (Horner) and a few others . . . but it didn't happen. A missed opportunity.'[112] Even so, the Report *was* revived in late 1979 by Senator Arthur Tremblay.

Tremblay had been a noted Quebec academic who was recruited into the Quebec civil service in 1960 by Paul Gérin-Lajoie. In 1971 Tremblay succeeded Claude Morin as the Deputy Minister for Intergovernmental Affairs where he remained until 1977, when Robert Normand took over. In 1977 he returned to education, only to be suddenly recruited by Clark himself in 1979 following the Conservative victory. Appointed somewhat reluctantly to the Senate, he was put in charge of a Task Force on the 'renewal of the Federation'. In the short (six-page) document where its 'terms of reference' are defined, the Task Force was given as 'a starting point: the Pepin-Roberts Report . . . while we clearly recognize the value of other studies, that of the Pepin-Roberts Committee clearly must be given the greatest consideration when developing a federal proposal for renewing the Federation'.[113] So Pepin-Roberts was making something of a comeback until as he says, 'le treize décembre est arrivé, et mes conditions de travail ont radicalement changé!'[114]

At the same time the Quebec Liberal Party, under Claude Ryan, was preparing to issue its own report, which it did in the first week of January, 1980. Entitled *A New Canadian Federation* (and often referred to as '*le Livre beige*' because of the colour of its cover), it echoed many of the themes stressed by the Task Force, and tried to deal with the same difficulties in much the same ways. Thus, for example, although all the provinces were equal in law and had the same powers, rights, and obligations, Quebec 'must enjoy certain prerogatives consistent with its responsibilities . . . the constitution will never be able to take account in an explicit way of all the differences inherent in the reality of Canada.'[115] It took a comprehensive approach to the entire range of issues before it, containing twenty-nine sets of recommendations in all. On the amending question it went back to a slightly modified Victoria formula, which would have required the assent of two of the four western provinces, including one of the two more populated ones. The Report also suggested ratification via a simple national referendum once proposals had been approved by the legislatures and Parliament. On the key subject, Quebec, in a rather elegant turn of phrase the authors said: 'Within the Canadian political family, Quebec society has all the characteristics of a distinct national community', thus avoiding the trap of defining sovereignty in nation-state terms without surrendering Quebec's claim that it was a nation. Claude Ryan was to become the official leader of the 'No' capaign during the 1980 referendum. Even so, all the work that had gone into *A New Canadian Federation* was for naught. No attention was paid either to Ryan or the Liberal Party's proposals once the referendum was over. Trudeau no more wanted to hear from Ryan than he did from Pepin.[116]

But Tremblay's time was to come, once more, with the return to power of the Conservatives under Mulroney in 1984, for Tremblay was to be a key player in the construction of the Meech Lake Accord in 1987, discussed in greater detail in Chapter Six. It was in Meech that, for the first time, an attempt was made, by a federal government, to entrench a statement that Quebec was a 'distinct society'. Meech was more than this (Tremblay recalls that it was he who suggested the word 'compatible' with regard to the opting out of federal programs in provincial areas of responsibility, with compensation), but in this respect it followed in the traditions of Loranger, Laurendeau, and all those who, in Quebec, had pursued the idea of a compact 'inscribed in time'. It changes, it develops, but it is always there. Pepin-Roberts (and the *Livre beige*) had tried to give expression to this different vision.

Shortly after the Report was released one of the Commissioners, Senator Gérald-A. Beaudoin, advanced the argument that the real strength of the Report was that it had a philosophy: it left to the federal government 'all the powers necessary to keep this country together', and at the same time a province or provinces could use, if they so wished, 'the delegation clause, the opting out formula and the paramountcy provision to acquire a distinctive status. . . . This was asymmetric federalism *de facto* and not *de jure*.'[117] He concludes that Quebeckers would have had a choice not between the *status quo* and sovereignty, but between the *status quo* and a restructured federalism. 'We offered guidelines, we devised a philosophy . . . a federal constitution *shall not include too many silences*'[118] (my emphasis). This is and was a key point. When does one attempt to come to terms with such matters; or do we leave them alone and hope pragmatism will prevail?

Precisely the opposite of the Beaudoin view is encapsulated in Forsey's comment that:

> It (constitutional change) should emphatically not involve filling in all the 'gaps', the 'silences', in the existing constitution. Most of these 'silences', far from being defects in the BNA Act, are among its greatest glories. They leave us room to breathe, to develop, to improvise, to innovate....[119]

We have already seen that this line of argument was not accepted by the Task Force. Their perception was that the time had come to restate the fundamental questions the nation faced, and the Report stands out as a landmark because it:

> recognized, accepted and sought to accommodate the very forces in Canadian life and politics that Trudeau was combating . . . it frankly accepted the structural role of Quebec as the 'foyer' of the Francophone community in North America and the role of the other provinces in expressing the regional loyalties of Canadians in other parts of the country.[120]

In this sense it is part of what is called the 'communitarian' tradition of liberal nationalism, a tradition that now runs head-on into an individual-rights-based procedural constitutionalism. Trudeau's distrust of provincialism is understandable. Whether he was right in this estimate, or whether he had forgotten his earlier writings on the need for genuine balance, is another question.[121] After a decade of dealing with the provincial premiers, it must have been difficult to retain a sense of academic distance from the topic. The premiers' distrust of Ottawa is also easy to fathom. Such is the Canadian condition.

At the very least the work of the Task Force educated those who were a part of it and many of the key personnel, now wiser and more experienced, went on to play very important roles in later events and debates.[122] By 1980 Robarts was dead by his own hand after a struggle with a debilitating illness. Pepin himself, after much soul-searching, went back into the Trudeau government in 1980 as the Minister of Transport, and threw himself into other Canadian battles, like Via Rail, freight rates, and airport administration. He was under no illusions that his constitutional days were over, at least as long as he was in the cabinet. He knew that acceptance meant that, on the constitution, he had to shut up.[123] Given his experiences, given the directions the Report had taken, and given Jean-Luc Pepin's roots and personality, this was hard to accept: even in 1984 it still caused him obvious concern and regret. In 1983, in a cabinet shuffle, Lloyd Axworthy was made the Minister of Transport, and in a demotion accepted with his usual philosophical good humour, Mr Pepin became a Minister of State (external relations). He had apparently not endeared himself to Mr Trudeau before these changes because, when asked if he planned to run in the next election, he 'replied by asking Mr Trudeau about his plans, which were by then a sensitive issue in Liberal ranks'.[124] He was offered a seat in the Senate by Trudeau but declined; he could not see himself in such a role given his views on the second chamber (and the Task Force's recommendation to reform it).[125]

There remains the question of historical 'what ifs'. Answers to 'what if' —counterfactual—questions, if they are to be of any use in the world not of theory and speculation but of practical judgments, must be made cautiously, about particular cases. In a work entitled *Plausible Worlds*, the British political sociologist Geoffrey Hawthorn has investigated the nature of counterfactual history. His study raises very difficult questions about how we know what we think we know, and how 'possibilities haunt history' and form an essential part of our explanation of events.[126]

Hawthorn argues that 'in explanation possibilities at once decrease and increase' and this constitutes an important paradox.[127] Thus if we wish to explain the failure of the Pepin-Robarts Report we could do so in general terms. We would adduce such propositions as the following. Trudeau was in firm control of his party. His key advisors—Tellier, Lalonde, Robertson, et al.—were in sympathy with his views. The natural ally of the Report, the government of René Lévesque, was intransigent, at least until after the referendum. Other natural allies, such as Alberta, had their own agendas. The country was changing; deep social, demographic, and economic forces rendered the old dualist view suspect. It seemed as if the provinces were becoming too powerful, and that province building was a serious rival to the continued viability of a strong centre. The electoral system produced bizarre results, and the Quebec electorate showed its ambivalence in sending strong centralists to Ottawa and in placing strong decentralists or separatists in the Assembly. The Conservative Party was badly split, the NDP weak, and the Senate a tame ally of the Liberals. The House of Commons itself was so subject to party discipline that nothing radical could be expected from it. Change came down to executive power and initiative.

Our explanation would also emphasize more specific events and particular actions. The Task Force may have neglected to pay sufficient attention to its press release.[128] The Report may have been too hesitant in trying to accommodate both Quebec's special claims and in allowing the extension of these to the rest of the provinces. It may have been far too ambitious. Academic critics and the press picked up on the decentralizing theme. Not a single provincial premier championed the cause, and Robarts was ill and Pepin disheartened. Trudeau and Lalonde were easily able to sidestep the Report and did not meet the full group of Commissioners at any stage once the Report was released. Before the crucial meeting with the co-chairs (plus Dr Ronald Watts), Trudeau had time to read only half the document. Lalonde, taking the more traditional busy-man approach, had simply read the summary of its conclusions. This, suggests David Cameron, reveals their cast of mind, and is to Trudeau's credit.[129] Trudeau must have had a good idea what was coming, and was not prepared to sit down and discuss it as a realistic alternative (even though he was often prepared to listen to extended debates in cabinet). Given his later role, Gordon Robertson's comments are instructive:

I was against it then and I'd be against the Report now, so that I was not surprised when it got knocked over. There are some first class pieces of work in there and one can say with hindsight perhaps it would have been a good idea to adopt one thing or another. The Senate I think was impossible . . . on the whole the Report was not in tune with the times.

What happens as our explanations unfold is that 'it is quite natural, having sketched an explanation, to try to make it all but impossible to resist. We will want to make it difficult to believe in any alternative course of events that does not take us so far away from what did happen, or so far back, as to be indeterminate and uninteresting.'[130] What else could *possibly* have happened? Yet the very act of explaining 'suggests alternatives. Possibilities increase under it.'[131] If Clark had not been defeated on that fateful day in December, a radically different approach might have been proposed on language policy, on dualism, on the Charter, and on asymmetrical federalism. The referendum campaign would have proceeded very differently. Lévesque would not have confronted Trudeau as the French-Canadian leader of a party with a huge majority in Quebec.

We are therefore well aware, by implication, that the victory of the Trudeau agenda was not a foregone conclusion even if it has taken deep root. The explanation of what happened suggests an alternative, an alternative that still looks interesting given what was to come later and the state of the country now.[132]

Trudeau's deep and implacable hostility to any form of special status for Quebec, and to any recognition of equality between 'cultures' or 'peoples' or 'nations' within a single state, and his view that 'federalism cannot work unless all the provinces are in basically the same relation to the central government' found extensive support.[133] Individual rights were to be the basis of the Charter, and although the collective rights of French speakers were to be protected, French 'culture' was to be only one of many, for the country was irrevocably multicultural.[134] These propositions are now taken for granted by many, who hold them as self-evident truths (or fictions perhaps). We are all equal, we recognize and tolerate and promote all cultures (within the law), French rights are protected outside Quebec so that English rights in Quebec are accorded equal treatment, all provinces are equal. A right is a right is a right.

These ideas can easily be challenged by an equally plausible set of assumptions: group rights are prior to and essential for individual rights; federalism may require differentiation among sub-units; national bilingualism in Canada is unnecessary and unrealistic and should be a matter of local choice;[135] the protection of English in Quebec is not dependent on the same protection for French outside Quebec; there is no need to have state-sponsored multiculturalism; Quebec is the home of a nation and a people, and this distinct society should be formally recognized. Rereading the Pepin-Robarts report can make one wonder, even now, why we chose one set of assumptions over the other.

And the irony is, as previously noted, that the policies designed to thwart Quebec nationalism and outflank it have not done so, and may have had the very opposite results.[136] Many Canadians detest official bilingualism and blame Quebec for it. Many suspect that multiculturalism is undermining Canadian values and traditions, and some ethnic Canadians feel that it ghettoizes them. Other critics now view the Charter with suspicion and see it as élitist and as favouring special interests. Quebec is blamed because it will not accept mere provincial status in a redesigned Senate designed to promote provincial powers. So the fact remains that if Pepin-Robarts was vulnerable to criticism, and it was, so too is the Trudeau vision.[137] Trudeau's efforts to end-run the dualism abeyance brought the idea of a constitutionalized distinct society into irreconcilable conflict with a new set of operational principles. These principles led to the Constitution Act, 1982, after which many in Quebec would say, as Alain-G. Gagnon now does, that 'I feel that what has saved Canada up until now is that we have had those abeyances. We have agreed, in many ways, to disagree. That is what has made Canada possible. And now, since 1982, we have stopped agreeing that we have the right to disagree.'[138]

Therefore when we reread the documents of yesteryear we can reflect on what has happened since and consider how else it might have turned out, and why it happened as it did: 'explanations . . . are not fixed. . . . Explanations, we can say, are dependent, *as* explanations, on context.'[139] Our inquiries may, as Hawthorn notes, reduce our certainty 'and in that sense our knowledge' as they add to it. And this brings us back to the problems mentioned in the Introduction to this book and its discussion of history, structure, agency, cause and effect. We are back to personality, to Fortuna, and to the relationship between long-term forces and the improvisational, competitive skills of the politician. There is no one better at these skills than Trudeau.

The final irony is that someone who avoided military service during the war and who had trouble accepting a job, or responsibility, or even making up his mind; someone who was regarded as an academic, a legal philosopher, and a dilettante, should turn out to be so different. Not a philosopher but a master of rhetoric; tough, decisive, and a ruthless competitor; not an ivory tower academic but a brilliant communicator and debater, and probably, as Jean-Luc Pepin put it not quite in jest, 'our best actor since Sarah Bernhardt'. In the last chapter we now turn to yet more attempts to put our abeyances back into the graveyard, and Trudeau's role in thwarting them.

Notes

1. Edmund Burke, 'Speech on moving his Resolutions for Conciliation with the Colonies' in Gerald B. Chapman, *Edmund Burke: The Practical Imagination* (London: Oxford University Press, 1967), 29.
2. See, for example, J.R. Maddicott, 'Trade, Industry and the Wealth of King Alfred', *Past and Present* 123 (May 1989), 3–51 and the debate which follows about the 'essential strangeness' of the past and our tendency to ascribe modern motives to

those involved. The idea that 'the past is a foreign country; they do things differently there', is taken from the prologue to L.P. Hartley's 1953 novel *The Go-Between*, popularized in the 1971 film of the same name (script by Harold Pinter). Jeremy Rayner uses the useful term 'present-centredness' in his discussion of the problems facing revisionist historians. See 'The Very Idea of Canadian Political Thought', *Journal of Canadian Studies* 26, 2 (1991), 7–24.

3 Charles Taylor's essay on this subject, entitled 'Shared and Divergent Values', has been widely quoted and noted, and this piece, and many of his other works, are particularly important contributions to the debate over Quebec's claims to recognition. See Charles Taylor, 'Why Do Nations Have to Become States?' in *Philosophers Look at Confederation*, ed. Stanley French (Ottawa: Canadian Philosophical Association, 1978); Charles Taylor, 'Legitimacy, Identity and Alienation in Late Twentieth Century Canada' in *Constitutionalism, Citizenship and Society in Canada*, eds Alan Cairns and Cynthia Williams, Royal Commission on the Economic Union and Development Prospects for Canada (Toronto: University of Toronto Press, 1985), vol. 33, 183–229; Charles Taylor, 'Shared and Divergent Values' in *Options for a New Canada*, eds Ronald L. Watts and Douglas M. Brown (Toronto: University of Toronto Press, 1991); Charles Taylor, 'Multiculturalism and the Politics of Recognition' in *Multiculturalism and the Politics of Recognition*, ed. Amy Gutmann (Princeton: Princeton University Press, 1992); Charles Taylor, *Reconciling the Solitudes: Essays on Canadian Federalism and Nationalism* (Montreal and Kingston: McGill-Queen's University Press, 1993).

4 Not that such subjects are unimportant; far from it. The question is whether to constitutionalize them.

5 For discussions of this question note: Kenneth McRoberts and Patrick J. Monahan, eds, *The Charlottetown Accord, the Referendum, and the Future of Canada* (Toronto: University of Toronto Press, 1993); Curtis Cook, ed., *Constitutional Predicament: Canada After the Referendum of 1992* (Montreal and Kingston: McGill-Queen's University Press, 1994); Leslie A. Pal and F. Leslie Seidle, 'Constitutional Politics 1990–1992: The Paradox of Participation' in *How Ottawa Spends: A More Democratic Canada?* ed. Susan D. Phillips (Ottawa: Carleton University Press, 1993); Andrew Heard, 'When Must Constitutional Change Be Achieved By Amendment?', paper presented at the Annual Meeting of the Canadian Political Science Association (Calgary, 1994).

6 Both Gordon Robertson and Robert Normand made the point in the interviews that this was a mistake on Quebec's part, and they represent two different perspectives. Others would argue that this is hindsight, and that there was no chance of Quebec agreeing to the social policy clause.

7 See Janet Ajzenstat, ed., *Canadian Constitutionalism 1791–1991* (Ottawa: Canadian Study of Parliament Group, 1992). The constitutionalist-communitarian debate is the theme of this collection.

8 Robertson interview. It is possible that his use of the phrase 'in abeyance', both here and in other quotes, may have been influenced by a prior reading of an earlier article that I had written, and had sent to him before the interview. See 'Turning a Blind Eye: Constitutional Abeyances and the Canadian Experience', *International Journal of Canadian Studies* 7–8 (Spring-Fall 1993), 63–80. However, *in this context*, I think it likely that the term was used quite naturally.

9   Pierre Elliott Trudeau, 'Quebec and the Constitutional Problem' in *Federalism and the French Canadians* (Toronto: Macmillan of Canada, 1968), 36.

10 Pierre Elliott Trudeau, *Fatal Tilt: Speaking Out About Sovereignty* (Toronto: Harper-Collins, 1991), 14–15.

11 H.D. Forbes, 'Trudeau's Moral Vision: Reflections on His Memoirs', paper presented at the Annual Meeting of the Canadian Political Science Association (Calgary, 1994).

12 Kenneth McRoberts notes that in practice Trudeau had very little knowledge of Canada outside Quebec and had not travelled widely within the country. See Kenneth McRoberts, *English Canada and Quebec: Avoiding the Issue* (North York: Robarts Centre for Constitutional Studies, 1991), 11.

13 For a review of these questions and the 'new federalism' see David Milne, *Tug of War: Ottawa and the Provinces Under Trudeau and Mulroney* (Toronto: James Lorimer, 1986), ch. 1.

14 For a summary of Trudeau's cosmopolitan and centralist views see Andrew Stark, 'English-Canadian Opposition to Quebec Nationalism' in *The Collapse of Canada?* ed. R. Kent Weaver (Washington: The Brookings Institution, 1992), 123–58.

15 Over half of the essays in *Federalism and the French Canadians* are devoted to attacks on Quebec nationalism and his most substantial piece of work, the lengthy introduction to *La grève de l'Amiante. Une étape de la révolution industrielle au Québec* (Montreal: Cité Libre, 1955) is a biting dissection of Quebec's development. David Cameron has attacked the Trudeau view that nationalism is liberal or illiberal as a 'misconception of what the doctrine is about'. To really find out we must get 'down on the ground', and see the details of untidy reality. 'A mistake on this point may have serious consequences, and an example may be found in Canadian experience in the case of Pierre Trudeau.' See David Cameron, *Nationalism, Self-Determination and the Quebec Question* (Toronto: Macmillan, 1974), 69–70.

16 For a discussion of this phrase, and Trudeau's approach to federalism, see also Samuel V. LaSelva, 'Re-imagining Confederation: Moving Beyond the Trudeau-Lévesque Debate', *Canadian Journal of Political Science* 26, 4 (December 1993), 699–720 at 705.

17 Ibid.

18 According to Reg Whitaker, Trudeau is, to some extent, a Hobbesian in his distrust of nationalism; he sees federalism as the agent of liberalism in the management of nationalism. Whitaker does not, however, see him as an anti-nationalist and says that to label him thus is invalid. Reg Whitaker, 'Reason, Passion, and Interest: Pierre Trudeau's Eternal Liberal Triangle' in *A Sovereign Idea: Essays on Canada as a Democratic Community*, ed. Reg Whitaker (Montreal and Kingston: McGill-Queen's University Press, 1992), 151. See also Kenneth McRoberts, *English Canada and Quebec,* and Andrew Stark, 'English Canadian Opposition to Quebec Nationalism'.

19 Yael Tamir, *Liberal Nationalism* (Princeton, New Jersey: Princeton University Press, 1993). Given Trudeau's views, Tamir's work is particularly important within a Canadian context, where we are wrestling with culture, rights and identities in such an overt way. Her carefully built case for a far more accepting (and pragmatic) view of nationalism is one that I believe has considerable merit.

20 This is Stark's view. He says that 'probably no other Prime Minister has been as guided by a coherent political theory.' See 'English Canadian Opposition to Quebec Nationalism', 127.

21 Forbes, 'Trudeau's Moral Vision', 2–3.

22 Ibid., 5.

23 Ibid., 11. For a discussion of Canada's approach to cultural differences see Kenneth McRoberts, 'Living With Dualism and Multiculturalism', in François Rocher and Miriam Smith, eds, *New Trends in Canadian Federalism* (Peterborough: Broadview Press, 1995), 109–32.

24 For a full chronological account of the development of Trudeau's views see Stephen Clarkson and Christina McCall, *Trudeau And Our Times, Volume 1: The Magnificent Obsession* (Toronto: McClelland and Stewart, 1991).

25 Peter W. Hogg, 'Federalism Fights the Charter of Rights' in *Federalism and Political Community*, eds David P. Shugarman and Reg Whitaker (Peterborough: Broadview Press, 1989), 254.

26 See Richard Bird, 'Fiscal Decentralization' in his *Financing Canadian Government: A Quantitative Overview* (Toronto: Canadian Tax Foundation, 1979), 64. This theme is echoed also in Bird's other works, and by Thomas Courchene. See Thomas J. Courchene's *Economic Management and the Division of Powers*, Royal Commission on the Economic Union and Development Prospects for Canada (Toronto: University of Toronto Press, 1986), vol. 67, 19: 'comparisons hide as much as they reveal . . . it is important to recognize that overseeing a given percentage of expenditures is not the same as having the freedom to allocate these expenditures'.

27 Milne, *Tug of War*, 18. This debate still rages on. See John E. Trent, Robert Young, and Guy Lachapelle, eds, *Québec-Canada. What is the Path Ahead?* (Ottawa: University of Ottawa Press, 1996). In this volume of essays, Sylvia Bashevkin argues that research shows clearly that we live in one of the most decentralized federal systems in the world, and David Elton contends that, paradoxically, Canada is 'at one and the same time the most centralized and the most decentralized federation in the world'.

28 See, for example, the views of federalism outlined in Ronald Watts, *Multicommunal Societies and Federalism* (Ottawa: Studies of the Royal Commission on Bilingualism and Biculturalism, 1970).

29 See Rocher and Smith, eds, *New Trends in Canadian Federalism*, ch. 2. There are numerous other commentaries and discussions. For a recent useful overview from Quebec see Alain-G. Gagnon and Daniel Latouche, *Allaire, Bélanger, Campeau et les autres: Les Québécois s'interrogent sur leur avenir* (Montreal: Éditions Québec, 1991).

30 Donald Johnston, ed., *Pierre Trudeau Speaks Out on Meech Lake* (Toronto: General Paperbacks, 1990), 75. This turns all distinct-society arguments into mere province-building.

31 Pepin interview.

32 John L. Hiemstra, 'Trudeau's Political Philosophy: The Role of Federalism in Assimilating the "French Canadians"', paper presented at the Annual Meeting of the Canadian Political Science Association (Victoria, 1990).

33 For a more extensive review of these organizational moves see Cristine Andrea Beauvais de Clercy, 'Holding Hands With the Public: Trudeau and the Task Force on Canadian Unity' (MA thesis, Saskatchewan, 1992), especially ch. 4. I am indebted to Ms de Clercy for her pioneering account of the creation and work of the Task Force.

34 David R. Cameron, 'Not Spicer and not the B & B: Reflections of an Insider on the Workings of the Pepin-Robarts Task Force on Canadian Unity,' *International Journal of Canadian Studies* 7–8 (Spring-Fall 1993), 333–46. This essay is a particularly useful source of information on the work of the Task Force. Trudeau's speech to the House of Commons spoke of the need for 'wide input . . . the debate on fundamental change must not be confined to closed rooms or privileged élites . . . the government wishes to enable individual Canadians and their non-governmental organizations to play a more informed role. . . .' Canada, House of Commons *Debates*, 30th Parliament, vol. 2 (Ottawa: Government of Canada, 1977), 7314–15.

35 Ibid., 34. Also confirmed by Cristine Andrea Beauvais de Clercy, 'Holding Hands With the Public', and in interviews.

36 See Jeffrey Simpson, 'Jean-Luc Pepin: the bundle of energy with ideas of his own', *The Globe and Mail*, 27 January 1979, 13.

37 Pepin interview.

38 Jean-Luc Pepin, 'Closing Address', Inaugural Ceremonies for the Robarts Centre for Canadian Studies, York University, May 1984.

39 Louis Balthazar in a recent article called them 'two most loyal and distinguished Canadians'. See 'Within the Black Box: Reflections from a French Quebec Vantage Point', *The American Review of Canadian Studies* 25, 4 (Winter 1995), 519–41.

40 Cameron, 'Not Spicer and not the B & B', 337.

41 Pepin interview.

42 Among those who turned down an appointment were Claude Castonguay, Michel Bélanger, and Arthur Tremblay. These are all interesting names in view of later events.

43 See his address to the Montmorency Conference, 9 August 1967, *Journal of Canadian Studies* 2, 3 (August 1967), 52–8.

44 For a full account of Robarts's career see A.K. McDougall, *Robarts* (Toronto: University of Toronto Press, 1986). I am indebted to Professor McDougall for his advice regarding Robarts in general, and Robarts's work on the Task Force in particular.

45 Ibid., 174.

46 Ibid., 190.

47 Ibid., 200.

48 Ibid., 201. Robarts once confided to Claude Ryan that Trudeau's presence as the head of the federal government made it very difficult for the Premier of Ontario to assume a leadership role that was more accommodating to Quebec than the Prime Minister was prepared to be (private correspondence).

49 Pepin, 'Closing Address', 114.

50 The quotations which follow are taken from a wide-ranging interview.

168 **Whistling Past the Graveyard**

51 All three continued to have distinguished academic and public careers. Professor Dion is currently engaged in the writing of a multi-volume history of Quebec. John Meisel served, amongst other things, as the Chairman of the CRTC, and has recently retired from his academic chair at Queen's University. Edward McWhinney is currently the Liberal MP for Vancouver-Quadra.

52 Ibid.

53 See David Cameron, 'Not Spicer and not the B & B', 341. (The two so entrusted were Ronald Watts and David Cameron.)

54 Ibid., 336. All of the *Task Force on Canadian Unity Documents and Papers* are contained in the National Archives in Ottawa. They are set up as Record Group 33: Royal Commissions, Series 118, Volumes 1–33. Volumes 1–7 contain the drafts of the report. Loretta Czernis has offered a very different interpretation of the Task Force's work. In *Weaving a Canadian Allegory: Anonymous Writing, Personal Reading* (Waterloo: Wilfrid Laurier Press, 1994) she argues that the report was the work of a 'federal writing machine', and, because it 'was written by a number of civil servants . . . (therefore) it is not productive to find one writer and ask him/her what was intended.' We should, she argues, focus instead upon its allegorical and 'contextural' meanings. I can imagine what Jean-Luc Pepin would have had to say about this!

55 Pepin, 'Closing Address', 115.

56 Alan C. Cairns, 'Recent Federalist Constitutional Proposals' in *Disruptions: Constitutional Struggles from the Charter to Meech Lake*, ed. Douglas E. Williams (Toronto: McClelland and Stewart), 47. J. Stefan Dupré and Paul J. Weiler in their opening sentence speak of the 'elegantly written' Report. See 'A Sense of Proportion and a Sense of Priorities: Reflections on the Report of the Task Force on Canadian Unity', *The Canadian Bar Review* 57 (1979), 450–71.

57 Canada, *A Future Together: Observations and Recommendations,* Task Force on Canadian Unity (Ottawa: Queen's Printer, 1979), 4–5. They spoke with deep regret of 'a diversity in ignorance of itself, where each fragment of opinion is inclined to think that it is the whole'. See 6.

58 Ibid., 12–14.

59 Ibid., 17.

60 Ibid., 23–5.

61 Ibid., 26–7. J. Stefan Dupré and Paul C. Weiler disagree. They argue that the second problem should have been defined as Western Canadian alienation, not regionalism or provincialism as such. See 'A Sense of Proportion and a Sense of Priorities'.

62 Ibid., 48.

63 Ibid., 50.

64 Ibid., 51.

65 Ibid., 49.

66 Ibid., 52. This was one of the recommendations that Eugene Forsey, amongst numerous others, opposed so strongly. It would, he said 'mean leaving both minorities defenceless'. See 'The "Third Option"'. *The Canadian Bar Review* 57 (1979), 472–91

at 483. Gerard V. La Forest concluded that "There must be few more pious expressions of hope in a public document than this one'. See 'Towards a New Canada: The Canadian Bar Association's Report on the Constitution', *The Canadian Bar Review* 57 (1979), 492–512 at 501. In the Association's Report, it had been argued that, without language guarantees, 'Canada's existence as a nation is in danger'.

67 *A Future Together*, 87.

68 Ibid., 113.

69 Dupré and Weiler, 'A Sense of Proportion and a Sense of Priorities', 450–1.

70 *A Future Together*, 87.

71 Cairns, 'Recent Federalist Constitutional Proposals', 53. The same criticism is made by Alain-G. Gagnon and Daniel Latouche in *Allaire, Bélanger, Campeau et les autres*. They also note that 'Ainsi, d'une seule société distincte on passait à dix.' (Thus where there had been a single distinct society there were now ten.) However, they recognize the line of argument from Tremblay through Laurendeau-Dunton to Pepin-Robarts, and add that the Macdonald Royal Commission also endorsed the Pepin-Robarts approach to Quebec's distinctiveness and asymmetry. See 70–71 and 65.

72 Both Pepin and Watts made this observation in the interviews.

73 *A Future Together*, 103.

74 Milne, *Tug of War*, 21. Forsey, in 'The "Third Option"', 491, saw it as leading to a choice between 'a territory split between two sovereign states, and a North American ghost of the deceased Holy Roman Empire, sitting crowned upon the grave thereof.'

75 The Canadian Bar Association's Report did not recommend this, and saw the superior courts as performing a national function, and as preventing the emergence of a complex system of dual courts.

76 Watts interview.

77 This is Gordon Robertson's view.

78 Tremblay interview, 'and here it is important, in my opinion, to pose the question: why did Trudeau introduce Bill C-60 in June *without waiting for* (my emphasis) the Pepin-Robarts Report?'

79 Other strong critics included, as already noted, Senator Eugene Forsey. See 'The "Third Option"'. J. Stefan Dupré and Paul C. Weiler, 'A Sense of Proportion and a Sense of Priorities', also provide an extensive and detailed critique of the Report's whole approach, arguing that not only was it far too decentralizing but that it should never have tackled such a broad range of problems. They were 'emphatically' opposed to the new Senate, and thought that the recommendations constituted a 'laundry list'. They defended executive federalism as a pragmatic response, and thought that constitutionalizing economic questions was a mistake. The one reform they did entertain was partial proportional representation for the House of Commons.

80 Cairns, 'Recent Federalist Constitutional Proposals', 48.

81 Ibid.

82 For a comprehensive discussion of linguistic questions see David Schneiderman, ed., *Language and the State: The Law and Politics of Identity* (Cowansville: Les Éditions Yvon Blais, 1989). Note also Kenneth McRoberts, 'Making Canada Bilingual: Illusions and Delusions of Federal Language Policy' in *Federalism and Political Community*, eds David P. Shugarman and Reg Whitaker (Peterborough: Broadview Press, 1989), 141–72.

83 See, for example, his comments on the provinces and the later 1982 amending formula: 'worked on and agreed to by eight provincial governments, it was indifferent to the interests of the national government and the national community.' 'The Politics of Constitutional Renewal in Canada' in *Disruptions*, ed. Douglas E. Williams, 100.

84 'I view the Meech Lake process as a failure in constitutional morality'. See Cairns, 'Ottawa, the Provinces, and Meech Lake', 143.

85 Cairns, 'The Politics of Constitutional Renewal in Canada', 196–7.

86 He agrees with Roger Gibbins's concern that 'the federal government was a referee but not a player aggressively pursuing its own interests and vision.' See Cairns, 'Citizens and Governments in Constitution Making', 127.

87 Cairns, 'Recent Federalist Constitutional Proposals', 54.

88 Ibid., 50.

89 Without agreement on first principles we are in grave difficulty. See Cairns, 'Ritual, Taboo, and Bias in Constitutional Controversies in Canada, or Constitutional Talk Canadian Style', in *Disruptions*, ed. Douglas E. Williams, 205.

90 Cairns, 'The Fragmentation of Canadian Citizenship' in *Belonging: The Meaning and the Future of Canadian Citizenship*, ed. William Kaplan (Montreal and Kingston: McGill-Queen's University Press, 1994), 181–220 at 210.

91 *A Future Together*, 32.

92 See *Disruptions*, ed. Douglas E. Williams, 32. For a view from Quebec see Serge Denis, *Le Long Malentendu. Le Québec vu par les intellectuels progressistes au Canada anglais 1970–1991* (Montreal: Boréal, 1992), chs. 5 and 6. Denis argues that Cairns does not come to terms with the centrality of Quebec's collective claims and sees the Canada Act, 1982, as a compromise which, for Quebec, it was not.

93 None of the volumes were ever examined by a parliamentary committee 'and subsequent calls for reprints of the report were ignored'. See Cristine Andrea Beauvais de Clercy, 'Holding Hands With the Public', 98.

94 Every interview confirmed this.

95 Confirmed in interviews.

96 Cameron interview.

97 Clark interview.

98 In a work published in 1983 entitled *The Progressive Conservatives and the Constitution: No Small Measure*, Nathan Nurgitz and Hugh Segal discuss a number of issues, yet the only place that the Unity Task Force Report is even mentioned is in their brief chronology of events.

99 Clark interview. Clark also notes that he and Senator Arthur Tremblay believed that a final effort should have been made to bring Lévesque in, or to show conclusively that he was being obstructive. Clark phoned Bennett, Lougheed, and others to be told that it was 'too late' to make such an attempt. 'There was never enough effort made to bring Lévesque's government in, or enough discussion on it . . . bad temper prevailed. Trudeau and Lévesque were beyond the stage of talking to each other.'

100 Broadbent interview. Note Reg Whitaker's comment that the NDP has never been able to cope with Quebec. 'If Canada has a permanent Quebec problem, Canadian social democracy has a permanent Quebec crisis.' See 'Quebec Question', in Simon Rosenblum and Peter Findlay, *Debating Canada's Future: Views from the Left* (Toronto: James Lorimer, 1991), 248.

101 A comprehensive collection of press clippings is to be found in the National Archives amongst the collected papers of the Task Force. See *Task Force on Canadian Unity Documents and Papers*, vols 23–4.

102 Michael Goldbloom, *The Gazette*, 2 February 1979. It is still favourably referred to. See Louis Balthazar, 'Within the Black Box: Reflections from a French Quebec Vantage Point', *The American Review of Canadian Studies* (Winter 1995), 519–41. He argues that had its recommendations been followed the 1980 referendum might well not have taken place.

103 William Johnson, 'Task Force Making a Mistake', *The Globe and Mail*, 29 January 1979, A7. Johnson said that although he was 'most impressed with the quality of the Task Force's work and equally depressed by the cogent reasons which lie behind their recommendations, I think they are mistaken.'

104 *The Globe and Mail*, 26 January 1979.

105 Gilles Paquin, 'Le rapport Pepin-Robarts adopte la vision Trudeau', *La Presse*, 25 January 1979.

106 Normand interview. Robert Normand is in a position to know. He was Deputy Minister in the Quebec Justice Department from 1971–7. He then became Quebec's Deputy Minister of Intergovernmental Affairs from 1977–82, and ended his bureaucratic career as the Deputy Minister in Finance. He later served on the *Citizens' Forum on Canada's Future*, and wrote a dissenting opinion.

107 The headline in *The Globe and Mail* of 26 January 1979 read: 'Unity proposals will just make Quebec hungry for more, Lévesque'. He added that the proposals would leave Quebec 'like a half pregnant woman'.

108 Ramsay Cook, 'Why It Won't Work', *The Globe and Mail*, 5 February 1979, A7.

109 Denis Smith, *The Globe and Mail*, 5 February 1979, A7.

110 Canada, House of Commons *Debates*, Fourth Session, 30th Parliament, vol. 3 (Ottawa: Government of Canada, 1979), 2551–2.

111 Ibid.

112 Pepin interview.

113 Tremblay interview.

114 Ibid. 'On 13 December my working conditions changed radically.'

115 *A New Canadian Federation,* The Report of the Constitutional Committee of the Quebec Liberal Party. Montreal, 9 Jan. 1980.

116 See Claude Ryan, *Regards sur le fédéralisme canadien* (Montreal: Boréal, 1995), 123–138. Ryan discusses the events of this period, including the very delicate situation the Quebec Liberal Party found itself in after the referendum had been defeated. He, and the Party, were in agreement with a good number of the federal government's objectives—including the need for a Charter of Rights.

117 Gérald-A. Beaudoin, 'Devolution, Delegation, Centralization and Decentralization of Powers as seen by the Pepin-Robarts Commission' in *The Cambridge Lectures, 1979,* ed. Derek Mendes da Costa (Toronto: Butterworths, 1981), 79–92, 84. See also Gérald-A. Beaudoin, 'La philosophie "constitutionnelle" du Rapport Pepin-Robarts', in *Essais sur la constitution,* ed. Gérald-A. Beaudoin (Ottawa: l'Université d'Ottawa, 1979), 377–95.

118 Ibid., 90–1.

119 Forsey, 'The "Third Option"', 491.

120 Cameron, 'Not Spicer and not the B & B', 344.

121 This particular point is one that Ronald Watts recalls reminding the Prime Minister of at the time of the meeting on the Report; his recollection was confirmed by Jean-Luc Pepin.

122 There are reports that in 1991 Gordon Smith, the Secretary to the Cabinet for federal-provincial relations, read the Report from cover to cover and found it very helpful. Dr Watts noted that when the Senate came back as a subject of debate, that it was the academics who now had to talk the politicians out of a Council of the Federation approach!

123 He has of course been involved in constitutional debate since his retirement. He was, for example, a member of the 'Group of 22' who put out a set of 'Practical Suggestions for Canada' in 1991.

124 Obituary, *The Globe and Mail,* Sept. 7, 1995. In 1984 he had undergone heart surgery, a condition no doubt exacerbated by his incredible working hours and working habits. He was 70 years old when he died. Jeffrey Simpson, who had come to know him well during the days of the Task Force, summed up Jean-Luc Pepin's career in words that all politicians should want to be remembered by: 'Jean-Luc Pepin gave political life a good name. He was honest, courageous, dedicated to public service, a fighter for his beliefs, a lover of his province and a patriot for his country.' *The Globe and Mail,* 13 Sept. 1995, A4.

125 Pepin interview.

126 Geoffrey Hawthorn, *Plausible Worlds* (Cambridge: Cambridge University Press, 1991).

127 Ibid., 10.

128 Ronald Watts makes the explicit point that far too little attention was paid to the Report's initial press release, which was simply delegated and was not worked on by the Commissioners, and so what got picked up was the 'decentralising' theme, when in fact the Report contained so much more.

129 See Cameron, 'Not Spicer and not the B & B'. This was also confirmed in the interviews.

130 Hawthorn, *Plausible Worlds*, 13.

131 Ibid., 13.

132 Another counterfactual possibility was suggested during the interviews. The 'what if' was this: 'But another juncture was what if Stanfield had won the election and not Trudeau? What kind of prime ministership would that have been? A very, very different one. And somebody who is, I think, attuned much more to not having to be absolutely clear about everything, and not having ideas which are fixed and finished, but having convictions and principles which act as guides, and not as theorems. And ... I think ... what I am convinced of is that Trudeau's was not the only possible response to the kinds of nationalist pressures that were coming on. Could you have recaged that beast if you had been a little more like Pearson, or a little more like Stanfield, as just accommodating without trying to clarify the ultimate absurd direction in which it might conceivably have gone if you didn't ever stop? Because you always do stop. Societies always do stop.'

133 Stephen Clarkson and Christina McCall, *Trudeau and Our Times*, 106.

134 For a classic dissection of the idea that the Charter contains only individual rights see David Elkins, 'Facing Our Destiny: Rights and Canadian Distinctiveness', *Canadian Journal of Political Science* 22, 4 (December 1989), 699–716. Also note Alan C. Cairns, 'The Fragmentation of Canadian Citizenship', 208. The Charter, says Cairns, mobilizes people 'in terms of these (Charter) categories'.

135 See McRoberts, 'Making Canada Bilingual'.

136 The ironies of the Trudeau legacy, and their counterproductive effects, have been explored in particular by Kenneth McRoberts. See *English Canada and Quebec: Avoiding the Issue*.

137 Robert Vipond has commented, in what one can see as yet another irony, that: 'Canadians have accommodated themselves to a constitutional process that is *Calhounian* in its implications' (my emphasis). 'Seeing Canada Through the Referendum: Still a House Divided', *Publius* 23, 3 (Summer 1993), 39–55.

138 Gagnon interview.

139 Hawthorn, *Plausible Worlds*, 26.

6

Unsettled Settlement

Gentlemen, you will be pleased to take into your consideration the phrase and the manner as well as the matter.[1]

We need to remember that Quebec found out in 1981–2 that it did not have a veto over major constitutional change, and that its idea of a partnership was not the rest of the country's understanding. The views of successive Quebec governments as to what was needed to reform federalism were certainly not encapsulated either in the Charter, or in the new provincially inspired amending formulae contained in the Constitution Act, 1982. Quebec's collective goals, and its desire for the recognition of its rights as a distinct political community, were thwarted. Trudeau's promise of reformed federalism, given in his famous and controversial speech at the Paul Sauvé Arena in May 1980, was reform designed to keep Quebec firmly in its federal place. Those who knew Trudeau's work and ideas certainly should not have been surprised. Senator Arthur Tremblay was there the night of the speech. He has known Trudeau since their days at Harvard. He had been a prominent supporter in print of the 'no' campaign, but he turned to his wife after the event and said: 'nous sommes floués' (we've been had/swindled). He nearly changed his vote in the referendum, because he knew that what Trudeau seemed to be promising was not what federalists in Quebec wanted or expected.[2] They were not demanding a Charter of Rights (Quebec already had one) and the amending formula itself was far from the only issue for those who remained federalist.

Guy Laforest has undertaken a dissection of the Sauvé Arena speech.[3] He uses the Quentin Skinner view that consideration must always be given to two things: what an author actually says, as well as what he or she claims was the obvious intent. Trudeau solemnly promised renewed federalism and change, and warned English Canada that it was coming, 'I'm solemnly appealing to you Canadians in all the other provinces when I tell you we're putting our heads on the line by telling Quebeckers to vote "no".' Trudeau's use of the phrase 'renewed federalism' must, in Quebec, (in Laforest's opinion) be seen in the context of the traditional Quebec view of what this would mean. This is the point made by those who, like Morin and Adam, have attacked Trudeau's intentions.[4] Laforest's analysis is more subtle. He does not question Trudeau's intentions so much as what he actually said—and what he did not say. In order to understand the real meaning of a text it is necessary, following Skinner, to place its key concepts in a particular ideological and political context.[5] Trudeau had been silent on many issues during the brief Clark government and Laforest notes, in particular, his reluctance to comment on the key propositions in either the Pepin-Robarts Task Force Report or the Quebec Liberal Party's *Livre beige*. Both of these documents had, in the tradition of Laurendeau-Dunton, been a part of the same intellectual family that saw dualism as the central fact of Canadian political life. Laforest contrasts Trudeau's silence with the studious attention to the details of renewed federalism shown in Pepin-Robarts and the *Livre beige*. Trudeau's speech must be placed, he says, in this context of ambiguity and the renewed effort to redefine federalism that had gone on:

> Pierre Elliott Trudeau, fils du Québec et plus important leader politique de la fédération canadienne, a choisi d'être ambigu au moment sans doute le plus important dans l'histoire du peuple québécois. Le 14 mai 1980, au Centre Paul-Sauvé, sorte de temple du nationalisme québécois, dans un atmosphère lourde de solennité, il s'engagea à renouveler le fédéralisme canadien. . . .[6]

It is easy to understand why many in Quebec did not expect, after voting no and after a *warning* had been issued to the *rest* of Canada, to get what they got.

The package that was passed in 1982 put paid to the idea that Quebec was (a) going to be recognized formally as different to the other provinces, or (b) that there was an equal partnership between French and English Canada or (c) that there was going to be any redistribution of powers. Trudeau's whole strategy, already touched upon in Chapter Five, was to elevate the Charter and the notion of individual rights as the key counterweight to the centrifugal forces of federalism and provincialism. 'Quebeckers for some time previously had refused to assert that there was a contradiction between the Trudeau vision of a Canada for French Canadians and the Quebec government's vision of a strong provincial state.'[7] But 1982 chose one vision and entrenched it, forcing those in Quebec to realize that these visions were no longer compatible. 'In short', says Janet Ajzenstat, it was 'the federal government's injection of a particular political conception into the debate' that pushed Quebec into feeling it must choose.[8] When the Meech Lake Accord came along to tamper with the 1982 arrangements Trudeau was to say, 'For those who dreamed of the Charter as a new beginning for Canada, where everyone will be on an equal footing and where citizenship would finally be founded on a set of commonly shared values, there will be nothing left but tears.'[9] Setting aside for the moment the rhetorical excesses of this statement, his reasoning shows the centrality of the Charter to his arguments.

This is the issue that Charles Taylor tackles in his 1992 essay 'Can Canada Survive the *Charter*?' He argues that what now binds Canada together, *outside* Quebec, is not a common history but 'political institutions and ways of being'.[10] He is not suggesting that these ways of being are a total break from an older identity that was focused largely on Britishness and differentiation from the United States, defined through the political institutions of parliamentary government, and juridical traditions.[11] The Constitution Act, 1982, marked a break with Canada's past in several important ways, and helped to set up differing perceptions of our institutions inside and outside the province. James Tully develops this idea further in his essay 'Diversity's Gambit Declined', when he presents the argument that there have been three 'conventions of justification' which have provided the touchstone for Canadian federal relationships and constitutional negotiations.[12] These conventions involve recognition, procedural fairness, and the consent of those affected; taken together, 'the three conventions of justification comprise the Canadian tradition of federalism, which is complementary to the liberal tradition of citizenship'.[13] The Constitution Act, 1982, was perceived in Quebec, says Tully, as a violation of all three conventions, as a breach of trust, as a loss of middle ground—and as unjust.[14]

Like Tully, Charles Taylor has also pursued the argument that there is a distinction between the different philosophical bases of a liberal society. He argues that a society with collective goals, like Quebec, violates the assumptions of an individually anchored procedural liberalism of the kind so ably defended by liberal thinkers in the United States. Taylor concludes that what we have are two incompatible views of a liberal society that now square off against each other.[15] One view, the procedural liberalism espoused by Trudeau, claims to define the very essence of liberalism and this 'is erroneous and in a sense arrogant'.[16] What we should do, according to Taylor, is recognize that there are other models for a liberal society, including ones that recognize levels of diversity and difference. 'In a way, accommodating difference is what Canada is all about.'[17] For Taylor, recognition of second-level or deep diversity is essential and is what federalism should attempt to entrench, as others around the world are finding out.[18] However, this view runs counter to the expectation that the Charter is a new basis for national unity.

It also raises very difficult questions about how we are to define identities, and which groups are to obtain distinct political rights. As Katherine Fierlbeck has noted, if we blithely accept the claims made by groups and base this simply upon the demands for a secure cultural context, we run the risk that this could lead us to the recognition of cultural practices we would rather not endorse.[19] We must, she says, 'be intensely cautious' about accepting the normative claims of cultural identity, otherwise we may find ourselves in situations of diminished political tolerance, with fewer individual rights.

Even so, Tully, Taylor, and others make a strong case for the view that historical and contractual arguments apply in the Canadian situation.[20] As briefly discussed in Chapter Five, Yael Tamir has offered a detailed defence of 'liberal-nationalism', in which she shows how claims to national identity can and should operate within the framework of liberalism and the state. She, like Fierlbeck, suspects the authenticity/tradition arguments of Burke, based as they are on the idea 'that a nation that has undergone a slow and organic process of development is more authentic than one that has developed in a less stable and continuous way.'[21] Such views should be treated 'with some suspicion'. Authenticity claims can be a vehicle of oppression, especially towards women. Each case has to be judged on its merits, and individuals must be allowed to make their own choices. Hers is a world of great moral complexity, in which there will be frequent collisions between rights and values, and untidy compromise will often result. But tidiness, as Isaiah Berlin has noted, 'is not a proper end for heterogeneous societies'.[22]

At a crucial testing time for cultural and national communities, political communities strive to preserve both an ongoing commitment to a national vision and a commitment to a set of liberal beliefs. Tamir probes deeply into such vital problems as where our identities come from, what role society plays in identity formation, and why the existence of a state, with all as its citizens, *does not remove the claims of a group to national recognition within such a state.* For her, the right to national self-determination is a cultural rather than a political claim, although she is careful not to grant the right to a culture an overly predominant role. Certain claims are far more defensible than others. In a world full of minorities, the liberal-nationalist position advocates 'taking cultural and national differences into account and acknowledging that members of national minorities, even within the most liberal of states, have legitimate grievances, and formulating ways of alleviating them.'[23] She is not arguing that the claims of all can be met, or that suffering and persecution are sufficient grounds for the bestowal of national rights (if they were, women, homosexuals, religious groups, political parties, unions, could all qualify). However, 'most claims for national self-determination are advanced by groups to whom the term "nation" applies without great difficulty.'[24] The response to such a claim will be based upon factors that are outside the community's control, and which really amount to luck (such as geography, resources, climate), and the size of the communities involved. Tamir is able to use size as a key because she sees the right to national self-determination as a 'cumulative individual right'. In so doing she avoids the trap that lies in wait for those who see these claims purely as collective rights: in which case, why are larger groups entitled to more extensive rights than smaller ones?[25] Although different nations will have differing degrees of self-determination due to the unequal distribution of chance factors, and to their size and power, all are 'entitled to enjoy the widest degree of national self-determination allowed by their specific circumstances.'[26]

In Canada's case, this sentiment is crucial to bear in mind, for toleration and even encouragement of diversity in a single state are key ideas behind federalism. Tamir's point of view, in a Canadian context, has been forcefully expressed by Alain-G. Gagnon. For him, Canadian citizenship does not mean Quebeckers should have to give up their national identity, and preserving this identity does not mean that they cease to be liberal, or democratic, or Canadians. Gagnon puts it thus:

To wish a long life to Canada is to encourage 'deep diversity' and to recognize the multinational nature of the country. The resistance to do so on the part of many Canadians is incomprehensible to those whose federal vision is based on communitarian principles.[27]

For him, it is the lack of recognition of political communities as nations that leads those communities to seek nation-state status. Yet all would recognize how difficult it is to maintain a balancing act that juggles tensions within the state with the need for some overarching sense of national cohesion, at a time when global and regional rules and market constraints have altered so much.[28] Maintaining, and even strengthening, sub-national identities within federal units is undoubtedly one strategy to cope with the demands of global competition. Recognizing that the best solution will depend upon specific circumstances in each case is also vital. The Unity Task Force had tried to make similar points in 1979. So had the *Livre beige* in 1980.

Altered States: Meech Lake

Charles Taylor's thoughts on diversity and the Charter were written in the shadow of the failure of the Meech Lake Accord, after which, in his opinion, 'something snapped' in Quebec.[29] From the standpoint of abeyances Meech is particularly important because it attempted to put Canada's greatest abeyance into writing. This is not the recommended way to handle such volatile questions, as we have seen: abeyances are not subject to satisfactory definition or 'even to the prospect of being definable', according to Foley. They are ways of adjusting to issues 'left unresolved'; they exist—and must exist—because of the absence of definitive constitutional settlement. It is therefore highly unlikely that a major abeyance will survive 'a journey into print', for to put one into print is to have to tackle its illogical, contradictory nature. It can no longer remain unfathomable but acceptable, and so it will lose its 'essential character' which was based upon 'intuitive social acquiescence'. And when we discover that our previously held expectations were a chimera and are no more, the natural corollary will be disillusionment, frustration, anger, and a sense of loss. Also perhaps a sense of betrayal: it was thought there was an implicit bargain, but now it is clear that the rules have changed. No matter that it was as much Quebec's fault as any for breaking an implicit truce and opting for confrontation in the 1970s; or that it was Daniel Johnson's administration and 'Égalité ou Indépendance' that put onto the constitutional agenda demands that forced the abeyance to the surface.[30] Meech was an attempt to get the abeyance under control, not to up the ante.

For a time, after 1982, it appeared that the Quebec abeyance had been put to sleep; that the question of Quebec's 'real' status in Confederation had been buried by the combined defeat of the referendum of 1980, the seeming demise of the PQ, and the successful introduction of the Charter and the amending formulae. Whatever one thinks of Trudeau's approach to Quebec and the Constitution prior to 1982—whether he is seen as right or wrong—

there is a case to be made that he had succeeded in laying to rest the question of Quebec's status. This line of reasoning, though powerful and developed later by Trudeau himself ('impudent meddlers') must, nevertheless, be treated with some caution. If the abeyance was buried, it was a shallow grave.[31]

Constitutional debate was reopened once again in May of 1986 when Gil Rémillard presented what was thought by all present to be a 'modest, restrained and manageable' list of Quebec's conditions for accepting the arrangements of 1982.[32] The debate that followed and which led to the Meech Lake Accord precipitated a new crisis, a crisis that had at its centre the fact that this was the first time that the federal government of Canada was prepared to write into the constitution a statement recognizing duality and the special role of Quebec. Trudeau was under no doubts on this score. Of Meech he was to say:

> We have made peace with Quebec by letting it believe that 'Distinct Society' means Two Nations. If the courts hold that it does have that meaning, then Canada is doomed. If they hold otherwise, Quebec will have been tricked and the howls of protest will strengthen separatism. One way or another, Meech Lake may mean the peace of the grave for the Canada we know and love.[33]

This polarized view, that either the distinct society provisions of Meech meant nothing or spelled doom with a capital 'D', does not accord with the argument to be presented in this chapter that Meech was an ingenious, subtle attempt to deal with an abeyance by both recognizing and constitutionalizing it *and* by making it so vague as to leave in doubt whether or not it really meant anything at all.

It is not the intent to retell the whole sorry Meech tale of opportunities lost and battles fought. There are several excellent full-length accounts, notably those by Andrew Cohen and Patrick Monahan, several consolidations of readings, and hundreds of articles.[34] Accounts of the Charlottetown Accord also have to draw heavily upon the events of Meech and cast further light upon them. For the purposes of the argument presented here, Meech is far more important than the abortive Charlottetown Accord, although it too wrestled with similar problems and had the same implacable antagonist.

This chapter is devoted, first, to showing how we can think of the Meech Lake Accord as a way of dealing with an abeyance that had haunted us for decades, and how it should be understood 'only in the light of the years of non-recognition, of the *mariage de raison* that had failed to engage the heart and reflect dignity'.[35] This is not an argument about process and whether it was democratic or not; it deals with the 'vision thing', as George Bush might call it. Secondly, it is argued that Pierre Trudeau's style of debate in itself epitomizes the absolute *antithesis* of the kind of thinking necessary to preserve and protect our abeyances, and prevent them from colliding. Trudeau wants to confront and exaggerate and 'win'; he wants to have crystal-clear principles at work. (This is not the same as arguing that there comes a time when an issue must be faced, nor is it a comment upon the need for a strong centre.) Trudeau's rhetoric was challenged by Gordon Robertson's public refutation: their exchange of views is particularly illustrative of two entirely different approaches to Quebec and abeyances. Trudeau's approach is also seen as a stark contrast to the kind of political advice and wisdom found in Burke. Thirdly, and to conclude, there is a discussion of the ways in which the Scottish question has been handled in the United Kingdom, because this too involves claims to national recognition, in this case within a non-federal state. Is there anything to be learned from the Westminster/Edinburgh relationship that can give us a much-needed perspective on the Canada/Quebec situation, and on the approaches and attitudes we have taken? This brings us back to the Foleyan question of political temperament, to the whole idea of abeyances, and to the constitutional strait-jacket we have created for ourselves.

Alan Cairns, Roger Gibbins, and many others have argued that the Meech Lake Accord lacked vision, and that this was a fundamental defect because 'our written constitution becomes a critically important means of articulating the Canadian political community, (and) constitution making has become the definitive act of Canadian nation building.'[36] In this respect, says Gibbins, the Meech Lake Accord failed to develop a *Canadian* vision 'because the federal government and Prime Minister Mulroney failed to bring any national vision to the bargaining table'.[37] Others have argued that it enshrined the *wrong* vision and would have taken on a moulding role that would have the overall effect of the rewriting of political relationships in Canada.

> Perhaps the most significant implication of the new s.2 (distinct society) is its potential to affect the perceptions that Canadians have of themselves. The Accord officially divides us into French-speaking Canadians and English-speaking Canadians. . . . A constitution is the fundamental link between a society and its government and should be the expression of its vision of itself as a political and social unit.[38]

These charges need to be revisited in the light of the idea of abeyances and how they must be handled, for such critiques can be turned around entirely; it was precisely because Meech was *not* dominated by a single vision that it could have succeeded.

Meech was able (or at least tried) to reconcile competing constitutional agendas just as was the case in 1867. No single party could impose a settlement; all wanted one but not, this time, for external or economic reasons; all could proclaim a victory and could immediately offer conflicting versions of the settlement. Honour was saved, and it was hard to sort out any clear winners and losers, or so it initially appeared. As the basis of the Accord, Quebec had put forward its five 'demands', which were also indisputably the most modest list of requests from Quebec in 20 years. These five items entailed: explicit recognition of Quebec's unique character as a distinct society; increased powers in immigration; participation in the appointment of judges to the Supreme Court; provincial approval for federal spending in areas of exclusive provincial authority; and a Quebec veto over constitutional amendments which affected its interests.[39] To them were later added other items bargained for by the provinces, plus some federal counters, but these five points remained the heart of the Accord that was agreed to by the Prime Minister and the provincial premiers on June 3, 1987. In the final flurry of negotiations this text was later altered, but it and not what followed constitutes the crux of the matter.

Undoubtedly the most controversial clauses were the reference to Quebec as a 'distinct society' contained in section 2.1 (b): *'The recognition that Quebec constitutes within Canada a distinct society'* along with the statement that 'The role of the legislature and Government of Quebec is to preserve and promote the distinct identity of Quebec referred to (in 2.1b).' These two clauses were sandwiched between other important interpretive clauses which specified that the presence of French-speaking Canadians outside Quebec and English-speaking Canadians within Quebec was a 'fundamental characteristic of Canada', and that it was the responsibility of the federal Parliament and the provincial legislatures to preserve this. Meech quite clearly attempted to be a delicate and carefully crafted balancing act, especially with regard to the distinct society clause, which did not make the attempt to define what made Quebec distinct. (It could include, for example, the presence of a large anglophone minority.) Distinct society had finally made it into constitutional print, but it was on a leash. 'Quebec had no guarantees whatsoever that the distinct society clause—the flag-bearer of political duality—would have carried the day in any particular occasion.'[40] Provincial equality was mentioned also, but only in the preamble, 'Whereas the amendment proposed in the schedule hereto also recognizes the equality of all the provinces. . . .' The division of powers remained the same, and 'nothing in section 2' was to affect aboriginal and multicultural rights in sections 25 or 27 of the Charter.

Even so, the reactions produced were extraordinary. Some argued that distinct society would mean nothing at all and that this was a danger because Quebec would be disillusioned. Trudeau himself used this line of thought, claiming that Meech might be 'insulting' to Quebec,[41] whilst he was, at the same time, arguing that Meech was the end of a constitution that could have lasted 'a thousand years'.[42] His concerns for Quebec's honour seem a trifle feigned. Some said Meech Lake constitutionalized the *status quo*; others saw it ripping apart the work of Sir John A. Macdonald and his successors. It let the Quebec genie out of the bottle, or it put the stopper back in before the genie woke up again. It would have paradoxically enshrined the essence of Trudeau's Charter and the arrangements of 1982 but Trudeau simply could not see this, or it would have wrecked the grand scheme because 'the process of *constitutionalizing* the people of Canada . . . was stopped in its tracks'[43] (my emphasis). The new section 2 would not override the Charter; it was an interpretive provision and would be 'subordinate to the Charter of Rights and Freedoms'[44] and would work with it, in that any limitations on rights in Quebec would have to be 'demonstrably justified in a free and democratic society, albeit one that is distinct culturally and linguistically.'[45] Or it meant that for those who saw the Charter as a new unifying force, a new beginning where everyone would be on an equal footing, as equal citizens, there will be 'nothing left but tears'.[46] It was seen by many as strongly decentralizing in its allocation of reasonable compensation to the provinces if they opted out of federal shared-cost programs and would mean, it was said, the end of any grand federal initiatives such as national daycare. Others noted that the programs in question were in areas of exclusive provincial jurisdiction, and so this gave to the federal government something it had always lacked—the constitutional right to legislate in these areas, and it also demanded that any province opting out must have a 'program or initiative that is compatible with the national objectives'.[47] Even in areas like immigration there were those, like Garth Stevenson, who saw it as a return to the spirit of the immediate post-1867 years, for 'The significant role the provinces once played in immigration policy, as well as the real origins of co-operative federalism, have thus almost been forgotten.'[48] In Stevenson's view there was nothing on immigration in Meech that was 'either unprecedented or contrary to the spirit of Canada's constitution'.[49] Others, who usually knew far less history on the subject, saw the immigration provisions as disastrous.

The list of utterly irreconcilable opinions could go on and on. It seems fairly safe to argue that people could find in Meech what they wanted to find. They could also find missing those things they thought should have been stated, many of which were to surface in the Charlottetown Accord. Meech provided only a very general statement of provincial equality in the preamble; it did not create a Senate based upon such a principle. It did not deal at all with the question of aboriginal sovereignty and distinctiveness. It avoided language questions except in the very general provisions of section 2.

It is a hopeless and unrewarding task to sort out who was right and who was wrong because so much was speculative. The distinct society clause would have meant something—but what? It is quite possible that provisions that people did not see as earth-shattering, such as provincial nominees for the Senate, could have had the most dramatic effects of all. Within a short time all the Western provinces might have been submitting the names of individuals who had been elected to the Senate, elected furthermore to a Senate with full powers if it but chose to exercise them.[50] Given the track record of unanticipated consequences emanating from 1982, when the possibility of provincial referenda was not on the table, it is foolish to think that constitutional prophecy is, or ever has been, a very advanced science.[51] Therefore those who feared the unanticipated effects of change did have grounds for concern. This, however, is not a precise but a vague objection, and usually assumed precision was the order of the day in terms of concerns.[52]

Meech was like a mini-version of 1867. It was precise in places; it assumed a great deal; it contained ambiguities and clauses that would mean what the Courts wanted them to mean; it left a great deal to be worked out between Ottawa and the provinces; it avoided, quite deliberately, stating certain things. If 1867 had been put to the test of public opinion it would probably have lost; but, had the Meech Lake Accord been accepted, Guy Laforest argues that:

> the constitution of Canada would have remained faithful to what was, according to Ramsay Cook writing 20 years ago, the meaning of Confederation. In 1867 the founders of Confederation, in Cook's opinion, had been wise enough to produce a constitution in which an equilibrium between principles, a tension between visions, had been devised.[53]

If we think once again in terms of abeyances, what the Meech Lake Accord clearly tried to do was tackle one and avoid the rest: it had to tackle the problem that had bedevilled debate since the 1960s. Was there to be any recognition in the Constitution that Quebec had a special place in Confederation?

Without actually using the word 'abeyance', Richard Simeon has come as close as anyone to outlining, in abeyance-like terms, exactly why Meech was trying to avoid the trap of either picking one vision or clarifying things where there was no agreement. His assessment accords perfectly with the thesis that there are things better left unsaid, unresolved, and in a state of suspension—and that the Meech Lake Accord was quite clearly in the tradition of 1867.[54]

Simeon notes that the expectation that the Constitution can 'encapsulate' Canada is unreasonable, as is the assumption that we can all see ourselves reflected in it; 'our expectations should be much more modest.'[55] There is, says Simeon, no single vision of Canada, and if one starts from this proposition the task:

> is not to enshrine one (vision) to the exclusion of others, but to provide the framework for a continuous dialectic among them, both by balancing and compromising existing ideas, and by accommodating shifts in perceptions and values which occur over time. . . . I do not want a government, much less a Constitution, to prescribe or define my identity for me.[56]

Simeon sees Meech as a careful compromise whose specific terms soon got lost in rhetorical excesses, where critics assumed sweeping motives and consequences and/or searched for minute pieces of evidence. Simeon's argument is based upon the need to see the Accord in historical perspective: yet another in a long line of events which tilt the federation slightly in one direction or another. Events in 1982 tilted the country further towards bilingualism but 'made virtually no concession to a conception of Quebec as a distinct society'.[57] Meech, says Simeon, tilts the balance the other way and is somewhat more provincialist, but there were precedents for virtually all the elements in it. Meech, in other words, was nothing new, and like our previous arrangements, it refused to pick a winner in terms of either the old problems (French-English relations, federal-provincial relations, provincial and national communities) or the new (issue and group focused). The genius of Meech was that it refused to make clear choices, whilst it did take the all-important step of recognizing dualism:

Meech Lake does not select any of the competing conceptions. Instead, it embodies elements of all of them. . . . And perhaps more important, it signals the end of the polarized debate between mutually exclusive images of the country which so poisoned constitutional debate over the last 20 years.[58]

If Simeon was right, and if new forces and issues could then have become the focus of attention, Quebec and Canada would not still be locked into such a fierce debate about nationalism and duality within a single state. Not that the topic would ever disappear, but it might at the very least have been set aside. The state would have been able to get on with grappling with other problems—like its economy and its cultural survival.[59] And the expectation expressed by Simeon is that we could, at least for some time, have laid to rest the issue of the recognition of Quebec as special, as something other than a province, which has haunted us for so long. An abeyance very nearly survived a journey into print, and in print it would still have been appropriately vague and indeterminate. Even Quebec nationalists saw in Meech a compromise between the vision of Laurendeau and Scott. It was a partial victory for the heirs of Laurendeau, like Claude Ryan and Arthur Tremblay.[60] The 'taboo par excellence' against pronouncing the words 'unique status' would have been broken, but the world would not have fallen apart.[61] The Supreme Court could have become, like its US counterpart, a key abeyance avoidance mechanism through its interpretive powers over the meaning of 'distinct society'. Ralph Heintzman has concluded that, 'Whatever else may be said for or against it, the Meech Lake Accord was a dramatic and eloquent expression of a high moral ideal; the ideal of a Canadian political space to be shared on some basis of equity by two great languages.'[62]

In sum, Meech did what its authors thought *had* to be done; it was not constraining, and it left things undetermined or even contradictory, whilst preserving a fundamental characteristic of the country: 'In this, it is [was] like all our constitutional documents.'[63] Simeon is far from alone in this judgment. Carolyn Tuohy entitled her 1993 study of key policy problems *Policy and Politics in Canada: Institutionalized Ambivalence*. We are, she says:

> ambivalent about the appropriate roles of the state and the market, about national and regional conceptions of political community, and about individualistic and collectivist concepts of rights and responsibilities. This ambivalence arises from tensions that are endemic to three fundamental features of the Canadian context: the relationship with the United States, the relationship between anglophones and francophones within Canada, and the regionalized nature of the Canadian economy and political community.[64]

Shades of Pepin-Robarts! She too shows how this ambivalence was reflected in the Meech Lake Accord. But one person was not ambivalent in the slightest, and it is to his abeyance-confronting role that we now turn.

States of Mind: Pierre Trudeau

Gordon Robertson knows Pierre Trudeau well. He has known him for over 40 years. They worked together as juniors in the Privy Council Office (1949–50). He was Trudeau's boss when Trudeau joined the federal bureaucracy. In 1968, when Trudeau became Prime Minister, the roles were reversed. Robertson was the Clerk of the Privy Council (the secretary to the federal cabinet), a post he held from 1963 until 1975, after which, for the next four years, he became the Secretary to the Cabinet for Federal-Provincial Relations (and therefore the senior advisor for all federal-provincial conferences). He finally retired in 1979. During his time as secretary, 'Virtually every working day (from 1968–75) . . . began with a meeting in Mr Trudeau's office on all the problems of government a Prime Minister has to resolve.'[65] Friend, confidant, colleague, and senior advisor though he was or had been, Gordon Robertson broke publicly with Pierre Trudeau in early October 1992. Ostensibly it was over the former Prime Minister's comments on the Charlottetown Accord published in *Maclean's* magazine, but it had built up since the demise of the Meech Lake Accord. 'It took a lot because of my friendship with Trudeau. It wasn't a matter of courage . . . I didn't like quarrelling with him publicly, but I decided finally that I disagreed with him so profoundly.'[66]

Robertson, in an article entited 'How Pierre Trudeau Misleads the People', accused Trudeau of making unsupported judgments and of exercising to the full his 'imagination and demagogic skill'.[67] Essentially, he says Trudeau was totally wrong when he spoke and wrote of Charlottetown in terms of 'blackmail' and of being 'in the presence of dictatorship', and Robertson could not—'to my great regret'—stand by and let it pass.[68] This is an extraordinary turn of events, when someone as restrained and circumspect as a Gordon Robertson ventures into the press to take on his own Prime Minister in this way. The further exchange of views makes things even more unusual, as will be seen.[69] However, before this correspondence is discussed it is important to note that Robertson had been a supporter of the 1982 changes and that it was not until Trudeau's opposition to Meech that he broke with the Trudeau vision.

He had been in accord with Bill C-60 (in 1979) and the federal strategy of going it alone to show that movement was possible. When asked when he would date the commencement of his differences with Trudeau he replied:

> I was conscious, I suppose, from . . . I have trouble putting a date on it. I don't think his views and mine differed at all—really in any significant way—up until the time of the Liberal defeat in the election [of 1984]. I was conscious that he took a more rigid view than I did of special status. I was prepared to have all sorts of special status. . . . I personally negotiated the opting-out for Quebec. . . . Well, then when Meech Lake came along, I became aware that he drew the line much more firmly than I did. I accepted the distinct society clause, he rejected it.[70]

Robertson had seen the arrangements of 1982 as the least of the available evils, 'not good, but better than failure', but he recognized that it was a 'very serious blow to Quebec' and thought that something had to be done, in principle, to make it possible for Quebec to swallow 1982.[71] Obviously, Trudeau did not.

Trudeau's objections to the distinct society clause of the Meech Lake Accord he views as 'utter nonsense. I think he's got away with murder on this'.[72] The reason that the clause was so central was that:

> it was one of the classic demonstrations of a very, very shrewd attempt to leave a number of things in abeyance, unstated. Did the distinct society give new and special powers to Quebec or not? I'm clear in my mind that it did not, but it wasn't answered. That was part of the genius of the thing.[73]

It is still galling for those who believed so much in the Meech Lake Accord to have seen it come so close to passing, and to know that one of the key reasons that it did not was Trudeau's brutal intervention. Before returning to the Robertson-Trudeau exchange of correspondence over Charlottetown, it is important to get a sense of the Trudeau style. We cannot ignore its tone and tactics, and should remember that:

> As soon as a political thinker commits himself to paper in an effort to communicate his ideas to people, the persuasive methods he adopts to convey and give vitality to those ideas become matters of critical importance. The one cannot be dissociated from the other—in a very real sense 'the phrase and the manner' give the character to 'the matter'.[74]

Trudeau's phrase and manner are a combination of personal attacks, selective detail, deliberate and crucial omissions, sweeping denunciation, exaggeration and pure vitriol, always put together in such a way that opponents are kept off balance.

His opponents in Quebec—those who demanded changes to 1982—are a 'bunch of snivellers'.[75] We are 'governed by eunuchs' and the 'wimp' who took over from Trudeau. Of the proposed amending formula in Meech he said, 'Well, the least we can say about the new formula is that whatever consensus there may be in Canada, however broad that consensus, we will never be able to take Canada in that direction if one province was opposed to it.'[76] This statement does two things. It makes it appear as if the Accord made unanimity the rule for all constitutional change. It did not; it extended unanimity to amendments to the Supreme Court of Canada (already partially covered by the existing unanimity provisions), changes to the proportion of members of the House of Commons elected from each province, and the extension of existing provinces into the Territories. None of these were problematic. Only the proposals to extend unanimity to cover significant changes to the Senate, and the creation of new provinces, were at issue. Otherwise the rule of 7/50 stayed in place. If there is to be a unanimity rule at all in a federal system, surely changes in these two key areas of federal-provincial powers (and the balance of federal arrangements) qualify for its application? The second thing that this statement ignores is who agreed to a unanimity rule in the first place. It wasn't Quebec, it was the government of Pierre Elliott

Trudeau. He gave the country an amending formula that was devised by the provinces. His Charter and this formula make very uneasy bedfellows.[77]

He denounces what Quebec politicians are claiming the clause means, knowing full well that every politician has to play to the home crowd, just as Moe Sihota did in 1992 when he discussed Charlottetown in British Columbia. Trudeau could just as easily have chosen the comments of a David Peterson or an Arthur Tremblay and he knew also, as did everyone else in Quebec, that those who would be the most delighted if the Accord failed were the stalwarts in the PQ. This is impossible to guess from his writings. According to Trudeau the provinces 'got everything they wanted'.[78] This should be news to Alberta supporters of a Triple-E Senate. He comments that Quebec had 'not got *everything* in November of 1981'.[79] The implication is, given the italics, that they had got *almost* everything, and came back to get the rest. This conclusion too will come as news to those in Quebec who believe that 1982 was an attempt to outflank and outwit historic claims to special status, and that the Charter was designed to be an instrument of federal control. But Trudeau claims that Quebec, in 1987, 'was not attempting to correct the things that happened in 1981'.[80]

The last twenty years had been 'a struggle to establish the sovereignty of the people over all levels of government'.[81] In 1981 'the battle for people's rights was won'[82] and was now being thrown away; it would be 'the end of the peaceable kingdom' for with Meech Lake 'there is no national will left'.[83] Such statements are pure hyperbole by anyone's standards—and there are many more examples to choose from. (Many could argue that comments such as these might more appropriately have been addressed to the Free Trade Agreement.) As one final example, it is interesting to note how he argues that Quebeckers actually voted in favour of the 1982 Accord. He simply adds up the number of federal and provincial Quebec MPs and MNAs who voted for it, and the result comes out as 109 to 74. One wonders what the residents of any other province would say if their legislative assembly voted one way and their federal MPs another. Would they just add up the votes and declare a winner?[84]

It is interesting to examine such tactics in the light of Marc Gold's discussion of rhetoric mentioned briefly in Chapter Two.[85] Gold, we will recall, emphasises the importance of the anticipated audience and *its* expectations. He notes how any sustained debate on the merits of an entrenched Charter was avoided in 1981; Trudeau derided those who were prepared to trade 'individual rights for fish'. (In retrospect, Newfoundlanders might well still take the fish, if they could be found, for without it their individual rights look rather bleak.) The Court, says Gold, relies on the rhetoric of individualism whilst claiming to be objective. It exaggerates. It chooses which facts to highlight or render banal. It characterises legislation by using negative terms. It denigrates the character and competence of opponents and their arguments, yet manages to maintain its image as a neutral balancing forum, situated above the fray. This is part of its means of persuasion. Trudeau obviously does not stay above the fray, yet he too manages to convey the impression that he intervenes only to set the record straight and to get things back on track. All the rhetorical devices Gold ascribes to the Court, and more, are present in Trudeau's written and oral interventions. Trudeau is brilliant in debate. He knows what messages he wants to get across; he does not deviate from his themes; history doesn't stand in his way; opponents are rarely a match, and, if they are, the ground for debate gets switched.[86] Every photograph placed in *Pierre Trudeau Speaks Out on Meech Lake* carries a message: here are the weaklings and villains (starting with Robert Stanfield), here are the heroes.

This brings us back to the confrontation with Gordon Robertson. In his *Maclean's* magazine piece[87] Trudeau had charged that the Charlottetown Accord was the payment of 'ransom' to Quebec and the 'master blackmailer' would just be back for more; the ransom changed from year to year. Changes to the 'Canada clause', (it had been expanded and if anything the distinct society clause had been weakened), including the statement that Quebec was a distinct society, would of course be the end of equality because the clause would prevail over the Charter. The Accord spelled 'the end of social programs in the poorer provinces' and the end of new national programs, because it contained a spending clause similar to the one in the Meech Lake Accord. One does not need to remember all the details of Charlottetown to see that these were the core of the objections he had raised over Meech. (There was certainly far more to attack in Charlottetown: its index alone was two pages of single-spaced type.) There is no doubt that Trudeau was consistent in his claims.

Robertson's rebuttal, and his charge that the former Prime Minister was now 'misleading the people of Canada' focused on three key points.[88] First, no *constitutional* ransom had been paid to Quebec in response to its demands over the previous forty years. Quite the contrary; the Charter of Rights and Freedoms was imposed on Quebec without its agreement. 'In short, there has been no constitutional change to this day—not one—to pay any "ransom" or "blackmail".'[89] All provinces made demands that changed somewhat with circumstances, but Quebec 'has probably been the most consistent of all the provinces in its basic objectives, but so far it has achieved none of them.'[90] We must remember that this comment comes from someone who was a key party to the events of the past forty years; someone who had phoned Pierre Trudeau in 1964 to congratulate him for his speech on the dangers of opening up the constitutional debate;[91] someone who was hardly a constitutional radical, and who knew the history of federal-provincial dealings on the subject inside and out. Secondly, Robertson took Trudeau to task for his view that the Charter would be overridden and would not remain the key interpretive document. His allegations about the loss of equality 'cannot stand up'. Thirdly, there was the restriction on federal spending power in areas of exclusive provincial jurisdiction. 'What alternative,' asked Robertson, 'does Mr Trudeau propose?' Should the federal government be able to impose a program in a provincial area of jurisdiction against the wishes of a province? 'We had enough of that trouble in the 1960s.'[92] So Trudeau's rigid interpretations and sweeping denunciations ran up against someone who was there, on the inside and on the federal side, and whose historical memory would be difficult to refute.

The Trudeau response was a classic case of ships passing in the night. The style of the reply was odd. Virtually every paragraph began with Trudeau referring to himself in the third person: 'Pierre Trudeau had said'; 'Pierre Trudeau's reply'. What kind of effect this was designed to produce is difficult to say.[93] His reply to the three charges discussed above was that 'of course no constitutional changes were made' because Quebec had 'moved the goal posts'.[94] So what Quebec got, for example, was the Quebec pension plan and various opting-out arrangements. The Charter which Robertson says Quebec had not wanted 'is precisely what the Lesage government had asked for. Admittedly, it came twenty years late; but this is because Premier Lesage killed the process of constitutional change in 1964.' He repeats his charge that the Canada clause will prevail over the Charter. And he asserts that 'that trouble' over spending power which Robertson referred to 'gave Canada nation-wide programs such as hospitalization, medicare and post-secondary education funding'. Any new plans along these lines will be 'rendered impossible'. (In his next sentence they are still possible but no federal politician would raise the money only to see it spent on programs merely 'compatible' with federal objectives.)

What was an unsuspecting member of the public to make of all of this? You either believed Pierre Trudeau or you did not. Robertson, however, had the last word. He was offended by Trudeau's reply and considered it 'third class'.[95] In a long letter he relaid his charge that Trudeau's rhetoric was misleading, and now had other examples to quote, especially Trudeau's amazing claim that Lesage and Quebec had demanded the Charter and that, twenty years late, he had delivered 'precisely what they had asked for'.[96] Robertson takes this 'effrontery' to task, pointing out how the Charter was always a key federal initiative.[97] He agrees that there were changes in such areas as various shared-cost arrangements and pensions, but reiterates that none of these were related to 'any constitutional change that Quebec had sought'. He then argues that the Trudeau assertions on the Canada clause and the Charter are misleading, and takes pains to show how the courts will apply the various portions of the Charter. There was no further reply from Trudeau.

What is made abundantly clear in these exchanges is that any attempt to tilt the federal balance or to constitutionalize Quebec's claims to distinctiveness in any way whatsoever, would be met by a former Prime Minister who remained the best debater in the country, a master of phrase and image making, with a simplicity that promised truth, and with a view of federalism that does not brook any other. It is a view that is easy to explain because it seems so clear. Everything hinges on 'equality'—equality between individuals, and equality between provinces, all under the Charter. Does this imply a Triple-E Senate or recognition of aboriginal claims? Should this mean an end to the privileged status of French outside Quebec? These are not the kinds of details and consequences that need be discussed when one's objective is to defend the *status quo* and a particular view of rights.[98] The fact is, there is no way of knowing who won the war of words that had erupted in *The Globe and Mail*. However, Trudeau's extraordinary reputation and public profile translated into enormous political power, regardless of the merits of the detailed points under consideration.

The Trudeau approach has had obvious consequences in terms of how we treat our abeyances. It is a strategy of confrontation. The abeyances surrounding the idea of two nations have to be beaten into submission; the problem is named and the assault launched. It is a vicious war, using every available weapon. Trudeau gives no quarter and expects none. Losing is for wimps. Saving face, avoiding insult, not pushing a single principle too far, accepting an 'œconomy of truth', exercising prudence, attending to specific circumstance, not letting theory drive practice, and seeing Quebec's nationalism as liberal and positive, as well as threatening, were not on Trudeau's agenda.

A new vision of federalism may have taken root and could now unfold. We may have broken with the past and the traditions of Trudeau's Liberal predecessors. A far more Diefenbaker-like view prevails, certainly in the Western provinces: unhyphenated Canadianism, provincial equality, no recognition of distinct society, institutional reform, and less pandering to Quebec, are all part of the agenda now. So also is what has been termed 'secular fundamentalism', by which is meant that people hold uncompromising convictions on a wide range of questions (intransigent self-righteousness might also be a description).[99] The ghost of John George, not Sir John A., lives on in such attitudes.

Is this approach really the best way to tackle deep-seated contradictions that have been a part of the Canadian state's constitutional life for so long? Does it make an abeyance more or less likely to return to the graveyard? The 'phrase and the manner' as well as the matter do count: manners may be as important politically as laws.[100] Certainly, in Burke one finds a very different approach to the dangerous and the intractable. As we know from the discussion of Burke at the end of Chapter Two, he wrote of the need to avoid extremes, to distrust theory, to always see things in the light of 'circumstances' and to rely on our 'feelings'—meaning our feelings for each other and for the human condition. If one reads, say, *Pierre Trudeau Speaks Out* juxtaposed with the writings of Burke, the contrasts are startling. Burke attacks those who are so intransigent in their beliefs in the rights of man that they will brook no argument.[101] He even pleads for 'an œconomy of truth. It is a sort of temperance, by which a man speaks truth with measure that he may speak it longer.'[102] But first of all there is the importance of plain good intention 'which is as easily discovered at the first view as fraud is surely detected at last, is let me say, of no mean force in the government of mankind.'[103] We must try to avoid injured pride; 'When a man is robbed of a trifle on the highway, it is not the tuppence lost that constitutes the capital outrage.'[104] It is not that Burke is always opposed to taking action. Timely action to redress a wrong can be crucial, because if not taken 'the concessions which had satisfied in the beginning could satisfy no longer; because the violation of tacit faith required explicit security.'[105] Burke warns us not to judge people when they are politically agitated and highly partisan: 'It is not fair to judge of the temper or dispositions of any man or any set of men, when they are composed and at rest, from their conduct or their expressions in a state of disturbance and irritation.'[106] Of course, 'We Englishmen stop very short of the principles upon which we support any given part of our Constitution, or even the whole of it together.'[107] In the case of the Americas there was the desirability of a simple peace 'sought in its natural course and in its ordinary haunts'.[108] Those habits which politicians acquire after a life 'too much conversant in office' will suffice in normal circumstances but will not do when 'the high roads are broken up, and the waters out, when a new and troubled scene is opened, and the file affords no precedent'.[109] Of course, Burke too was guilty of exaggeration, purple prose, rhetorical excess, sarcasm and invective, yet there still shines through his works a distrust of the impractical and, above all, a very different approach to the intractable.

Have we therefore been guilty of not understanding or taking our full circumstances into account, of picking one principle over another, of underestimating complexity, of ignoring our past and exaggerating our present, of lacking a spirit of principled wisdom? If the ghost of Burke had been sitting in the Maison Egg Roll on the night Pierre Trudeau attacked the Charlottetown Accord, what would it have made of the way in which Trudeau presented his argument? It could be judged as conduct 'in a state of disturbance' and, as such, excusable. Or it could be seen as a violation of the cardinal principle of moderation:

> The pretended rights of those theorists are all extremes; and in proportion as they are metaphysically true, they are morally and politically false. The rights of men are in a sort of *middle*, incapable of definition, but not impossible to discern.[110]

Burke would and did argue that it 'is better that the whole should be imperfectly and anomalously answered than that while some parts are provided for with great exactness, others might be totally neglected, or perhaps materially injured, by the over care of a favourite member.'[111] It is not a great stretch to recognize we all pick our favourites, and that for Pierre Trudeau the Charter came before all else.

Of course it is unfair in some respects to simply compare eighteenth-century political wisdom with twentieth-century concerns. Yet there is a clear contrast between the approach that Burke took to deep political problems—the whole tenor of his argument—and the way in which Trudeau attacks both 'the manner and the question'. He is not in search of Burke's simple peace, as a rereading of Burke's *Speech on Conciliation with the Colonies* will confirm. Trudeau often encourages us to read Mill, Acton, and Madison. Burke should be added to the list.

Let us move from what has happened—our sins of omission and commission—to what we may have learned, and to the light that an abeyance perspective sheds on constitutional practice and temperament. Canada is an extraordinary model for those who wish to study the complexities of formal constitutional change in late twentieth-century, supposedly postmodern, federal democracies. It illustrates the emergence of a Foleyan abeyance and our inability to resolve it. It shows how impossibly difficult it is to write things down. It reveals old federal forces at work, and new ones taking shape. It tells us a great deal about the country and about the power of symbols—and about the roles individuals can play.

It may be that pluralist systems are better at dealing with distributional questions than they are at handling the deep and divisive problems of language, nationalism, and history.[112] It takes a long time to bury such issues; it does not take nearly as long for them to re-emerge. What can be done, within the confines of a democratic polity, to return an abeyance from whence it came? A number of possibilities suggest themselves. Measured against the Canadian experience, how do they fare? Is there something to be learned by looking abroad for clues?

States of Being

One place to look is certainly Scotland in its relationship to England. Scotland is not so remote that it cannot be understood and appreciated; it is perhaps not as difficult as making comparisons with, say, Catalonia or Northern Italy about which less may be known. In fact, if asked whether or not Scotland is a 'country', and whether or not the Scots constitute a 'nation' separate from the English, most Canadians are likely, in my view, to answer 'yes', even (perhaps especially) if they are of British origin. There is a relatively easy and straightforward acceptance of a Scottish heritage, of Scotland as a 'transcendent idea which runs through history'.[113] Scottish symbolism is overt and powerful, even if it has become what to some is the 'monster' of tartanry in all its forms.[114] So Scotland can easily be accepted as a sort of mini-state, with the Scots as a unique people, and with Scotland as a country with the potential to be a full state. Yet, in spite of the fact that Quebeckers, unlike most Scots, work and live in a different language, if Canadians are asked if Quebec is a country and if those in it comprise a nation, the answers are likely to be 'no'. When pressed on this point, people will often reply that Quebec is a province, ergo it is not a country, and those in it are just citizens like the rest of us. (If in doubt, try this question out.) Why are we ready to separate state from nation in the one case, and so unwilling to do it in the other?

Perhaps at this point we should note the similarities between Quebec and Scotland, or at least many of the key ones. They were both thriving cultures 'with genuine claims to linguistic, legal, religious and educational differences, swallowed up by superior military power masquerading as political process'.[115] The underlying tensions in the settlements that emerged were never really resolved. Matters were put into abeyance in both cases. A recent review of a spate of books on the Scottish question had this to say about Scottish nationalism:

> The Treaty of Union came just in time to bury a nascent Scottish nationalism, but could only put it in a shallow grave. Consent was the key to its remaining there. Yet to give such continuing consent it could never be really buried and forgotten. . . . In 1707 it was decreed undead, not dispatched to genuine oblivion. Embalmed by Union, it has not ceased to exert the most profound influence on each new generation.[116]

The reviewer, Tom Nairn, goes on to make the equally important points that:

> All recent experience suggests how persistent and apparently indelible nationhood can be. Once modernity reaches or crosses the threshold of modern development it is rare indeed for it not to attain political realization, or at least go on struggling towards it. The autonomy of modern Scotland was intended to be a stable, self-reproducing system of dependency. But however artfully designed and maintained, dependency depends: it assumes the permanence of a wider system. If the latter collapses or shrinks, then it may have been an odd way of cold-storing nationhood. The corpse may simply step out from temporary retirement to resume his rights. He was never really sleeping anyway.[117]

It takes little imagination to change the date and substitute Quebec for Scotland, for in both cases we are whistling past a constitutional graveyard.

Thus there is widespread agreement that the settlements made (in both cases) were above all pragmatic: constitutional means to economic and cultural ends. The Act of Union of 1707 gave Scotland access to a free market without sacrificing Scottish control over such matters as local government, education, the church, and the courts.[118] The arrrangements were characterised by amity and flexibility (in general) and by an acceptance of pluralism. What emerged in Britain was a 'Union State', in which integration was far from perfect, where pre-union rights and infrastructures were carried over and accepted, and where regional autonomy was preserved and even protected.[119] As in Quebec, patronage was managed by local élites, who were willing to settle for less than complete autonomy. (Lindsay Paterson calls this 'realistic utopianism'.[120]) After the creation of the Scottish Office in 1885, all domestic policy except social security and taxation came under its purview. As late as the 1980s 'there were about 4,000 positions of patronage in the economic sphere available to the Secretary of State for Scotland.'[121] In many ways Quebec and Scotland became self-regulating polities, dominated by moderate nationalists who were proud members of a larger Empire, whose élites were able to take advantage of the economic opportunities this provided. In both cases civil society—those institutions lying between the state and its citizens—was strong, and its distinct institutions were staunchly defended.[122] Given the nineteenth-century reliance on the rule of law as the foundation of the state, the carrying over of previous legal systems helped legitimize local authority, and in both cases the nation did not require 'sovereignty' to survive. The essence of the nation was cultural and in both cases this 'was over and over interpreted as the family', with which the state must not interfere.[123] There was also an idealization of rural life and its virtues.

Thus although Unionism and federalism are different, they were alike in this key respect: to be a Unionist in Scotland meant insisting on, and asserting, 'true' union rights, and so also to be a federalist in Quebec meant asserting the need for a 'true' federation. It still does. These were the only real counters to full-scale nationalism and to nationalists.

To this abbreviated list of historical similarities we can add some that are far more current. For both, the idea of a nation is an aspiration; it is a state of feeling and a source of obligation, and if Scots or Quebeckers are forced to choose, their natural allegiance will go to the closer and smaller community in which they live their daily lives. Seven out of ten Scots give priority to being Scottish, and a further 19 per cent gave equal weighting to their loyalties.[124] In Quebec, support for nationalism has grown significantly, although much depends upon the wording of any question asked, and there is more support for softer options. The percentage of francophones identifying themselves as Québécois increased from 21 per cent in 1970 to 59 per cent in 1990.[125] Yet people in both countries have clearly wanted to preserve dual loyalties, and have in Paterson's words 'mutually dependent dual patriotisms', which erode slowly as the welfare state declines and once-dominant centres lose their lustre. The question grows: who is to control what is left? At the same time, at the centre, there is less and less desire to defend either Scotland's or Quebec's perceived expenditure differential and advantages in public policy (the nature of the advantages and disadvantages of having been on the periphery, and of being captives of a market economy, are hotly disputed). The context for choice has thus changed in both cases; there has been, in Keating's apt phrase, 'a reinvention of territory' as the old states weaken, as new powers emerge (the European Union in particular) and as we witness 'the rise of the regional state with more limited ambitions'.[126] There is no longer the need to modernise and liberalise via association with a single stronger power. In some ways both Quebec and Scotland see theirs as civic cultures that are more likely to preserve Keynesianism, and a 'progressive' and principled view of economic affairs, in the face of assault from neo-conservatism/reductionist capitalism and Thatcherism.[127] The society which gave birth to Adam Smith now seems to reject his modern disciples, and in another irony the separatist Bloc Québécois defends national programs in the federal parliament. Both societies have been remarkably peaceful in their twentieth-century political practices; the few terrorist groups have received little support, and in the Scottish case were utterly incompetent.

In 1976, a devolution bill for Scotland and Wales was introduced in the House of Commons, and, after much manoeuvring, in 1977 the Scotland Bill, providing for a Scottish assembly (and a separate one for Wales) went to a second reading. In 1978, an amendment to the Scotland Bill was passed, against government wishes, which provided for the repeal of the Bill if 40 per cent of *the registered electorate* did not agree to devolution in a referendum. The referendum duly took place in Scotland and Wales on March 1, 1979. Wales voted heavily against devolution, but in Scotland the 'yes' side won, with 51.6 per cent of the votes cast. Yet the referendum was *lost*, because only 62.9 per cent of the electorate had voted. More than one out of every three voters had stayed home, and so the 40 per cent level was not reached. This failure to produce the originally expected overwhelming majority for the setting up of a Scottish assembly was devastating for all those who had anticipated victory.[128] There had never been a majority against devolution in any opinion poll, and the 40 per cent rule was bitterly resented as having favoured the 'no' side and as having helped galvanize its campaign. But the aftermath of this campaign, a campaign that had proved to be a formative moment in Scottish history, was entirely peaceful.

Even more remarkable was the aftermath of the referendum vote in Quebec on October 30, 1995. The question was far harder in tone than the one asked in the 1980 referendum. It read:

> Do you agree that Québec should become sovereign, after having made a formal offer to Canada for a new economic and political partnership, within the scope of the Bill respecting the future of Québec and of the agreement signed on June 12, 1995?

The participation rate was an astonishing 93.48 per cent. The 'no' side won by the skin of its teeth with 50.56 per cent. A clear majority of francophones, over 60 per cent, voted 'yes'. Yet there was no violent aftermath, not even a single sizeable rampage through the streets. There were some charges of electoral fraud, but although these were serious, the number of ballots declared spoiled in fact rose only to 1.82 per cent as compared with 1.74 per cent in the 1980 referendum. In other words, the whole thing was amazingly peaceful, and this was a tribute to Canada's and, above all, to Quebec's civil society. We do not appreciate this enough; as Wayne Reilly has noted, 'where else in the world have people so passionately debated the termination of the most basic and important political bonds with such care for the democratic process?'[129]

Both Quebec and Scotland face the dilemma of knowing that (a) there is no clear way to negotiate differences constitutionally, and (b) independence within either the European Union or the NAFTA can come only with full statehood—which they may not want, as it involves a repudiation of the constitution. In 1979 the Scots shied away from devolution out of caution, but it is now on the agenda once again, along with the thorny question of what rights Scottish MPs at Westminster would have after Scotland obtained its own assembly.[130] For Quebec, fifteen years after the 1980 referendum defeat, repudiation of the entire constitution almost became a reality. Anyone who doubts this should read a transcript of the remarks Lucien Bouchard made in his reply to Jean Chrétien's speech to the nation, just prior to the October 1995 referendum, or should review the speech Jacques Parizeau never got to give:

> My friends:
> Quebec is standing tall. The people of Quebec, by its majority vote today, has just affirmed to the world that it exists. This affirmation, serene and democratic, cannot be erased by anything or anyone.
> A simple and strong decision was made today: Quebec will become sovereign. Prepare a place for it at the table of nations. And because Quebec is now standing up, it can first extend its hand to its Canadian neighbour, offering it a new contract, a new partnership, based on the principle of equality between peoples....[131]

With a majority 'yes' vote, Quebec was therefore going to stay a province only in order to prepare, within a year, for a transition to sovereign status, whereas the Scots are still discussing devolution.

And, of course, there have also always been other differences, starting with those that are elementary but vital. If Scotland became independent it would not cut England in two, and although territorial contiguity is not logically essential for a state's existence, it is usually assumed to be vital. (Alaska's and Hawaii's existence as US states are obvious exceptions.) For centuries the northern border was a *border*: behind Hadrian's Wall lay a different kingdom. Scotland was never a mere colony, and Wallace, Bruce, Bannockburn, and the Union itself prove this to the Scots. Eventually war became a unifying factor, and the great regiments of Scotland fought for the same causes as the rest of Britain's forces. It must, however, be remembered that initially highland soldiers were used to put down their fellow Scots and were 'the first of Britain's colonial levies, called to arms to police their own hills'. They were treated with disdain and suspicion until, as regular, disciplined battalions of the line, their peculiar identity and traditions 'had become a harmless military caricature'.[132]

The Scots, as noted, have been asking for home rule and a parliament of their own; Quebec has always had far more formal, institutional, power than Scotland, including control over such key matters as taxation. Quebec, with roughly a quarter of the Canadian population (Scotland's is less than 9% of England's) has had a larger role in the party system, and there has been alternation in leadership from within and without Quebec, at least within the Liberal party. Class ties are more important in Britain, and Scottish ties to the Labour party have been strong. Many of the standard 'identity garments' of nationalism 'do not fit the Scots with any ease' and are far more applicable to Quebec (particularly language and religion).[133] Quebec's nationalism is far more ethnic, and its minority problem far more pronounced.[134] In the main, Scottish élites ran Scotland's economy; English élites ran Quebec's.[135] Quebec must also wrestle with its native populations and their rights (although Scotland too would have to consider the rights of the islands to separate from the mainland). Perhaps the image of Scotland in England and in Scotland itself has been more masculine and muscular, whereas Quebec is often described in feminine terms indicative of weakness and vacillation.[136] This latter may be misleading and therefore dangerous, and the former, let us not forget, is tied to the brutality of Scottish history, when all too often Scot was pitted against Scot.

Scotland has in some ways done better on the symbolic front, where it can take on the rest of the sporting world as Scotland, in events with a great deal of visibility: the five-nations cup in rugby; world championships in rugby and soccer; international matches; participation in the Commonwealth games. On the other hand, Quebec has created 'délégations générales' abroad to foster Quebec's interests in culture, education, immigration, investment, and trade. Quebec has its own pension plan, is seated at the table at meetings of 'la Francophonie', and plays a major role in immigration, often renting space in certain Canadian embassies to do so. There have also been 'accords-cadres' developed with other countries that allow Quebec to enter into agreements with them. Above all, there have been a whole range of special federal-provincial arrangements, such as opting-out of certain programs and the transfer of tax powers as a consequence. And of course the federal government itself has spent millions of dollars attempting to implement bilingualism in federal institutions, and provides substantial assistance in support of Quebec's cultural infrastructure, while within Quebec the province has had the power to establish French as the official language.[137]

Both countries may, nevertheless, evidence a certain 'chippiness' and quickness to take offence, as both have suffered, understandably, from a cultural inferiority complex.[138] Yet the English aristocracy developed strong ties to Scotland, and popular monarchs also played a part in the assertion of Scottish culture. The monarchical tie has played a far different role in Canada, but even here it would be wrong to overstate the differences. It is entirely possible that, like Scotland, an independent Quebec could choose to stay in the Commonwealth—and could theoretically even accept the British crown as the rest of Canada does. This would have the advantage, for Quebec, of showing that it was a legitimate successor-state, becoming what it could have been if Confederation had not arrived! It could also, by maintaining the links to the Royal Proclamation of 1763 and aboriginal ties to the Crown, help to ameliorate somewhat the aboriginal problems Quebec would face.

As always, there is so much that is paradoxical in all of this. At a time when old ideas of state, nation, sovereignty, and citizenship are in such disarray, and other organizational forms are pushing both state and nation 'to a lower rung on the ladder or hierarchy of identities', Scotland and Quebec are asserting their nationalism.[139] This can be seen as looking backwards in tribal fashion, or it can be viewed far more positively (as McCrone does) because it uses nationalism to strengthen civil society, to help create living and working communities in which there will continue to be multiple allegiances. Quebec and Scotland are examples of the fissiparous tendencies remaking the political world; they are both attempting to preserve a coherent domestic social order as other levels of organization, above and below, mutate: 'Scotland, like other societies, may be entering a post-nationalist age. The vehicle on that journey, ironically, seems to be nationalism itself.'[140] Contrary to much of what one hears and reads, in *both* cases it is a nationalism that is 'overwhelmingly liberal and democratic'.[141]

The State We're In

Let us now return to Canada's problems, and ask again what we are to do when abeyances are no longer buried. When tombstones are scattered across the landscape like signposts, and more are unearthed regularly, we can see clearly what a pickle we are in. Elite accommodation, consociationalism, and executive federalism have had a rough ride, so rough that we may forget how close agreement came on two occasions. Yet there is little choice in Canada but to return to these mechanisms privately, if not publicly. They are, however, showing signs of heavy damage under the combined fire of Charterphiles, interest groups, aboriginals, and those who believe that executive federalism is entirely inappropriate as a way of dealing with constitutional problems. It has proved to be impossible to separate the question of Quebec's distinctiveness from the often contradictory ideas of the importance of provincial equality, aboriginal rights, individual rights, multiculturalism, and majoritarianism.[142]

During the period of constitutional debate that preceded the Charlottetown Accord and the referendum, following the first of the constitutional conferences in Halifax, it seemed as if asymmetrical federalism might well be a possible agenda item (a series of conferences was held from January to March 1992). This would have been a major break-through from the federal point of view. Accordingly, Constitutional Affairs Minister Joe Clark phoned all the provincial premiers, save for Quebec, as well as the leaders of the opposition parties, only to find that not one would support it (i.e., asymmetry).[143] Asymmetrical arrangements, though widely practised, can be difficult to constitutionalize: 'Asymmetry is a social reality. It is a fact of life, but it is not necessarily a fact of political life. This depends upon the "politics of recognition".'[144]

Canadians, says Alan Cairns, are now playing a 'multinational game by rules that presuppose that they are essentially a federal people'.[145] These rules acquire a federal inertia all their own, while the government of Quebec 'conducts itself in terms of what it hopes to become and thus denies what it constitutionally is.'[146] Yet the Rest of Canada (familiarly, RoC), although it rejects asymmetry, 'clearly sees itself as participating in a two-nation constitutional game'.[147] Under the Charlottetown Accord, the real winner was not Quebec. Cairns argues that it was the aboriginal peoples who made astonishing and far-reaching gains, and that 'their achievement of a third order of government underlined the failure of Quebec, constrained by the equality of the provinces principle, to attain asymmetrical status.'[148] Instead, the provincial equality principle 'is reiterated like a reassuring mantra on page after page'.[149] Something else that had been avoided in 1867 had now come back in a new guise, and people in the periphery, as David Milne has noted, invest a great deal in the notions of provincial status and equality because they feel such anger at what they consider to be central Canada's grievous lack of appreciation for their aspirations and rights.[150]

Also back again, and on the upsurge, is populism, and populism by its very nature is unlikely to be receptive to the idea that there are things we don't talk about and problems best left well alone:

> Populism is often described as being as much a mood or syndrome as a systematic philosophy. It is built on a number of factors: a common sense celebration of the average citizen, a preference for direct democracy devices ... an identification with small-scale business capitalism ... a tendency to blame outside forces for economic and social problems and to see solutions in simple or even simplistic terms....[151]

Populism, in spite of its reliance on a strong leader, is anti-élitist in tone and temper. When Reform Party leader Preston Manning speaks of his new Canada, he is talking of a country that will operate according to a few seemingly straightforward principles; ambiguity and equivocation are not the dominant theme. And if Quebec doesn't like it, it can leave—but not on its own terms. Populism demands referendums, but because abeyances are 'the product of long historical experience and accumulated practice of which the public is but dimly aware' they are exceptionally difficult to handle during a referendum campaign.[152] Populism has had its base in Western Canada, and was rooted in the perception that the West was a colony of the East.[153] The Reform Party's views on Quebec's demand for distinct society status make any accommodation extremely difficult for Western Canadian premiers, including British Columbia's Glen Clark who, as an NDP leader, might have been expected to be more open on the subject. Reform provides evidence to Quebeckers that English Canada will never understand Quebec nationalism—or Quebec's pride.[154]

Michael Lusztig has argued that 'mass input/legitimization is incompatible with successful constitution-making in deeply divided societies. As a result, given prevailing conditions, the Canadian constitution remains in a state of paralysis, with new constitutional initiatives doomed to fail.'[155] He now sees three or possibly four 'mega-constitutional orientations' (MCOs) in play which he styles the 'Trudeau, Quebec and Western orientations' plus possibly a fourth, 'the minoritarian'.[156] All four MCOs came into play during the Meech and Charlottetown debates. He reaches the interesting conclusion that those who supported the Trudeau MCO were the most likely to sacrifice their constitutional preferences for the sake of national unity, and that the supporters of the new MCOs were and are the most intractable.[157] This is bad news because it means that the Western and minoritarian views do not lend themselves to élite accommodation and that 'where significant compromise is required, consociational constitutionalism will not succeed.'[158]

Michael Atkinson contends that the system of constitutional bargaining has become *less* integrative and more aggregative.[159] In aggregative processes 'politics is understood as a means of satisfying the interests or preferences of citizens as individuals.'[160] Aggregative processes are innately competitive, and will tend to produce institutional equilibrium. Integrative processes are not based upon competition but upon beneficial exchanges: 'emphasis is placed, instead, on achieving consensus through deliberation and debate.'[161] Preferences are shaped and not merely aggregated. Thus, says Atkinson, where aggregation dominates, there we will also find an emphasis on equal citizenship notions, whereas where integrative processes prevail, there we are likely to find élite accommodation and a trustee rather than a brokerage approach to issues. Canadians have savaged the integrative practices of yesteryear and have attempted to substitute far more aggregative ones. The result of this mix of old and new is still deadlock. And it reveals a move closer to the American rights-based, aggregative model.[162]

Such deeply held orientations do not augur well for the exclusion of ideas and views on the basis that they are taboos. Our taboos seem to be breaking down, even those surrounding aboriginal issues. Public opinion is hardening. The publication of numerous books on Canada's break-up, and how the boundaries of Quebec will have to be redrawn, shows how far we have come since 1980.[163] The role of television, talk shows, and the media as 'art forms' with their own 'working assumptions' cannot be ignored, nor can the influence of the United States' media. The public's right to know transcends all. Edwin R. Black is one of the few authors to investigate these crucial questions:

> Scholars too have left almost totally unexplored questions about the ways in which mass media professional, craft, and vocational ideologies have shaped our federalism and our system of political communication. The new reality for federalist politics in Canada can be simply stated: so far as the voters are concerned, if it's not on TV, it doesn't exist.[164]

We live in an age where few things are sacrosanct; our leaders must use the media and are caught in their supposedly populist glare.

A democracy can get out of an impasse, and cope with a crisis, if it has a leader capable of what might be termed a certain 'Gaullism' of action. But this is only possible if one has a de Gaulle, and it is even more difficult in a federal than a unitary system. Pierre Trudeau got away with a certain Gaullist high-handedness in 1981, but in this situation the rules were in his favour, and in yet another irony the Empire struck back and saved him. He was able to play the imperial card against the provinces, and although there was public debate, the procedures were not set. A Quebec premier is perhaps more likely to be able to engage in dramatic steps than is a Prime Minister. (In the wake of the failure of the Meech Lake Accord, Robert Bourassa could probably have led Quebec to independence had he chosen to do so.)

Formal, seriatim change is also unlikely because of the problem of linkages between subjects. Apropos of this question, Janet Ajzenstat takes issue with the Charles Taylor view that it is the tension between the 'procedural constitution' and Quebec's collective goals that is at the root of our constitutional problems.[165] She sees the cause as the 'erosion of confidence in procedural institutions'. Quebec can now have little or no confidence that anything short of secession will bring about change, and the battle is not really about different forms of liberalism, but about how to change things. 'We can hope that the habits of 125 years of settled political life under the procedural constitution will suffice.'[166] (We also must bear in mind how extraordinarily difficult it is to change anything now that certain provinces require that a referendum be held prior to the formal legislative vote.)

On this basis there might be hope that we can put our abeyances back where they belong, and scurry past the graveyard once more. In addition to the habits of 125 years, we may now be constitutionally wiser. We have had 30 years of 'constitutional consciousness raising'[167] and the last round of debate over the Charlottetown Accord was unprecedented even by Canadian standards.[168] Since then, there was the precipice of the October referendum. What this may mean is that Canadians, both inside and outside Quebec, are sadder and wiser, and that the momentum of constitutional change has finally been brought to a halt by a combination of things: exhaustion, frustration, the press of other problems, the realization that we have asked the constitution to do too much, the sheer gridlock of the amending processes, uncertainty over the rules for change, and perhaps increased appreciation of the intractability of the problems.

This latter point is particularly speculative, but particularly important insofar as abeyances are linked to constitutional temperament and historical experience. The Meech Lake Accord was primarily about Quebec's needs (the distinct society clause, Supreme Court appointees, spending powers, immigration, and amendment/veto) but Charlottetown was not, and all could see what we had opened up for 'resolution', and why we were in difficulty. We may decide to narrow our options again in order to avoid dealing with such a broad range of questions.

We are now back to a focus on Quebec and what is to be done, and back, in many ways, to the answers put forward by the Unity Task Force in 1979. This is because the questions, and circumstances, are so similar. By 1979 the country had experienced:

- The failure of major attempts at constitutional reform even though there had appeared to be initial agreement amongst the First Ministers and the Prime Minister;[169]
- The rise to power of the Parti Québécois;
- Western Canadian economic growth, particularly in Alberta and British Columbia;
- A western Canadian desire for institutional reform;
- A parliamentary opposition rooted in the West;
- A debate over centralization and decentralization, with strong provincial support for the latter;
- Attempts at national redefinition, with deep divisions as to what course should be pursued;
- Disputes over national policies, national standards, and federal control, including a debate over health care;

- Hostility towards either the bicultural compact view of Canada and special status for Quebec, or the national bilingualism federal antidote;
- A growing emphasis on provincial equality in Canada outside Quebec, and the rejection of this by Quebec, which rooted its views in the two-nations theory;
- A national government headed by a Prime Minister from Quebec.

This is a fairly extensive list of similarities, but they should not blind us to major differences. In 1979 a Quebec referendum was awaited, whereas we know the outcome. The 1995 result was significantly different from that of 1980, and was directly linked to the formal failure of two major constitutional initiatives. In 1979, the Task Force paid little attention to aboriginal questions: dualism came first. Now, demands for a fundamental restructuring of aboriginal/non-aboriginal relationships cannot be so ignored. The federal government's position due to its debt and deficit load is radically altered.[170] Alberta is not about to become the Kuwait of North America, even if the West is growing economically. Mike Harris's Ontario is clearly not the Ontario of 1979. Canada is now a member of the North American Free Trade Agreement. Liberalism is under siege, and although the current clash over liberalism's ingredients had its origins in the 1970s (not in the 1980s), the cumulative effects of globalization on liberalism have been extensive.[171] In 1979 the Charter was not in place, and neither were the amending formulae (with the addition later of provincial and probably federal referendums). We must also remember that patronage too has ceased to serve as the cement it once was, and that even in the one, perhaps the sole, area where French and English Canadians came together for a common purpose, namely the federal political parties, French-Canadian representation has been changed dramatically. The Liberals are now Canada's only national party, but lack strong Quebec support. The Reform Party has no base in Quebec at all. Our partisan divisions have become aligned with our constitutional problems, and our constitutional abeyances are a part of partisan debate. Thus while some things have not really changed—as the Spicer Commission (the *Citizens' Forum on Canada's Future*) found out in 1991 when it toured the country—others have made matters *far more difficult* than they were in 1979. This is why there is such academic pessimism.

Optimistically we can hope that Canada has, by some miracle of miscalculation and temperament, found a new way of dealing with abeyances: expose them to full frontal scrutiny and debate. While this raises the level of the rhetoric, and the use and abuse of symbols and myths, it could also make a clear majority opt for an ambiguous *status quo*. If this happens, then the Supreme Court becomes a key agent of constitutional change, and Canada moves even more towards an American model of abeyance avoidance, via the politics of the judiciary and the kinds of creative avoidance mechanisms that are available to the court.[172] A great deal has been written on this, and Canada's Supreme Court would have to face a number of hurdles before it acquired the stature of its American cousin.[173] But certain sections of the Charter, especially section 1, give Canada's courts more leeway in working creatively with ambiguity. Recourse to the law does not, however, deal particularly effectively with the demands made by populism, or the views of those in Quebec who think that the present federal system has run its course. Those who hold the four differing mega-constitutional orientations identified previously may not give up the struggle even after what we have been through, and may, increasingly, come to resist what the Court does. So will those who prefer an aggregative and competitive approach. But even so, outside Quebec there may be a new consensus that constitutional questions should be set aside as too dangerous. Or there could arise the view that we've got to 'settle it once and for all'.

If pragmatism triumphs over the forces demanding dramatic change, particularly those in Quebec, then the politics of issue displacement could take over as the realization settles in that 'the best (constitutional) strategy is no strategy at all'.[174] Existing arrangements, a major restructuring of the welfare state, cultural difficulties, aboriginal issues, and economic relationships within the Free Trade Agreement, the NAFTA and the General Agreement on Tariffs and Trade will hold our attention. However, this assumes away the Quebec question, and presumes that issues such as federal-provincial restructuring will not raise serious constitutional and structural problems for the federal state, problems that will prevent us from putting our abeyances back to sleep. What has to hold things together in such circumstances, when collective narratives and Keynesian assumptions fall apart, and indeterminacy reigns, is our sense of self and past, our myths and our fictions, and our parties and leaders.[175]

However, historians, educators, and those who write about Canadian culture lament the emergence of a pastless Canada. As Robert Fulford notes, 'newcomers to Canada find themselves in a curiously pastless country, where the oldest writers anyone quotes were living ten years ago and the political parties seem rarely to mention traditions that stretch back further than the 1960s.'[176] He says that we have feared our past:

> Divisiveness, many Canadians decided long ago, is not to be tolerated, and if possible not even mentioned. The year 1759 cannot be permitted to echo in our 'mystic chords of memory'.[177]

Mackenzie King embodied this avoidance of the articulation of national beliefs to perfection, and therefore 'drove intellectuals like [F.R.] Scott to distraction'.[178] In William Kaplan's view we need a coherent and principled approach to questions of citizenship and the relationship of individuals to the state.[179] C.E.S. Franks has shown how divisive are our symbols and myths and he concludes that, 'To those who would like Canada to remain together, the crude, mutually incompatible myths and symbols are the greatest obstacles to seeing a possible future of mutual cooperation and harmony'.[180] Whilst one may not agree that they are our 'greatest' obstacle, nation building and state building are indeed heavily dependent upon symbolic rallying points, as

Trudeau himself stressed. And the fact remains that we have neither agreed upon the kind of federal system we should have, nor have we been able to accommodate duality within it to the satisfaction of many in Quebec.[181]

The argument presented throughout this book is that we have tried to keep certain key problems in abeyance, and succeeded in so doing by a combination of luck and leadership, buttressed by patronage, geography, federalism itself, and perhaps by political temperament and political tradition. Abeyances, as discussed in Chapters One and Two, are protected by layers of meaning above them, including fictions, myths, and symbols. Yet they will never be completely hidden, and as we search for a common notion of who and what we are, this in itself can drive abeyances to the surface.

We also cannot exclude the more hopeful possibility that something intractable that was clearly not (or had ceased to be) an abeyance can nevertheless become one. In the 1992 discussions over the Charlottetown Accord:

> The language question was quite deliberately set aside... the federal proposals which laid the agenda for Charlottetown, there's very little on the language question there and that was a deliberate strategic decision, that to open up that issue was one you could not win... and the word had come from Bourassa that he would be quite happy to see that issue left alone and not raised. So while the language issue was an important one in the Pepin-Robarts Report, I think that since Pepin-Robarts, Bill 101 and all the things that had happened, that at this stage of the deliberations language was an issue that should be left in abeyance. That was a strategic, definite, decision ... and nobody pushed to have it on the agenda.[182]

Even the Bloc Québécois has taken to defending the Official Languages Act when it is debated in the House of Commons. It would be another irony if the language issue dropped off the table at precisely the time that duality, partnership, and provincialism become more acute. Recent events in Quebec have, however, shown how easy it is for language questions, and all the baggage associated with them, to burst into flames again just when the fires seemed dim. Lucien Bouchard has to struggle to keep the linguistic hard-liners in the party under control, and the anglophone minority is becoming more vocal about such matters as the sign laws.

Above all, the mere presence of the Bloc Québécois in the House reminds us how far we have come from our traditional techniques for managing our constitutional incoherence. We can no longer rely on the same strategies to resolve our problems because, as is the case with abeyances elsewhere, what is needed to maintain them is restraint. They are therefore dangerously exposed, and even though the strategy of the Liberal party has been to try to avoid them, this is going to be exceptionally difficult to do.

The notion of abeyances does make it apparent that, as Foley says, constitutions become 'more equivocal in nature ... significantly more porous'.[183] It also makes it apparent that political sophistication in the avoidance of whatever a society deems necessary to avoid can take different forms, for there are many ways to defer or evade. One such illustration from a non-Western system might be the case of Japan.[184] The thesis of Karel Van Wolferen's work *The Enigma of Japanese Power* is that it is *impossible* to understand, or theorize successfully, about the ways in which power is exercised in Japan without understanding that there 'are several commonly cherished fictions', including the fiction of responsible government. These fictions are maintained:

> because it is socially acceptable in Japan for 'reality' to consist not so much of the results of objective observation as of an emotionally constructed picture in which things are portrayed the way they are supposed to be.[185]

Thus, says Wolferen, in Japan 'reality' is not seen as we see it in the West—as something that can be logically managed, moulded, and understood in all its aspects. Contradictions, delusions, and illusions are something that Wolferen sees Western philosophy and practice as attempting to counter. A reading of Morgan and Foley might give him pause. Nevertheless, the fact remains that in his description of the foundations of Japanese political practice, he may have hit upon some important points applicable to the Western world of constitutional development. Japanese political reality is 'managed' because there is an acceptance of multiple and contradictory truths. A rationally argued claim made by one side may be countered by arguments belonging to an altogether different frame of reference—at which point the exchange reaches a dead end.

To reach such a dead end is not, however, to then assume that one's opponents are totally wrong. This would be to make the assumption that there is a single transcendent and definable truth. Instead the Japanese will ask for 'understanding'; but *wahatte kudasai* means please understand 'in the sense of please accept my explanation, regardless of whether it has any basis in fact'.[186] It is a plea for acceptance or tolerance and in this sense 'understanding' is another word for agreeing to differ.

In such a world of understandings, where reality is not an absolute, it is easier to maintain fictions and tolerate abeyances. And 'in a world of competing realities appearances are crucial.'[187] There are even words to describe the difference between the façade of ostensible truth—the way things are supposed to be—and the real, the genuine, the truth you sense and 'know' (*honne*). So contradictions can be complementary facets of the same truth, and there is a suspicion of people who are too narrowly logical and who cannot appreciate these contradictions. They are referred to as *rikutsuppoi*—reason freaks.[188]

What we can take from this is that in our world of constitutional debate there is also, often, a need to 'understand' in the Japanese sense, a need to maintain appearances in a world of conflicting realities, where the situational and the particularistic must have a place with the universal and the transcendent. Social harmony is also, for us, a paramount constitutional goal; we perhaps need a word like *honne*; certainly *rikutsuppoi* would come in handy, and several to whom it would apply spring readily to mind.

There are those, both inside and outside Quebec, who think that Canada has reached a stage where if Quebec stays within Confederation it is like a cancer in the body politic, and that no amount of 'understanding' will suffice. There are those who hope that Quebec has gone through one of its periods of periodic upheaval and that things can settle down. There are others who still hope that some significant constitutional changes can be made, especially if they are symbolic. And there are many who, given the state of our world, will want to believe that we can put our abeyances back into obscurity, and that we will find the wisdom to do so as we struggle to retain and build a binational and truly federal country, a country that is tolerant and pluralistic, economically strong, and still differentiated from a more unruly United States. To return to the metaphor used at the outset, we know the black holes are there, and have proved their existence by the behaviour of the things around them. There is still a danger that we cannot prevent ourselves from being sucked in. The other possibility is that we are already in one—and cannot get out.

Notes

1 Advice to the jury at Tom Paine's trial. See James T. Boulton, *The Language of Politics in the Age of Wilkes and Burke* (Toronto: Routledge and Kegan Paul, 1963), 250.

2 Tremblay interview. In 1995, Tremblay was reported as indicating that he would vote 'yes' this time. To anyone who knew Canada's constitutional players, this was a very telling sign. On 6 October Jacques Parizeau announced the names of the first five members of the Committee that was to 'oversee' negotiations on a new partnership with Canada. They included Jean Allaire and Arthur Tremblay.

3 Guy Laforest, *Trudeau et la fin d'un rêve canadien* (Montreal: Septentrion, 1992), ch. 1. Claude Ryan believes that this was the finest speech of Trudeau's political career, notwithstanding what happened later. See *Regards sur le fédéralisme canadien* (Montreal: Boréal, 1995), 130.

4 An English version of these exchanges is appended in Donald Johnston, ed., *Pierre Trudeau Speaks Out on Meech Lake* (Toronto: General Paperbacks, 1990), 110–38.

5 Laforest, *Trudeau et la fin d'un rêve canadien,* 32.

6 Ibid., 50. 'Pierre Elliot Trudeau, son of Quebec and the most important political leader of the Canadian federation, chose to be ambiguous at what was no doubt the most important moment in the history of the Québécois people. On 14 May 1980, at the Centre Paul-Sauvé, a kind of temple of Québec nationalism, in an atmosphere pregnant with solemnity, he vowed to renew Canadian federalism. . . .' Note also the similar point made by Peter M. Russell in *Constitutional Odyssey. Can Canadians Become a Sovereign People?* (Toronto: University of Toronto Press, 1992), 109, and by Jeremy Webber in *Reimagining Canada. Language, Culture, Community and the Canadian Constitution* (Montreal and Kingston: McGill-Queen's University Press, 1994), 107.

7 Janet Ajzenstat, 'Decline of Procedural Liberalism: The Slippery Slope to Secession', paper presented at the Annual Meeting of the Canadian Political Science Association (Calgary, 1994), 12.

8 Ibid., 14. The Right Honourable Joe Clark has commented, in the same vein, that 'the 1982 exclusion was so terribly defining'. Seminar, University of Calgary, 24 November 1993.

9 Johnston, ed., *Pierre Trudeau Speaks Out on Meech Lake*, 10.

10 Charles Taylor, 'Can Canada Survive the *Charter?*', *Alberta Law Review* 30, 2 (1992), 427–47 at 428.

11 Ibid. Political institutions are also regarded as what continue to distinguish Canada from the United States. See Roger Gibbins, 'The Impact of the American Constitution on Contemporary Canadian Constitutional Politics' in *The Canadian and American Constitution in Comparative Perspective*, ed. Marian C. McKenna (Calgary: University of Calgary Press, 1993).

12 James Tully, 'Diversity's Gambit Declined', in *Constitutional Predicament: Canada After the Referendum of 1992*, ed. Curtis Cook (Montreal and Kingston: McGill-Queen's University Press, 1994), 149–98.

13 Ibid., 173.

14 Ibid., 181–4.

15 Taylor, 'Can Canada Survive the *Charter?*', 443. Kenneth McRoberts makes the same point in 'Disagreeing on the Fundamentals: English Canada and Quebec' in *The Charlottetown Accord, the Referendum, and the Future of Canada*, eds Kenneth McRoberts and Patrick J. Monahan (Toronto: University of Toronto Press, 1993), 249–63. He notes that 'Quebec's constitutional vision has been clearly defined for close to thirty years now' and that there are 'profoundly different perceptions of political community'.

16 Taylor, 'Can Canada Survive the *Charter?*', 444.

17 Ibid., 445.

18 See Michael Burgess, 'Is Quebec's Distinct Society Exportable?', paper presented at the Annual Meeting of the British Association for Canadian Studies (Cambridge, 1993). His optimistic view must be tempered, in practice, by the realities of the problems caused by the idea that communities have rights. For an unusual and useful look at this in a Canadian context see Don Desserud, 'The Exercise of Community Rights: Language Rights and New Brunswick's Bill 88,' paper presented at the Annual Meeting of the British Association for Canadian Studies (York, 1994). Desserud argues that either the New Brunswick constitutional amendment is purely symbolic, or 'we will be faced with the prospect of an Acadian community logically and justifiably demanding state and territory.'

19 Katherine Fierlbeck, 'The Ambivalent Potential of Cultural Identity', *Canadian Journal of Political Science* 29, 1 (March 1996), 3–22. Note also Frederick Johnstone, 'Quebeckers, Mohawks and Zulus: Liberal Federalism and Fair Trade', *Telos* 93 (Fall 1992), 71–91.

20 Jeremy Webber's *Reimagining Canada* is an especially useful and comprehensive discussion of the language, culture, community, and constitutional linkages. He too pleads for a recognition of Quebec as a distinct society, for the recognition and implementation of aboriginal self-government, and for the acceptance of the value

of multiple loyalties. Above all, we have to recognize that we do not want to push the 'logic' of arguments to simplistic conclusions. The whole purpose of his book 'is to show how language and culture shape political community and to argue for more effective means of accommodating the differences they create', 201.

21 Yael Tamir, *Liberal Nationalism* (Princeton: Princeton University Press, 1993), 51.

22 Ibid., 6.

23 Ibid., 145.

24 Ibid., 68–9. While I am not as sanguine on this point, as the scope for 'national' self-delusion seems large indeed (e.g., are cossacks a people, or a class, or a military organization?), Quebec's case is clear.

25 Ibid., 75.

26 Ibid.

27 Alain-G. Gagnon, 'From Nation-State to Multinational State: Quebec and Canada facing the challenge of modernity', keynote speech to the British Association of Canadian Studies, Exeter, 12 April 1996. I wish to thank Dr Gagnon for providing me with a copy of this paper.

28 For a lucid overview of gobalization's iterative effects see Vincent Cable, 'The Diminished Nation-State: A Study in the Loss of Economic Power', *Daedalus* 124, 2 (Spring 1995), 23–53.

29 Taylor, 'Can Canada Survive the *Charter*?' 436.

30 For an attack on Johnson's views see William Johnson, *A Canadian Myth: Quebec, Between Canada and the Illusion of Utopia* (Montreal: Robert Davies Publishing, 1994), 58–68.

31 Perhaps the very holding of the referendum was an example of another abeyance (the right to secede) which surfaced and was dealt with rapidly and successfully, at least until now, with the demands that we rethink the 'rules' to be applied. For a succinct defence of the need to accept that a simple majority would be sufficient, see Thomas Flanagan, 'Should a supermajority be required in a referendum on separation?' in John E. Trent, Robert Young, and Guy Lachapelle, eds, *Québec-Canada. What is the Path Ahead?* (Ottawa: University of Ottawa Press, 1996), 129–34.

32 Patrick Monahan, *Meech Lake: The Inside Story* (Toronto: University of Toronto Press, 1991), 57. There are still many who blame Mulroney for 'opening' the question and for flagrantly flirting with those who had been overt separatists. For a recent restatement of this view see Mordecai Richler's 'Letter from Canada: O Quebec', *The New Yorker*, 30 May 1994: 'He (Mulroney) enlisted the support of the P.Q. in exchange for a promise that he would reopen the constitutional can of worms, for Quebec's sake' (52). In my view, this line of argument is unfair, and does not do justice to the depth of the problem and the underlying abeyances.

33 Johnston, ed., *Pierre Trudeau Speaks Out on Meech Lake*, 35. In this particular volume one can find Trudeau's initial article first published in *The Toronto Star*, plus later pieces, as well as his testimony before various committees. It also includes some criticisms, and Trudeau's rebuttals.

Unsettled Settlement 209

34 The 1991 edition of *Canada: The State of the Federation*, ed. Douglas M. Brown (Kingston: Institute of Intergovernmental Relations, 1991) contains an extensive Meech Lake bibliography, and much has been written since. See, for example, Webber, *Reimagining Canada*, ch. 5.

35 Taylor, 'Can Canada Survive the *Charter*?', 437.

36 Roger Gibbins, 'The Interplay of Political Institutions and Political Communities' in *Federalism and Political Community*, eds David P. Shugarman and Reg Whitaker (Peterborough: Broadview Press, 1989), 427.

37 Ibid., 431.

38 Joan Boase, 'The Spirit of Meech Lake' in *Federalism and Political Community*, 214.

39 See Monahan, *Meech Lake: The Inside Story*, 56.

40 Guy Laforest, 'Interpreting the Political Heritage of André Laurendeau' in *After Meech Lake: Lessons for the Future*, eds. David E. Smith, Peter Mackinnon, and John C. Courtney (Saskatoon: Fifth House Publishers, 1991), 102.

41 Johnston, ed., *Pierre Trudeau Speaks Out on Meech Lake*, 34.

42 Ibid., 20.

43 Ibid., 95. For a further development of this constitutionalising theme see Barry Cooper, 'Looking Eastward, Looking Backward: A Western Reading of the Never-Ending Story' in *Constitutional Predicament*, ed. Curtis Cook, 89–107.

44 Peter Hogg, *Meech Lake Constitutional Accord Annotated* (Toronto: Carswell, 1988), 15.

45 See Katherine Swinton, 'Of Federalism and Rights' in *Federalism and Political Community*, 286.

46 Johnston, ed., *Pierre Trudeau Speaks Out on Meech Lake*, 10.

47 Ex-Premier Peter Lougheed saw this recognition as an important federal gain. Howard Pawley had insisted on Section 106A precisely on grounds 'that it would solidify the constitutional basis for future federally driven programs'. See Nelson Wiseman, 'In Search of Manitoba's Constitutional Position, 1950–1990', *Journal of Canadian Studies* 29, 3 (Fall 1994).

48 See Garth Stevenson, 'The Origins of Cooperative Federalism' in *Federalism and Political Community*, 29. Stevenson reminds us that by 1870 there had been no less than four federal-provincial conferences on the subject of immigration.

49 Ibid.

50 Andrew Heard notes that as things stand the Alberta Senate election may have been unconstitutional, but would not have been so had the Meech Lake Accord passed, for a legal right 'would have been created'. See Andrew Heard, 'When Must Constitutional Change Be Achieved By Amendment?', paper presented at the Annual Meeting of the Canadian Political Science Association (Calgary, 1994), 23.

51 Note, for example, J. Stefan Dupré's comment that he did not foresee the role that legislative assemblies would play. See 'Canadian Constitutionalism and the Sequel to the Meech Lake Accord' in *Federalism and Political Community*, 243.

52 This is not a new phenomenon. In the United States in 1787, even though there was agreement on principles in a general sense (a republican government with checks to keep those in power honest), opponents could seize on particular provisions and predict dire consequences: 'the federal judiciary would preempt the functions of the state judiciaries and abolish trial by jury ... the Presidency would turn into a lifetime office and the Senate into a hereditary aristocracy.' Proponents could not acknowledge defects 'for fear of opening the whole document to revisions....' See Edmund S. Morgan, 'Power to the People?' *The New York Review of Books*, 21 December 1993, 27.

53 Laforest, 'Interpreting the Political Heritage of André Laurendeau', 102.

54 Richard Simeon, 'Meech Lake and Visions of Canada' in *Competing Constitutional Visions: The Meech Lake Accord*, eds K.E. Swinton, and C.J. Rogerson (Toronto: Carswell, 1988). Note also Roderick A. Macdonald, 'Meech Lake to the Contrary Notwithstanding', *Osgoode Hall Law Journal* 29, 2 (Summer 1991), 253-328 and 3 (Fall 1991), 483-572. Macdonald provides a particularly useful and comprehensive review of the 'demands' made (originally six not five), the symbolism of the Accord, the effects of Bill 178, the current role and place of Quebec's anglophones, and the whole history of dualism. Amendments are, he says, exercises in 'studied ambiguity', and the Accord was complementary to the 1982 Constitution Act, and would have led to further, positive restructuring of the federation.

55 Simeon, 'Meech Lake and Visions of Canada', 295.

56 Ibid., 296. Guy Laforest makes the same point when he says that 'these checks, ambiguities, and blurred sovereignties between visions were necessary to the flourishing of complex federalism in Canada.' This is an interesting statement coming from a cultural and educational tradition that has often been seen as demanding exactitude and precision in such matters. It represents a far more British point of view. See 'Interpreting the Political Heritage of André Laurendeau', 102.

57 Richard Simeon, 'Meech Lake and Visions of Canada', 298.

58 Ibid., 302.

59 Peter Russell makes the same point about the high price of constitutional navel-gazing in his conclusion to *Constitutional Odyssey* (Toronto: University of Toronto Press, 1992). The linkages between economic changes, federalism, our conception of the role of government, and whether we need to undertake a wholesale rethinking of our 'constitutional underpinnings,' has been explored in particular by Thomas Courchene. See 'Mon pays, c'est l'hiver: reflections of a market populist,' *Canadian Journal of Economics* 25, 4 (1992).

60 Guy Laforest, *Trudeau et la fin d'un rêve canadien*, 115. The ultimate failure to pass the Accord was certainly extraordinarily welcome news to hard-line PQ nationalists, just as it was an affront to Quebec federalists.

61 Christian Dufour, *A Canadian Challenge/Le défi québécois* (Lantzville: Oolichan Books, 1990), 137.

62 Ralph Heintzman, 'Political Space and Economic Space: Quebec and the Empire of the St. Lawrence', *Journal of Canadian Studies* 29, 2 (Summer 1994), 55.

63 Richard Simeon, 'Meech Lake and Visions of Canada', 305.

64 Carolyn Tuohy, *Policy and Politics in Canada: Institutionalized Ambivalence* (Philadelphia: Temple University Press, 1993), 4.

65 'How Pierre Trudeau misleads the people', *The Globe and Mail*, 8 October 1992, A29.

66 Robertson interview.

67 'How Pierre Trudeau misleads the people'.

68 Ibid.

69 There was an article in response by Trudeau in *The Globe and Mail* on 21 October 1992 entitled 'Trudeau to Robertson: "So where is the demagogy"?' and a long letter from Robertson in response to Trudeau on 24 October.

70 Robertson interview.

71 Ibid.

72 Ibid.

73 Ibid.

74 Boulton, *The Language of Politics in the Age of Wilkes and Burke*, 264.

75 Donald Johnston, ed., *Pierre Trudeau Speaks Out on Meech Lake*, 18. Webber notes that Trudeau's portrayal of Brian Mulroney as the 'Sorceror's apprentice' was omitted from the published version of this speech. Webber also criticizes Trudeau's attack on the Supreme Court. *Reimagining Canada*, 344-5.

76 Ibid., 31.

77 See Alan C. Cairns, 'Constitutional Refashioning of Community' and 'The Charter and the Constitution Act, 1982' in his *Charter Versus Federalism: The Dilemmas of Constitutional Reform* (Montreal and Kingston: McGill-Queen's University Press, 1992). In the latter essay he discusses the amending formula as the work of the 'Gang of Eight' and sees it as embodying 'very different visions of our country.' Note especially 86–93. For a more favourable view of the unanimity provisions from a Western Canadian standpoint, see Roger Gibbins and Sonia Arrison, *Western Visions: Perspectives on the West in Canada* (Peterborough: Broadview Press, 1995), 56.

78 Donald Johnston, ed., *Pierre Trudeau Speaks Out on Meech Lake*, 35.

79 Ibid., 62.

80 Ibid., 87.

81 Ibid., 94.

82 Ibid.

83 Ibid., 100.

84 See Ryan, *Regards sur le fédéralisme canadien*, 136-7. He discusses the very difficult situation facing the Quebec Liberal Party, and its refusal to support the federal proposals. He too takes exception to the way the voting has been portrayed by Trudeau: 'Cette prétention est une déformation de l'histoire'.

85 Marc Gold, 'The Rhetoric of Rights: The Supreme Court and the Charter' in *Making the Laws: The Courts and the Constitution*, eds. John Saywell and G. Vegh (Toronto: Copp Clark Pitman, 1991), 364–389.

86 His opposition to the Charlottetown Accord was conducted in exactly the same style. See Pierre Elliott Trudeau, *A Mess That Deserves A Big No* (Toronto: Stewart House, 1992). He calls its creators 'doddering fools' (17), claims that the Charter has 'clear and precise' language (20), claims that the Accord leaves out Rostand's 'little people, the privates, marching footsore' (22). The Accord will trap us all 'irremediably in a constitution which will destroy the Canada we know, a Canada of equality for all without distinction' (38). We should see Bosnia, he says, as an example of where we are headed with the Accord.

87 'Trudeau Speaks Out', *Maclean's Magazine,* 28 September 1992.

88 'How Pierre Trudeau misleads the people'.

89 Ibid.

90 Ibid.

91 Robertson interview.

92 'How Pierre Trudeau misleads the people'.

93 Someone else who did this was not a person with whom Trudeau would want to be associated. Richard Nixon 'was in the habit of referring to himself in the third person, something I had never heard anyone do before—not even members of the British Royal Family. "When Nixon was President and Leader of the Free World . . ." he would say.' See Michael Korda, 'Nixon, Mine Host', *The New Yorker*, 9 May 1994, 77.

94 'Trudeau to Robertson: "So where is the demagogy?"'

95 Robertson interview.

96 'Trudeau to Robertson: "So where is the demagogy?"'

97 *The Globe and Mail*, 24 October 1992.

98 See Mary Ann Glendon, *Rights Talk* (New York: Free Press, 1991). She discusses the ways in which legal discourse has come to define political debate.

99 For a full discussion of attitudes in the West, accompanied by recent empirical data, see Roger Gibbins and Sonia Arrison, *Western Visions*. In some senses they see 'the West' as a byproduct of the challenge posed by Quebec; Quebec gave the West leverage.

100 See James T. Boulton, *The Language of Politics in the Age of Wilkes and Burke,* 100.

101 'They have "the rights of men". Against these there can be no prescription; against these no argument is binding: these admit no temperament and no compromise.' See *Reflections on the Revolution in France*, in *Edmund Burke on Government, Politics and Society*, ed. B.W. Hill (New York: International Publications Service, 1976), 324.

102 Edmund Burke, *Three Letters Addressed to a Member of the Present Parliament on the Proposals for Peace With the Regicide Directory of France, Letter I: On the Overtures of Peace,* in *The Works of the Right Honourable Edmund Burke in Twelve Volumes* (London: John C. Nimmo, 1887), vol. 5, 340.

103 Edmund Burke, *Speech on Conciliation with the Colonies*, in *Edmund Burke on Government, Politics and Society*, ed. B.W. Hill, 160.

104 Ibid., 176.

105 Edmund Burke, *A Letter to the Sheriffs of Bristol*, in *Edmund Burke on Government, Politics and Society*, ed. B.W. Hill, 204–5.

106 Edmund Burke, *Speech on Conciliation with the Colonies*, 185.

107 Ibid.

108 Ibid., 160.

109 Edmund Burke, *On American Taxation*, in *Edmund Burke on Government, Politics and Society*, ed. B.W. Hill, 122–23.

110 Edmund Burke, *Reflections on the Revolution in France*, 328.

111 Ibid.

112 Constitutional democracies may in fact be very difficult systems to transform institutionally. Their constitutions are respected and established, interests are embedded, and norms and values entrenched. At the same time, our democratic practices are in themselves under scrutiny: there is an understandable public demand for consultation and involvement. For discussion of these issues see, for example, John E. Trent, Robert Young, and Guy Lachapelle, eds, *Québec-Canada*.

113 David McCrone, *Understanding Scotland: The Sociology of a Stateless Nation* (London: Routledge, 1992), 28.

114 There is an ongoing debate about the ancestry of Scottish traditions. This includes the possibility that wearing of kilts, and the use of clan tartans, came via their promotion by English businessmen.

115 Mark Kingwell, *The Globe and Mail*, Feb. 24, 1996. Kingwell was reviewing Ludovic Kennedy's *In Bed With An Elephant: A Journey Through Scotland's Past and Present* (Bantam Press).

116 Tom Nairn, 'Upper and Lower Cases', *London Review of Books*, vol. 17, no. 16, 24 Aug., 1995, 18. I was already using the metaphor of a shallow burial and the 'constitutional undead' when I came across Nairn's review.

117 Ibid.

118 Lindsay Paterson, *The Autonomy of Modern Scotland* (Edinburgh, 1994), 28–31. This line of argument should not, however, obscure the harsh realities of the English-Scottish relationship. Scotland was, in Prebble's words, 'a despised political partner' for a long time. See John Prebble, *Mutiny: Highland Regiments in Revolt 1743–1784* (London: Penguin Books, 1975), 20.

119 See James Mitchell, *Strategies for Self-Government: The Campaigns for a Scottish Parliament* (Edinburgh, Polygon, 1996), 38. Also note the discussion of the union state concept in Michael Keating, *Nations against the State: The New Politics of Nationalism in Quebec, Catalonia and Scotland* (New York: St Martin's Press, 1996), 163–4.

120 Paterson, *The Autonomy of Modern Scotland*, 9.

121 Ibid., 121.

122 See Mitchell, *Strategies for Self-Government*, 52.

123 Paterson, 18.

124 David McCrone, *Understanding Scotland: The Sociology of a Stateless Nation*, 198. McCrone provides an excellent overall analysis, and he shows how Scotland's culture is 'periodically remade'. Michael Keating's recent book *Nations Against the State* also contains up-to-date survey and electoral data for all three cases studied.

125 Keating, 83.

126 Ibid., 219.

127 The idea that Quebec is a more egalitarian and collectivist political culture has been put forward by Quebec's leaders. Whether this is true is a moot point. Data from the World Values Survey of 1990 show that Quebeckers may be less rather than more inclined than other Canadians to prefer equality. See John Heliwell, 'Canada's Economic and Social Union. Past, Prospects and Proposals' in Trent, Young, and Lachapelle, *Québec-Canada*, 194–5.

128 For a discussion of the campaign, and the tactics used, see John Bochel, David Denver and Allan Macartney, eds, *The Referendum Experience: Scotland 1979* (Aberdeen: Aberdeen University Press, 1981).

129 Wayne G. Reilly, 'The Quebec Sovereignty Referendum of 1995: What Now?' *The American Review of Canadian Studies*, 25, 4 (Winter 1995), 495. Our willingness to rely on democratic processes appears to be receding; we are now turning to the courts for answers and judgments, and the reference case now sent to the Supreme Court on the Quebec secession issue is clearly illustrative of this. This is a dangerous turn of events.

130 This is often referred to as the 'West Lothian problem', raised forcefully by Tom Dalyell, MP for this constituency.

131 'The speech that Jacques Parizeau never got to give', *The Globe and Mail*, translation supplied by the Canadian Press. Bouchard spoke of an equal footing, peoples who have never understood each other, 'the first authentic meeting of our two collective minds', and other clear indicators of what was to follow.

132 Prebble, *Mutiny*, 20.

133 McCrone, *Understanding Scotland*, 220.

134 For a useful typology of ideal types of nationalism, both ethnic and civic, with or without a state, see Keating, *Nations Against the State*, 22.

135 See McCrone, *Understanding Scotland*, for a full discussion of these masculine aspects (e.g., fathers, brothers, Stakhanovite male work ethic, tartanry, the lad o' pairts, Kailyardism, Clydesidism). Lindsay Paterson, however, makes the point that Scotland was often seen as female, while England was male. Paterson, *The Autonomy of Modern Scotland*, 65.

136 Mitchell's *Strategies for Self-Government*, 265–6 contains an interesting discussion of symbolism and identity. He shows how the British governments have been very conscious of the importance of political symbols, including such items as postage stamps, and discussed them at cabinet level. In 1958, the bicentenary of Robbie

Burns' birth did not get a special stamp: it was too associated with Scottish nationalist sentiment.

137 I have not listed here all of Quebec's constitutional powers, which include the right to veto, under s. 41, any changes to the Constitution respecting: the use of French or English; the composition of the Supreme Court, which includes three judges from Quebec; the amending formula itself. If Quebec opts out of an amendment transferring provincial legislative powers regarding education and culture to Ottawa, Canada must provide reasonable compensation to Quebec. Within the Constitution Quebec is of course given a wide range of responsibilities under the terms of section 92.

138 See Arnold Kemp, *The Hollow Drum: Scotland Since the War* (Edinburgh: Mainstream Publishing, 1993). Kemp describes Scotland as 'divided by regional jealousies' and 'tortured by self-doubt'.

139 See David Elkins, *Beyond Sovereignty: Territory and Political Economy in the Twenty-First Century* (Toronto: University of Toronto Press, 1995), 34. Elkins discusses the ways in which the idea of the state became 'bundled' with other notions, and how we are now 'unbundling' it.

140 McCrone, *Understanding Scotland*, 196.

141 Keating, *Nations Against the State*, 220.

142 See Michael B. Stein, 'Tensions in the Canadian Constitutional Process: Elite Negotiations, Referendums and Interest Group Consultations, 1980–1992' in *Canada: The State of the Federation 1993*, eds Ronald L. Watts and Douglas O. Brown (Kingston: Institute of Intergovernmental Relations, 1993).

143 Seminar, the University of Calgary, 24 November 1993. This puts optimism about how far English-Canadians had really moved into perspective. Alain Nöel expresses some of this optimism in 'Deliberating a Constitution: The Meaning of the Canadian Referendum of 1992' in *Constitutional Predicament*, 78. In the same volume Alan Cairns notes that 'it was only to be expected that asymmetrical federalism ... disappeared when the "provincial powerbrokers" took charge in the final negotiations.' See 'The Charlottetown Accord: Multinational Canada v. Federalism', 35.

144 See Michael Burgess and Franz Gress, 'Asymmetrical Federalism in Canada, the United States and Germany', paper presented at the 16th World Congress of the International Political Science Association (Berlin, August 1994), 20.

145 Alan C. Cairns, 'The Charlottetown Accord', 27.

146 Ibid., 34.

147 Ibid., 33.

148 Ibid., 49. He offers a number of reasons why this was so, not all of them flattering to the RoC. He also makes the important point that in terms of dealing with Quebec, a 'well developed discourse' was already available.

149 Ibid., 55.

150 David Milne, 'Exposed to the Glare', in F. Leslie Seidle, ed. *Seeking a New Canadian Partnership: Asymmetrical and Confederal Options* (Ottawa: Institute for Research on Public Policy, 1994), 115.

151 Peter McCormick, 'The Will of the People: Democratic Practice in Canada and the United States' in *Canada and the United States: Differences that Count*, ed. David M. Thomas (Peterborough: Broadview Press, 1993), 189. See also David Laycock, *Populism and Democratic Thought in the Canadian Prairies 1910–1945* (Toronto: University of Toronto Press, 1990); Patrick Boyer, *Direct Democracy in Canada* (Toronto: Dundurn Press, 1992). Populism is a complex phenomenon, and is capable of important mutations. For a European perspective see Hans-George Betz, 'The New Politics of Resentment: Radical Right-Wing Populist Parties in Western Europe', *Comparative Politics* 25, 4 (July 1993), 413–427. For a discussion of the added complexities of a conservative postmodern populism see Richard Sigurdson, 'Preston Manning and the Politics of Postmodernism in Canada', *Canadian Journal of Political Science* 27, 2 (June 1994), 249–276. For empirical evidence of hostility towards special status for Quebec see Keith Archer and Faron Ellis, 'Opinion Structure of Party Activists: The Reform Party of Canada' in the same journal, 277–308.

152 Roger Gibbins and David Thomas, 'Ten Lessons From the Referendum,' *Canadian Parliamentary Review* 15, 4 (Winter 1992–3). The difficulties of dealing with constitutional change via referendum were realized by the framers of the American Constitution. They did not submit it to a popular referendum. It went instead to special popularly elected conventions. Rhode Island refused to agree and submitted the question to a referendum, in which the Constitution was overwhelmingly defeated (even allowing for a federalist boycott). The Federalists argued that this was not a valid expression of the popular will, because 'Without the opportunity to meet together and exchange views, no-one could decide what was good for the whole state'. See Edmund S. Morgan, 'Power to the People?', 28.

153 See Roger Gibbins and Sonia Arrison, *Western Visions: Perspectives on the West in Canada* (Peterborough: Broadview Press, 1995); also see Don Braid and Sydney Sharpe, *Breakup: Why the West Feels Left Out Of Canada* (Toronto: Key Porter Books, 1990).

154 See David Laycock, 'The Reform Party of Canada and right-populist parties in Western Europe: a comparative analysis', paper presented at the annual conference of the British Association of Canadian Studies, Exeter, 1996. I wish to thank Dr Laycock for sending me a copy of this paper.

155 Michael Lusztig, 'Constitutional Paralysis: Why Canadian Constitutional Initiatives Are Doomed To Fail', *Journal of Political Science* 27, 4 (Dec. 1994), 770.

156 Ibid., 752.

157 This argument must be treated with caution. Johnston et al. conclude that 'Trudeau fanciers, who started the campaign most likely to vote "Yes", ended up the least likely to do so.' They argue that he remains a 'pivotal figure'. See Richard Johnston, et al., 'The People and the Charlottetown Accord' in *Canada: The State of the Federation, 1993*, eds Ronald L. Watts and Douglas O. Brown.

158 Michael Lusztig, 'Constitutional Paralysis', 771.

159 Michael M. Atkinson, 'What Kind of Democracy Do Canadians Want?' *Canadian Journal of Political Science* 27, 1994, 717–745. For an earlier version of the integrative theory see Michael B. Stein, *Canadian Constitutional Renewal, 1960–1981: A*

Case Study in Integrative Bargaining (Kingston: Institute of Intergovernmental Relations, 1990).

160 Atkinson, 723.

161 Ibid., 724.

162 See Alan C. Cairns, 'The Charlottetown Accord: Multinational Canada versus Federalism' in Douglas Williams, ed., *Reconfigurations*.

163 For example, Roger Gibbins has commented that a Canada without Quebec would provide an opportunity for the RoC 'to get out from under the dead weight of old ideas and old issues'. See 'Speculations on a Canada Without Quebec' in *The Charlottetown Accord, the Referendum and the Future of Canada*, 272.

164 Edwin R. Black, 'Going Public: Mass Communications and Executive Federalism' in *Federalism and political community*, eds. David P. Shugarman and Reg Whitaker, 358.

165 Janet Ajzenstat, 'Decline of Procedural Liberalism: The Slippery Slope to Secession'.

166 Ibid., 21.

167 Cairns, 'The Charter, Interest Groups, Executive Federalism, and Constitutional Reform', in *After Meech Lake*, 20.

168 It should have been. It cost at least $300 million in federal spending alone, without counting for release time and some of the advertising. For a summary and discussion of the process see Leslie A. Pal and F. Leslie Seidle, 'Constitutional Politics 1990–92: The Paradox of Participation' in *How Ottawa Spends: A More Democratic Canada,* ed. Susan D. Philips (Ottawa: Carleton University Press, 1993).

169 For a full account of this and Canada's other 'mega-constitutional' events and crises see Peter H. Russell, *Constitutional Odyssey*.

170 See Thomas J. Courchene, '*Staatsnation* vs *Kulturnation*: The Future of RoC' in Kenneth McRoberts, ed., *Beyond Quebec: Taking Stock of Canada* (Montreal and Kingston: McGill-Queen's University Press, 1995), 390.

171 Anthony King's classic piece on the overloaded state was written in 1974. See 'Overload: Problems of governing in the 1970s', *Political Studies* 23, 2–3 (1974), 284–296. William Lawton notes that the policy choice which unravelled the 'Keynesian consensus' was the abandonment of the commitment to full employment and the attack on inflation, and that this 'predated the electoral success of neo-conservatism, notably in Britain'. See 'The State of the Welfare State in Canada and Britain', paper presented at the Annual Meeting of the Canadian Political Science Association, Montreal 1995.

172 This point is in fact made in the *Report of the Commission on the Political and Constitutional Future of Quebec:* 'In 1982 the Canadian Constitution drew closer to the American political culture' and the new arrangements had 'altered the spirit of the 1867 Act and the compromise established at that time', 30.

173 Note in particular F.L. Morton, 'Judicial Politics Canadian-Style: The Supreme Court's Contribution to the Constitutional Crisis of 1992', in *Constitutional Predicament*.

174 See Roger Gibbins, 'The Evolution of Canada's Constitution' in *Canadian Politics in the 1990s*, 4th edn, eds Michael Whittington and Glen Williams.
175 See Thomas J. Courchene, '*Staatsnation* vs *Kulturnation*'.
176 Robert Fulford, 'A Post-Modern Dominion: The Changing Nature of Canadian Citizenship' in *Belonging: The Meaning and the Future of Canadian Citizenship*, ed. William Kaplan (Montreal and Kingston: McGill-Queen's University Press, 1994), 116. He also notes that the two major federal parties reversed their traditional positions on Canada-United States relations in the mid-1980s, which further confuses everyone.
177 Ibid., 111.
178 Ibid., 112. The F.R. Scott who had such an influence on Pierre Trudeau.
179 See Kaplan's introduction to *Belonging*, 22. In the same volume note especially Alan C. Cairns, 'The Fragmentation of Canadian Citizenship'. Also see Alan C. Cairns, *Charter Versus Federalism*.
180 C.E.S. Franks, *The Myths and Symbols of the Constitutional Debate in Canada* (Kingston: Institute of Intergovernmental Relations, 1993), 66.
181 It might be useful if more attention were paid to the idea of *federalism* as a 'value concept' and to the idea of *federation* as an organizational form. See Michael Burgess, 'Federalism and Federation: A Reappraisal' in *Comparative Federalism and Federation*, eds Michael Burgess and Alain-G. Gagnon (Toronto: University of Toronto Press, 1993).
182 Watts interview.
183 Michael Foley, *The Silence of Constitutions* (London: Routledge, 1989), 130.
184 I am grateful to Joy Kogawa for giving me this idea. I had occasion to explain the idea of abeyances to her, whereupon she exclaimed, 'But that is so Japanese!'
185 Karel Van Wolferen, *The Enigma of Japanese Power* (Tokyo: Charles E. Tuttle, 1993), 10.
186 Ibid., 14.
187 Ibid., 308.
188 Ibid., 309.

Conclusion

How do I get to Biddicombe? ... I wouldn't start from here if I were you.

There is clearly a desire on the part of many Canadians to let things rest awhile. An understanding and appreciation of the role and nature of constitutional abeyances inevitably reinforce such a view. As Michael Foley has argued, all functioning political systems—all constitutions construed very generally—will house such areas of indecision and disjunction, and will avoid them. Does this therefore mean that to talk of constitutional abeyances is merely a truism, a statement of the obvious? To put it another way, should we not simply say, 'So what? All democratic systems set things aside, such things change over time, and Canada is no different.'

This is not a reply to be given if one accepts either the idea that the existence of deep, profound abeyances is a functional requirement for mature constitutions, which do not simply unfold and become ever clearer and more logical, or that this examination of abeyances in a Canadian setting has merit. The evidence shows that Canada's abeyances, as one might well expect, are very different from those elsewhere, and have some particularly intractable elements even for something that has intractability as a defining feature. My contention is that the idea of 'abeyances' should be added to our constitutional lexicon, and should become a part of the way we view constitutional issues. However, do we have the temperament and consensus necessary to admit to them? This is not merely a matter of discussing Canada's political culture, or a particularly important part of it, such as views of citizenship. Abeyances lie at the heart of constitutional values and, because of our inability to deal with them satisfactorily, the constitution has become a battleground that now affects our political culture probably far more than is the case in Britain or the United States. In order to understand the debate over Canadian values, we have to realize how and why our abeyances have not become ever more deeply hidden, how our instinctual constitutional behaviour has changed, and why our mechanisms of abeyance evasion have not worked.

Chapters One and Two therefore took up the task of discussing in what ways the terms and concepts *already* in use do not capture what an abeyance is. They set out what an abeyance is, and what it is not, and why the notion fits so well with the other terms routinely employed in the service of constitutional analysis. Chapter Two also emphasized that abeyances are not merely the result of common sense in action, for they are often not common-sensical at all.

Chapter Three then dealt with the pivotal events of 1867 to show that the conditions were appropriate for abeyance creation as well as avoidance, and that in Sir John A. Macdonald we had a leader who thought in Burkean terms—and Burke of course acted and wrote in a manner that leaves little doubt that there are things best left unsaid and undone, and that extremism in the pursuit of political virtue is a vice. In the 1867 settlement there were conflicting visions and everyone lived to fight another day. For almost 100 years the country managed, with some exceptions, to prevent a reopening of the terms of the federal bargain, and patronage was the lubricant of the party systems both provincially and federally. Chapter Four discussed how the one abeyance capable of tearing things apart—the status, place, and powers of the province of Quebec and what people inside and outside the province thought that these were, remained buried. However, what might be called the mega-abeyance was in a shallow grave, and there was always a danger that the bones would be exhumed during a crisis. The crises that did occur were often external to Quebec itself and had to do with the place of the French language and Catholicism in the other provinces: important symbolically but a different question than that of the status of the province and its government. Quebec itself, whilst not exactly asleep, maintained its traditional demands, but remained relatively quiescent under a very conservative regime of church and state control. The most serious crises involved questions of citizenship and conscription, and whether one should be prepared to die for a country called Canada. But from the 1960s on it became increasingly impossible to maintain a policy of strategic avoidance of the black hole that many knew deep constitutional debate to be. What had protected us before would no longer suffice. Chapter Four concluded by tracing the rise of Quebec's specific claims to constitutional recognition.

Chapter Five examined what happened when the 'mega-abeyance' was no longer in abeyance. Chances for agreement were missed. From the mid-1960s to the late 1970s the federal government struggled to respond, and in 1979 the *Report of the Task Force on National Unity* took up the challenge in an unprecedented manner. It built upon the work of both the Tremblay and the Laurendeau-Dunton Reports, and it came under sustained criticism both for its views on dualism and for what was perceived as its strongly decentralist approach to federalism. The Quebec question was to bring with it others that had long been ignored, including questions of sovereignty, democracy, power, and provincial rights. The settled unsettlement of the preceding century had given way to 'unsettled unsettlement'. And in the person of Pierre Elliott Trudeau the country found someone who was prepared, once he had decided to accept the constitutional challenges posed by Quebec and the increasingly aggressive provinces, to tackle an abeyance vigorously, first by outflanking it, secondly by erecting counterweights, and thirdly by confrontation. The country as a whole was convinced that, on Quebec at least, Trudeau was right, even though there was widespread opposition to his government's program of national bilingualism. His solutions stood squarely in the way of those proposed by the Task Force. We are now left with thought-provoking questions as to what might have been if this had not been so.

After 1982, with the passage of the Constitution Act of that year, it appeared for a time as if the country had its abeyances under control and was back to its usual institutionalized ambivalence. This was deceptive. Quebec's quiescence was not consent and the problems created by the Act were far from being resolved. At best, we might just have returned to settled unsettlement, but the attempt to bring Quebec into the constitutional family, in a constitutional way, via the Meech Lake Accord, blew up into a major constitutional and political crisis, a crisis from which some believe there is no turning back. Chapter Six showed how the Accord was a graphic illustration of an attempt—for the first time—to entrench a definition of Quebec's distinctiveness into the Constitution. We were trying to write an abeyance down. It was a clever compromise, an attempt to balance 'visions', much in the spirit of 1867, and it might have worked. But the temperament needed to sustain such a compromise was not often in evidence. Process became a key problem, and Pierre Trudeau rallied the opposition to any concessions to Quebec that smacked of dualism. Distinctiveness was taken to imply a claim to superiority or preferential treatment, not merely difference, and was seen as dangerously open-ended. Chapter Six also examined the highly illustrative confrontation between the former Prime Minister and someone who had been his colleague and confidant for almost his entire administration. It illustrates the extent to which rhetoric had displaced caution and reason. The Trudeau interventions in both the Meech and Charlottetown Accords represent a sharp contrast to the kind of imagination, advice, and wisdom to be found in Burke—which had played such an important part in the world of Sir John A. It also runs counter to the idea that we should take a positive view of the kind of liberal nationalism that can come with the claims to national recognition put forward by a Scotland or a Quebec (or a Catalonia): small nations accommodated within the framework of a federation or a union-state.

Chapter Six concluded by discussing democracies and abeyances, in particular Canada's unique situation, and by asking how abeyances are to be buried once raised. The only seemingly easy answer is to ignore them—if we can. Recent events have shown, yet again, that our problems and approach differ markedly from those of either Britain or the United States. We have tried, in a manner truly Canadian, to educate ourselves about the constitution and to discuss it. If our present disposition is any indication, we may not have achieved much by it. Our federal and constitutional structure, the problems left untackled until now, and our lack of overarching symbols or even strong notions of citizenship all come back to haunt us. The idea of abeyances, if added to our constitutional vocabulary, at least gives us a broader frame of reference and enables us to see constitutional and political questions in a different and perhaps more realistic light. It does not further obscure our explanatory world—it makes it more nuanced.

We have a uniquely Canadian situation with regard to abeyances, one that

Foley does not discuss. We have 'unsettled settlement' and do not know if it can last, or change. It was far harder for the federalists to win the referendum in 1995 than it had been in 1980. Lawrence Leduc has used David Easton's well-known analysis of political 'authority' to explain why this was so. Easton distinguishes amongst *political authorities* (e.g., those individuals who hold formal political power, including those who run political parties); *political regimes* (the rules of the game, including institutions and constitutional practices); and the *political community* (the people in a given territory who share common feelings of political identity, as well as common institutions).[1] Of these three, political community is not only the most general and elusive, it is also the most essential because it is the foundation for regimes and authorities.

In terms of all three Eastonian categories, as Leduc has shown, the federalists were significantly weaker in 1995.[2] None of the federal 'authorities' had the stature that Pierre Trudeau had in 1980, including Pierre Trudeau himself (and he was therefore asked not to intervene). Chrétien ranked well behind Bouchard in every popular dimension in Quebec. Federalists could not offer meaningful 'regime' change; renewed federalism promises would not wash a second time, certainly not after the failure of the Meech and Charlottetown Accords. What could still be stressed was the most important but most nebulous of all—community. The idea of belonging, or not belonging, to a *Canadian community* was not the ground on which sovereignists wished to fight. Leduc in fact argues that:

> the most striking feature of the comparison of the 1980 and 1993 Canadian National Electoral Study figures however may be the shrinkage of the number of respondents with strongly held or immovable positions on the issue. After twenty years of debate, the number of Quebeckers who truly have no view on the issue of sovereignty is relatively small. But the proportion strongly attached to the more sharply drawn concept of 'sovereignty' also seems to have declined. . . . The data seem to suggest that Quebeckers in the 1990s were becoming more oriented than ever to a flexible middle ground.[3]

Thus, on the central question of community, there is still good reason to believe that Quebeckers want to remain Canadians—but there must be a perceived middle to retreat to.[4]

So what, if anything, should or could change? We could opt for a far more vigorous defence of our existing arrangements, including in this defence the fact that the system allows for enormous change as it is without recourse to formal amendment. We could combine such a defence with the oft-touted solution of asymmetrical federalism, but this runs into several of our most intractable abeyances. Asymmetrical proposals tend to produce gridlock: the cry always goes up that if they have it, we must have it too.

An eminently sensible and moderate agenda and timetable for change has now been put forward by a group of twenty-two distinguished academics, mainly political scientists. Their report, entitled *Making Canada Work Better*, recommends starting with fiscal and economic matters and moving finally to the dualism question, after real progress has been made on the other issues. Their suggestions on dualism include aiming for 'the substance of Meech', possibly accompanied by a fiscal equality clause ('culturally distinct, fiscally equal'). An amended Meech Lake formulation could state, they argue, in clause 2.(1) (b), that:

> the Constitution of Canada shall be interpreted in a manner consistent with 'the recognition of the fact that Canada is characterized by a fundamental duality in that, unlike other countries in the Americas, public life in Canada does not tend to converge to a single language. On the contrary, both English and French constitute languages of public life, each having preponderance in its own geographic area.'[5]

The preferred back-up position if this approach fails is 'inspired by the Pepin-Robarts Task Force'. It would preserve bilingualism in areas of federal jurisdiction, would recognize certain official minority language rights but, beyond that, would 'accord jurisdiction over the public use of language to the provinces'. (Two signatories preferred this approach to a distinct society clause, but 'most of us remain unconvinced'.) The entire report is brief and well worth reading, and it reaffirms one thing very clearly: twenty-two of our best constitutional minds are still convinced that there needs to be a formal recognition of the separate identity that a majority of French-speaking Quebeckers cherish.

Therefore, while it has been argued throughout that it is advisable for us to add to our constitutional vocabulary the term abeyance not only to denote the place one puts things into—a state of abeyance—but also to denote the thing itself and the temperament necessary to allow such mysteries, I also believe that it is time to confront an abeyance, and lay it to rest. There are abeyances out there in the graveyard at the bottom of our constitutional garden, and one in particular has always haunted us. We have summoned them and have not prevented their emergence into the constitutional light of day. We need a Burkean temperament to put them back where they came from, and we are not able to rely on the mechanisms available to other political systems. We do not have their history and their traditions; we do not look at our ideological and even institutional incoherence and accept it, as they do.

Americans can simultaneously believe in free enterprise and the need to attack special interests, in individualism and community, in equality in the midst of rampant inequality, in democracy as decided by a specialist judiciary—to mention but a few obvious paradoxes. The British really do let sleeping abeyances lie and have come to condone their constitutional obscurities, although even this could change if the Labour Party wins the next election and Scottish and Welsh devolution and a Charter of Rights end up on the political agenda. Then the paradoxical view that Britain has a flexible constitution, but one that must not be bent or it will break, will really be tested. (Foley goes so far as to say that if there were a breakdown of abeyances in Britain 'the subsequent sectional demands for a clarified constitution might well represent the prelude to a civil war as they were in the seventeenth century.'6) Americans can worship their constitution even as they argue about it all the time, the British can see theirs as pragmatic and responsive when it often isn't. Certainly neither Britain nor the United States lack deep constitutional problems and abeyances, but both strive to avoid having political divisions allied to constitutional differences, particularly if these involve territorial problems. History provides an explanation: constitutions survive in this world not by settling matters decisively but by deflecting them.

We do not, however, have to take an extreme view and see written constitutions as things that do not really matter, or believe that what counts are Oakeshott-style traditions of behaviour, modes of experience, which may appear unintelligible to the uninitiated. Federal systems require more than this. Canadian federalism has, in some respects, shown great flexibility; in others it has not. Comparing Canada's abeyance exposure problems to the experiences of other mature political systems may help to reassure us that we can and should continue to ignore profound questions, just as others do. Irresolution is not necessarily a sign of weakness or a dereliction of political duty. But if an abeyance cannot be avoided, *and in our case it cannot*, then change, if we follow Burke, must be brought about with the utmost care: imaginatively and wisely, prudently and honourably. Feelings and recognition count. Principles are not absolutes; they must be weighed and judged and applied in the light of particular circumstances and historical experience. This does not mean however that principles are not important for, in certain respects, we always have to choose which principles, in our particular situation, are to be regarded as trumps. We must also always bear in mind that at times of deep divisiveness there will be, in Robert Young's descriptive phrase, 'mutually profitable antagonisms' which political leaders can exploit, particularly in a federal system.[7]

My own preference for a much clearer statement of dualism and Quebec's distinctiveness must by now be clear. Such an assertion may seem to ignore the heterogeneity of Quebec society, marginalize Quebec's anglophone community and its historic contributions, and omit other claims to recognition. Perhaps more fundamentally we must always be aware that generalizations about what large groups of people believe, or what they see themselves as, are deeply suspect. What we are talking about are *individual* choices, which are far more complex than the labels we use indicate.[8] Yet having admitted the inadequacies of labels we are still faced with the fact that individuals can and do choose which communities matter most to them; how we define ourselves becomes a collective concern.

As noted at the very outset, I believe that what we are talking about, as Keating so clearly shows, is the nationalism of a smaller nation within a federal state in which the majority have not honestly recognized what we are dealing with. Quebec's francophone majority do not see themselves as simply rights-bearing individual citizens of a state called Canada. They now define themselves as Québécois and as a distinct, small, historically-rooted, French-speaking society that agreed to become a part of a federation. By virtually all normal standards Quebeckers constitute a nation, and one not merely based on ethnicity, as many outside Quebec assume.[9] Quebec nationalism has changed and modernized, but it is always there. It has redefined itself, for, as Jane Jenson notes 'there have always been competing ways to achieve this end' (the preservation of language and culture) and there have been 'different political strategies for doing so.'[10] It is surely time to take stock of the ways in which we were able to avoid the recognition that Quebec is the homeland of a people whose separate existence predates Canada's and who, if they so choose, could secede. The terms of such a departure are of course another matter. The Unity Task Force Report said essentially the same thing.

To recognize Quebec as different does not have to mean that Quebeckers would cease to be part of an overarching federal state. All in Quebec would remain Canadian citizens; for many this would be their primary allegiance, just as some form of union-state remains the preference of most Scots. There would be recognized dual loyalties. Aboriginal peoples would preserve their multiple national allegiances also. It was ever thus. To many outside and even inside Quebec this may seem an insupportable proposition: using a word such as 'nation' raises so many hackles that it may not be possible to discuss matters in these terms. This is why we retreated into what was thought to be the relative safety of such phrases as 'distinct society'. One of the legacies of the Meech Lake Accord is that this term is now a shibboleth; its use by either 'side' produces instant reactions. Any term we use as a replacement is likely to be just as contentious: too strong or too weak; too demeaning or too dangerous. Yet we *are* talking about nationalism, how to contain it, and how it might play a positive role in a modern federation which is itself trying to redefine its nationhood. Federalism is still, at least theoretically, capable of coping with such tensions. An avoidance strategy is unlikely to work any longer, and other methods have failed.

Trudeau chose to use the Charter, pan-Canadianism, and universal individual rights as his main counterweights to Quebec nationalism. This has not prevented the further fragmentation of our identities and in fact may have exacerbated it. Belgium, which followed a completely different route and sought to compartmentalize and separate linguistic and community differences, has ended up reinforcing excessive particularism. Neither approach has worked.[11] We have to find a uniquely Canadian solution which recognizes identities, in particular Quebec's, in a symbolic and respectful way, without creating the conditions for excessive and exclusive nationalism and compartmentalization. How do we do this, given what we have gone through, and given what we rejected? We have to find the way to Biddicombe, and we have to start from here.

Readers may think that I have a responsibility to go beyond these observations, and should provide more detail regarding possible remedies. That we need to think hard about what to do there is no doubt, for our situation is dangerous and volatile. Old taboos and restraints have been cast aside. Our new economy may be radicalizing our politics and alienating (and marginalizing) many of our citizens.[12] Political leaders are viewed with disdain. Media pundits often oversimplify, feed on every mistake, and proffer their own solutions. The Chrétien government's quasi-constitutional manoeuvres in response to the fact that a majority of Quebec francophones voted for sovereignty, or at least for the possibility of sovereignty, may have made matters very much worse. This is particularly true from a Western-Canadian perspective, but it is also true for Quebec.[13] The Liberals seem unlikely to move boldly into any new arrangement and are, understandably, far more prone to a political approach; which is to say, to see nothing fundamentally wrong, and to hope things sort themselves out as the economy changes and Bouchard's popularity wanes. At the same time attitudes may be hardening as we get used to seeing Quebec as 'not part of us', although we claim, paradoxically, to be tolerant and pluralistic.[14] We also have to remember that Canada's population has grown at a rate 'unmatched in other liberal democracies in the twentieth century'.[15] It grew by almost 50% between 1945 and 1960. This has meant that a very large number of new voters were socialized and mobilized. These were voters who did not see Quebec in historical context, and the geographic distribution of this electorate has created 'five-region politics' at the federal level along with extraordinary volatility.[16] In 1993 over 200 of the nearly 300 MPs were new to Ottawa. Thus personal friendships ('acquaintance') across a linguistic divide, a knowledge of Quebec's historical perspectives on dualism and federalism, and a familiarity with the details of Ottawa life are inevitably in short supply.

Even so, I am not going to move to a prescriptive mode and suggest in any detail what we must and should do to change things. I am unwilling to do so for two reasons, First, I do not have a magic formula in mind, either procedurally or substantively. I am simply joining those who argue—who plead—for an open-minded, tolerant, and historically sensitive approach to the underlying nature of our constitutional difficulties when it comes to Quebec's future within a federal system.[17] I am all too sure that many people still appear to believe that our difficulties stem from Canada having been too generous and accommodating to Quebec, which was beaten but has refused to abide by the assumed rules for the vanquished. Since when has a military defeat meant that people abandon their sense of who they are and what they wish to be? Using the perspective of abeyances has, I hope, made a contribution to our understanding, and helps to counter such notions.

My second reason for not offering possible solutions or alternatives is that there are already extant a goodly number of recent blueprints for change. One has already been noted. Others are provided in the endnotes, along with brief comments.[18] *Whistling Past the Graveyard* is not an attempt to provide specific answers, although some are implicit in the arguments presented. It is rather a plea for a more balanced and detailed consideration of the Quebec question, of constitutional abeyances, and of federalism itself, set against our Burkean past and our unBurkean present. It is not, I should add, an argument for decentralization (although some may be appropriate) or for a weakened and diminished federal government. It is an argument for less rhetoric and more genuine sympathy of feeling. John Trent, Robert Young, and Guy Lachapelle reflect just such a spirit in a ten-point set of 'cultural conditions' that they have set out for an ethnically/nationally divided and diverse federation. This list is derived from the writings of Alan Cairns, and it includes a capacity for self-restraint, an acceptance of tension and contradiction, mutual recognition and appreciation, and 'incessant symbolic confirmation' of cultural and racial pluralism as well as of an overarching common citizenship. Like many, I now fear that we may not adequately recognize and appreciate what we have had until it is too late, and that we are not building on our strengths, which do include tolerance, a respect for diversity, and strong federal and democratic traditions.[19] Surely most Canadians inside and outside Quebec want, above all, a vibrant economy, a tolerant society, and to stay as Canadians within a federal political culture where important differences are recognized and affirmed.[20] What we could stress is 'the Canadian advantage' over the United States. It includes a far more rational and less costly health care system, lower crime rates, more affordable higher education, and a whole host of other specific but often forgotten differences that, cumulatively, matter a great deal.

Approaches such as these ask us to appreciate what we have been able to achieve—and to accommodate—as we continue to evolve as a political community. In this sense there is no '*status quo*', for as Claude Ryan has noted, to believe that we can actually maintain our institutions in their present state 'testifies to a profound lack of understanding of the ways in which the country has not ceased to change since 1867, and the very small role that the Constitution itself has played in this'.[21] Above all, we must remember that the question we face is not whether Quebec's spirit deserves praise or blame, but 'what in the name of God, shall we do with it?' Do we continue to try our best to avoid the very hard questions that are raised? Is the new strait-jacket of popular sovereignty via referendums a blessing (for it protects us from change) or is it a curse because leaders cannot now act as they once could? Should we put some honest and direct questions to the Canadian people, questions which ask whether or not we are prepared to recognize that Quebec has been, and is, fundamentally different and that this should be formally recognized and respected?[22] Could Canada outside Quebec alter its views if we had someone like a George Brown to lead it: an individual with a reputation for being resolutely hostile to notions of special status but who has a change of heart?[23] Preston Manning seems unlikely to assume such a role.

In reaching these conclusions, and in asking such questions, I am not ignoring other concerns, especially the need for principled settlements with aboriginal peoples. There would still be room for equivocation, for balance, for other forms of change, and for constitutional silences. Not all matters have to or can be resolved, but in certain key areas hard choices have to be made. Quebec's status still poses the greatest and toughest challenge of all. We have to stop whistling past the graveyard; it is time to go in, pay our respects, and come to terms with our past and present.

And even in our pseudo-participatory, media-dominated times, although the burden of this responsibility rests upon us all as individual political actors, it still rests primarily upon those we elect. Academic comparisons and discourse, however informative, are merely helpful at best: they are no substitute for political leadership; no substitute for vision, empathy, intelligence, pragmatism, and perhaps those greatest of all political commodities—timing and luck.

Notes

1. Lawrence Leduc, 'Framing the Question: The Politics of Question Wording in the 1980 and 1995 Quebec Referendums', paper presented at the Annual Meeting of the British Society for Canadian Studies, Exeter, 1996.

2. Easton's categories are set out in full in David Easton: *A Framework for Political Analysis* (Englewood Cliffs, N.J.: Prentice Hall, 1965).

3. Leduc, 'Framing the Question', 10.

4. For a discussion of what this might be see Donald G. Lenihan, Gordon Robertson, and Roger Tassé, *Canada: Reclaiming the Middle Ground* (Montreal: The Institute for Research on Public Policy, 1995).

5. The Group of 22, *Making Canada Work Better* (May 1996). Copies of this report, in English or French, can be obtained from the C.D. Howe Institute, the Canada West Foundation, the McGill Institute for the Study of Canada, and the Royal Bank of Canada. It is important not to confuse this report with the report of a different 'Group of 22' in June 1991.

6. Michael Foley, *The Silence of Constitutions: Gaps, 'abeyances' and political temperament in the maintenance of government* (New York: Routledge, 1989), 114.

7. Robert Young, *The Breakup of Czechoslovakia* (Kingston: Institute of Intergovernmental Relations, 1994), 16. Young also notes that the new Czech constitution 'contained significant abeyances on the issue of territorial division'.

8. For a discussion of this point see Brian Slattery, 'Rights, Communities and Traditions', *University of Toronto Law Journal* 41 (1991), 447–67.

9. The Bélanger-Campeau Commission, in its 1992 report on the future of Quebec in the aftermath of the Meech Lake failure, made the explicit point that Quebec was now a multi-ethnic community united by language, shared common values, and a 'collective life'. Léon Dion has argued that while French Canadians form a nation, the Québécois do not. See *Le duel constitutionnel Québec-Canada* (Montreal: Boréal, 1995), 350. I prefer the line of argument used by Michael Keating (and others). See *Nations Against the State* (New York: St Martin's Press, 1996).

10. Jane Jenson, 'Naming Nations. Making nationalist claims in Canadian Public discourse', *Canadian Review of Sociology and Anthropology* 30, 3 (1993), 340.

11. See Dimitrios Karmis and Alain-G. Gagnon, 'Fédéralisme et identités collectives au Canada et en Belgique: des itinéraires différents, une fragmentation similaire', *Canadian Journal of Political Science* 29, 3 (Sept. 1996), 435–68.

12. For a discussion of the new economic realities, and their effects, see Jocelyn Létourneau, *Les Années sans guide. Le Canada à l'ère de l'économie migrante*. Note in

particular Chapter Seven, 'Fragmentation du sujet politique et dispersion civique', and the conclusions reached. See also Richard Gwyn, *Nationalism Without Walls* (Toronto: McClelland and Stewart, 1996).

13 Roger Gibbins has provided a sobering denunciation of the steps taken by the federal government. His conclusion is that 'this is a strategy designed to heighten regional unrest . . . it is a strategy fraught with danger'. If Ontario rejects the Reform Party and accepts the Chrétien strategy, 'it may not be Reformers who silently fold their tents and go away. It may be the West.' See 'Western Canada in the Wake of the Events of 1995' in John E. Trent, Robert Young, Guy Lachapelle, eds, *Québec-Canada. What is the Path Ahead?* (Ottawa: University of Ottawa Press, 1996), 255–62.

14 See Charles Taylor, 'Sharing Identity Space', in Trent, Young, and Lachapelle, eds, *Québec-Canada*, 121–4. Taylor points out that the American and French models of a standard state with a single clear identity do not fit the Canadian experience or the realities of turn-of-the-millennium conditions throughout the world. And in Canada, 'Both refusals to share identity space can't see themselves as such'.

15 Kenneth Carty, 'The Electorate and the Evolution of Canadian Electoral Politics', *The American Review of Canadian Studies* 26, 1 (Spring 1996), 8.

16 Ibid., 22.

17 For a Quebec example of such an approach, see Claude Ryan, *Regards sur le fédéralisme canadien* (Montreal: Boréal, 1995). Ryan offers a clear and spirited defence of pan-Canadian nationalism as well as of Quebec's need for recognition as a distinct society. He also offers a strong defence of the federal Charter of Rights, and of federalism itself. Based upon considerable experience as a provincial cabinet minister, in portfolios which included higher education, science, language law application, public security, municipal affairs, and housing, Ryan concludes that in these areas, for which he had responsibility, there is absolutely no need for any major or urgent constitutional change. See pp. 99–108.

18 See, for example:

- André Burelle, *Le mal canadien. Essai de diagnostic et esquisse d'un thérapie* (Éditions Fides, 1995). Burelle sets out his recommendations for a new model of federalism.

- Claude Ryan, *Regards sur le fédéralisme canadien*. In addition to his defence of federalism noted above, Ryan also advocates changes in four specific areas as well as (a) recognition of Quebec as a distinct society and (b) changes to the amending formula.

- Jeremy Webber, *Reimagining Canada. Language, Culture, Community, and the Canadian Constitution* (Montreal and Kingston: McGill-Queen's University Press, 1994).

- *Today and Tomorrow, An agenda for action*. Ideas and recommendations of the Confederation 2000 conference participants (Ottawa: 3–4 May 1996). The Confederation 2000 Conferences were organized by the Business Council on National Issues.

- *Recognition and Interdependence*, the Report of the Quebec Liberal Party's Committee on the Evolution of Canadian Federalism, Dec. 1996.

Other reform-oriented discussions are included in the bibliography.

19 See John Berry, 'Ethnic Attitudes and Identities' in Trent, Young, and Lachapelle, eds, *Québec-Canada*, 221–34.

20 See Alan Cairns, 'Constitutional Government and the Two Faces of Ethnicity: Federalism is not enough' in Karen Knop, Sylvia Ostry, Richard Simeon, and Katherine Swinton, eds, *Rethinking Federalism: Citizens, Markets and Governments in a Changing World* (Vancouver: University of British Columbia Press, 1995), 15–39.

21 Ryan, *Regards sur le fédéralisme canadien*, 209.

22 Or must Quebeckers simply choose to be 'an ethnic nation or a civic nation', and, if the latter, accept the gradual restructuring of the federation, and not independence? For a clear presentation of the view that this is the fundamental choice that Quebec itself must make see Ramsay Cook, 'Challenges to Canadian Federalism in the 1990s' in James Littleton, ed., *Clash of Identities. Media, Manipulation, and Politics of the Self* (Englewood Cliffs, N.J.: Prentice Hall, 1996), 89–100. In the same volume note also the essays by Alain Fienkielkraut, Reg Whitaker, and Louis Balthazar.

23 For further historical details see Roderick A. Macdonald, 'Meech Lake to the Contrary Notwithstanding', *Osgoode Hall Law Journal* 29, 3 (1991), 567.

Bibliography

With a few exceptions, only those sources actually utilised in the text, and acknowedged in the endnotes, have been included in the bibliography. There has been no attempt to create a complete bibliography of works available. A particular essay which appears in a collection of readings has sometimes been noted separately, along with the edited collection, if it was used extensively or is particularly pertinent. This was done so as to make locating them easier for the interested reader. Unpublished papers presented at conferences have been noted only if quotations were used.

Interviews

Beaudoin, Senator Gérald-A., Ottawa, Ontario, 9 May 1994.

Black, Dr Edwin R., Kingston, Ontario, 9 May 1994.

Broadbent, Dr Edward G., Montreal, Quebec, 10 May 1994.

Cameron, Dr David R., Toronto, Ontario, 2 May 1994.

Clark, The Right Honourable Joseph, Calgary, Alberta, 22 November 1993.

Gagnon, Dr Alain-G., Montreal, Quebec, 10 May 1994.

Heintzman, Dr Ralph R., Ottawa, Ontario, 9 May 1994.

Kovitz, Dr Muriel, Calgary, Alberta, 1993.

Normand, Robert, Quebec City, Quebec, 12 May 1994.

Pepin, The Honourable Jean-Luc, Edmonton, Alberta, 23 April 1994.

Robertson, Dr Gordon, Ottawa, Ontario, 6 May 1994.

Simeon, Dr Richard, Toronto, Ontario, 2 May 1994.

Tremblay, Senator Arthur, Quebec City, Quebec, 13 May 1994.

Watts, Dr Ronald L., Kingston, Ontario, 5 May 1994.

Books, Articles, and Manuscript Sources

Ajzenstat, Janet. 'Comment: The Separation of Powers in 1867', *Canadian Journal of Political Science* 20, 1 (March 1987), 117–20.

Bibliography

Ajzenstat, Janet. *The Political Thought of Lord Durham.* Montreal and Kingston: McGill-Queen's University Press, 1988.

Ajzenstat, Janet, ed. *Canadian Constitutionalism 1791–1991.* Ottawa: Canadian Study of Parliament Group, 1992.

Ajzenstat, Janet. 'Constitution Making and the Myth of the People' in *Constitutional Predicament: Canada After the Referendum of 1992,* ed. Curtis Cook. Montreal: McGill-Queen's University Press, 1994.

Ajzenstat, Janet. 'Decline of Procedural Liberalism: The Slippery Slope to Secession'. Paper presented at the Annual Meeting of the Canadian Political Science Association (Calgary, 1994).

Ajzenstat, Janet. 'Reconciling Parliament and Rights: A.V. Dicey Reads the Canadian Charter of Rights and Freedoms'. Paper presented at the Annual Meeting of the Canadian Political Science Association (St Catherines, 1996).

Anderson, Benedict. *Imagined Communities: Reflections on the Spread of Nationalism,* 2nd edn. New York: Verso, 1991.

Arès, Richard S.J. *Dossier sur le Pacte Fédératif de 1867. La Confédération: pacte ou loi?* Montreal: Bellarmin, 1967.

Armstrong, Christopher. *The Politics of Federalism: Ontario's Relations With the Federal Government.* Toronto: University of Toronto Press, 1981.

Armstrong, Christopher. 'Ceremonial Politics: Federal Provincial Meetings Before the Second World War' in *National Politics and Community in Canada,* eds R. Kenneth Carty and W. Peter Ward. Vancouver: University of British Columbia Press, 1986.

Atkinson, Michael. 'What Kind of Democracy do Canadians Want?' *Canadian Journal of Political Science* 27, 4 (December 1994), 717–45.

Axworthy, Thomas and Pierre Elliott Trudeau, eds. *The Trudeau Years: Towards the Just Society.* Montreal: Le Jour, 1990.

Bakvis, Herman. *Federalism and the Organization of Political Life: Canada in Comparative Perspective.* Kingston: Institute of Intergovernmental Relations, 1981.

Bakvis, Herman and William M. Chandler, eds. *Federalism and the Role of the State.* Toronto: University of Toronto Press, 1987.

Bakvis, Herman, ed. *Representation, Integration and Political Parties in Canada.* Toronto: Dundurn Press, 1991.

Balthazar, Louis. *Bilan du nationalisme au Québec.* Montreal: L'Hexagone, 1990.

Balthazar, Louis. 'Conscience nationale et contexte international' in *Le Québec et la restructuration du Canada—1980–1992,* eds Louis Balthazar, Guy Laforest, and Vincent Lemieux. Sillery, Quebec: Septentrion, 1991.

Balthazar, Louis, Guy Laforest, and Vincent Lemieux, eds. *Le Québec et la restructuration du Canada—1980–1992.* Sillery, Québec: Septentrion, 1991.

Balthazar, Louis. 'Within the Black Box: Reflections from a French Quebec Vantage Point', *American Review of Canadian Studies* 25, 4 (1995), 519–41.

Banting, Keith G. and Richard Simeon, eds. *And No-One Cheered: Federalism, Democracy and the Constitution Act.* Toronto: Methuen, 1983.

Banting, Keith G. and Richard Simeon, eds. *Redesigning the State: The Politics of Constitutional Change in Industrial Nations.* Toronto: University of Toronto Press, 1985.

Banting, Keith G., ed. *State and Society: Canada in Comparative Perspective.* Research Studies of the Royal Commission on the Economic Union and Development Prospects for Canada. Toronto: University of Toronto Press, 1986, vol. 31.

Beaudoin, Gérald-A. 'Devolution, Delegation, Centralization and Decentralization of Powers as seen by the Pepin-Robarts Commission' in *The Cambridge Lectures, 1979*, ed. Derek Mendes da Costa. Toronto: Butterworths, 1981.

Beaudoin, Gérald-A. 'La philosophie "constitutionnelle" du Rapport Pepin-Robarts' in *Essais sur la constitution,* ed. Gérald-A. Beaudoin. Ottawa: l'Université d'Ottawa, 1979.

Bégin, Monique. 'Debates and Silences: Reflections of a Politician', *Daedalus* 117, 4 (Winter 1988), 335–62.

Behiels, Michael. *Prelude to Quebec's Quiet Revolution: Liberalism versus Nationalism, 1945–1960.* Montreal and Kingston: McGill-Queen's University Press, 1985.

Behiels, Michael, ed. *Quebec Since 1945: Selected Readings.* Toronto: Copp Clark Pitman, 1987.

Bell, David V.J. *The Roots of Disunity: A Study of Canadian Political Culture,* rev. edn. Toronto: Oxford University Press, 1992.

Bercuson, David J. and Barry Cooper. 'From Constitutional Monarchy to Quasi Republic: The Evolution of Liberal Democracy in Canada' in *Canadian Constitutionalism 1791–1991,* ed. Janet Ajzenstat. Ottawa: Canadian Study of Parliament Group, 1992.

Bergeron, Gérard. 'Le devenir de l'État du Québec', *Le Québec et la restructuration du Canada—1980–1992,* eds Louis Balthazar, Guy Laforest, and Vincent Lemieux. Sillery, Quebec: Septentrion, 1991.

Bernard, André. Introduction to René Lévesque, *Option Québec,* ed. André Bernard. Montreal: Les Éditions de l'Homme, 1988.

Bernard, André. *What Does Quebec Want?* Toronto: James Lorimer & Company, 1978.

Bernier, Ivan. 'Meech Lake and Constitutional Visions' in *Competing Constitutional Visions: The Meech Lake Accord,* eds K.E. Swinton and C.J. Rogerson. Toronto: Carswell, 1988.

Betz, Hans-George. 'The New Politics of Resentment'. *Comparative Politics* 25, 4 (July 1993), 413–27.

Birch, Anthony. 'Political Authority and Crisis in Comparative Perspective' in *State and Society: Canada in Comparative Perspective,* ed. Keith G. Banting, Research Studies of the Royal Commission on the Economic Union and Development Prospects for Canada. Toronto: University of Toronto Press, 1986, vol. 31.

Bishay, Susan. 'Conformist Federalism', *Telos* 95 (Spring 1993), 77–108.

Black, Edwin R. *Divided Loyalties: Canadian Concepts of Federalism.* Montreal and Kingston: McGill-Queen's University Press, 1975.

234 Bibliography

Black, Edwin R. 'Going Public: Mass Comunications and Executive Federalism' in *Federalism and Political Community*, eds David P. Shugarman and Reg Whitaker. Peterborough: Broadview Press, 1989.

Black, Eric. *Our Constitution: The Myth That Binds Us.* Boulder: Westview Press, 1988.

Blais, André and Richard Nadeau. 'To Be or Not To Be Sovereigntist? Quebeckers' Perennial Dilemma', *Canadian Public Policy* 18, 1 (1992), 89–103.

Boase, Joan. 'The Spirit of Meech Lake' in *Federalism and Political Community*, eds David P. Shugarman and Reg Whitaker. Peterborough: Broadview Press, 1989.

Bonenfant, J.C. 'Cartier, George-Étienne', *Dictionary of Canadian Biography*. Toronto: University of Toronto Press, 1988, vol. X.

Bonenfant, J.C. *The French Canadians and the Birth of Confederation*. Ottawa: Canadian Historical Association, 1966.

Bothwell, Robert. *Canada and Quebec: One Country, Two Histories*. Vancouver: University of British Columbia Press, 1995.

Boulton, James T. *The Language of Politics in the Age of Wilkes and Burke*. Toronto: Routledge and Kegan Paul, 1963.

Bourassa, Henri. 'The French-Canadian in the British Empire' in *Canadian Political Thought*, ed. H.D. Forbes. Toronto: Oxford University Press, 1984.

Bourassa, Henri. 'The Spectre of Annexation' in *Canadian Political Thought*, ed. H.D. Forbes. Toronto: Oxford University Press, 1984.

Braid, Don and Sydney Sharpe. *Breakup: Why the West Feels Left Out of Canada*. Toronto: Key Porter Books, 1990.

Breton, Eric D. 'The Preliminary Report of the Royal Commission on Bilingualism and Biculturalism as a Looking Glass to Canadian Political Culture'. Paper presented at the Annual Meeting of the Canadian Political Science Association (Charlottetown, 1991).

Breton, Gilles and Jane Jenson. 'La nouvelle dualité canadienne' in *Le Québec et la restructuration du Canada—1980–1992*, eds Louis Balthazar, Guy Laforest, and Vincent Lemieux. Sillery, Quebec: Septentrion, 1991.

Brooks, Stephen, ed. *Political Thought in Canada: Contemporary Perspectives*. Irwin Publishing: Toronto, 1984.

Brooks, Stephen and Alain-G. Gagnon. 'Politics and the Social Sciences in Canada' in *Canadian Politics: an introduction to the discipline*, eds Alain-G. Gagnon and James P. Bickerton. Peterborough: Broadview Press, 1990.

Brooks, Stephen and Alain-G. Gagnon. *Social Scientists and Politics in Canada: Between Clerisy and Vanguard*. Montreal and Kingston: McGill-Queen's University Press, 1988.

Brown, Douglas M., ed. *Canada: The State of the Federation 1991*. Kingston: Institute of Intergovernmental Relations, 1991.

Brown, Douglas M. and Jonathan W. Rose, eds. *Canada: The State of the Federation 1995*. Kingston: Institute of Intergovernmental Relations, 1995.

Brown-John, Lloyd. 'The Meech Lake Accord in historical perspective' in *Canadian Federalism: Past, Present and Future*, ed. Michael Burgess. Leicester: Leicester University Press, 1990.

Brun, Henri and Guy Tremblay. *Droit Constitutionnel.* Cowansville: Éditions Yvon Blais, 1982.

Bumsted, J.M. ed. *Interpreting Canada's Past, Volume Two, Post-Confederation*, 2nd edn. Toronto: Oxford University Press, 1993.

Burelle, André. *Le mal canadien. Essai de diagnostic et esquisse d'une thérapie.* Montreal: Éditions Fides, 1995.

Burgess, Michael, ed. *Canadian Federalism: Past, Present and Future.* Leicester: Leicester University Press, 1990.

Burgess, Michael. 'Canadian imperialism as nationalism: the legacy and significance of the imperial movement in Canada' in *Canadian Federalism: Past, Present and Future*, ed. Michael Burgess. Leicester: Leicester University Press, 1990.

Burgess, Michael and Alain-G. Gagnon, eds. *Comparative Federalism and Federation.* Toronto: University of Toronto Press, 1993.

Burgess, Michael. 'Federalism as Political Ideology: Interests, Benefits and Beneficiaries in Federalism and Federation' in *Comparative Federalism and Federation*, eds Michael Burgess and Alain-G. Gagnon. Toronto: University of Toronto Press, 1993.

Burgess, Michael. 'Is Quebec's Distinct Society Exportable?'. Paper presented at the Annual Meeting of the British Association for Canadian Studies (Cambridge, 1993).

Burgess, Michael. *The British Tradition of Federalism.* London: Leicester University Press, 1995.

Cable, Vincent. 'The Diminished Nation-State: A Study in the Loss of Economic Power', *Daedalus* 124, 2 (Spring 1995), 27–54.

Cairns, Alan C. 'The Politics of Constitutional Conservatism' in *And No-One Cheered: Federalism, Democracy and the Constitution Act*, eds Keith G. Banting and Richard Simeon. Toronto: Methuen, 1983.

Cairns, Alan C. 'The Politics of Constitutional Renewal in Canada' in *Redesigning the State: The Politics of Constitutional Change in Industrial Nations*, eds Keith G. Banting and Richard Simeon. Toronto: University of Toronto Press, 1985.

Cairns, Alan and Cynthia Williams. 'Constitutionalism, Citizenship and Society in Canada: An Overview' in *Constitutionalism, Citizenship and Society in Canada*, eds Alan Cairns and Cynthia Williams, Research Studies of the Royal Commission on the Economic Union and Development Prospects for Canada. Toronto: University of Toronto Press, 1985, vol. 33.

Cairns, Alan C. *Constitution, Government and Society in Canada*, ed. Douglas E. Williams. Toronto: McClelland and Stewart, 1988.

Cairns, Alan C. 'The Limited Constitutional Vision of Meech Lake' in *Competing Constitutional Visions: The Meech Lake Accord*, eds K.E. Swinton and C.J. Rogerson. Toronto: Carswell, 1988.

Cairns, Alan C. 'The Charter, Interest Groups, Executive Federalism, and Constitutional Reform' in *After Meech Lake: Lessons for the Future*, eds David E. Smith, Peter MacKinnon, and John C. Courtney. Saskatoon: Fifth House Publishers, 1991.

Cairns, Alan C. 'Constitutional change and the three equalities' in *Options for a New Canada*, eds Ronald L. Watts and Douglas M. Brown. Toronto: University of Toronto Press, 1991.

Cairns, Alan C. 'Ritual, Taboo, and Bias in Constitutional Controversies in Canada, or Constitutional Talk Canadian Style', in *Disruptions: Constitutional Struggles from the Charter to Meech Lake*, ed. Douglas E. Williams. Toronto: McClelland and Stewart, 1991.

Cairns, Alan C. *Charter Versus Federalism: The Dilemmas of Constitutional Reform*. Montreal and Kingston: McGill-Queen's University Press, 1992.

Cairns, Alan C. 'The Fragmentation of Canadian Citizenship' in *Belonging: The Meaning and Future of Canadian Citizenship*, ed. William Kaplan. Montreal and Kingston: McGill-Queen's University Press, 1994.

Cairns, Alan C. 'The Charlottetown Accord: Multinational Canada v. Federalism' in *Constitutional Predicament: Canada After the Referendum of 1992*, ed. Curtis Cook. Montreal and Kingston: McGill-Queen's University Press, 1994.

Cairns, Alan C. *Reconfigurations: Canadian Citizenship and Constitutional Change*, ed. Douglas E. Williams. Toronto: McClelland and Stewart, 1995.

Cairns, Alan C. 'The Constitutional World We Have Lost' in *Reconfigurations: Canadian Citizenship and Constitutional Change*, ed. Douglas E. Williams. Toronto: McClelland and Stewart, 1995.

Cameron, David R. *The Social Thought of Rousseau and Burke: A Comparative Study*. London: Weidenfeld and Nicholson, 1973.

Cameron, David R. *Nationalism, Self-Determination and the Quebec Question*. Toronto: Macmillan, 1974.

Cameron, David R. 'Lord Durham Then and Now', *Journal of Canadian Studies* 25, 1 (1990), 5–23.

Cameron, David R. 'Not Spicer and Not the B & B: Reflections of an Insider on the Workings of the Pepin-Roberts Task Force on Canadian Unity', *International Journal of Canadian Studies* 7–8 (Spring-Fall 1993), 333–46.

Camp, Dalton. *Whose Canada Is This Anyway?* Vancouver: Douglas and McIntyre, 1995.

Canada. *Final Report*, Special Joint Committee of the Senate and the House of Commons on the Constitution, ed. Molgat-MacGuigan. Ottawa: Queen's Printer, 1972.

Canada. *A Time For Action: Toward the Renewal of the Canadian Federation*. Ottawa: Ministry of Supply and Services, 1978.

Canada. *A Future Together: Observations and Recommendations*, Task Force on Canadian Unity. Ottawa: Queen's Printer, 1979.

Canada. *Coming to Terms: The Words of the Debate*, Task Force on Canadian Unity. Ottawa: Queen's Printer, 1979.

Canada. *A Time to Speak: The Views of the Public*, Task Force on Canadian Unity. Ottawa: Queen's Printer, 1979.

Canada. *Papers,* Task Force on Canadian Unity. Ottawa: Library of Canada, Archives, Record Group 33, Royal Commission Series 118, vols. 1–33.

Canada. *Report of the Royal Commission on the Economic Union and Development Prospects for Canada*. Ottawa: Supply and Services Canada, 1985.

Canada. *Constitution Amendment Act, 1987*. Ottawa: Queen's Printer, 1987.

Canada. *The Process for Amending the Constitution of Canada: the Report of the Special Joint Committee of the Senate and the House of Commons*. Ottawa: Queen's Printer, 1991.

Canada. *A Renewed Canada,* Special Joint Committee of the Senate and the House of Commons. Ottawa: Supply and Services, 1992.

Canadian Bar Association. *Towards a New Canada*. Ottawa, 1978.

Carty, R. Kenneth and W. Peter Ward. 'Canada as Political Community' in *National Politics and Political Community in Canada*, eds R. Kenneth Carty and W. Peter Ward. Vancouver: University of British Columbia Press, 1986.

Carty, R. Kenneth, ed. *Canadian Political Party Systems*. Peterborough: Broadview Press, 1992.

Carty, R. Kenneth and W. Peter Ward. 'The Making of a Canadian Political Citizenship' in *National Politics and Political Community in Canada*, eds R. Kenneth Carty and W. Peter Ward. Vancouver: University of Vancouver Press, 1986.

Chapman, Gerald B., ed. *Edmund Burke: The Practical Imagination*. London: Oxford University Press, 1967.

Cheffins, R.I. and P.A. Johnson, eds. *The Revised Canadian Constitution: Politics as Law*. Toronto: McGraw-Hill Ryerson, 1986.

Christie, Ian R. *Myth and Reality in Late-Eighteenth-Century British Politics*. Berkeley: University of California Press, 1970.

Clark, Joseph. *A Nation Too Good To Lose: Renewing the Purpose of Canada*. Toronto: Key Porter Books, 1994.

Clarkson, Stephen and Christina McCall. *Trudeau And Our Times, Volume 1: The Magnificent Obsession*. Toronto: McClelland and Stewart, 1991.

Clarkson, Stephen and Christina McCall. *Trudeau And Our Times, Volume 2: The Heroic Delusion*. Toronto: McClelland and Stewart, 1994.

Cohen, Andrew. *A Deal Undone: The Making and Breaking of the Meech Lake Accord*. Vancouver: Douglas and McIntyre, 1990.

Coleman, William D. *The Independence Movement in Quebec 1945–1980*. Toronto: University of Toronto Press, 1984.

Comeau, Robert, ed. *Jean Lesage et l'éveil d'une nation*. Sillery, Quebec: Les Presses de l'Université de Québec, 1989.

Conklin, William E. *Images of a Constitution*. Toronto: University of Toronto Press, 1989.

Conway, John F. *Debts to Pay: English Canada and Quebec from the Conquest to the Referendum*. Toronto: James Lorimer and Company, 1992.

Cook, Curtis, ed. *Constitutional Predicament: Canada After the Referendum of 1992*. Montreal and Kingston: McGill-Queen's University Press, 1994.

Cook, Ramsay. *Canada and the French Canadian Question*. Toronto: Macmillan, 1966.

Cook, Ramsay. *Provincial Autonomy, Minority Rights and the Compact Theory, 1867–1921*, Studies of the Royal Commission on Bilingualism and Biculturalism. Ottawa: Queen's Printer, 1969.

Cook, Ramsay. *The Maple Leaf Forever: Essays on Nationalism and Politics in Canada*. Toronto: Macmillan, 1971.

Cook, Ramsay. 'Alice in Meechland or the Concept of Quebec as a Distinct Society', *Queen's Quarterly* (Winter 1987).

Cook, Ramsay. *Canada, Quebec and the Uses of Nationalism*. Toronto: Macmillan, 1986.

Cook, Ramsay. 'The Evolution of Quebec Nationalism', *British Journal of Canadian Studies* 1 (1989), 306–17.

Cooper, Barry. 'Looking Eastward, Looking Backward: A Western Reading of the Never-Ending Story' in *Constitutional Predicament: Canada After the Referendum of 1992*, ed. Curtis Cook. Montreal and Kingston: McGill-Queen's University Press, 1994.

Cooper, Barry. 'Western Political Consciousness' in *Political Thought in Canada*, ed. Stephen Brooks. Irwin Publishing: Toronto, 1984.

Courchene, Thomas J. *Economic Management and the Division of Powers*, Research Studies of the Royal Commission on the Economic Union and Development Prospects for Canada. Toronto: University of Toronto Press, 1986, vol. 67.

Courchene, Thomas J. 'Meech Lake and Federalism: Accord or Discord?' in *Competing Constitutional Visions: The Meech Lake Accord*, eds K.E. Swinton and C.J. Rogerson. Toronto: Carswell, 1988.

Courchene, Thomas J. 'Mon pays, c'est l'hiver: reflections of a market populist', *Canadian Journal of Economics* 25, 4 (November 1992), 759–89.

Courchene, Thomas J. '*Staatsnation* vs *Kulturnation*: The Future of RoC' in *Beyond Quebec: Taking Stock of Canada*, ed. Kenneth McRoberts. Montreal and Kingston: McGill-Queen's University Press, 1995.

Creighton, Donald. 'Eugene Alfred Forsey: an introduction' in *Freedom and Order: Collected Essays*, ed. Eugene Forsey. Toronto: McClelland and Stewart, 1974.

Creighton, Donald. *John A. Macdonald*. 2 vols. Toronto: Macmillan, 1955.

Creighton, Donald. *The Road to Confederation*. Toronto: Macmillan, 1964.

Creighton, Donald. 'Sir John A. Macdonald and Canadian Historians' in *Approaches to Canadian History*, eds Ramsay Cook, Craig Brown, and Carl Berger. Toronto: University of Toronto Press, 1967.

Crepeau, P.A. and C.B. MacPherson, eds. *The Future of Canadian Federalism*. Toronto: University of Toronto Press, 1965.

Crête, Jean and Pierre Favre, eds. *Générations et politique*. Quebec: Les Presses de l'Université Laval, 1989.

Crick, Bernard. 'The English and the British' in *National Identities*, ed. Bernard Crick. Oxford: Basil Blackwell, 1991.

Crick, Bernard. *Essays on Politics and Literature.* Edinburgh: University of Edinburgh, 1989.

Crick, Bernard. *In Defence of Politics*, 4th edn. London: Weidenfeld and Nicholson, 1992.

Crick, Bernard, ed. *National Identities: The Constitution of the United Kingdom.* Oxford: Basil Blackwell, 1991.

Cuthbertson, Gilbert Morris. *Political Myth and Epic.* Ann Arbor: Michigan State University Press, 1975.

de Clercy, Cristine Andrea Beauvais. 'Holding Hands With The Public: Trudeau and the Task Force on Canadian Unity'. MA thesis, University of Saskatchewan, 1992.

Denis, Claude. 'Quebec-as-distinct-society and conventional wisdom: the constitutional silence of anglo-Canadian sociology', *Canadian Journal of Sociology* 18, 3 (1993), 252–69.

Denis, Roch, ed. *Québec: dix ans de crise constitutionnelle.* Montreal: VLB éditeur, 1990.

Denis, Serge. *Le Long Malentendu. Le Québec vu par les intellectuels progressistes au Canada anglais 1970–1991.* Montreal: Boréal, 1992.

Dewar, Kenneth. 'The Flight From Politics', *Chronicle-Herald*, 2 July 1991, A7.

Dickinson, John A. and Brian Young. *A Short History of Quebec*, 2nd edn. Toronto: Copp Clark Pitman, 1993.

Dion, Léon. *À la recherche du Québec.* Quebec: Les Presses l' Université Laval, 1987.

Dion, Léon. 'The Mystery of Quebec', *Daedalus* 117, 4 (1988), 283–318.

Dion, Léon. *Nationalismes et politiques au Québec.* Montreal: Hurtubise HMH, 1975.

Dion, Léon. 'Pepin-Roberts', *Le Devoir*, le 9 février 1978.

Dion, Stéphane. 'Explaining Quebec Nationalism' in *The Collapse of Canada*, ed. R. Kent Weaver. Washington: The Brookings Institution, 1992.

Dion, Stéphane. 'The Quebec Challenge to Canadian Unity', *Political Science and Politics* 26, 1 (March 1993), 38–43.

Djwa, Sandra. *The Politics of the Imagination: The Life of F.R. Scott.* Toronto: McClelland and Stewart, 1987.

Dobel, Patrick J. *Compromise and Political Action: Political Morality in Liberal and Democratic Life.* Savage, Md: Rowman and Littlefield, 1990.

Dodge, William. *Boundaries of Identity: A Quebec Reader.* Toronto: Lester Publishing, 1992.

Drache, Daniel and Roberto Perrin, eds. *Negotiating With A Sovereign Quebec.* Toronto: James Lorimer and Company, 1992.

Duchacek, Ivo D. 'National Constitutions: A Functional Approach', *Comparative Politics* 1 (October 1968), 91–102.

Dufour, Christian. *A Canadian Challenge/Le défi québécois.* Lantzville: Oolichan Books, 1990.

Dufour, Christian. 'Le mal canadien' in *Le Québec et la restructuration du Canada—1980–1992*, eds Louis Balthazar, Guy Laforest, and Vincent Lemieux. Sillery, Quebec: Septentrion, 1991.

Dufour, Christian. *La Rupture Tranquille*. Montreal: Boréal, 1992.

Dufresne, Jacques. *Le courage et le lucidité: essai sur la constitution d'un Québec souverain.* Sillery, Quebec: Septentrion, 1990.

Dumont, Fernand. *Genèse de la Société Québécoise*. Montreal: Boréal, 1993.

Dumont, Fernand. *The Vigil of Quebec*. Toronto: University of Toronto Press, 1974.

Dumont, Fernand. *Idéologies au Canada français, 1900–1929*. Quebec: Les Presses de l'Université Laval, 1974.

Dumont, Fernand, ed. *La société québécoise après 30 ans de changement.* Quebec: Institut québécois de recherches sur la culture, 1991.

Dumont, Fernand, Jean Hamelin, et Jean-Paul Montminy, eds. *Idéologies au Canada français, 1940–1976*. Quebec: Les Presses de l'Université Laval, 1981.

Dupré, J. Stefan and Paul C. Weiler. 'A Sense of Proportion and a Sense of Priorities: Reflections on the Report of the Task Force on Canadian Unity', *The Canadian Bar Review* 57 (1979), 450–71.

Dupré, J. Stefan. 'Reflections on the Workability of Executive Federalism' in *Intergovernmental Relations*, Research Studies of the Royal Commission on the Economic Union and Development Prospects for Canada, ed. Richard Simeon. Toronto: University of Toronto Press, 1985, vol. 63.

Edelman, Murray. *Constructing the Political Spectacle*. Chicago: University of Chicago Press, 1988.

Eden, L. and M. Molot. 'Canada's National Policies: Reflections on 125 Years', *Canadian Public Policy* 19, 3 (1993), 232–51.

Elazar, Daniel J. 'Constitution-making: The Pre-eminently Political Act' in *Redesigning the State: The Politics of Constitutional Change in Industrial Nations*, eds Keith G. Banting and Richard Simeon. Toronto: University of Toronto Press, 1985.

Elkins, David K. and Richard Simeon. 'A Cause in Search of Its Effect, or What Does Political Culture Explain?' *Comparative Politics* 11 (1979), 127–45.

Elkins, David K. 'Facing Our Destiny: Rights and Canadian Distinctiveness', *Canadian Journal of Political Science* 22, 4 (December 1989), 699–716.

Elkins, David K. 'Parties as National Institutions: A Comparative Study' in *Representation, Integration and Political Parties in Canada*, ed. Herman Bakvis, Royal Commission on Electoral Reform and Party Financing. Toronto: Dundurn Press, 1991, vol. 14.

Elkins, David K. *Beyond Sovereignty: Territory and Political Economy in the Twenty-First Century*. Toronto: University of Toronto Press, 1995.

Elshtain, Jean Bethke. *Democracy On Trial,* CBC Massey Lectures Series. Concord: Anansi Press Ltd., 1993.

English, John. 'The End of the Great Party Era' in *Canadian Political Party Systems*, ed. R.K. Carty. Peterborough: Broadview Press, 1992.

English, John. 'The "French Lieutenant" in Ottawa' in *National Politics and Community in Canada*, eds R. Kenneth Carty and W. Peter Ward. Vancouver: University of British Columbia Press, 1986.

Fidler, Richard. *Canada, Adieu? Quebec Debates its Future.* Lantzville, Ontario: Oolichan Books, 1991.

Fierlbeck, Katherine. 'The Ambivalent Potential of Cultural Identity', *Canadian Journal of Political Science* vol. 29, 1 (March 1996) 3–22.

Foley, Michael. *American Political Ideas: Traditions and Usages.* Manchester: Manchester University Press, 1991.

Foley, Michael. *Laws, Men and Machines: Modern American Government and the Appeal of Newtonian Mechanics.* New York: Routledge, 1990.

Foley, Michael. *The Silence of Constitutions: Gaps, 'abeyances' and political temperament in the maintenance of government.* New York: Routledge, 1989.

Forbes, H.D., ed. *Canadian Political Thought.* Toronto: Oxford University Press, 1984.

Forbes, H.D. 'Trudeau's Moral Vision: Reflections on His Memoirs'. Paper presented at the Annual Meeting of the Canadian Political Science Association (Calgary, 1994).

Forsey, Eugene. *Freedom and Order: Collected Essays.* Toronto: McClelland and Stewart, 1974.

Forsey, Eugene. 'The "Third Option"', *The Canadian Bar Review* 57 (1979), 472–91.

Forsey, Eugene. *A Life on the Fringe: The Memoirs of Eugene Forsey.* Toronto: Oxford University Press, 1990.

Fournier, Pierre. *A Meech Lake Post-Mortem: Is Quebec Sovereignty Inevitable?* Montreal and Kingston: McGill-Queen's University Press, 1991.

Franks, C.E.S. *The Myths and Symbols of the Constitutional Debate in Canada.* Kingston: Institute of Intergovernmental Relations, 1993.

Fraser, Graham. *P.Q.: René Lévesque and the Parti Québécois in Power.* Toronto: Macmillan, 1984.

French, Stanley G., ed. *Philosophers Look at Canadian Confederation.* Montreal: The Canadian Philosophical Association, 1979.

Friedrich, Carl J. *Trends of Federalism in Theory and Practice.* New York: Praeger, 1968.

Fulford, Robert. 'A Post-Modern Dominion: The Changing Nature of Canadian Citizenship' in *Belonging: The Meaning and the Future of Canadian Citizenship*, ed. William Kaplan. Montreal and Kingston: McGill-Queen's University Press, 1994.

Gagnon, Alain-G. and Joseph Garcea. 'Quebec and the Pursuit of Special Status' in *Perspectives on Canadian Federalism*, eds R.D. Olling and M.W. Westmacott. Scarborough: Prentice Hall Inc., 1988.

Gagnon, Alain-G. and Mary Beth Montcalm. *Quebec: Beyond the Quiet Revolution.* Scarborough: Nelson, 1990.

Gagnon, Alain-G. 'Quebec-Canada relations: the engineering of constitutional arrangements' in *Canadian Federalism: Past, Present and Future*, ed. Michael Burgess. Leicester: Leicester University Press, 1990.

Gagnon, Alain-G. and Daniel Latouche. *Allaire, Bélanger, Campeau et les autres: Les Québécois s'interrogent sur leur avenir*. Montreal: Éditions Québec, 1991.

Gagnon, Alain-G. 'Everything old is new again: Canada, Quebec, and constitutional impasse' in *How Ottawa Spends 1991: The politics of fragmentation*, ed. Frances Abele. Ottawa: Carleton University Press, 1991.

Gagnon, Alain-G. 'The Political Uses of Federalism' in *Comparative Federalism and Federation*, eds Michael Burgess and Alain-G. Gagnon. Toronto: University of Toronto Press, 1993.

Gagnon, Alain-G., ed. *Quebec: State and Society*. Toronto: Methuen, 1984.

Gagnon, Alain-G., ed. *Quebec: State and Society*, 2nd edn. Scarborough: Nelson, 1993.

Gagnon, Alain-G. 'Quebec: Variations on a Theme' in *Canadian Politics: an introduction to the discipline*, eds James P. Bickerton and Alain-G. Gagnon, 2nd edn. Peterborough: Broadview Press, 1994.

Gagnon, Alain-G. 'The Role of the Intellectual in Modern Quebec: The Drive for Social Hegemony' in *Political Thought in Canada*, ed. Stephen Brooks. Toronto: Irwin Publishing, 1984.

Gagnon Alain-G. 'From Nation–State to Multinational State: Quebec and Canada facing the challenge of modernity', paper presented at the Annual Meeting of the British Association for Canadian Studies, Exeter, 1996.

Gagnon, Lysiane. 'Canada, where compromise is the stuff of daily life', *The Globe and Mail*, 21 November 1992.

Gérin-Lajoie, Paul. *Constitutional Amendment in Canada*. Toronto: University of Toronto Press, 1950.

Gibbins, Roger. 'Federal Societies, Institutions, and Politics' in *Federalism and the Role of the State*, eds Herman Bakvis and William M. Chandler. Toronto: University of Toronto Press, 1987.

Gibbins, Roger. 'The Impact of the American Constitution on Contemporary Canadian Politics' in *The Canadian and American Constitutions in Comparative Perspective*, ed. Marian C. McKenna. Calgary: University of Calgary Press, 1993.

Gibbins, Roger. 'The Interplay of Political Institutions and Political Communities' in *Federalism and Political Community*, eds David P. Shugarman and Reg Whitaker. Peterborough: Broadview Press, 1989.

Gibbins, Roger, ed. *Meech Lake and Canada: Perspectives from the West*. Edmonton: Academic Printing and Publishing, 1988.

Gibbins, Roger and David Thomas. 'Ten Lessons From the Referendum', *Canadian Parliamentary Review* 15, 4 (Winter 1992–3), 3–6.

Gibbins, Roger and Sonia Arrison. *Western Visions: Perspectives on the West in Canada*. Peterborough: Broadview Press, 1995.

Gingras, François-Pierre and Neil Nevitte. 'The Evolution of Quebec Nationalism' in *Quebec: State and Society*, ed. Alain-G. Gagnon. Toronto: Methuen, 1984.

Gold, Marc. 'The Rhetoric of Rights: The Supreme Court and the Charter' in *Making the Laws: The Courts and the Constitution*, eds John Saywell and G. Vegh. Toronto: Copp Clark Pitman, 1991.

Granatstein, J. L. 'The "Hard" Obligations of Citizenship: The Second World War in Canada' in *Belonging: The Meaning and the Future of Canadian Citizenship*, ed. William Kaplan. Montreal and Kingston: McGill-Queen's University Press, 1994.

Green, Ian. 'The Myths of Legislative and Constitutional Supremacy' in *Federalism and Political Community*, eds David P. Shugarman and Reg Whitaker. Peterborough: Broadview Press, 1989.

Guindon, Herbert. *Traditions, modernité et aspiration nationale de la société québécoise*. Montreal: Éditions Saint-Martin, 1990.

Gutmann, Amy, ed. *Multiculturalism and the Politics of Recognition*. Princeton: Princeton University Press, 1992.

Gwyn, Sandra. *Tapestry of War: A Private View of Canadians in the Great War*. Toronto: HarperCollins, 1992.

Gwyn, Richard. *Nationalism Without Walls: The Unbearable Lightness of Being Canadian*. Toronto: McClelland and Stewart, 1996.

Hall, D.J. 'The Spirit of Confederation: Ralph Heintzman, Professor Creighton, and the bicultural compact theory', *Journal of Canadian Studies* 9, 4 (1974), 24–43.

Harney, J.P. 'A Matter Of Respect' in *Debating Canada's Future: Views From The Left*, eds Simon Rosenblum and Peter Findlay. Toronto: James Lorimer and Company, 1991.

Harvey, Louis-Georges. 'The First Distinct Society: French Canada, America and the Constitution of 1791' in *Canadian Constitutionalism 1791–1991*, ed. Janet Ajzenstat. Ottawa: Canadian Study of Parliament Group, 1992.

Hawthorn, Geoffrey. *Plausible Worlds*. Cambridge: Cambridge University Press, 1991.

Heard, Andrew. *Canadian Constitutional Conventions: The Marriage of Law and Politics*. Toronto: University of Toronto Press, 1991.

Heard, Andrew. 'When Must Constitutional Change Be Achieved By Amendment?' Paper presented at the Annual Meeting of the Canadian Political Science Association (Calgary, 1994).

Heintzman, Ralph. 'The Political Culture of Quebec, 1840–1960', *Canadian Journal of Political Science* 16, 1 (March 1983), 3–60.

Heintzman, Ralph. 'Political Space and Economic Space: Quebec and the Empire of the St Lawrence'. *Journal of Canadian Studies* 29, 2 (Summer 1994) 19–64.

Heyman, Richard. 'A Political Economy of Minority Group Knowledge Demands.' *Compare* 8, 1 (1978), 3–13.

Hiemstra, John L. 'Trudeau's Political Philosophy: The Role of Federalism in Assimilating the "French Canadians"'. Paper presented at the Annual Meeting of the Canadian Political Science Association (Victoria, 1990).

Hill, B.W., ed. *Edmund Burke on Government, Politics and Society*. New York: International Publications Service, 1976.

Hobsbawm, E.J. *Nations and Nationalism Since 1780: Programme, Myth, Reality*. Cambridge: Cambridge University Press, 1990.

Hobsbawm, Eric. 'The New Threat to History', *The New York Review of Books*, 16 December 1993, 62–4.

Bibliography

Hockin, Thomas. 'Federalist Style in International Politics' in *An Independent Foreign Policy for Canada*, ed. Stephen Clarkson. Toronto: McClelland and Stewart, 1968.

Hogg, Peter. *Constitutional Law of Canada*, 2nd edn. Toronto: Carswell, 1985.

Hogg, Peter. 'Federalism Fights the Charter of Rights' in *Federalism and Political Community*, eds David P. Shugarman and Reg Whitaker. Peterborough: Broadview Press, 1989.

Hogg, Peter. 'Formal Amendment of the Constitution of Canada', *Law and Contemporary Problems* 55, 1 (1992).

Hogg, Peter. *Meech Lake Constitutional Accord Annotated*. Toronto: Carswell, 1988.

Horton, Donald. *André Laurendeau: French Canadian Nationalist*. Toronto: Oxford University Press, 1992.

Howes, David. 'In the Balance: The Art of Norman Rockwell and Alex Colville as Discourses on the Constitutions of the United States and Canada', *Alberta Law Review* 29, 2 (1991), 475–97.

Hueglin, Thomas O. 'Legitimacy, Democracy, and Federalism' in *Federalism and the Role of the State*, eds Herman Bakvis and William M. Chandler. Toronto: University of Toronto Press, 1987.

Hurley, James Ross. *Amending Canada's Constitution. History, Processes, Problems and Prospects*. Ottawa: Canada Communication Group, 1996.

Ignatieff, Michael. *Blood and Belonging: Journeys Into The New Nationalism*. Toronto: Viking, 1993.

Johnson, Daniel. *Égalité ou Indépendance, 25 ans plus tard*. Montreal: VLB éditeur, 1990.

Johnson, J.K. and P.B. Waite. 'Macdonald, John Alexander' in *Dictionary of Canadian Biography*. Toronto: University of Toronto Press, 1990, vol. 12.

Johnson, William. *A Canadian Myth: Quebec, Between Canada and the Illusion of Utopia*. Montreal: Robert Davies Publishing, 1994.

Johnston, Donald, ed. *Pierre Trudeau Speaks Out on Meech Lake*. Toronto: General Paperbacks, 1990.

Johnston, Richard and André Blais. 'Meech Lake and Mass Politics: The "Distinct Society" Clause' *Canadian Public Policy* 14, 3 (1988), 25–42.

Johnston, Richard et al. 'The People and the Charlottetown Accord' in *Canada: The State of the Federation 1993*, eds Ronald L. Watts and Douglas O. Brown. Kingston: Institute of Intergovernmental Relations, 1993.

Johnstone, Frederick. 'Quebec, Apartheid, Lithuania and Tibet: The Politics of Group Rights', *Telos* 95 (Fall 1993), 56–62.

Johnstone, Frederick. 'Quebeckers, Mohawks and Zulus: Liberal Federalism and Fair Trade', *Telos* 93 (Fall 1992), 2–20.

Jones, Richard. *Community in Crisis: French-Canadian Nationalism in Perspective*. Toronto: McClelland and Stewart, 1972.

Kaplan, William, ed. *Belonging: The Meaning and the Future of Canadian Citizenship*. Montreal and Kingston: McGill-Queen's University Press, 1994.

Keating, Michael. *Nations Against the State: The New Politics of Nationalism in Quebec, Catalonia and Scotland.* New York: St Martin's Press, 1996.

Karmis, Dimitrios and Alain-G. Gagnon. 'Fédéralisme et identités collectives au Canada et en Belgique: des itinéraires différentes, une fragmentation similaire', *Canadian Journal of Political Science* 29, 3 (Sept. 1996), 435–68.

Kemp, Arnold. *The Hollow Drum: Scotland Since the War.* Edinburgh: Mainstream Publishing, 1993.

Knop, Karen, Sylvia Ostry, Richard Simeon, and Katherine Swinton, eds. *Rethinking Federalism: Citizens, Markets and Government in a Changing World.* Vancouver: UBC Press, 1995.

Kwavnick, David. 'Quebec and the Two Nations Theory: a Re-examination', *Queen's Quarterly* (Fall 1974), 357–76.

Kwavnick, David, ed. *The Tremblay Report: Report of the Royal Commission of Inquiry on Constitutional Problems.* Toronto: McClelland and Stewart, 1973.

La Forest, Gerard V. 'Towards A New Canada: The Canadian Bar Association's Report on the Constitution', *The Canadian Bar Review* 57 (1979), 492–512.

Laforest, Guy. 'L'Esprit de 1982' in *Le Québec et la restructuration du Canada—1980–1992*, eds Louis Balthazar, Guy Laforest, and Vincent Lemieux. Sillery, Quebec: Septentrion, 1991.

Laforest, Guy. 'Interpreting the Political Heritage of André Laurendeau' in *After Meech Lake: Lessons for the Future*, eds David E. Smith, Peter Mackinnon, and John C. Courtney. Saskatoon: Fifth House Publishers, 1991.

Laforest, Guy. 'Protéger et promouvoir une société distincte au Québec'. Submission to the Commission on the Political and Constitutional Future of Québec (the Bélanger-Campeau Commission), 1990.

Laforest, Guy. *Trudeau et la fin d'un rêve canadien.* Sillery, Quebec: Septentrion, 1992.

Laing, R.D. *The Politics of the Family and Other Essays.* New York: Pantheon Books., 1971.

Langford, Paul, ed. *The Writings and Speeches of Edmund Burke, vol. II: Party, Parliament and the American Crisis 1766–1774.* Oxford: Oxford University Press, 1981.

LaRue, Richard and Jocelyn Létourneau. 'De l'unité et de l'identité au Canada. Essai sur l'éclatement d'un État', *International Journal of Canadian Studies* 7–8 (Spring-Fall 1993), 81–94.

LaSelva, Samuel V. 'Re-imagining Confederation: Moving Beyond the Trudeau–Lévesque Debate', *Canadian Journal of Political Science* 26, 4 (December 1993), 699–720.

Latouche, Daniel. *Canada and Quebec, Past and Future: An Essay*, Research Studies of the Royal Commission on the Economic Union and Development Prospects for Canada, vol. 70. Toronto: University of Toronto Press, 1986.

Latouche, Daniel, Guy Falardeau, and Michel Lévesque, eds, *Politique et Société au Québec: guide bibliographique.* Montreal: Boréal, 1993.

Laurendeau, André. *The Diary of André Laurendeau 1964–1967.* Toronto: James Lorimer and Company, 1991.

Laurier, Wilfrid. 'Political Liberalism' in *Canadian Political Thought*, ed. H.D. Forbes. Toronto: Oxford University Press, 1984.

Laxer, Gordon. 'Constitutional crises and continentalism: Twin threats to Canada's continued existence', *Canadian Journal of Sociology* 17, 2 (1992), 199–222.

Lederman, W.R. 'Canadian Constitutional Amending Procedures: 1867–1982', *American Journal of Comparative Law* 32 (1984), 339–59.

Lederman, W.R. *Continuing Canadian Constitutional Dilemmas.* Toronto: Butterworths, 1982.

Leduc, Lawrence. 'Framing the Question: The Politics of Question Wording in the 1980 and 1995 Quebec Referendums', paper presented at the Annual Meeting of the British Association for Canadian Studies, Exeter, 1996.

Legare, Anne and Nicole Morf. *La société distincte de l'État, Québec-Canada 1930–1980.* Montreal: Hurtubise HMH, 1989.

Legault, Josée. *Les nouveaux démons.* Montreal: VLB éditeur, 1996.

Lenihan, Donald G. 'Squaring Politics and Principles: Institutional Reform in Canada', *Network Analyses* 3 (January 1992).

Lenihan, Donald G., Gordon Robertson, and Roger Tassé. *Canada: Reclaiming the Middle Ground.* Montreal: Institute for Research on Public Policy, 1994.

Leslie, Peter M., ed. *Canada: The State of the Federation 1985.* Kingston: Queen's University Press, 1986.

Leslie, Peter M. and Ronald L. Watts, eds. *Canada: The State of the Federation 1987–88.* Kingston: Institute of Intergovernmental Relations, 1988.

Létourneau, Jocelyn. *Les Années sans guide. Le Canada à l'ère de l'Économie migrante.* Montreal: Boréal, 1996.

Levitt, Joseph. *A Vision Beyond Reach: A Century of Images of Canadian Destiny.* Ottawa: Deneau, 1982.

Lewontin, R.C. 'Women Versus the Biologists', *The New York Review of Books*, 41 (7 April 1994), 31–5.

Lijphart, Arend. 'Consociation and federation: conceptual and empirical links', *Canadian Journal of Political Science* 12, 3 (September 1979), 499–515.

Lijphart, Arend. 'Cultural Diversity and Theories of Political Integration', *Canadian Journal of Political Science* 4, 1 (March 1971), 1–14.

Lijphart, Arend. *Democracies: Patterns and Consensus Government in Twenty-One Countries.* New Haven: Yale University Press, 1984.

Lijphart, Arend. *Democracy in Plural Societies: A Comparative Explanation.* New Haven: Yale University Press, 1977.

Linteau, P.A. et al. *Histoire du Québec contemporain: De la Confédération à la crise (1867–1929).* Montreal: Boréal Express, 1979.

Linteau, P.A. et al. *Histoire du Québec contemporain: Le Québec depuis 1930.* Montreal: Boréal Express, 1986.

Livingston, William S. *Federalism and Constitutional Change.* Oxford: Clarendon Press, 1956.

Lusztig, Michael. 'Constitutional Paralysis: Why Canadian Constitutional Initiatives Are Doomed to Fail', *Canadian Journal of Political Science* 27, 4 (December 1994), 747–71.

McConkey, Mike. 'Individuals, Communities and Federalism—Reply to Johnstone', *Telos* 93 (Fall 1993), 21–6.

McCrone, David. *Understanding Scotland: The Sociology of a Stateless Nation.* London: Routledge, 1992.

Macdonald, Roderick A. 'Meech Lake to the Contrary Notwithstanding', *Osgoode Hall Law Journal* 29, 2 (1991), 253–328 and 29, 3 (1991), 483–572.

McDougall, A.K. *Robarts.* Toronto: University of Toronto Press, 1986.

MacKay, A. Wayne. 'Linguistic Duality and the Distinct Society in Quebec: Declarations of Sociological Fact or Legal Limits on Constitutional Interpretation' in *Competing Constitutional Visions: The Meech Lake Accord,* eds K.E. Swinton and C.J. Rogerson. Toronto: Carswell, 1988.

McKenna, Marian C., ed. *The Canadian and American Constitutions in Comparative Perspective.* Calgary: University of Calgary, 1993.

McNaught, Kenneth. 'The National Outlook of English-Speaking Canadians' in *Nationalism in Canada,* ed. Peter Russell. Toronto: McGraw-Hill, 1966.

McNaught, Kenneth. 'Three Myths and the Canadian Continuum', *The Round Table* 327 (1993), 315–22.

McRae, Kenneth D., ed. *Consociational Democracy: Political Accommodation in Segmented Societies.* Toronto: McClelland and Stewart, 1974.

MacRae-Buchanan, Constance. 'American Influence on Canadian Constitutionalism' in *Canadian Constitutionalism 1791–1991,* ed. Janet Ajzenstat. Ottawa: Canadian Study of Parliament Group, 1992.

McRoberts, Kenneth. 'Making Canada Bilingual: Illusions and Delusions of Federal Language Policy' in *Federalism and Political Community,* eds David P. Shugarman and Reg Whitaker. Peterborough: Broadview Press, 1989.

McRoberts, Kenneth. *Quebec: Social Change and Political Crisis,* 3rd edn. Toronto: McClelland and Stewart, 1993.

McRoberts, Kenneth. *English Canada and Quebec: Avoiding the Issue.* York University: Robarts Centre for Constitutional Studies, 1991.

McRoberts Kenneth, ed. *Beyond Quebec: Taking Stock of Canada.* Montreal and Kingston: McGill-Queen's University Press, 1995.

McRoberts, Kenneth and Patrick J. Monahan, eds. *The Charlottetown Accord, the Referendum, and the Future of Canada.* Toronto: University of Toronto Press, 1993.

McWhinney, Edward. *Constitution Making: Principles, Processes, Practice.* Toronto: University of Toronto Press, 1981.

McWhinney, Edward. *Quebec and the Constitution 1960–1978.* Toronto: University of Toronto Press, 1979.

Mallory, J.R. 'The Continuing Evolution of Canadian Constitutionalism' in *Constitutionalism, Citizenship and Society in Canada*, eds Alan Cairns and Cynthia Williams, Studies of the Royal Commission on the Economic Union and Development Prospects for Canada. Toronto: University of Toronto Press, 1985, vol. 33.

Mallory, J.R. 'The Macdonald Commission', *Canadian Journal of Political Science* 19, 3 (September 1986), 597–613.

Marquand, David. 'Nations, Regions and Europe' in *National Identities*, ed. Bernard Crick. Oxford: Basil Blackwell, 1991.

Marr, Andrew. *The Battle for Scotland.* Harmondsworth: Penguin, 1992.

Martin, Ged, ed. *The Causes of Canadian Confederation.* Fredericton: Acadiensis Press, 1990.

Martin, Ged. 'The Canadian Question and the Late Modern Century', *British Journal of Canadian Studies* 7, 2 (1992), 215–47.

Martin, Ged. 'What We Know and What We Think We Know: The Great Coalition of 1864 in The Province Of Canada'. Paper presented at the Annual Meeting of the British Association for Canadian Studies (Nottingham, 1991).

Martin, Ged. *Britain and the Origins of Canadian Confederation, 1837–67.* Vancouver: University of British Columbia Press, 1995.

Martin, Pierre. 'Générations politiques, rationalité économique et appui à la souveraineté au Québec', *Canadian Journal of Political Science* 27, 2 (June 1994), 345–59.

Milne, David. 'Equality or asymmetry: why choose?' in *Options for a New Canada*, eds Ronald L. Watts and Douglas M. Brown. Toronto: University of Toronto Press, 1991.

Milne, David. 'Politics and the Constitution' in *Canadian Politics: an introduction to the discipline*, eds Alain-G. Gagnon and James P. Bickerton. Peterborough: Broadview Press, 1990.

Milne, David. *Tug of War: Ottawa and the Provinces Under Trudeau and Mulroney.* Toronto: James Lorimer, 1986.

Milne, David. 'Whither Canadian Federalism? Alternative Constitutional Futures' in *Comparative Federalism and Federation*, eds Michael Burgess and Alain-G. Gagnon. Toronto: University of Toronto Press, 1993.

Milne, David. 'Exposed to the Glare: Constitutional Camouflage and the Fate of Canada's Federation' in *Seeking a New Canadian Partnership: Asymmetrical and Confederal Options*, ed. F. Leslie Seidle. Ottawa: Renouf Publishing Company, 1994.

Mitchell, James. *Strategies for Self-Government. The Campaigns for a Scottish Parliament.* Edinburgh: Polygon, 1996.

Monahan, Patrick J. *Meech Lake: The Inside Story.* Toronto: University of Toronto Press, 1991.

Monahan, Patrick J. 'The Sounds of Silence' in *The Charlottetown Accord, the Referendum, and the Future of Canada*, eds Kenneth McRoberts and Patrick J. Monahan. Toronto: University of Toronto Press, 1993.

Monet, Jacques. *The Last Cannon Shot: A Study of French-Canadian Nationalism 1837–1850.* Toronto: University of Toronto Press, 1969.

Monière, Denis. 'Currents of Nationalism in Quebec' in *Political Thought in Canada*, ed. Stephen Brooks. Toronto: Irwin Publishing, 1984.

Monière, Denis. *Ideologies in Quebec: The Historical Development.* Toronto: University of Toronto Press, 1981.

Montcalm, Mary Beth. 'Quebec Separatism in Comparative Perspective' in *Quebec: State and Society*, ed. Alain-G. Gagnon. Toronto: Methuen, 1984.

Morgan, Edmund S. *Inventing the People: The Rise of Popular Sovereignty in England and America.* New York: W.W. Norton, 1988.

Morton, F.L. 'Judicial Politics Canadian-Style: The Supreme Court's Contribution to the Constitutional Crisis of 1992' in *Constitutional Predicament: Canada After the Referendum of 1992*, ed. Curtis Cook. Montreal and Kingston: McGill-Queen's University Press, 1994.

Nairn, Tom. 'Upper and Lower Cases', *London Review of Books*, 24 Aug. 1995.

Neatby, Blair. *Laurier and a Liberal Quebec.* Toronto: McClelland and Stewart, 1973.

Nemni, Max. 'Canada in Crisis and the Destructive Power of Myth', *Queen's Quarterly* (Spring 1992), 222–39.

Nemni, Max. 'La Commission Bélanger-Campeau et la construction de l'idée de sécession au Québec', *International Journal of Canadian Studies* 7–8 (Spring-Fall 1993), 285–314.

Nemni, Max. 'Le "des"accord du Lac Meech et la construction de l'imaginaire symbolique des Québécois' in *Le Québec et la restructuration du Canada—1980–1992*, eds Louis Balthazar, Guy Laforest, and Vincent Lemieux. Sillery, Quebec: Septentrion, 1991.

Noël, Alain. 'Deliberating a Constitution: The Meaning of the Canadian Referendum of 1992' in *Constitutional Predicament: Canada After the Referendum of 1992*, ed. Curtis Cook. Montreal and Kingston: McGill-Queen's University Press, 1994.

Noel, S.J.R. 'Canadian responses to ethnic conflict: Consociationalism, federalism and control' in *The Politics of Ethnic Conflict Regulation*, eds John McGarry and Brendan O'Leary. New York: Routledge, 1993.

Nutbrown, Richard. 'State Images and the Writing of English Canadian Political Science' in *Canadian Politics: an introduction to the discipline*, eds Alain-G. Gagnon and James P. Bickerton. Peterborough: Broadview Press, 1990.

O'Brien, Conor Cruise. *The Great Melody: A Thematic Biography of Edmund Burke.* Chicago: University of Chicago Press, 1992.

Oakeshott, Michael. *Rationalism in Politics and Other Essays.* New York: Barnes and Noble, 1974.

Oliver, Michael. 'The Impact of the Royal Commission on Bilingualism and Biculturalism on Constitutional Thought and Practice in Canada', *International Journal of Canadian Studies* 7–8 (Spring-Fall 1993), 315–32.

Oliver, Michael. 'Laurendeau et Trudeau: leurs opinions sur le Canada' in *L'engagement intellectuel*. Sainte-Foy: Les Presses de l'Université Laval, 1991.

Oliver, Michael. *The Passionate Debate: The Social and Political Ideas of Quebec Nationalism 1920–1945*. Montreal: Véhicule Press, 1991.

Ouellet, Fernand. 'The Socialization of Quebec Historiography Since 1960', *Robarts Centre Occasional Papers*, 1988.

Owram, Doug. *The Government Generation: Canadian Intellectuals and the State 1900–1945*. Toronto: University of Toronto Press, 1986.

Pal, Leslie A. and F. Leslie Seidle. 'Constitutional Politics 1990–92: The Paradox of Participation' in *How Ottawa Spends: A More Democratic Canada? 1993–1994*, ed. Susan D. Phillips. Ottawa: Carleton University Press, 1993.

Palti, Elias José. 'Liberalism vs. Nationalism: Hobsbawm's Dilemma', *Telos* 95 (Spring 1993), 109–26.

Paterson, Lindsay. *The Autonomy of Modern Scotland*. Edinburgh: 1994.

Pelletier, Réjean. 'L'État du Québec, dix ans plus tard (1980–1990)' in *Le Québec et la restructuration du Canada—1980–1992*, eds Louis Balthazar, Guy Laforest, and Vincent Lemieux. Sillery, Quebec: Septentrion, 1991.

Pepin, Jean-Luc. 'Closing Address'. York University: Inaugural Ceremonies for the Robarts Centre for Canadian Studies, 1984.

Phillips, Susan D., ed. *How Ottawa Spends: A More Democratic Canada?* Ottawa: Carleton University Press, 1993.

Piccone, Paul. 'The Case Against Liberal Federalism and Protectionism–Reply to Johnstone', *Telos* 93 (Fall 1993), 27–41.

Pocock, J.G.A. 'The devil has two horns', *London Review of Books*, 24 February 1994, 9–11.

Preece, Rod. 'The Political Wisdom of Sir John A. Macdonald', *Canadian Journal of Political Science* 17, 3 (September 1984), 459–86.

Québec. *Les positions traditionnelles du Québec en matière constitutionnelle 1936–1990*. Québec: Secrétariat aux affaires intergouvernementales canadiennes, document de travail, 1991.

Québec. *Les positions traditionnelles du Québec sur le partage des pouvoirs 1900–1976*. Québec: Ministère des Affaires intergouvernementales, 1978.

Québec. *Quebec-Canada: A New Deal: The Quebec Government Proposal for a New Partnership Between Quebec and Canada*. Québec: Conseil Exécutif, 1979.

Québec: *A New Canadian Federation*. Report of the Constitutional Committee of the Québec Liberal Party, 9 Jan. 1980.

Québec. *A Québec Free to Choose*. Report of the Constitutional Committee of the Québec Liberal Party, 28 Jan. 1991.

Québec. *L'avenir politique et constitutionnel du Québec*. Québec: Éditeur Officiel du Québec, 1991.

Rayner, Jeremy. 'The Legend of Oakeshott's Sceptical Philosophy and Limited Politics', *Canadian Journal of Political Science* 18, 2 (June 1985), 313–52.

Rayner, Jeremy. 'The Very Idea of Canadian Political Thought', *Journal of Canadian Studies* 26, 2 (1991), 7–23.

Bibliography

Reesor, Bayard. *The Canadian Constitution in Historical Perspective.* New Jersey: Prentice Hall, 1992.

Reid, Darrell R. *Bibliography of Canadian and Comparative Federalism.* Kingston: Institute of Intergovernmental Relations, 1988.

Remillard, Gil. 'Legality, Legitimacy, and the Supreme Court' in *And No-One Cheered: Federalism, Democracy and the Constitution Act*, eds Keith Banting and Richard Simeon. Toronto: Methuen, 1983.

Resnick, Philip. *Towards a Canada-Quebec Union.* Montreal and Kingston: McGill-Queen's University Press, 1991.

Resnick, Philip. *Thinking English Canada.* Toronto: Stoddart Publishing, 1994.

Riker, William H. *Liberalism Against Populism.* Prospect Heights: Waveland Press, 1982.

Riker, William H. 'Six books in search of a subject or does federalism exist and does it matter?' *Comparative Politics* 2 (October 1969), 135–46.

Robarts, John P. 'Address to the Montmorency Conference', *Journal of Canadian Studies* 2, 3 (August 1967), 52–8.

Robarts, John P. *Papers.* The Archives of Ontario, F15, Series 5, MU8050.

Rocher, François, ed. *Bilan québécois du fédéralisme canadien.* Montreal: VLB éditeur, 1992.

Rocher, François and Miriam Smith, eds. *New Trends in Canadian Federalism.* Peterborough: Broadview Press, 1995.

Rodal, Berel. 'State and Nation in Conflict' in *Boundaries of Identity: A Quebec Reader*, ed. William Dodge. Toronto: Lester Publishing Ltd, 1992.

Rodgers, Daniel T. *Contested Truths: Keywords in American Politics.* New York: Basic Books, 1987.

Rogers, Norman McLeod. 'The Compact Theory of Confederation' in *Proceedings of the Canadian Political Science Association*, 1931, 205–30.

Romney, Paul. 'Why Lord Watson Was Right' in *Canadian Constitutionalism 1791–1991*, ed. Janet Ajzenstat. Ottawa: Canadian Study of Parliament Group, 1992.

Romney, Paul. 'Confederation: The True Story', paper presented at the biennial meeting of the Association for Canadian Studies in the United States, Seattle, 1995.

Rudin, Ronald. 'Revisionism and the Search for a Normal Society: A Critique of Recent Quebec Historical Writing', *Canadian Historical Review* 73, 1 (1992), 30–61.

Ruel, Jacinthe. 'Le passé au service du présent. Les mémoires de la Commission Bélanger-Campeau, entre la mémoire et la rhetorique'. Paper presented at the Annual Meeting of the British Association for Canadian Studies (Cambridge, 1993).

Russell, Peter H. 'Attempting Macro Constitutional Change in Australia and Canada: The Politics of Frustration', *International Journal of Canadian Studies* 7–8 (Spring-Fall 1993), 41–62.

Russell, Peter H. 'Can Canadians Be a Sovereign People?' *Canadian Journal of Political Science* 24, 4 (December 1991), 691–711.

Russell, Peter H. *Constitutional Odyssey: Can Canadians Become a Sovereign People?* Toronto: University of Toronto Press, 1992 (2nd edn 1993).

Russell, Peter H. et al. *The Court and the Constitution: Comments on the Supreme Court Reference on Constitutional Amendment*. Kingston: Institute of Intergovernmental Relations, 1982.

Russell, Peter H. 'The jurisdictional pendulum within Canadian federalism 1867–1980' in *Canadian Federalism: Past, Present and Future*, ed. Michael Burgess. Leicester: Leicester University Press, 1990.

Ryan, Claude. *Regards sur le fédéralisme canadien*. Montreal: Boréal, 1995.

Schechter, Stephen L. 'Amending the United States Constitution: A New Generation on Trial' in *Redesigning the State: The Politics of Constitutional Change in Industrial Nations*, eds Keith G. Banting and Richard Simeon. Toronto: University of Toronto Press, 1985, 160–203.

Schmitt, Carl. 'The Constitutional Theory of Federation', *Telos* 91 (Spring 1992), 16–56.

Schneiderman, David, ed. *Language and the State*. Cowansville: Éditions Yvon Blais Inc., 1989.

Scott, Frank R. *Essays on the Constitution*. Toronto: University of Toronto Press, 1977.

Scott, Frank R. *A New Endeavour: Selected Political Essays, Letters, and Addresses*, ed. Michiel Horn. Toronto: University of Toronto Press, 1986.

See, Katherine O'Sullivan. *First World Nationalisms: Class and Ethnic Politics in Northern Ireland and Quebec*. Chicago: University of Chicago Press, 1986.

Séguin, Maurice. *L'idée d'indépendance au Québec: Genèse historique*. Trois-Rivières: Boréal Express, 1968.

Seidle, Leslie F., ed. *Seeking a New Canadian Partnership*. Ottawa: Renouf Publishing Company, 1994.

Sheldrick, Byron M. 'Constitutional Evolution and Constitutional Reform: Prospects for the Judicial Modification of the Canadian Federal "Arrangement"', paper presented at the Annual Meeting of the Canadian Political Science Association, St Catharines, 1996.

Shugarman, David P. and Reg Whitaker, eds. *Federalism and Political Community*. Peterborough: Broadview Press, 1989.

Siegfried, André. *The Race Question in Canada*, reprinted 1966 edn. Toronto: McClelland and Stewart, 1970.

Silver, A.I. *The French-Canadian Idea of Confederation*. Toronto: University of Toronto Press, 1982.

Simeon, Richard. *Federal-Provincial Diplomacy: The Making of Recent Policy in Canada*. Toronto: University of Toronto Press, 1972.

Simeon, Richard. 'Meech Lake and Visions of Canada' in *Competing Constitutional Visions: The Meech Lake Accord*, eds K.E. Swinton and C.J. Rogerson. Toronto: Carswell, 1988.

Simeon, Richard and Ian Robinson. *State, Society, and the Development of Canadian Federalism*, Research Studies of the Royal Commission on the Economic Union and Development Prospects for Canada. Toronto: University of Toronto Press, 1990, vol. 71.

Slattery, Brian. 'The Constitutional Priority of the Charter' in *Competing Constitutional*

Visions: The Meech Lake Accord, eds K.E. Swinton and C.J. Rogerson. Toronto: Carswell, 1988.

Slattery, Brian. 'Rights, Communities and Traditions', *University of Toronto Law Journal* 41 (1991) 447–67.

Smiley, Donald V. *Canada in Question: Federalism in the Eighties.* Toronto: McGraw-Hill Ryerson, 1980.

Smiley, Donald V. *The Canadian Political Nationality.* Toronto: Methuen, 1967.

Smiley, Donald V. 'A Dangerous Deed: The Constitution Act, 1982' in *And No-One Cheered: Federalism, Democracy and the Constitution Act*, eds Keith G. Banting and Richard Simeon. Toronto: Methuen, 1983.

Smiley, Donald V. and Ronald L. Watts. *Intrastate Federalism in Canada,* Research Studies of the Royal Commission on the Economic Union and Development Prospects for Canada. Toronto: University of Toronto Press, 1985, vol. 39.

Smiley, Donald V. *The Federal Condition in Canada.* Scarborough: McGraw-Hill Ryerson, 1987.

Smiley, Donald V. 'The Rowell-Sirois Report, Provincial Autonomy and Post-War Canadian Federalism', *Canadian Journal of Economics and Political Science* 28, 54 (1962).

Smith, Anthony D. *National Identity.* Harmondsworth: Penguin Books, 1991.

Smith, David E. 'Party Government, Representation and National Integration in Canada' in *Party Government and Regional Representation in Canada*, Research Studies of the Royal Commission on the Economic Union and Development Prospects for Canada, ed. Peter Aucoin. Toronto: University of Toronto Press, 1985, vol. 36.

Smith, David E. 'Perennial alienation: the prairie west in the Canadian federation' in *Canadian Federalism: Past, Present and Future*, ed. Michael Burgess. Leicester: Leicester University Press, 1990.

Smith, David E. *The Invisible Crown: The First Principle of Canadian Government.* Toronto: University of Toronto Press, 1995.

Smith, Jennifer. 'Canadian Confederation and the Influence of American Federalism', *Canadian Journal of Political Science* 21, 3 (September 1988), 443–63.

Smith, Jennifer. 'Intrastate Federalism and Confederation' in *Political Thought in Canada*, ed. Stephen Brooks. Toronto: Irwin Publishing, 1984.

Smith, Jennifer. 'Political Vision and the 1987 Constitutional Accord' in *Competing Constitutional Visions: The Meech Lake Accord*, eds K.E. Swinton and C.J. Rogerson. Toronto: Carswell, 1988.

Smith, Jennifer. 'The Unsolvable Constitutional Crisis' in François Rocher and Miriam Smith, eds, *New Trends in Canadian Federalism.* Peterborough: Broadview Press, 1995.

Smith, Peter J. 'The Ideological Origins of Canadian Federalism', *Canadian Journal of Political Science* 20, 1 (March 1987), 3–29.

Stark, Andrew. 'English-Canadian Opposition to Quebec Nationalism' in *The Collapse of Canada?* ed. R. Kent Weaver. Washington: The Brookings Institution, 1992.

254 Bibliography

Stein, Michael B. 'Tensions in the Canadian Constitutional Process: Elite Negotiations, Referendums and Interest Group Consultations, 1980–1992' in *Canada: The State of the Federation 1993*, eds Ronald L. Watts and Douglas O. Brown. Kingston: Institute of Intergovernmental Relations, 1993.

Stevenson, Garth. 'Intrastate Federalism in Nineteenth Century Canada'. Paper presented at the Annual Meeting of the Canadian Political Science Association (Charlottetown, 1992).

Stevenson, Garth. 'The Origins of Cooperative Federalism' in *Federalism and Political Community*, eds David P. Shugarman and Reg Whitaker. Peterborough: Broadview Press, 1989.

Stewart, A.T.Q. *The Narrow Ground: The Roots of Conflict in Ulster*. London: Faber and Faber, 1989.

Stewart, Gordon T. *The Origins of Canadian Politics*. Vancouver: University of British Columbia Press, 1986.

Stewart, Gordon T. 'The Origins of Canadian Politics and John A. Macdonald' in *National Politics and Community in Canada*, eds R. Kenneth Carty and W. Peter Ward. Vancouver: University of British Columbia Press, 1986.

Stewart, Gordon T. 'Political Patronage Under Macdonald and Laurier 1878–1911' in *Canadian Political Party Systems*, ed. R.K. Carty. Peterborough: Broadview Press, 1992.

Stewart, Ian. 'Putting Humpty Dumpty Together: The Study of Canadian Political Culture' in *Canadian Politics: an introduction to the discipline*, eds Alain-G. Gagnon and James P. Bickerton. Peterborough: Broadview Press, 1990.

Sulet, Marc Henry. *Le silence des intellectuels: radioscopie de l'intellectuel québécois*. Montreal: Éditions Saint-Martin, 1987.

Swinton, K.E. and C.J. Rogerson, eds. *Competing Constitutional Visions: The Meech Lake Accord*. Toronto: Carswell, 1988.

Swinton, Katherine. 'Competing Visions of Constitutionalism: Of Federalism and Rights' in *Competing Constitutional Visions: The Meech Lake Accord*, eds K.E. Swinton and C.J. Rogerson. Toronto: Carswell, 1988.

Swinton, Katherine. 'Federalism Under Fire: The Role of the Supreme Court', *Law and Contemporary Problems* 55, 1 (1992), 121–45.

Tamir, Yael. *Liberal Nationalism*. Princeton: Princeton University Press, 1993.

Taylor, Charles. 'Can Canada Survive the *Charter*?' *Alberta Law Review* 30, 2 (1992), 427–47.

Taylor, Charles. 'Legitimacy, Identity and Alienation in Late Twentieth Century Canada' in *Constitutionalism, Citizenship and Society in Canada*, eds Alan Cairns and Cynthia Williams, Studies of the Royal Commission on the Economic Union and Development Prospects for Canada. Toronto: University of Toronto Press, 1985, vol. 33.

Taylor, Charles. 'Multiculturalism and the Politics of Recognition' in *Multiculturalism and the Politics of Recognition*, ed. Amy Gutmann. Princeton: Princeton University Press, 1992.

Taylor, Charles. *Reconciling the Solitudes: Essays on Canadian Federalism and Nationalism*, ed. Guy Laforest. Montreal and Kingston: McGill-Queen's University Press, 1993.

Taylor, Charles. 'Shared and Divergent Values' in *Options for a New Canada*, eds Ronald L. Watts and Douglas M. Brown. Toronto: University of Toronto Press, 1991.

Taylor, Charles. 'Why Do Nations Have to Become States?' in *Philosophers Look at Confederation*, ed. Stanley French. Ottawa: Canadian Philosophical Association, 1978.

Taylor, Rupert. 'South Africa: Consociation or Democracy', *Telos* 85 (Fall 1993), 17–32.

Thomas, David, ed. *Canada and the United States: Differences that Count*. Peterborough: Broadview Press, 1993.

Thorburn, Hugh. 'Federalism, Pluralism, and the Canadian Community' in *Federalism and Political Community*, eds D.P. Sugarman and Reg Whitaker. Peterborough: Broadview Press, 1989.

Thorburn, Hugh. 'Needed! A New Look at the Two Nations Theory', *Queen's Quarterly* (Summer 1974), 268–73.

Trent, John E., Robert Young, and Guy Lachapelle, eds. *Québec-Canada. What is the Path Ahead?* Ottawa: University of Ottawa Press, 1996.

Tribe, L. *American Constitutional Law*. New York: Foundation Press, 1988.

Trofimenkoff, S. *The Dream of a Nation: A Social and Intellectual History of Quebec*. Toronto: Macmillan, 1982.

Trudeau, Pierre Elliott. *Fatal Tilt: Speaking Out About Sovereignty*. Toronto: HarperCollins, 1991.

Trudeau, Pierre Elliott. 'Convocation Speech at the Opening of the Bora Laskin Law Library', *University of Toronto Law Journal* 41 (1991), 295–306.

Trudeau, Pierre Elliott. *Federalism and the French Canadians*. Toronto: Macmillan, 1968.

Trudeau, Pierre Elliott, ed. *La grève de l'Amiante: Un étape de la révolution industrielle au Québec*. Montreal: Cité Libre, 1955.

Trudeau, Pierre Elliott. *A Mess That Deserves A Big No*. Toronto: Stewart House, 1992.

Trudeau, Pierre Elliott. 'Trudeau Speaks Out', *Maclean's Magazine*, 28 September 1992.

Tully, James. 'Diversity's Gambit Declined' in *Constitutional Predicament: Canada After the Referendum of 1992*, ed. Curtis Cook. Montreal and Kingston: McGill-Queen's University Press, 1994.

Tuohy, Carolyn J. *Policy and Politics in Canada: Institutionalized Ambivalence*. Philadelphia: Temple University Press, 1992.

Tupper, Allan. 'English Canadian Scholars and the Meech Lake Accord', *International Journal of Canadian Studies* 7–8 (Spring-Fall 1993), 347–57.

Verney, Douglas V. *Three Civilizations, Two Cultures, One State: Canada's Political Traditions*. Durham: Duke University Press, 1986.

Vipond, Robert C. *Liberty and Community: Canadian Federalism and the Failure of the Constitution*. Albany: State University of New York Press, 1991.

256 Bibliography

Vipond, Robert C. '1767 and 1867: The Federal Principle and Canadian Confederation Reconsidered', *Canadian Journal of Political Science* 22, 1 (March 1989), 3–25.

Vipond, Robert C. 'Seeing Canada Through the Referendum: Still a House Divided', *Publius* 23, 3 (1993), 39–55.

Vipond, Robert C. 'Whatever Became of the Compact Theory? Meech Lake and the New Politics of Constitutional Amendment in Canada', *Queen's Quarterly* (Winter 1989), 793–811.

Waddell, Eric. 'Language, Community and National Identity: Some Reflections on French-English Relations in Canada' in *Canadian Politics: an introduction to the discipline*, eds Alain-G. Gagnon and James P. Bickerton. Peterborough: Broadview Press, 1990.

Wade, Mason. *The French Canadians: 1760–1967*. 2 vols. Toronto: Macmillan, 1968.

Wagenberg, Ronald et al. 'Federal societies and the founding of federal states: an examination of the origins of Canadian Confederation' in *Canadian Federalism: Past, Present and Future*, ed. Michael Burgess. Leicester: Leicester University Press, 1990.

Waite, P.B., ed. *The Confederation Debates in the Province of Canada*. Toronto: McClelland and Stewart, 1963.

Waite, P.B. *The Life and Times of Confederation, 1864–1867: Politics, Newspapers, and the Union of British North America*, 2nd edn. Toronto: University of Toronto Press, 1962.

Walsh, W.H. *Introduction to the Philosophy of History*. London: Hutchinson, 1967.

Watkins, Mel. 'Coming Apart Together: The Report of the Task Force on Canadian Unity', *This Magazine*, May 1979.

Watts, Ronald L. and Douglas M. Brown. *Canada: The State of the Federation 1993*. Kingston: Institute of Intergovernmental Relations, 1993.

Watts, Ronald L. 'The Macdonald Commission and Canadian Federalism' in *Canadian Federalism: Past, Present and Future*, ed. Michael Burgess. Leicester: Leicester University Press, 1990.

Watts, Ronald L. *Multicultural Societies and Federalism,* Studies of the Royal Commission on Bilingualism and Biculturalism. Ottawa: Information Canada, 1970.

Watts, Ronald L. and Douglas M. Brown, eds. *Options for a New Canada*. Toronto: University of Toronto Press, 1991.

Watts, Ronald. 'The Survival or Disintegration of Federation' in *One Country or Two?* ed. R. M. Burns. Montreal and Kingston: McGill-Queen's University Press, 1971.

Weaver, R. Kent. 'Political Institutions and Canada's Constitutional Crisis' in *The Collapse of Canada?* ed. R. Kent Weaver. Washington: The Brookings Institution, 1992.

Webber, Jeremy. *Reimagining Canada. Language, Culture, Community, and the Canadian Constitution*. Montreal and Kingston: McGill-Queen's University Press, 1994.

Whitaker, Reginald A. 'Apprehended Insurrection? RCMP Intelligence and the October Crisis', *Queen's Quarterly* (Spring 1993), 383–406.

Whitaker, Reginald A. 'Democracy and the Canadian Constitution' in *And No-One Cheered: Federalism, Democracy and the Constitution Act*, eds Keith G. Banting and Richard Simeon. Toronto: Methuen, 1983.

Whitaker, Reginald A. 'The Quebec Cauldron: A Recent Account', in *Quebec: State and Society*, ed. Alain-G. Gagnon. Toronto: Methuen, 1984.

Whitaker, Reginald A. 'Quebec Question,' in *Debating Canada's Future: Views From The Left*, eds Simon Rosenblum and Peter Findlay. Toronto: James Lorimer and Company, 1991.

Whitaker, Reginald A. *A Sovereign Idea: Essays on Canada as a Democratic Community*. Montreal and Kingston: McGill-Queen's University Press, 1992.

Whyte, John D. 'The 1987 Constitutional Accord and Ethnic Accommodation' in *Competing Constitutional Visions: The Meech Lake Accord*, eds K.E. Swinton and C.J. Rogerson. Toronto: Carswell, 1988.

Whyte, Donald. 'Sociology and the constitution of society: Canadian experiences' in *Fragile Truths: 25 Years of Sociology and Anthropology in Canada*, ed. W.K. Carroll. Ottawa: Carleton University Press, 1992.

Williams, Cynthia and Douglas Williams. 'Political Entanglements: Ideas and Identities in Canadian Political Life' in *Canadian Politics: an introduction to the discipline*, eds Alain-G. Gagnon and James P. Bickerton. Peterborough: Broadview Press, 1990.

Williams, Melissa S. 'Burkean "Descriptions" and Political Representation: A Reappraisal', *Canadian Journal of Political Science*, 29, 1 March 1996, 23–45.

Wiseman, Nelson. 'In Search of Manitoba's Constitutional Position, 1950–1990', *Journal of Canadian Studies* 29, 3 (Fall 1994) 85–107.

Woehrling, José. 'La Constitution canadienne et l'évolution des rapports entre le Québec et le Canada anglais, de 1867 à nos jours', *Points of View* 4 (1993).

Woehrling, José. 'La crise constitutionnelle et le réaménagement des rappports entre le Québec et le Canada anglais', *International Journal of Canadian Studies* 7–8 (Spring-Fall 1993), 9–40.

Wolferen, Karel Van. *The Enigma of Japanese Power*. Tokyo: Charles E. Tuttle, 1993.

Young, Robert A. 'How Do Peaceful Secessions Happen?' *Canadian Journal of Political Science* 27 (March, 1994).

Young, Robert A. *The Breakup of Czechoslovakia*. Kingston: Institute of Intergovernmental Relations, 1994.

Young, Robert A. *The Secession of Quebec and the Future of Canada*. Montreal and Kingston: McGill-Queen's University Press, 1995.

Index

abeyances, constitutional, and Burke's approach, 33–41, 190–1; distinguished from other terms, 9–12, 19–31; expanded view of constitution, 8, 9; Foley's explanation, xvii, 1–3; illustrations of the idea, 3–4; important concept for Canada, xvi-xx, 37, 40–1; issues unclear at Confederation, 20, 51–2, 54, 56, 61–71, 76–8, 102, 121, 220; maintenance of, 56, 58–60, 71–6, 91–102, 106, 115, 120, 220; persistence of the Quebec abeyance, 198–206, 219–27; power lost in crises, 92, 102–4, 121; rising up of the Quebec abeyance, 106–12, 117; tackling an abeyance, 112–23, 137–63, 220; Trudeau's approach, 141, 162–3, 175, 178–9, 190, 220–1, 225; writing down an abeyance (Meech), 178–84, 186, 221

aboriginal peoples, 198, 227; in Pepin-Robarts Commission, 152; rights, 67–8, 182

accommodative framework, 97

aggregation vs. integration, 199–200

Ajzenstat, Janet, 32, 164n7, 175, 200–1

amending formula, omitted from BNA Act, 67, 87n130, 121–2; Victoria provisions, 119

Archer, Keith, 216n151

Arès, Richard, 84n82, 88n132, 128

Arrison, Sonia, 211n77, 212n99

asymmetrical federalism, 69–70, 75, 111, 159, 198, 222

Atkinson, Michael, 199–200

Balthazar, Louis, 39, 171n102

Banting, Keith G., 78n5

Bashevkin, Sylvia, 42n15, 166n27

Bateman, Thomas M.J., 18n47

Beaudoin, Gérald-A., 144–5, 159

Becker, Carl L., 51, 78n3

Bégin, Monique, 66

Bélanger, Réal, 99

Bélanger-Campeau Commission, xiv, 228n9

Bercuson, David J., 16n30

Bertrand, Jean-Jacques, 112

Betz, Hans-George, 216n151

bilingualism, 111, 113–16, 154; Confederation, 68, 70, 76, 102; public opposition to, 163

Bilingualism and Biculturalism Commission, xviii, xix, 92, 106, 113–17, 121, 122

Bill C-60, 152–3

bill of rights, absent from 1867 arrangements, 70, 77; Charter of Rights and Freedoms (1982), 174, 175–6, 188, 203

Bird, Richard, 141

Bishay, Susan, 123n2

Black, Edwin R., xiii, 73, 83n66, 84n94, 87n120, 131n117, 200

Black, Eric, 25

Bloc Québécois, 204

BNA Act. *See* Confederation

Bothwell, Robert, 99

Bouchard, Lucien, 195, 204, 214n131

Bourassa, Henri, 56, 104, 105

Bourassa, Robert, 117, 119, 200

Britain, civil war in, xv, 89, 90–1; constitution, 11–12; influence on 1867 Confederation, 54–6; Scottish nationalism, 192–8

Brooks, Stephen, xiin14

Brown, George, 72–3, 227

Index 259

Brun, Henri, 10, 17n41
Burelle, André, 229n18
Burgess, Michael, 11–12, 207n18, 218n181
Burke, Edmund, xix, 19, 33–41, 48n82, 49nn87,88, 176–7, 220; approach contrasted with Trudeau's, 190–1; views relevant to the present Quebec problem, 38–41, 48n76

Cairns, Alan C., xiv, xxvn29, 9, 17n31, 20–1, 28, 41n7, 86n107, 100, 113, 151, 170nn84,86, 198, 211n77, 215nn143,148, 230n20; criticism of Pepin-Robarts Commission, 138, 153–5, 156
Cameron, David R., xxviin47, 15n9, 27, 35, 48n81, 143–4, 145, 147, 156, 165n15, 167n34
Cartier, Sir George-Étienne, 51, 55, 56, 57, 58, 72
Carty, R. Kenneth, 85n95
cause and effect, xv-xvi
centralism, 71, 72–3, 74, 75, 76, 84n82. *See also* Trudeau, Pierre
Chaput-Rolland, Solange, 145
Charlottetown Accord, xix, 179, 182
Charlottetown Accord (1992), 201, 204; Trudeau's opposition, 188, 212n86, 221
Charter of Rights and Freedoms, Canadian, 174, 175–6, 188, 203
citizenship, not defined in BNA Act, 70
civil war, in Britain, xv, 43n33, 89, 90–1; in US, 61, 89–91
Clark, Glen, 199
Clark, Joe, 156–7, 158, 163, 171n99, 198, 207n8
common sense, 28–9, 31
community, 222
'community of communities', 152
compact theory, 74–5, 84n82, 108, 122, 141
compromises, 19–20, 31, 76; Laurier as the great compromiser, 98–9
Confederation, abeyances, 20, 51, 54, 56, 61–71, 76–8, 102, 220; bill of rights absent, 70, 77; British political influence, 54–6; conflicting visions, 69, 220; differing views, 61–3, 72–3, 76; distinct status for Quebec left open, 56, 57, 68–9, 74, 75–6, 77; French-Canadian views in the 1860s, 54–9; myths, 22, 23;
pragmatism, 62, 83n67; unsettled problems, 56, 62; wishful thinking, 71–6
confrontation strategy of Trudeau, 190, 220
Conklin, Charles, 6–7, 8
conscription crises, 104–5
consociationalism, 95–6
constitution, 1982 Act, xix-xx, 5–6, 163, 174, 175, 176, 221; amendment. *See* amending formula; BNA Act (1867). *See* Confederation; British, 11–12; Cairns's view, 9; Conklin's concept, 6–7, 8; expanded views of, 6–9; United States, 12–14, 25
convention, distinguished from abeyance, 9–10, 12
Cook, Ramsay, 157, 230n22
Cooper, Barry, 16n30, 43n29
Council of the Federation (Pepin-Robarts proposal), 150
Courchene, Thomas, 166n26, 210n59
Creighton, D.G., xxiin10
Crick, Bernard, xvii, 1, 46n62, 47n69
Crossman, Richard, xxiiin12
Crown, effect on constitutional developments in Canada, 8, 65
Czernis, Loretta, 168n54

de Clercy, Cristine Andrea Beauvais, xxviin47, 167n33
Denis, Claude, xxin10, xxvin37
Desserud, Don, 207n18
Dewar, Kenneth, 47n65
Diefenbaker, John, 112
Di Norcia, Vincent, 82n58
Dion, Léon, 128nn60,71, 228n9
distinct status for Quebec, xi, 59, 114–15, 224–5; distinct society clause in Meech, xix, 181–2; possibilities left open in 1867, 56, 57, 68–9, 74, 75–6, 77
divorce issue in abeyance at Confederation, 66–7
dualism, 56, 57, 68–9, 74, 75, 97, 102, 175, 179, 224; in Pepin-Robarts Report, 149, 154, 155; recognized by Meech, 183–4
Dumont, Fernand, 59, 99
Duplessis, Maurice, 106–7
Dupré, J. Stefan, 151, 168n61, 169n79, 209n51
Durham, Lord, 56

Easton, David, 222
élite accommodation, 96, 97–8
Elkins, David, xxvn31, 215n139
Ellis, Faron, 216n151
Elshtain, Jean Bethke, xxvn30, xxvin33
Elton, David, 166n27
Emberley, Peter, xxvin33
empiricism, 35
English, John, xxiiin19, 127n58

federal-provincial conferences, 112
federalism, xiii, 56, 60, 138, 177; asymmetrical, 69–70, 75, 111, 159, 198, 222; Livingston's views, 20–1; prevailing attitudes, 190, 198–201, 205–6; principle of Confederation, 57; proposals of Pepin-Robarts Commission, 148, 149, 150, 152; Quebec's view, 122; Trudeau's views, 165nn12–18, 174–5; view of Tremblay Commission, 108–10
fictions, relationship to abeyances, 25–7, 31, 44n43, 205
Fierlbeck, Katherine, 176
First Ministers' Conference (Nov. 1981), xxvin34
First World War, 104–5
Flanagan, Thomas, 208n31
Foley, Michael, xvi, 5, 40, 219, 223–4; definition of abeyances, xvii, 1–3; on the US Constitution, 12–13
Forbes, H.D., 139, 140
Forcese, Dennis P., xxin10
Forsey, Eugene, xiv, 160, 168n66
Franks, C.E.S., 23, 24, 203
Fulford, Robert, 203, 218n176

Gagnon, Alain-G., xiii, xxiin14, 130n94, 131n111, 163, 169n71, 177–8
Gagnon, Lysiane, 3, 45n53
Gauthier, David, 78n5
Gérin-Lajoie, Paul, 67, 84n92
Gérin-Lajoie doctrine, 110
Gibbins, Roger, xiii, 180, 211n77, 212n99, 216n152, 217n163, 229n13
Globe and Mail, The, 157
Gold, Marc, 30, 46n58, 187
Guay, Jean, 129n86
Gwyn, Sandra, 105, 130n90

Hailsham, Lord, 18n46
Hall, D.J., 79n12
Hawthorn, Geoffrey, 161
Heard, Andrew, 9–10, 209n50
Heintzman, Ralph, 58–9, 101–2, 127n59, 144, 145, 184
Heyman, Richard, 115, 116
Hobsbawm, Eric, xiv, xxiiin21
Hockin, Thomas, 126n41
Hogg, Peter, 5–6
Howes, David, 6, 16n17

Ignatieff, Michael, 15n9
instrumentalities, 20–1, 31
Irish nationalism, xxvin43
irresolution, 44n42

Japan, 205
Jenkins, Roy, xxiin12
Jenson, Jane, 225
Johnson, Daniel, 111–12, 178
Johnson, J.K., 87n130
Johnson, William, 171n102
Johnston, Richard, 216n157
Judicial Committee of the Privy Council, 103, 118
jury system, 4

Kaplan, William, 203
Keating, Michael, 49n90, 214n124
Kemp, Arnold, 215n138
keywords, 29–31
King, Anthony, 217n171
King, William Lyon Mackenzie, 99, 120, 203
Kogawa, Joy, 218n184
Kwavnick, David, 107–8

Lachapelle, Guy, 227
La Forest, Gerard V., 169n66
Laforest, Guy, 74, 116, 174–5, 183, 210n56
Laing, R.D., 3–4, 45n47
Lalonde, Marc, 142
language issue, 204
Lapointe, Ernest, 118
La Presse, 157
Latouche, Daniel, xxin6, 130n94, 169n71

Laurendeau, André, 113–14, 115, 121, 133n145, 134nn152,153
Laurendeau-Dunton Commission. *See* Bilingualism and Biculturalism Commission
Laurier, Sir Wilfrid, 98–9, 104
Lawton, William, 217n171
leadership, xxvn32, 98
Leduc, Lawrence, 222
Lesage, Jean, 110, 111, 132nn119,126
Létourneau, Jocelyn, 228n12
Lévesque, René, xv–xvi, 157, 162
Lewontin, R.C., 28
Lijphart, Arend, 95, 96
Livingston, William S., 20, 21
Livre beige (1980 Quebec Liberal proposals), 158–9, 175
Lord Chancellor in Britain, 11
Lower, A.R.M., 65
Lusztig, Michael, 199

McCrone, David, 135, 214nn124,135
Macdonald Commission, xii, 21
Macdonald, Roderick A., 81n42, 84n82, 210n54, 230n23
Macdonald, Sir John A., 19, 51, 53–4, 56, 72, 220
McDougall, A.K., 146
McNaught, Kenneth, xxvn30, 22
MacRae-Buchanan, Constance, 23
McRoberts, Kenneth, xix, xxivn25, 113, 165n12, 166n23, 207n15
McWhinney, Edward, 76, 168n51
Maddicott, J.R., 163n2
Making Canada Work Better, 222–3, 228n5
Mallory, J.R., 46n64, 85nn95,99
Manning, Preston, 199, 227
Maritimes: opposition to Confederation (1867), 71–2
Martin, Ged, xxin10, 53, 71, 78n7, 79n8, 87n128
Meech Lake Accord (1990), xix, 116, 137, 159, 175, 178–84, 201, 221; as abeyance, 186, 221; distinct society clause, xix, 181–2
mega-constitutional orientations, 12, 199, 203
Meisel, John, 168n51

Milne, David, xxvn28, 25, 46n64, 49n96, 69, 93, 141
Milne, Edmund, 44n35
Mitchell, James, 214n136
Monet, Jacques, 81n41
Monière, Denis, 80n36
Morgan, Edmund S., 25–7, 44nn36–41
Morton, F.L., 14, 130n94
Mulroney, Brian, 180, 208n32
multiculturalism, 22, 116, 140
myths, political, 21–5, 31, 203; relationship to abeyances, 25; unitary government, 11–12

Nairn, Tom, 193
nationalism in Quebec, 59, 225, 230n22
Native peoples. *See* aboriginal peoples
Nemni, Max, xxiiin20
New Democratic Party (NDP), 113
Nöel, Alain, 215n143
Noel, S.J.R., 49n98, 126n39
Normand, Robert, 157, 164n6, 171n106
North, Lord, 28–9
Nurgitz, Nathan, 170n98
Nutbrown, Richard, 32

Oakeshott, Michael, 32–3, 46n62, 47nn64,66, 124n15
Official Languages Act (1969), 114
Oliver, Michael, xxivn27, 23, 115

Pal, Leslie A., 217n168
Papineau, Talbot, 105
Parent, Étienne, 59
Parizeau, Jacques, 195–6, 206n2
Parti Québécois, 120, 123, 142
Paterson, Lindsay, 24, 214n135
Patriation Reference case (1981), 6, 10, 75
patronage, 97, 98, 101, 102, 202, 220
Pearson, Lester, 113, 115, 126n34, 145
Pepin, Jean-Luc, 141, 142, 144, 146–7, 148, 160–1, 172n124
Pepin-Roberts Commission, xviii–xix, 120, 123, 137–9, 141, 142, 220, 221; language recommendations, 149, 151; press response, 157, 172; principles, 150; reasons for failure, 138, 161–2; view of federalism, 148, 149, 150, 152

262 Index

Philips, Derek L., 49n89
Pocock, J.G.A., 47n64
populism, 199, 216n151
pragmatism, 62, 83n67, 120, 121
Preece, Rod, 53–4
provincial equality principle, 122, 162, 198; clear statement avoided at Confederation, 69–70, 75, 77; rejected by Pepin-Robarts Report, 150
provincial rights, at Confederation, 61–2, 63–4, 72, 76; in Pepin-Robarts Report, 152, 155

Quebec, a century of 'hibernation', 99–100, 220; compared with Scotland, 192–8; constitutional powers, 68–9, 74, 75–6, 77, 197, 215n137; distinct status. *See* distinct status for Quebec; referendum (1980), xix; referendum (1995), 39–40, 49n96, 195, 222; religion in, xxivn27, 58

rationalism, 35
referendums, 216n152, 227; on the Charlottetown Accord (1992), xix; on the Meech Lake Accord (1990); Quebec (1980), xix; Quebec (1995), 39–40, 49n96, 195, 222; in Scotland and Wales (1979), 195
regionalism, in Pepin-Robarts Report, 149, 154–5
Reilly, Wayne, 195
religion, church establishment in abeyance at Confederation, 66; in Quebec, xxivn27, 58
Rémillard, Gil, 179
Richler, Mordecai, 208n32
Riel, Louis, 103, 104
rights, aboriginal, 67–8, 182; bill of rights absent at Confederation, 70, 77; Charter. *See* Charter of Rights and Freedoms, Canadian; provincial, 61–2, 63–4, 72, 76
Riker, William H., 90, 123n4, 124n9
Robarts, John, 142, 143, 145–6, 148, 151
Robertson, Gordon, xvi, 120, 142, 161–2, 164nn6,8, 180, 188; argument with Trudeau, xvi, 185–6, 188–9
Robinson, Ian, xxivn27, 20
Rocher, François, 129nn80,86, 141
Rodal, Berel, 29

Romney, Paul, 23, 61
Rowell-Sirois Report, 109
Rudin, Ronald, 129n77
Ruel, Jacinthe, xxiiin19
Russell, Peter H., xxiin13, xxvn30, 12, 18n50, 43n32, 117–18, 210n59, 217n169
Ryan, Claude, 135n174, 158, 159, 172n116, 206n3, 211n84, 227, 229nn17,18

Savile, George, 55
Schechter, Stephen, xxiin15
Schneiderman, David, 170n82
Scotland: compared with Quebec, 192–8
Scowen, Reed, 144
Segal, Hugh, 170n98
Seidle, F. Leslie, 217n168
Seiler, Tamara Palmer, 42n18
Senate, 64, 65, 68, 69, 76, 77, 122; Pepin-Robarts Report proposes replacement, 150
Serge, Denis, 170n92
Sigurdson, Richard, 216n151
Silver, A.I., 57–8
Simeon, Richard, xxivn27, 20, 78n5, 183, 184
Simpson, Jeffrey, 172n124
Smart, Patricia, 114
Smiley, Donald, 20–1, 41n7, 43n32, 92–3, 94, 95
Smith, Anthony D., 43n33
Smith, David, 8
Smith, Dennis, 157–8
Smith, Gordon, 172n122
Smith, Jennifer, 64, 80n25, 83n79
Smith, Miriam, 141
Smith, Peter J., 62–3, 83nn66,70
special status for Quebec, 106–17; Gérin-Lajoie doctrine, 110; in Meech, xix, 181–2; Trudeau's opposition, 158, 161–3, 174–6, 179, 181
Spicer Commission, 202
Srebrnik, Henry F., 126n38
Stanfield, Robert, xviii, 112–13, 173n132
Stevenson, Garth, xxivn26, 182, 209n48
Stevenson, J.T., 125n31
Stewart, A.T.Q., xxviin43, 15n3
Stewart, Gordon T., xxvn31, 60, 80n21, 82n59, 97, 127n44

Index

Stewart, Ian, 125n18
Sulet, Marc Henry, xxiin14
Supreme Court, Canadian, 14, 16n20, 30, 202–3; Patriation Reference case (1981), 6, 10
Supreme Court, US, 12, 13–14
Sutherland, Stuart, xvii

taboos, 27–8, 31, 200
Tamir, Yael, 140, 165n19, 176–7
Taschereau, 118
Taylor, Charles, 86n106, 121, 164n3, 175–6, 178, 200, 229n14
Tellier, Paul, 142
'temperament', political, xviii, xix, 8
Thomas, David, 216n152
Thorson, Donald, 142
Time for Action, A (federal government, 1978), 153
Tremblay, Arthur, 153, 158, 171n99, 174, 206n2
Tremblay Commission, xix, 106, 107–10; Report (1956), 92, 121, 129n83, 131n112
Tremblay, Guy, 10, 17n41
Trent, John, 227
Trent, John E., xxivn22
Trudeau, Pierre, xvi, xix, xx, 104, 116, 122, 185–91, 220–1; attack on Charlottetown Accord, 188, 212n86, 221; comments on his views, 139–41, 165nn12–18; debating style, 186–8, 189; denunciation of Meech Lake Accord, xix, 181, 186–7, 221; dispute with Robertson, 185–6, 188–9; on federalism, 174–5; foe of Quebec nationalism, 123, 138, 139–40, 141, 162, 163, 179, 189–90, 225; initial success of 1982 Constitution, 178–9, 221; opposition to Pepin-Robarts

Report, 138, 139, 158, 161; Sauvé Arena speech, 174–6, 206n6; style of debate, 179–80
Tully, James, 17n39, 176
Tuohy, Carolyn, 30, 184
two-nations policy, 111–13

Underhill, Frank, 94–5
Union Nationale, 111–12
United States Constitution, 12–14
Unity Task Force. *See* Pepin-Robarts Commission

Vachon, André, 43n27
Verney, Douglas, 96, 97
Verney, Richard, 65
Victoria Charter (1971), 92, 117–20
Vipond, Robert, 63–4, 173n137
vocabulary, constitutional, 19–31

Wade, Mason, 55
Waite, P.B., 87n130
Walsh, W.H., xxivn24
Ward, W. Peter, 85n95
Watts, Ronald, xxviin48, 141, 144, 145, 172n128
Webber, Jeremy, 45n53, 125n24, 207n20
Weiler, Paul C., 151, 168n61
western Canada, 75, 122, 123, 137
Whitaker, Reg, 127n45, 165n18, 171n100
Whyte, John, 20
Williams, Melissa, 39
Woehrling, José, 102
Wolferen, Karel Van, 205
Wood, Gordon S., xiiin19

Young, Robert, 227, 228n7